D1406885

Data Communications and Networking Fundamentals Using Novell NetWare® (3.11)

Emilio Ramos
Al Schroeder
Ann Beheler

Richland College

Macmillan Publishing Company
New York

Maxwell Macmillan Canada
Toronto

Maxwell Macmillan International
New York   Oxford   Singapore   Sydney

Cover art: Marjory Dressler

Editor: Charles E. Stewart, Jr.

Cover Designer: Thomas Mack

Production Buyer: Pamela D. Bennett

This book was set in Times Roman and was printed and bound by Von Hoffman Press, Inc.. The cover was printed by Von Hoffman Press, Inc.

Copyright © 1994 by Macmillan Publishing Company, a division of Macmillan, Inc.

Novell NetWare is a registered trademark of Novell, Inc.

Printed in the United States of America

All rights reserved. No part of this book may be reproduced or transmitted in any form or by any means, electronic or mechanical, including photocopy, recording, or any information storage and retrieval system, without permission in writing from the Publisher.

The Publisher offers discounts on this book when ordered in bulk quantities. For more information, write to: Special Sales Department, Macmillan Publishing Company, 445 Hutchinson Ave., Columbus, OH 43235, or call 1-800-228-7854.

Macmillan Publishing Company
866 Third Avenue
New York, New York 10022

Macmillan Publishing Company is part of the
Maxwell Communication Group of Companies.

Maxwell Macmillan Canada, Inc.
1200 Eglinton Avenue East, Suite 200
Don Mills, Ontario M3C 3N1

Library of Congress Cataloging-in-Publication Data

Ramos, Emilio
       Data communications and networking fundamentals using Novell NetWare (3.11) / Emilio Ramos, Al Schroeder, Ann Beheler.
              p.   cm.
         Includes index.
         ISBN 0-02-407766-6 (spiral)
       1. NetWare (Computer file)   2. Local area networks (Computer networks)   I. Schroeder, Al.
       II. Beheler, Ann.   III. Title
       TK5105.7.R37   1994
       004.6--dc20   93-8780
                                                                                                                              CIP

Printing: 1 2 3 4 5 6 7 8 9   Year: 4 5 6

Preface

During the past decade, businesses have experienced unprecedented growth in the use of computer workstations by their employees. Although data communications and networking previously had been an integral part of data processing systems, this new growth area has brought these topics to the forefront in both the business and personal-use sectors.

While communications has been taught at the college level for many years, courses in networking only recently have become part of the core curriculum. This change has caused a shift in course structure for computer students. Some colleges have developed a networking course, while others have modified their data communications course to place a greater emphasis on networking. Whatever the approach, colleges and universities are trying to provide a strong introduction to both communications and networking for the computer literate student.

This book was written to serve both needs. The first half of the book serves as an orientation to communications and networking. The second half focuses on the use of networks. It features Novell's NetWare version 3.11 to illustrate local area network applications, and it provides hands-on tutorials for the student to implement NetWare 3.11.

NetWare 3.11 was chosen as the software to use because it currently has the largest share of the market. Therefore, it is likely that a student not only would want to study it, but would see it again in business use.

Objectives of This Text

1. To teach the fundamental terminology of communications.
2. To present the components needed to establish communications and the options available in applying each component.
3. To show the uses of both wide area and local area networks.
4. To teach the fundamental terminology relating to networks.
5. To illustrate the components required to configure a local area network and the options available in applying each of them.
6. To present fully the characteristics of NetWare 3.11.
7. To show the student how to install and operate NetWare 3.11.

Organization of the Text

The book is written in two parts, which provides the flexibility of using either or both of them, depending on the situation. The first half is an introduction to communications and networking. It provides the essential terminology and concepts for an introductory course in communications and networking. The

iii

second half of the book provides an introduction to the use of NetWare, including installing, managing, and using the software. This provides the student with a how-to look at applying the knowledge gained in the first half of the book, and it reinforces the concepts and terminology from the first half, particularly with respect to LANs.

The organization of the book assumes a level of computer literacy usually attained in college level Introduction to Computer Science courses or an equivalent continuing education course. This book provides a foundation in the concepts and terminology of communications and networking; it follows that with the study of a specific LAN product and the opportunity for hands-on use of that product. Exercises in the first part of the book focus on grasping communications terminology and studying specific network components. Hands-on tutorials in the second half of the book focus on installing, managing, and operating a specific local area network.

A degree of flexibility is inherent in the book's organization, which allows use of either the first or the second half or both parts, as need warrants. Chapters 1 through 7 can be used to teach a course in communications and networking through a variety of scenarios. Chapters 8 through 15 can be used to teach an introductory course in Novell NetWare to persons who already have a knowledge of networking concepts. The entire book provides an introduction to both communications and networking, with hands-on use of the most popular LAN product.

An appendix contains several lists of vendors for a variety of network products. You should review this material for familiarity, and use it as needed to identify vendors in any area of communications and networking.

Supplements

For the instructor there is a comprehensive instructor's guide that includes

1. Suggestions on how to organize the course, depending on the desired emphasis and focus

2. Answers to all end of chapter questions

3. Solutions to projects

4. Transparency masters of the art in the book and the chapter outlines

5. Hints for the presentation of material in the classroom

6. Test bank questions for examinations

7. Multimedia presentation software

Acknowledgements

We gratefully acknowledge the contributions of the following reviewers of our manuscript: Becky Ferguson, Garland, Texas; Lolita Gilkes, Richland College, Stephen Jordan, Cooke County College; James W. Koerlin, Golden Gate University; and George M. Whitson III, University of Texas at Tyler.

Our greatest source of support and encouragement has been our families. Without them we could not have written this book.

We would also like to thank the Macmillan staff who participated in this project and provided the opportunity to publish this book. Thank you all for your efforts in helping us complete this project.

This book is dedicated to my grandfather, Emilio Ramos, Sr.
Thank you for the strength and the love. Your gentle ways are
a source of inspiration.

ER

Contents

Communication Networks and Services Offered

Objectives

After completing this chapter you will

1. Understand the concept of data communication.
2. Have an overview of the history of data communication.
3. Understand the basic requirements of a communication system.
4. Understand the basic concepts of networking.
5. Have a general overview of some of the services offered through data communication networks.

Key Terms

Bulletin Board	Data Communication
E-mail	EBBS
Electronic Transfer	Home Banking
Information Service	Interexchange Facilities
Modem	Network
Public Network	Satellite
Telecommuting	Teleconferencing
Videotext	

Introduction

Before you devote many hours mastering the sophisticated concepts of communications and networking, you should gather a general understanding of the capabilities of such networks and communication systems. In addition, you must understand the general subdivisions or components of such systems along with some of the historical efforts that were required to create today's complex communication systems. That is the objective of this chapter.

The chapter begins with an introduction to the concept of data communication and its importance in the business world. It then provides a brief history of the most important developments that have shaped the data communication industry, followed by the most important functions that a data communication system must provide. And finally, the chapter closes with a discussion of some basic services that can be accessed through existing data communication networks.

Data Communication System

Definition

Data communication is the transmission of electronic data over some medium. The medium can be coaxial cable, optical fiber, microwave, or some of the other data-carrying media. The hardware and software systems that enable the transmission of data make up what are called data communication networks. These networks are an important component of today's information-based society, a society that is dominated by computers and the need to have access to accurate and timely information.

In this age of high-speed computers and data communication networks, many companies exist only to manage data and provide information to other corporations. As a result, a new type of industry has emerged in recent years that doesn't create any physical products. This industry is called the information service industry. Their main product is information. As such, information is a commodity that can be sold and purchased. In addition, many companies that create products for the consumer market also produce information that can be sold for a profit. One such case is a car manufacturer that sells data stored in its customer database to other companies that may offer products for the car sold. Companies that have large mailing lists sell them to other corporations that are interested in the same types of customers. Although the legal and moral implications of such transactions can be debated, the fact still remains that information is a commodity and its value depends on the accuracy and the timeliness of such information. The accuracy, of course, depends on how the data was acquired. Both accuracy and timeliness also depend on the accuracy and speed of the data communication network employed. If data transmitted through a network can't be trusted because it takes too long to reach its destination, the data communication system is a failure. Information consumers, such as a stock exchange, couldn't operate if the information in a file took hours to sort and display on monitors, or if portions of the data were lost in the transmission process.

It can be generalized that the value of the communication system depends on the knowledge transmitted by the system and the speed of movement of the knowledge. High-speed data communication networks transmit information that brings the sender and the receiver close together. Therefore, a good communication system is a major component of a successful business organization. The ability to provide information in a timely and accurate fashion is the key to survival in the 1990s and the decades ahead. Because of this, data communications is one of the fastest growing segments of the communication market.

Functions

An effective data communication system has a series of characteristics or functions that are easily recognized. These characteristics are the result of the behavior and functionality of the system as it provides information to its users, as it captures the information, and as it allows its users to communicate with each other. These characteristics can be further categorized by the features associated with them.

First, an effective data communication system must provide information to the right people in a timely manner. Having information at the proper place in a timely fashion can mean the difference between making a profit and sustaining a loss. Today's companies have networked data communication systems that can deliver text, voice, and graphical information at speeds that were thought impossible just a few years ago. By integrating communication and computer technology, a letter or report can be delivered anywhere in the world in seconds or minutes. Sometimes the information is delivered instantaneously as it is being produced, as in the case of video conferencing. This is more prevalent today as cellular data communication is currently making this need a reality for many corporations. A company employee can use a laptop computer, a modem, and a cellular telephone to access databases at a central location directly from a customer site where a telephone line may not be available.

Second, a data communication system needs to capture business data as it is being produced. Data communication systems are being used more and more as input mechanisms to capture data about the daily business operations of a corporation as the data is generated. On-line computer applications allow a business to enter customer information, produce an invoice to the customer, and provide inventory and shipping information while the customer is performing the transaction. In addition, once the information is entered into the system, it is available to other users instantaneously.

The survival of many businesses depends on having data available on a real-time basis. Imagine, for example, an airline reservation system that cannot provide timely notification of flight information to passengers or a bank that cannot post deposits on a timely basis. Transportation, finance, insurance, and other industries require complex, fast, and accurate data communication systems for their business survival. As a result, companies have developed parallel systems and proper backup systems to ensure that their communication networks have a minimal amount of "down time" (time when the network is not functioning). The survival of the company depends on the data communication network being accessible at all times.

Third and finally, data communication systems allow people and businesses in different geographical locations to communicate with one another. Data communication systems allow employees of companies separated by large distances to work as if they were in close proximity. Corporations can communicate with manufacturing operations in a geographical location far away from their administrative headquarters. Inventory, personnel, and other company data can be transmitted from one location to another through high-speed data communication networks. In this manner, the corporation can operate as a single entity. Managers can instantly review inventory levels in the manufacturing location. Engineers can deliver new designs in real-time, and managers can share timely and accurate information in order to make strategic decisions.

Data communication systems combined with computer technology are an integral part of today's companies. As a result, a business can become more effective and efficient in the world market than was possible a few years ago.

A Brief History

The first data communication systems were created in 1837 as a result of the invention of the telegraph by Samuel F. B. Morse. Even though the United States government declined to use the telegraph, in 1838 Morse created a private company to exploit his invention. By 1851, over fifty telegraph companies were in operation. Today's Western Union Telegraph was formed in 1856 and became the largest communication company in the United States ten years later.

In 1876, the U.S. patent office issued a patent to Alexander Graham Bell for his invention of the telephone, with the Bell Telephone Company then being formed in 1877. The first telephone system didn't have switching offices or exchanges. If a subscriber wanted to establish a communication with another subscriber, he had to have a pair of telephone wires attached directly to the phone at the location of the receiving call. Therefore, if a business needed communication with fifty other businesses, then it had to install fifty pairs of wires. When a call was made, the right wires had to be connected to the telephone. In addition, telephones didn't have bells or ringers. Therefore, both parties had to be on-line at the same time since there was no way for one party to know when the other was making a call.

However, technology progressed rapidly, and by 1878 Bell installed the first telephone exchange with an operator. By using wire jumpers a telephone operator could connect a user to different locations. Therefore, subscribers didn't require a pair of wires for each location they wanted to reach.

In 1885, American Telephone and Telegraph Company (AT&T) was formed to build and operate long distance lines in order to interconnect the regional phone companies. This allowed the connection of the individual Bell company subsidiaries operating throughout the country to connect all their subscribers together.

Technology continued to progress, and by 1892 automatic switching began with the introduction of the first dial exchange in La Porte, Indiana. This system worked by using a series of electromechanical selector switches, called relays, to automatically place the incoming call on the right outgoing line. This process took time to complete and that is the reason the first telephone used round dials. The round dials provided a deliberate waiting period after each digit was dialed, giving the switch time to set up the connections. The electromechanical switch was replaced later by the electronic switch. With this type of device the delay used for the relays was no longer required, and push-button telephones could then be used to make the connection.

The vacuum tube was invented in 1913, and in 1941 came the integration of computer and communication technology. This was an important step in the evolution of communication systems. The computer enabled the creation and management of faster and more sophisticated systems. With this integration, the usage and development of new systems accelerated, lowering the cost of communication and increasing quality and efficiency.

In 1943, submersible amplifiers and repeaters were developed, facilitating communication across large distances and among international customers. But it was the invention of the transistor in 1947 that revolutionized the telecommunication industry. The transistor allowed for the development of smaller and faster computers that, through mass production, became relatively inexpensive and within the reach of many companies and users. The integration of communication systems and computers would not be what it is today without the invention of the transistor and subsequent developments in integrated circuitry. This technology led to the development of satellites with the first satellite being launched in 1957, expanding the opportunity for worldwide data communications.

In 1968, an important decision, known as the Carterfone Decision, was made by the Federal Communication Commission (FCC). The FCC decided that a small Dallas-based company (Carter Electronics Corporation) could attach its Carterfone product to the public telephone network. The Carterfone allowed the connection of private radio systems to the phone network. When AT&T refused to allow Carter Electronics to attach its product to the phone system, Carter Electronics sued and won. This decision opened the door for the attachment of non-AT&T equipment to the public phone system and spawned a new era in the communication industry. It also help in breaking the monopoly that AT&T and the Bell companies had over the phone system.

Other antitrust suits against AT&T from the period of 1974 to 1982 ended in 1984, in the divestiture of AT&T from its 22 Bell companies. This allowed many other companies to provide phone services to individuals and corporations, ultimately increasing the quality, sophistication, and types of offerings that a communications company could provide. It also helped in reducing the cost of using data communication systems. Table 1-1 shows a summary of the history of data communication.

	Summary of Data Communication History
1837	Invention of the telegraph
1856	Western Union was created
1877	The Bell company was formed
1885	AT&T was created
1913	Invention of the vacuum tube
1941	Integration of computing and communication technology
1947	Invention of the transistor
1957	First satellite was launched
1968	Carterfone decision
1984	Divestiture of Bell company

Table 1-1. A summary of data communication history

Today, the network of available telephone lines, microwave stations, and satellite stations continues to expand. Computer technology continues to become faster and more economical. Data communication has become a worldwide enterprise. These systems, although complex, have three common characteristics that are used to subdivide them. These characteristics are what are called the data communication system basic components.

Basic Components

Data communication systems can be divided into three major components:

1. The source of communication. This is the originator of the message to be sent. This source can be a simple telephone used by a human or it can be a computer that calls another computer for the purpose of exchanging data.

2. The medium of communication. This is the physical path through which the message has to travel. It can consist of twisted pair wires, coaxial cable, optical fiber, microwave, or some other type of data carrying media.

3. The receiver (sometimes called the sink or host) of the communication. This is the receiver of the message. The receiver can be a telephone that is answered by a person or it can be a host computer answering the call from a calling computer or terminal.

The Sender

Although the communication established between two people through the use of the telephone is important, in this book we are more concerned with the communication requirements when two or more computers want to establish a communication link. This is because in many situations a computer is both the sender and receiver. If two computers have a communication link established and data is flowing from one machine to the other, one of the machines is transmitting data at times and at other times may be receiving data.

The Communication Medium

The medium can be a leased line from the telephone company (also called a common carrier), a proprietary coaxial line, optical fiber, microwave, satellite, or other facilities. Fig. 1-1 depicts a basic data communication system. This system includes computers or terminals that act as senders, modems, connector cables, telephone switching equipment, interexchange channel facilities, a receiver, and a host computer. The items in Fig. 1-1 will be explained in more detail in further chapters, but a general description follows.

The computer and terminal are used to enter information. This device can be a terminal attached to a minicomputer or mainframe, or a microcomputer with

Fig. 1-1. A basic
data communica-
tion system.

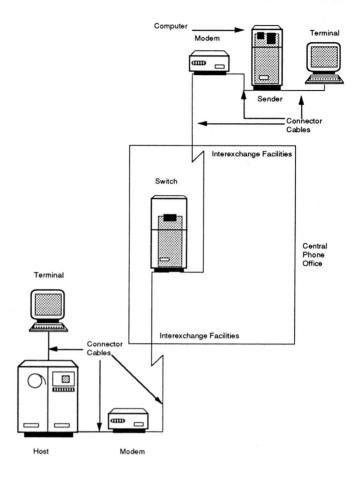

a keyboard and a printer, or it can be a FAX machine, or any other input device.

The connector cables in Fig. 1-1 connect the sender to a modem. The modem is an electronic device that converts digital signals originating from a computer or FAX machine into analog signals that the telephone equipment can transmit. The signals go from the modem to a local telephone switch that connects the home or office to the telephone company central office or some other carrier. Then, at the central office, switching equipment connects the sender's equipment to a line that terminates at the receiver's location and equipment.

The Central Office

The central office (sometimes called the exchange office) contains switching and control facilities operated by the phone company (see topic later in this chapter). All calls and data exchanges have to flow through these facilities unless there is a leased line. If there is a leased line, the phone company wires the line around the switching equipment in order to provide an unbroken path. An example of a commonly used lease line is the T1 line which will be discussed in Chapter 3.

The Interexchange Facilities

Interexchange channels (IXCs) are circuit lines that connect one central exchange office with another. These circuit lines can be microwave, satellite, coaxial cable, or other physical media. They simply relay communication data from one geographical location to another for the purpose of routing the call.

The Host

Finally, the receiving end has another modem to convert the analog signals from the telephone company back to digital format. These signals are then transferred to a host computer that processes the received message and takes appropriate action.

Many other components can be incorporated into the data communication system depicted in Fig. 1-1. Later chapters provide further details of these components, as well as an in-depth discussion of communication networks that incorporate computer technology. However, one component of the data communication system, the communication network, is worth discussing at this point.

The Data Communication Network

A network is a series of points that are connected by some type of communication channel. Each point (sometimes called a node) is typically a computer, although it can consist of switching equipment, printers, FAX machines, or other devices. A data communication network is a collection of data communication circuits managed as a single entity. Then what is the difference between a data communication system and a data communication network? The collection of data communication networks and the people who enter data, receive the data, and manage and control the networks make up the communication system. Fig. 1-2 shows examples of multiple networks which are part of a data communication system.

Even though almost anyone can establish a data communication network, successful network implementations have a common set of characteristics. These characteristics, sometimes called requirements, of a data communication network must be observed if the network is to be efficient and effective in its role. To create a successful implementation, a network designer must be aware of all the different configurations and possibilities that are at his or her disposal in designing the network. The network designer must be well schooled in design techniques as well as have an excellent understanding of the data communication field. This last point may seem trivial, but many companies leave network designing, especially local area network designing, to individuals without the proper background and training. The result is a

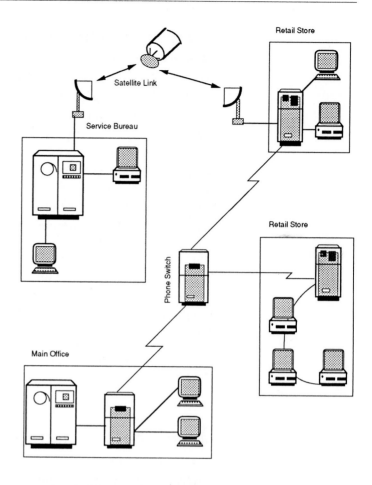

Fig. 1-2. Multiple networked data communications systems.

poorly configured system that is blamed for the difficulties and problems in communicating data within the company and a lack of user confidence in technology.

Requirements of a Data Communication Network

As discussed above, there is a set of major criteria that a successful data communication network must meet. These are performance, consistency, reliability, recovery, and security criteria.

Performance

A data communication network must deliver data in a timely manner. Performance is typically measured by the network response time. Response time is normally considered the elapsed time between the end of an inquiry to the network and the beginning of the response from the network or system. The response time of a communications network must meet the expectations of the users.

Many factors affect the response time of a network. Some of these factors are the number of users on the system, transmission speed, type of transmission medium, and the type of hardware and software being employed. For example, assume that a network was designed to handle the data communication needs of 20 individuals and their associated equipment. If the company that houses them has a growth period during which the number of users is doubled, then most likely the response time of the communication system will increase, in some cases by several orders of magnitude.

In addition, 20 users communicating through a medium at 10 megabits per second will get a different response time than the same number of users with a 2.1 megabit per second medium. Also, the type of data transmitted makes a difference in the response time of the network. If text files are transmitted through a 2.1 megabit transmission path, the response time will be less than the same network transmitting large graphics files and text files at the same time.

Although there is a tendency to relate the performance of a data communication network to its hardware, another big factor that will affect response time is the type of software running the system. The network operating system and the different protocols that must be handled by the network will have a large impact on the performance of the network. It is true that, if a network is slow, introducing faster hardware and a faster communication medium will decrease the response time. But, in many cases, the increase in speed of transmission gained by using this method is small compared to the gain obtained by using an efficient operating system and network operating system that are specifically designed to handle data communications between users. And just as important as the response time itself is the consistency of the response time across the network.

Consistency

Predictability of response time, accuracy of the data transmitted, and mean time between failures (MTBF) are important factors to consider when choosing a network. Inconsistency of response time is annoying to users, and sometimes it is worse than a slow but consistent response time. Users typically prefer having a consistent response time of three seconds that they can depend on to having, for example, a one-second response time that, on occasion, varies to 15 seconds. Unpredictable performance may motivate some users to rely on other means of acquiring and transmitting their data, making the data communication network inadequate as a data communication solution for the company.

Accuracy of data is important if the network is to be deemed reliable. If a system loses data, then the users will not have confidence in the information generated by the system. An unreliable system is often not used, and, if it is used, users tend to duplicate the data entered into the network by using manual systems. The result is that users spend additional time manually duplicating everything they send through the network, thus increasing the amount of time they spend on a function. This decreases their productivity, increases the cost to the company, and tends to demoralize the users of the system.

Reliability

In addition to the accuracy of the data transmitted, another factor that contributes to network reliability is how often the network is unusable. This is often called network failure and is measured by the mean time between failures.

Network failure is any event that prohibits the users from processing transactions. Network failure can include a breakdown in hardware, the data carrying medium, and/or the network controlling software (network operating system). With today's data communication networks as complex as they are, the number of components that can fail during the operation of the network is continually increasing. But modern equipment has a failure rate that is less than similar but older equipment. In addition, new monitoring techniques and redundancy in the network contribute to increasing the time during which the system is operational.

As mentioned above, the failure rate of the network and its equipment is measured by the mean time between failures. The MTBF is a measure of the average time a component is expected to operate between failures. This time is normally established by the manufacturer of the equipment, and users normally trust the numbers provided by the maker of the equipment. However, many user groups and trade publications have their own statistics, and users are advised to compare these numbers with those provided by equipment manufacturers. In addition, these statistics provide some indication of the time of recovery after a failure. This refers to the length of time for the equipment or the network to become operational after a failure.

Recovery

All networks are subject to failure. After a failure, the network must be able to recover to a prescribed level of operation. This prescribed level is a point in the network operation where the amount of lost data is nonexistent or at a minimum. Recovery procedures and the extent of recovery will depend on the types of hardware and software that control the network.

Some networks use log files that are saved continually to a hard disk. These log files contain all transactions performed since the system was turned on or since a predetermined date. If the network fails, then many network operating systems are capable of using the log file to rebuild transactions that were lost when the system went down. Less sophisticated systems rely on a network operator to rebuild the system based on the log file. In addition, many networks employ what are commonly known as mirror techniques with their hard drives. With this technique data can be saved to two different hard disks at the same time. In this manner, if a hard disk failure occurs, the other hard disk is brought on line and the system can stay operational. Mirror techniques enhance the reliability of the network, but they also enhance another critical aspect of the network, its security.

Security

Network security is another important component in communication networks, especially when computer data is involved. A business's data must be protected from unauthorized access and from being destroyed in a catastrophic event such as fire. Therefore, companies are placing more stringent security measures on networks in order to safeguard their data. When a communications network is being designed, security must be carefully considered and incorporated into the final design.

A network's security is enhanced by the use of identification numbers and passwords for all of its users. In addition, call-back units can be used to reduce the number of unauthorized callers. These units assure that the caller or user of the network is in an authorized location and/or terminal. However, even these measures are not enough in safeguarding the data transmitted through and stored in the network.

Another technique employed when security is a high priority is encryption. With this method, data that needs to be transmitted is encoded with a special security key. The result is that, to unauthorized users, the data looks like garbage. At the receiving end, the same key is used to decode the data and convert it to its original format. Security keys and encrypting are commonly used in the defense industry.

Data on a network is also threatened by computer viruses. A computer virus is a program that invades programs inside computers in the network and then performs unwanted functions on the programs themselves and the data stored on disks. These functions can be as simple as displaying annoying characters on the screens of network users, to destroying the data stored on the user hard disks and network servers. Several programs and monitoring software can be used to alert network administrators to the presence of such viruses.

Applications of Communication Networks

During the 1990s, data communication networks will be a faster growing industry than computer processing itself. Even though both industries are now integrated, we are moving from the computer era to the data communication era. A recent survey indicates that during this decade, the majority of new career opportunities will be related to the communication field, especially in local area networks and their connectivity to other systems. Data communication networks are appearing in all places where one computer needs to exchange data with another computer. Teaching institutions are connecting their students and administrative workstations. Companies connect each department with a local area network and then connect individual local area networks into a single network, and corporations that cover the world connect their regional networks into wider area networks through the use of satellites.

Also, many business systems currently use data communication networks as the "backbone" for carrying out their daily business activities. Data communication networks can be found in every segment of industry. On-line passenger systems, such as American Airlines' SABRE, have changed the way people travel. In addition, an airline's computer is normally connected to all other airlines via telecommunications. In this manner, reservation agents from United Airlines can make reservations for flights on American Airlines. Car rental companies, such as Avis, and hotel chains, such as Holiday Inn, could not function effectively without their reservation systems. The type and scope of communication networks are wide and extensive. But a few applications of data communication networks are commonly found in many modern companies. These types of applications are discussed in the following paragraphs and include videotext, satellite, public networks, teleconferencing, and telecommuting.

Videotext

Videotext is the capability of having a two-way transmission between a television or computer in the home and organizations outside the home. It allows people to take college courses at home, conduct teleconferences from the home, play video games with players in other locations, utilize electronic mail, connect with the bank and grocery stores, do on-line mail shopping, utilize voice store and messaging systems, and carry out many other functions.

Fig. 1-3 shows a screen display of a bulletin board that is used for discussing expert advice on computer topics. The conferencing system can be accessed from a home by using a microcomputer and special hardware to call a host computer and use it to "talk" to other people on the system. This is a common process used on many public and commercial bulletin boards (see topic below). With it, an electronic public forum or a question and answer session that involves dozens of people simultaneously can be conducted. In addition, it is a quick way to have on-line training between a customer and a service company.

Satellite

By using a home satellite TV receiver and transmitter, people will be able to communicate with others via a satellite dish located on their property. This antenna can receive and transmit voice or data to any other part of the world by relaying it to other satellites orbiting the earth.

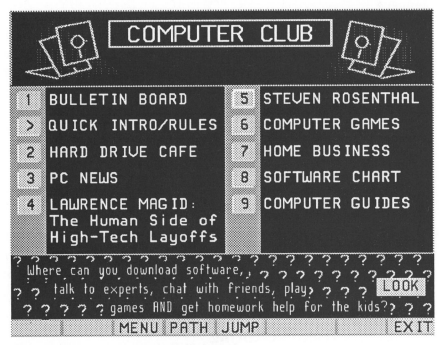

Fig. 1-3. A screen from a bulletin board.

Many steps have been taken to reduce the cost of transmitting data using this method. Today the cost of receiving data using a home satellite dish is relatively low. One use of this technology has been tested by politicians when they conduct electronic town meetings. When one of these "meetings" takes place, the satellite and frequency of transmission are normally available to the public. A person with the right equipment and information can tune into the satellite channel and receive the transmission without the interruption of commentators normally found in commercial television.

In addition to home satellite systems, many computer users have data communication through ham radio. With the appropriate equipment, a ham radio operator can transmit computer data through the radio waves without having to pay the fees normally associated with satellite transmission. Of course, the speed and clarity of the transmission is lower when using this method.

Public Communication Networks

Public communication networks have standard interfaces that allow almost any type of computer or terminal to connect to other computers or terminals. Many companies already have their own private telephone branch exchange (PBX). These systems can connect terminals and computers in the company to other systems anywhere in the world by using satellite, radio, and microwave transmission.

Using public networks an individual can use a terminal or computer and a modem from his or her home and connect to other computers and networks located in a different geographical location. This capability is used by many progressive companies to allow their employees to work from their homes. This has increased the efficiency of many employees since they can now spend the time required to travel back and forth from the office performing their jobs. Additionally, companies are now able to keep valuable employees that they could otherwise lose, such as new parents who want to stay home with their children. By using a personal computer, a modem, and a public network, these employees can now minimize the amount of time spent at the office.

In addition to traditional transmission media offered by public networks, cellular radio loops can be used to replace copper wire as the communication medium for computers. This increases the ability of an employee to be at a required location and still be in touch with the main office's network and host systems.

Teleconferencing

Video teleconferencing allows people located in different geographical regions to "attend" meetings in both voice and picture format. A video teleconference is accomplished by using a television camera and associated equipment to transmit voice and video signals through satellite networks. Many teleconferences have the same type of equipment at both sites, allowing all attendees to talk to and see each other, including selected computer displays. Other teleconferences have the projection equipment at a single location, and participants at remote locations can communicate back to the central transmitting site by using telephone communications.

Documents can also be made available to all people attending the teleconference almost instantaneously. This can be performed with the use of facsimile machines or by using a scanner and then transmitting the scanned image. However, if the required document exists in digital form, the data can simply be transmitted with the use of a modem and a receiving modem and computer system.

Telecommuting

This application, as explained before, allows employees to perform office work at home. Through the use of a terminal or a personal computer and a modem, an employee can be in constant communication with the company and perform his or her work more efficiently and without wasting the time required to travel to and from the office. This allows employees to have greater time flexibility, less stress, optimized scheduling, and many other benefits. The employee is then free to schedule his or her work to allow for maximizing use of the available time. In most of these cases, the employee visits the office once or twice per week for meetings or other duties, but this time is minimal when compared to the weekly schedule.

Electronic Mail

Electronic mail (e-mail) provides the ability to transmit written messages over short or long distances instantaneously through the use of a microcomputer or terminal attached to a communication network. The people communicating through electronic mail do not have to be on-line at the same time. Each can leave messages to the other and retrieve the replies at later times. Fig. 1-4 shows a screen that is typical of many electronic mail systems.

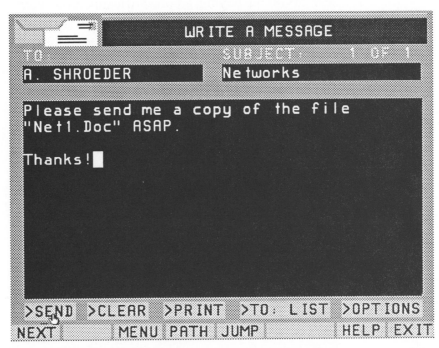

Fig. 1-4. Electronic mail screen.

Electronic mail has the ability to forward messages to different locations, send word processed or spreadsheet documents to any user of the network, and transmit the same message to more than one user by using a mail list. A mail list contains the names and electronic mailbox addresses of people to whom the message must be sent. The electronic mail system reads the names and addresses from the list and sends the message to all users on the mail list. Electronic mail significantly improves corporate and individual communications.

Home Banking

Computers can handle the traditional methods of making payments through home banking. A user with a terminal or microcomputer can connect to his or her bank's computer network through electronic mail and pay bills electronically, instead of writing paper checks. The user can indicate the amount of a payment and the receiver of the payment electronically, and the bank processes the transfer of funds. Additionally, new home banking systems offer many other services besides personal fund transfers. Some of these services are providing checking account balances, ticket purchasing, and stock information services. Fig. 1-5 shows a screen of a home banking service software program. The banking service displayed in the figure has services for bill paying, credit card acquisition, money markets, IRAs, loans, and mortgages.

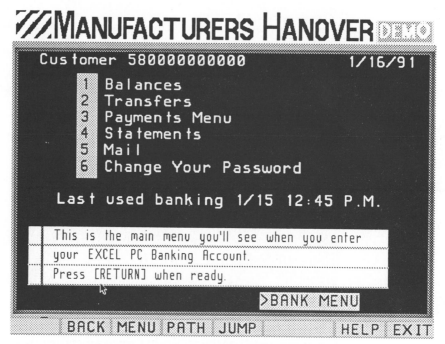

Fig. 1-5. A screen showing a home banking system.

Also, many electronic home banking services are being connected to other consumer services such as grocery stores. By using this service, an individual can use a personal computer and modem to dial a database of products belonging to a grocery company or store. The user selects the type and quantity of the products needed and then instructs the system to produce a balance. The balance is then forwarded to the electronic home banking system which transfers the balance to the grocer's account, and the bag of groceries can be picked up by the customer. Or, for a small fee, it can be delivered to the customer's address.

Electronic Funds Transfer

The ability to transfer funds electronically from one financial institution to another has become a necessity in today's banking world. Commercial banks transfer millions of dollars daily through their electronic funds transfer (EFT) system. The large number of transactions that are made every day by banks requires the use of computers and communication networks to increase speed and cost efficiency.

Imagine the amount of time that it would take to manually handle all fund transfer transactions that take place in a single day at the New York Stock Exchange. Although some people think that the use of technology in such settings is more harmful than good, today's financial transactions couldn't be accomplished without the use of effective data communication networks. The modern western world couldn't exist as we know it without such communication systems.

Information Utility Services

Information utility services offer general and specialized information that is organized and cross-referenced, much like subjects are in libraries. Items are organized into databases and each database contains several categories of services, such as access to news, legal libraries, stock prices, electronic mail services, conferencing, and games.

The desired information is located by signing onto the information service and then selecting the topic of interest from a menu. Once the topic is selected, search criteria can be entered and the system will display the information on the screen. This information can then be captured (downloaded) onto the hard disk of the user's microcomputer for further examination.

Electronic Bulletin Boards

The electronic bulletin board system (BBS or EBBS) consists of a computer or microcomputer that is used to store, retrieve, and catalog messages sent in by the general public through their modems. The telephone company provides the link between the person using the BBS and the host computer of the BBS. The primary purpose of BBS is for people to leave notes to others.

Additionally, some BBS are now being used for group conferencing. They offer a variety of messages and services to their users. Some of these services are electronic "chats" with other users, making airline reservations, playing games, and sending and receiving messages.

Value Added Networks

Value added networks (VANs) are alternative data carriers to the traditional public data carriers such as AT&T. VANs are now considered common carriers and are subject to all government regulations. They can be divided into public and private VANs.

Private VANs own and operate their networks and are not accessible to the public. One example of a private carrier is the SABRE system used by travel agents to make reservations and check prices. Public VANs offer a wide variety of communication services to the general public. These services include access to databases and electronic mail routing. An example of a public VAN is Telenet.

Summary

Data communication is the transmission of electronic data over some medium. The medium can be coaxial cable, optical fiber, microwave, or some of the other data-carrying media. The hardware and software systems that enable the transmission of data make up what are called data communication networks. For a data communication system to be effective, it must provide information to the right people in a timely manner, capture business data as it is being produced, and allow people in businesses in different geographical locations to communicate with one another. The basic components of a data communication system are the source of communication, the medium of communication, and the receiver of the communication. All data communication systems must meet a minimum set of requirements, which include performance, consistency, reliability, recovery, and security requirements.

Data communication systems are composed of data communication networks. A network is a series of points connected by some type of communication channel. Each point is typically a computer, although it can consist of many other electronic devices. The type and scope of data communication networks are wide and extensive. But a few applications of data communication networks are commonly found in modern companies. These types of applications include videotext, satellite, public networks, teleconferencing, and telecommuting.

Questions

1. Briefly describe the concept of data communications.
2. Name some of the possible data transmission media.
3. What are the functions of data communication systems?
4. Briefly name the most important historical events that shaped the communication industry up to the 1990s.
5. Describe the basic components of a data communication network.
6. What is a communication network?

7. What is the difference between a communication network and a communication system?

8. What are the major requirements that a data communication network must possess?

9. What is meant by mean time between failures (MTBF)?

10. Discuss three applications of a data communication network.

11. What is e-mail?

12. What is a bulletin board system?

13. What is an information service?

14. What services are provided by commercial bulletin board systems?

15. Name four commercial information services.

Projects

Project 1. Understanding an Existing Computer Communication System

This project will make the student familiar with a currently implemented data communication system. It provides a way to visualize the concepts and hardware discussed in the chapter. In addition, it allows the student to acquire a "feel" for how people use the components of data communication systems and to observe some of the equipment and processes that will be explained in more detail in subsequent chapters.

Visit the data center at your institution and find what types of network and data communication facilities are available for the private use of the institution and which facilities are available for general public access. Try to answer all of the following questions by asking data center personnel or by observing the daily operations and hardware present at the center.

a. What types of mainframes or minicomputers (hosts) are available?

b. What types of personal computers are available?

    o Laptops

    o Macintosh Classic/SE

    o Macintosh II family

    o IBM PC/AT

    o IBM PS/2

    o IBM-compatible clone

    o Other

c. Are the hosts networked?

d. Are the personal computers networked?

e. How are the personal computers connected to the host?

f. Is electronic mail available?

g. How is the electronic mail accessed?

h. What databases are available in the institution library?

i. How often do they experience down time?

j. Find out how the staff conducts business when their computer or terminal is down.

k. How is the data protected from unauthorized access and accidents?

Project 2. Understanding an Elementary Computer Network

Contact your local bank and write a report that describes how the bank personnel perform their daily routines. Use the following outline as a guide for your report.

a. What computer systems are in use at headquarters and at the branches?

    o Mainframes

    o Minicomputers

    o Personal computers

    o Terminals

b. What networks are used at each branch and between branch and headquarters?

c. How is electronic fund transfer handled?

d. What types of value added networks and public networks are used to perform e-mail and electronic fund transfer?

e. Are there any facilities available for home banking?

f. What types of disaster recovery plans do they have?

g. How do the managers at different branches communicate with each other?

Basic Communication Concepts and Hardware

Objectives

After completing this chapter you will

1. Differentiate between the various modes of data transmission.
2. Understand the ASCII code system and its importance.
3. Understand the concept and use of modems in the communication process.
4. Be able to design and use interfaces for serial (RS-232) ports.
5. Understand the role of microcomputers in data communication systems.

Key Terms

ASCII	Asynchronous Communication
Control Characters	Full-duplex
Half-duplex	Modem
Parallel Port	RS-232 Interface
Serial Port	Smart Modem
	Synchronous Communication

Introduction

Data communication hardware and software come in many different forms and levels of sophistication. However, at the basic level of transmissions, a few concepts and devices are standard across all computing and data communication platforms. The mode of transmission is one of these concepts. Regardless of the devices transmitting, the modes in which the data are transmitted remain basically constant. In this case data can be transmitted in simplex, half-duplex or full-duplex, and it can be a serial or parallel transmission. Data can be sent asynchronously or synchronously. These are the concepts that this chapter explores along with a description of the standard digital codes that constitute the data being transmitted.

In addition to the mode of data transmission, this chapter explores the concepts and uses of modems. Since modems are a basic and common way of communication in the microcomputer world, they deserve special treatment. Also, the port used to connect the modem to the computer, the RS-232 or EIA-232, as it is sometimes called, is explored and analyzed in detail.

Modes of Transmission

There are many different ways in which the transmission of data can be classified. However, data transmission is normally grouped into three major areas according to

1. How the data flows among devices.
2. The type of physical connection.
3. The type of timing used for transmitting data.

Data can flow in simplex, half-duplex, or full-duplex mode (see Fig. 2-1). The physical connection can be parallel or serial (see Fig. 2-2), and the timing can be synchronous or asynchronous.

Data Flow

In simplex transmission, data flows in only one direction on a data communication line. Examples of this type of communication are commercial television and radio transmission. A television station normally broadcasts a signal from an antenna connected to a production studio and it is received by a television receiver in the home. Once the signal is received by the television set, it is displayed but no data is sent back to the production studio.

Fig. 2-1. Modes of transmission.

Simplex. Data travels only in one direction.

Half-duplex. Data can travel in both directions, but only in one direction at a time.

Full-duplex. Data can travel in both directions simultaneously.

In half-duplex mode, transmission is allowed in either direction on a circuit, but in only one direction at a time. This type of transmission is widely used in data processing applications. If a computer is communicating with a terminal in this mode, then only one of them can be transmitting at any given time. Once the terminal sends data to the computer and the message is received, then the computer can send data back to the terminal. During this last phase, the terminal becomes the listener and the computer the sender. If two devices are communicating in half-duplex and both transmit at the same time, then the data sent is not received or simply becomes "garbage" in the lines.

Fig. 2-2. Serial and parallel communications.

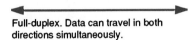

Serial Communication. One bit per clock pulse

Parallel Communication. All bits are transmitted at the same time.

25

Full-duplex mode allows for the transmission of data in both directions simultaneously. Most terminals and microcomputers are configured to work in full-duplex mode. This type of transmission requires more software and hardware control on both ends. This mode allows the computer and the terminal to send at the same time. Specialized software and hardware make sure that the messages are delivered to their destinations in a legible format. Although this is the most complex of the three modes, it is also the most efficient.

Physical Connection

Although data transmission can be classified according to the format of the data flow through the communication wires, it can also be classified as to how many bits of information are transmitted with every clock pulse. If data transmission is classified in this manner, then two possibilities arise. One is parallel communications and the other is serial communications.

The input/output ports of a data processing device can transmit data bit by bit or send an entire byte in a single parallel operation employing eight lines, one for each bit. The benefit of parallel transmission is its simplicity. A byte is placed on the output port of a device and a single pulse of the computer clock transfers the data to a receiving device. However, because of the number of wires involved and the loss of signal over relatively short distances, it is impractical to use parallel ports for communications over long distances. Parallel communication is achieved through the use of a parallel port or Centronics interface normally located at the back of the computer.

In serial transmission the data is sent one bit at a time using a single conductor to provide communication between devices. Standard telephone lines can be used to transmit data serially. Although transmitting data in this mode is slower than parallel transmission, it is currently a widely used data transmission mode. This is especially true in the case of communications between a microcomputer and a minicomputer or mainframe. In many situations, the microcomputer is simply working in a terminal emulation mode. That is, it is working as if it was the native terminal of the minicomputer or mainframe. In such cases, most managers want to use the least expensive communication schema. If the microcomputers are in close proximity to the host, serial communication is normally employed.

Timing

The type of timing used for the transmission of data is the last of the major categories for classifying data communications. Here, timing refers to how the receiving system knows that it received the group of bits that form a valid character. Two major timing schemas are used. One is asynchronous communication and the other is synchronous data communication.

Asynchronous communication is characterized by the use of a start bit preceding each character transmitted. In addition, there are one or more stop bits which follow each character. In asynchronous transmission, sometimes called async, data comes in irregular bursts, not in steady streams.

The start and stop bits form what is called a character frame. Every character must be enclosed in a frame. The receiver counts the start bit and the appropriate number of data bits. If it does not sense the end of a frame, then a framing error has occurred and an invalid character was received. When this happens, smart systems ask that the sender retransmit the last group of bits.

Asynchronous transmission is relatively simple and inexpensive to implement. It is widely used by microcomputers and commercial communication devices. However, it has a low transmission efficiency since at least two extra bits must be added to each character transmitted. Typically, asynchronous communication takes place at low speeds, ranging from 300 to 19,200 baud but in some cases the transmission speed can be higher.

The start and stop bits in asynchronous transmission add overhead to the bit stream. There is an alternate method of serial communication that doesn't use start and stop bits. It is called synchronous serial communication. With synchronous transmission, data characters are sent in large groups called blocks. These blocks contain synchronization characters that have a unique bit pattern. They are placed at the beginning and middle of each block with the synchronization characters ranging in number from one to four. When the receiver detects one of these special characters, it knows that the following bit is the beginning of a character maintaining, in this manner, synchronization.

This type of transmission is more efficient than asynchronous communication. As an example, assume that 10,000 characters are going to be sent serially. If the characters are sent via asynchronous transmission, then 10,000 char x (8 data bits + 2 bits per char) yields 100,000 bits that are sent in asynchronous communications. Using synchronous communication, the calculation (10,000 char + 4 synchronous char) x 8 bits per char yields 80,032 bits that are sent.

In this example, the synchronous transmission has a 22 percent increase in transmission efficiency over asynchronous transmission. The efficiency of synchronous over asynchronous transmission increases as the block of data gets larger. Many terminals use synchronous communication, including the IBM 3270 series. However, the actual efficiency of the transmission will also depend on many other factors such as how many times bits must be retransmitted.

Standard Digital Codes

As mentioned before, computers process information in digital form. That is, information is in the form of individual bits or digits with a bit being the smallest unit of data that the computer can represent. Normally, personal computers use 7 or 8 bits to represent the individual characters that are stored inside the computer. Individual characters for the English language that are stored in a computer include:

> Lower- and uppercase letters of the alphabet (a...Z)
>
> Digits (0...9)
>
> Punctuation marks (., ?, :, ...)
>
> Arithmetic operators (*, -, +, /, ...)
>
> Unit symbols (%, $, #, ...)

In addition to these characters, there is a set of special characters that some computer makers include with their machines. These are mostly graphical and language specific characters.

For many years, the computer industry has tried to standardize the representation of digital codes. As a result, two major code representations exist in the market today. The most popular and widely recognized is the code system employed by computer manufacturers in the United States and many other countries called the American Standard Code for Information Interchange (ASCII). The other major code is the Extended Binary Coded Decimal Interchange Code (EBCDIC), which is used by IBM mainframes and compatibles. Most other types of mainframes, minicomputers, and microcomputers employ the ASCII code.

ASCII is a seven-bit code in which 128 characters are represented. EBCDIC uses eight bits to represent each character. Table 2-1 shows the standard ASCII code representation. In addition to the standard 128 ASCII characters, there is a set of 128 special characters used by IBM personal computers and compatibles called the Extended ASCII. The characters represented in Extended ASCII vary among computer manufacturers and are used to represent foreign characters or graphic characters.

In this chapter we will concentrate on explaining the ASCII representation since it is the most popular. The ASCII code in Table 2.1 contains 128 unique items. The table shows 32 control characters and 96 printable characters. Table 2-1 uses the hexadecimal system to represent the ASCII value of each character. To find the ASCII value of a character the process is as follows. Assume that the ASCII value of "A" is required. The column number of "A" is four, therefore four is multiplied by 16 giving 64. The row number of "A" is one, so one is added to the previous result. The total is 65 and that is the ASCII value of the character "A". Notice that the rows jump from 9 to A, B,

	0	1	2	3	4	5	6	7
0	NUL	DLE	SP	0	@	P	`	p
1	SOH	DC1	!	1	A	Q	a	q
2	STX	DC2	"	2	B	R	b	r
3	ETX	DC3	#	3	C	S	c	s
4	EOT	DC4	$	4	D	T	d	t
5	ENQ	NAK	%	5	E	U	e	u
6	ACK	SYN	&	6	F	V	f	v
7	BEL	ETB	'	7	G	W	g	w
8	BS	CAN	(	8	H	X	h	x
9	HT	EM	)	9	I	Y	i	y
A	LF	SUB	*	:	J	Z	j	z
B	VT	ESC	+	;	K	[	k	{
C	FF	FS	`	<	L	\	l		
D	CR	GS	-	=	M	]	m	}
E	SO	RS	.	>	N	^	n	~
F	SI	US	/	?	O	-	o	DEL

Table 2-1. ASCII codes.

C, D, E, and F. In this case A represents 10, B is 11, C is 12, D is 13, E is 14, and F is 15. Using this example it is easily verified that the ASCII value of the character "O" is 79, because 4 x 16 = 64, and 64 + 15 = 79.

The printable characters can be generated by pressing the corresponding key on the keyboard or by pressing the shift key and the appropriate key. The control characters are generated by pressing a key labeled Control or CTRL on the keyboard and a corresponding key. For the rest of this chapter, the character ^ will be used to denote the CTRL key. These control codes are used for communicating with external devices such as modems, printers, and additional codes.

The control codes can be further subdivided into format effectors, communication controls, information separators, and others as described in the following sections.

Format Effectors

The format effectors provide functions analogous to the control keys used in document preparation. Each code name is followed by its hexadecimal representation, then a colon, and finally the key combination that can generate the code. A description of each follows.

BS (backspace) 08H:^H. It moves the cursor on a video display or the print head of a printer back one space.

HT (horizontal tab) 09H:^I. This is the same as the Tab key on a keyboard or typewriter.

LF (line feed) 0AH:^J. It advances the cursor one line on a display or moves the printer down one line.

CR (carriage return) 0DH:^M. It returns the cursor on a display or moves the printer head to the beginning of the line. This code is sometimes combined with the line feed to produce a new line character that is defined as a CR/LF sequence.

FF (form feed) 0CH:^L. It ejects a page on a printer. It also causes the cursor to move one space to the right on a video screen.

VT (vertical tab) 0BH: ^K. It line feeds to the next programmed vertical tab on a printer. It causes the cursor to move up one line on a video screen.

Communication Controls

Another series of control codes is used for communication. These controls facilitate data transmission over a communication network. They are used in both async and sync serial protocols for data transfer handshaking. These codes are:

SOH. It indicates the start of a message heading data block. Workstations in a network check the data following this header to determine if they are the recipients of the data that will follow the heading. Sometimes this character is used in asynchronous communications to transfer a group of files without handling each file as a separate communication session.

STX. It indicates the start of text.

ETX. It indicates the end of text.

EOT. It indicates the end of transmission.

ENQ. It indicates the end of an inquiry.

ACK. It indicates acknowledgment by a device.

NAK. It is negative acknowledgment.

EXT. This is an interrupt.

SYN. It is synchronous idle.

ETB. It indicates the end of a block.

These control codes are used in building data-transfer protocols and during synchronous transmission.

Information Separators

The information-separator codes are:

FS. It is used as a file separator.

GS. It is used as a group separator.

RS. It is used as a record separator.

US. It is used as a unit separator.

Most of the communication control and information-separator codes are not relevant to the material presented in the rest of this chapter. However, they are shown here for general information purposes.

Additional Control Codes

Of the remaining codes used by computers, the most important are:

NUL (null) OOH: ^@. It is used to pad the start of a transmission of characters.

BEL (bell) 07H:^G. It generates a tone from the speaker on the video monitor or the computer.

DC1, DC2, DC3, and DC4 (device control): ^Q,^R,^S,^T. These codes are used to control video monitors and printers. Of these four, the first (DC1) and the third (DC3) are of special interest. DC1 is generated by ^Q, and it is called X-On. DC3 is generated by ^S, and it is called X-Off. If a computer sends information to a printer too quickly, then the printer's buffer gets full before it can print the characters stored in it. The result is that characters are lost before they can be printed. In this situation, the printer sends a ^S (X-Off) to the computer before the buffer is completely full. This causes the computer to stop sending characters. When there is room in the printer buffer for more characters, a ^Q (X-On) is sent to the computer. This indicates to the machine that it can resume sending characters. This use of X-On and X-Off is called software handshaking.

ESC (escape) 1BH: ^[. Video terminals, computers, and printers interpret the next character after the escape code as a printable character.

DEL (delete) 7FH. It is used to delete characters under the cursor on video displays.

When two computers communicate with each other, the information will be exchanged by passing the individual bits that make up the characters. The flow of information is controlled by the use of control codes between communicating devices. The conventions that must be observed in order for electronic devices to communicate with one another are called the protocol. The bits that make up these control characters flow through some type of communication medium.

If the communicating devices are in close proximity then the medium of communication can be coaxial cable, twisted-pair cable, or optical fiber. If the computers are far apart, then microwave, satellite, or telephone line connections are used to connect the machines. The phone company provides one of the most common and inexpensive methods of connecting machines. However, if analog phone lines are used, a modem must be employed.

Modems

Normally data communication between terminals or microcomputers and other host systems is done over some type of direct cabling. Direct means that the cable goes directly from one device to the other. However, sometimes the distance between the devices is too large to have a direct connection. In such cases a device, called a modem, can be used to facilitate the transmission process using telephone lines.

Fig. 2-3 depicts the connection of a remote terminal or microcomputer to a host system via standard telephone lines. The terminal and host systems are connected through telephone lines with a modem at each end of the connection. A modem is an electronic device that converts (modulates) the digital communications between computers into audible tones that can be transmitted over telephone lines. The received data are then converted (demodulated) from the audible tones into digital information. This is the origin of the name modem (MOdulator-DEModulator).

Modems not only facilitate the transmission process, but many of them have smart features built in. For example, many modems can dial phone numbers automatically. Additionally, they can redial busy numbers and automatically set the proper communicating speed. These features and others are discussed later in this section.

Fig. 2-3. Connection between remote terminal and host through the telephone lines using modems.

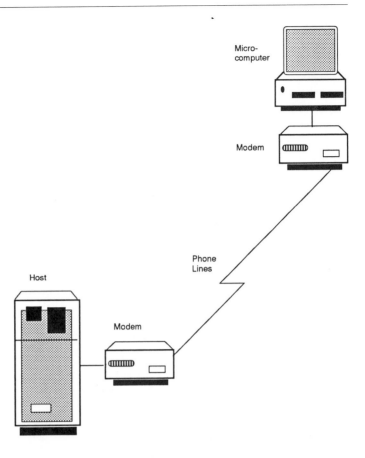

Although modems can be classified in many different ways, one way to classify them is according to the location of the modem with respect to the computer that it serves. Modems can be external or internal. An internal modem (Fig. 2-4) is placed inside the computer by using available bus expansion slots or bays. Then it is connected to a phone line with the use of a standard phone cord.

Fig. 2-4. Programmable half-card internal modem.

An external modem (Fig. 2-5) is placed next to the computer and connected to one of its serial ports with the use of a serial cable and to the telephone line with a phone cord. Once the modem is connected to the computer and the telephone, its function is normally controlled by software residing in the computer.

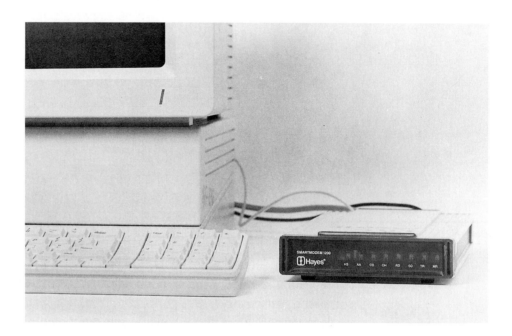

Fig. 2-5. Hayes external modem.

Modems transmit data at various speeds. The speed of data transfer through a modem can range from 300 bits per second to 9600 bits per second on microcomputers. On mainframe networks, modems operate at speeds of up to 1.5 million bits per second, and higher.

The speed of the modem determines the time required to transfer files. A higher speed of transmission means lower transfer time. The file transfer time can be estimated by using the formula:

Time = (characters to be transmitted x bits per character) / (modem speed in bits per second)

As an example, assume that a 100-page document is to be transmitted over telephone lines. Further assume that each page contains approximately 3300 characters and each character requires 7 bits for storage. This means that there will be 2,310,000 bits to be transmitted. The following table displays the approximate amount of time required to transmit the file.

Bits per second	300	1200	4800	9600
Time (seconds)	7700	1930	480	240

These are approximate times. The actual time required to transfer a file depends on many factors such as noise in the communicating lines, how the data is packed, and how many times a character must be retransmitted when an error occurs. However, the times shown in the table can be used to obtain an idea of how the transmission time is reduced by increasing the speed of the modem.

Types of Modems

There are several types of modems, each with a unique set of functions that make it suitable for a specific job. Some of the most common types are optical, short haul, acoustic, smart, digital, and V.32 modems. Of all of these, smart modems are the most commonly found in the microcomputer market.

Optical Modem

An optical modem transmits data over optical fiber lines. This type of modem, at the sender's end, converts electrical signals from a computer into pulses of light to be transmitted over optical fiber lines. At the receiver's end, the modem receives the light pulses and converts them back into a signal that the computer can understand. It operates using asynchronous or synchronous transmission modes.

Short Haul Modem

This type of modem uses paired wire cable to transmit electrical signals when the distances involved are approximately 20 miles or less. A short haul modem transmits at speeds of 9600 bits per second up to 5 miles, 4800 bits per second up to 10 miles, and finally at 2400 bits per second for distances of 10 to 20 miles. Normally, this type of modem is used to connect computers between different offices in the same building.

Acoustic Modem

This is an older type of modem, also called an acoustic coupler. It interfaces with any phone set and it is used for dialing another computer.

Smart Modem

A smart modem can perform functions by using a command language. The language can be accessed through communication programs and adds functionality to the modem. Among microcomputer users, the Hayes modem has become a standard. This device can automatically answer or dial other modems, switch communication parameters, set the modem's speaker volume, and perform many other functions under software control.

Digital Modem

If, instead of using analog conversion, the communication circuits use digital transmission, then a digital modem is used. This type of modem modifies the digital bits as needed. Its function is to convert EIA-232 digital signals into signals more suitable for transmission.

V.32 Modem

A V.32 modem works at full duplex at 9600 bits per second over normal telephone lines. It is typically used to back up leased phone lines on networks. That is, if data transmission through a leased line is interrupted, a V.32 and normal phone lines could be used as a temporary replacement for the leased line.

Features of Modems

Most newer modems have features that facilitate their use by inexperienced computer users. These features include the ability to change the speed of transmission, automatic dialing and redialing numbers, and automatic answering of incoming calls.

Speed

Modems are designed to operate at a set speed or a range of speeds. The speed can be set via switches on some modems or fall under program control. Typical speeds for modems under microcomputer control are 300, 1200, 2400, 4800, and 9600 bits per second.

Automatic Dialing/Redialing

Some modems can dial phone numbers under program control. If the modem encounters a busy line, it automatically redials the number until a connection is made.

Automatic Answering

Modems can automatically answer incoming calls and connect the dialing device to a host system. This is especially useful when setting up a private or home electronic bulletin board (see projects at the end of this chapter). In this case, you want the modem to answer calls automatically when a potential user calls in.

Self-testing

Most new modems have a self-testing mode. Each modem has electronic circuitry and software in ROM that allows the modem to check its electronic components and the connection to other modems, and to report any problems to the user. This includes memory checking, modem-to-modem transmission tests, and other self-tests.

Voice-over-data

Modems also allow the simultaneous transmission of voice and data. This allows a conversation to take place while data is being transmitted over the same phone line.

Other

Newer modems contain many other features in addition to the ones outlined above. Some of these features are:

> Auto-disconnect
>
> Manual connect/disconnect
>
> Speaker
>
> Full- or half-duplex
>
> Reverse channel
>
> Synchronous or asynchronous transmission
>
> Multiport

The RS-232 Port

Modems normally connect to the computer through an RS-232 or serial port. On most microcomputers, the connections between external modems, computers, and other devices conform to this RS-232 standard. The RS-232 is a connector that is found on the back panel of most computers. Fig. 2-6 shows a diagram of a 25-pin RS-232 connector.

The important pins to consider are pin numbers 1, 2, 3, 4, 5, 6, 8, and 20. Following is a description of these connectors with the capitalized abbreviations corresponding to the modem front panel.

> Pin 1. Frame ground: FG. It is used to connect the frame of the terminal or modem to earth ground. It protects the device from dangerous voltages. Normally, this pin is left unconnected.
>
> Pin 2. Transmit data: TD. Outgoing data travels from the terminal or computer to the modem via pin 2.
>
> Pin 3. Receive data: RD. Incoming data travels from the modem to the terminal or computer via pin 3.

Pin 4. Request to send: RTS. This is used to indicate to the terminal or computer that the modem has activated its carrier and that data transmission can start.

Pin 5. Clear to send: CTS. This pin is taken to an active level when the terminal or computer is ready to accept data.

Pin 6. Data set ready: DSR. An active DSR indicates to a device that it is connected to an active modem.

Pin 7. Signal ground: SG.

Pin 8. Data carrier detect: DCD. This pin is used by the modem to inform the computer or terminal that a remote connection has been made.

Pin 20. Data terminal ready: DTR. An active DTR indicates to the modem that it is connected to an active device.

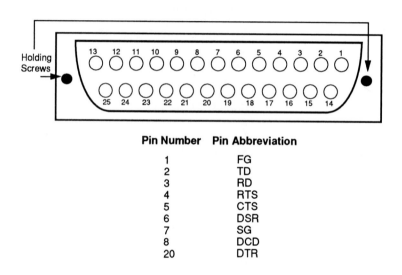

Pin Number	Pin Abbreviation
1	FG
2	TD
3	RD
4	RTS
5	CTS
6	DSR
7	SG
8	DCD
20	DTR

Fig. 2-6. 25-pin RS-232.

Handshaking is the manner in which the communicating computer knows when the other machine is sending or receiving data, or when it is doing some other task that might interfere with the transmission signals. This is also referred to as the communications protocol. Handshaking can be accomplished through the use of software by using control characters (X-On and X-Off). Pins 4, 5, 6, 8, and 20 are used for hardware handshaking. That is, these pins are used to make sure that there is cooperation between the devices exchanging data.

Another type of RS-232 connector is the nine-pin RS-232 connector found on some microcomputers. By using nine pins instead of twenty-five pins, space is saved on the back panels of computers and peripherals. The layout of the pin connections on this type of RS-232 differs from manufacturer to manufacturer. Fig. 2-7 shows the layout of the nine-pin RS-232 connector found on the IBM PC-AT.

The nine-pin connector in Fig. 2-7 has an extra pin (pin 9, RI) beyond the eight defined above. This is the ring indicator. This pin becomes active when the modem has received the ring of an incoming call.

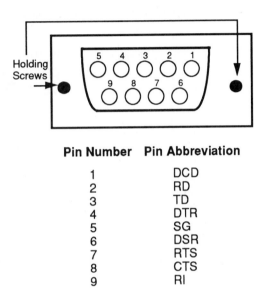

Pin Number	Pin Abbreviation
1	DCD
2	RD
3	TD
4	DTR
5	SG
6	DSR
7	RTS
8	CTS
9	RI

Fig. 2-7. 9-pin RS-232.

The process of using a modem to connect a microcomputer or terminal to a host system is as follows:

1. When the communicating devices are powered up, the terminal's DTR signal and the modem's DSR signal are activated.

2. When the terminal is ready to send data, it activates its RTS signal.

3. The modem activates the CTS signal of the analog carrier.

4. The user's modem dials the phone of the remote modem and waits for its response.

5. When the user's modem senses communication over the phone line, it activates its DCD signal.

6. A high level DCD signal tells the microcomputer or terminal that it is connected to a remote device and the data exchange can begin.

Summary

There are many different ways in which the transmission of data can be classified, but data transmission is typically grouped into three major areas according to

1. How the data flows among devices.
2. The type of physical connection.
3. The type of timing used for transmitting data.

Data can flow in simplex, half-duplex, or full-duplex mode. The physical connection can be parallel or serial, and the timing can be synchronous or asynchronous. Regardless of the mode of transmission, the data being transmitted is described by coding standards. One is the ASCII standard used by all microcomputers, non-IBM mainframes, and minicomputers. The other standard is the EBCDIC standard which is used by IBM mainframes and some of their minicomputers.

In the case of serial communications over telephone lines, modems have to be used. A modem is an electronic device that converts (modulates) the digital communications between computers into audible tones that can be transmitted over telephone lines. The received data is then converted (demodulated) from the audible tones into digital information. There are several types of modems each with a unique set of functions that makes it suitable for a specific job. Some of the most common types are optical, short haul, acoustic, smart, digital, and V.32 modems. Of all of these, smart modems are the most commonly found in the microcomputer market.

Modems connect to the computer, normally through an RS-232 or serial port. On most microcomputers that use the ASCII code, the connections between external modems, computers, and other devices conform to this RS-232 standard. The RS-232 is a connector that is found on the back panel of most computers.

Questions

1. What is data transmission in full-duplex mode?
2. Why is the synchronous mode more efficient than the asynchronous mode?
3. Since parallel transmission is faster than serial transmission, why don't we perform all data communication using parallel transmission?
4. What is the purpose of the ASCII standard?

5. Describe the function of a modem?

6. In the case of microcomputers, which modem are we most likely to use when sending data over phone lines? Why?

7. Describe three different types of modems?

8. What is the purpose of the RS-232 port?

9. Briefly describe the process of handshaking?

Projects

The projects in this chapter are intended to familiarize the student with the basic hardware required to connect computers and printers using standard RS-232 ports. The basic equipment required to perform the projects is outlined in Project 1. As an additional challenge, the instructor may provide unknown or lesser known serial printers and instruct the student to design the interface between the printer and a microcomputer.

Project 1. Interface between an External Modem and a Microcomputer

There are two methods of connecting an external modem to your computer. The first method is to purchase a serial cable from a local computer store, and connect the RS-232 or serial connector at the back of the computer with the serial connector at the back of the modem. This is the easier method. The second method is to construct your own serial cable. The tools required to make this cable are as follows:

1. Soldering iron and solder material.

2. Nine-wire (or more) cable.

3. Two serial connectors of the right gender. The gender can be "male" or "female." The male has pins coming out of the connector. In most cases the connector required for the PC will be female and that for the modem will be male. However, the gender of the connectors is not standard among all equipment manufacturers.

4. Wire strippers.

5. Clamps to hold the wires and connectors.

6. Breakout box (optional).

After all the tools and materials are gathered, use the connections outlined in Fig. 2-8 to connect a modem and a terminal.

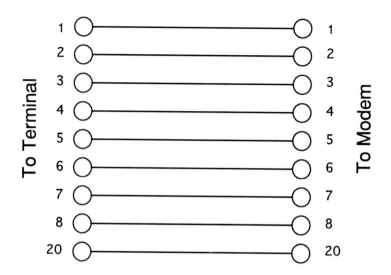

Fig. 2-8. Pin diagram for connector between a modem and a terminal.

Project 2. Serial Interface between Two IBM or IBM-compatible Microcomputers

To connect one computer directly to another without a modem, a modem eliminator or null modem is required. A null modem is a cable that has at a minimum the wires that connect pins 2 and 3 on both computers crossed over. Pin 2 on both computers is responsible for sending data, and pin 3 receives data. As you can imagine, if both of these pins were not crossed, then both the computers could talk but neither would be listening. Make these two connections now.

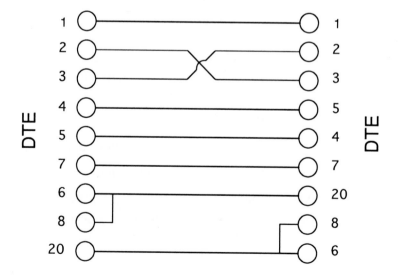

Fig. 2-9. Pin diagram for connector between two IBM or IBM-compatible microcomputers.

Making the connecting cable is only one aspect of connecting two microcomputers. Communication software will be required to perform the communication functions. The project in Chapter 5 explores this topic further and provides some hands-on experience. A general null modem can be created by crossing pins 2 and 3, 20 and 6, and connecting 8 to 6 on the RS-232 cable as in Fig. 2-9.

Advanced Communication Hardware

Objectives

After completing this chapter you will

1. Understand the use of concentrators, protocol converters, PBXs, cluster controllers, and matrix switches in a data communication system.

2. Understand the different line adapters that can be placed on a network and their application to data communication lines.

3. Understand the need for security in a data communication line and the equipment that can be used to enforce it.

4. Know the purpose of a breakout box.

5. Know the role of microcomputers, front end processor, and mainframes in a data communication system.

6. Know about multiplexers and their use.

Key Terms

Channel Extender	Cluster Controller
Concentrator	Digital Line Expander
Encryption	Line Monitor
Line Splitter	Multiplexer
Mainframe	Microcomputer
PBX	Protocol Converter

Introduction

Today's data communication systems have increased in sophistication and take advantage of equipment that was formerly reserved for voice communication systems only. Microcomputers, front end processors, mainframes, multiplexers, protocol converters, PBXs, matrix switches, and concentrators are among these devices. Additionally, the educated data communication system user and manager must understand the different devices that can be used to monitor these systems and the transmission media available to them.

It is important to point out that, although current tendencies in the data communication market are toward networks, a networking solution is in many situations not the best or the only solution to a data communication problem. The uneducated manager may try to solve any communication problem by using local or wide area networks, since these are solutions that usually seem to work. However, a network is not easy to install nor is it always the most cost effective solution for creating a media-sharing environment. Today's data communication managers must be aware of many devices that solve common data transmission problems quickly and effectively.

This type of thinking, along with the knowledge of the diversity of devices that can be used in different situations, indicates an informed manager who can make smart decisions. This type of individual is a rare commodity in a field that is crowded with so-called experts who don't have the proper training in the field of data communication. Any data communication manager can make decisions, but only knowledgeable and open-minded managers can make decisions that are efficient and cost effective. With this in mind, let's take a closer look at some of the data communication equipment that is commonly found in the market place.

Terminals and Microcomputers

A terminal is an input and/or output device that can be connected to a host computer. The terminal may depend on the host system for computational power and/or data. Obviously, many devices can meet this definition of a terminal. Among them is the microcomputer. Both the terminal and the computer to which it is connected are known as data terminal equipment (DTE). This type of equipment operates internally in digital format and produces digital output. The modem used to connect the terminal or computer to the communication line is known as data circuit-terminating equipment. Because the definition of data terminal is broad, there are several categories of terminals, each of which is defined in the following section.

Classifications

Microcomputer Workstation

A microcomputer workstation is a general purpose microcomputer or specialized input/output workstation with "smart" circuitry and a central processing unit. Technically, there is a difference between a microcomputer workstation and a microcomputer. The workstation includes the tools necessary for a professional to perform his or her daily work. These tools are specialized software applications such as CAD systems and mathematical modeling systems. In addition, today's workstations have the ability to use multitask software programs. This means they can run multiple programs simultaneously and can switch among them as the user needs to. The microcomputer may not have all of these capabilities built in. It may be used only for word processing or database access. Regardless of which system we are discussing, the microcomputer is an integral part of communication networks. It can be used as part of a local area network or as a terminal device connected to a host system. Fig. 3-1 shows a typical microcomputer system.

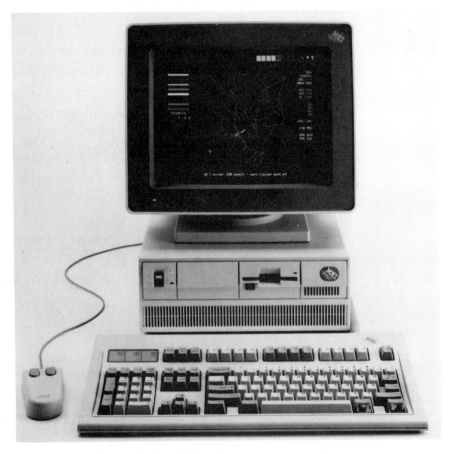

Fig. 3-1. A typical microcomputer system.

Microcomputer workstations are being increasingly used in networks since they can perform many processing functions internally before the data is passed on to a host system. Some of the ways in which they are used are:

1. Data stored in central systems is transmitted (downloaded) to the microcomputer. The data can be processed by the microcomputer using a word processor, database, spreadsheet, or some other software application. After processing, the data is transmitted back to the central system for further processing or storage.

2. Data stored on the microcomputer can be submitted as a batch job to the host system as required.

3. Applications on the microcomputer can be assisted by the processing power of the host system. For example, a scientific database can reside in part on the microcomputer system, but when large calculations or repetitious calculations are required, the microcomputer can rely on the host system for assistance.

4. Large projects can be divided among several microcomputers. The completed pieces can then be assembled on the host system.

5. Microcomputers can work as terminals to the host computer. In this role they emulate the native terminals of the central system.

6. Microcomputers that are part of a local area network can share storage and printer devices on the network or devices on the central system.

Remote Job Entry Station

A remote job entry station is a processor on a network or terminal workstation where several types of devices are connected. Data is often transmitted from the host system to a remote job entry station such as a video display terminal (VDT) or printer. Input can also be received by the host in a batch mode from entry stations.

Data Entry Terminal

This is a low cost terminal used in homes or offices. This device can establish an interactive dialog with the host system and obtain data from a business application and at the same time provide data to the application. Fig. 3-2 shows a picture of a data entry terminal. An example of a specialized data entry terminal is the transaction terminal employed by ATM machines in the banking industry for cash dispensing.

Facsimile Terminal (FAX)

A facsimile terminal (see Fig. 3-3) is able to transmit an exact picture of a hard copy document over telephone lines and satellite circuits anywhere in the world.

Fig. 3-2. A data entry terminal.

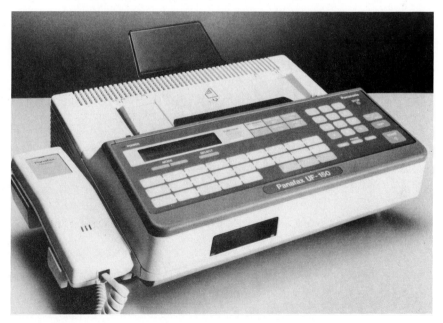

Fig. 3-3. The Panafax UF-150 facsimile is small and lightweight. It can also be used as a copying machine. (Courtesy of Panasonic Corporation)

FAX machines are divided into four major groups according to their technology and speed. Groups 1 and 2 are older analog machines, whereas groups 3 and 4 are digital technology machines. Most newer FAX machines are group 3 or 4. Group 3 machines can transmit a page in approximately one minute or less. Group 4 machines can transmit an 8 1/2- by 11-inch page in approximately 20 seconds. Additionally, group 4 FAX machines have a higher image transmission quality. Some newer models of FAX machines use "plain paper" to produce a hard copy of a digital transmission. This type of machine, also known as a laser FAX, can double as a scanner for the computer or as a plain paper copier. Its circuitry is based on laser printer engines, and it can serve as a multipurpose machine on a network.

Signals from a digital facsimile device can be read into a computer and stored because they are made up of bits. This has led to the development of FAX boards that can be added to microcomputers. With these boards, any document created on a personal computer can be transmitted to any FAX machine through phone lines. Messages sent by FAX machines can also be received by the FAX boards inside microcomputers and a picture of the document can be stored on a disk or sent to an attached printer.

Dumb/Intelligent Terminals

Dumb terminals are video terminals that do not participate in control or processing tasks. They do not contain storage systems, internal memory, or microprocessor chips. When a character is typed on one of these terminals, it is transmitted immediately to the host system. This forces the host or central system to create buffers for this type of terminal so the message can be assembled before acting on it.

Intelligent terminals are able to participate in the processing of data. These terminals contain internal memory and are capable of being programmed. Many intelligent terminals also contain auxiliary storage units and fast central processing units. Most of today's intelligent terminals are microcomputers and specialized microcomputer workstations.

Attributes of Terminals

Many terminal attributes should be considered when purchasing a terminal. Some of the most important are described next.

Keyboard

All terminals have some type of keyboard. Advanced or extended keyboards contain function keys that indicate functions to be performed on entered data. Also, some function keys act as interrupt keys. Additionally, most keyboards contain numerical key pads and control keys used to transmit sequences that can be acted on by a program. Specialized keyboards contain foreign language characters and job specific characters.

Light Pen

This device is used to select options from menus appearing on the screen. When the pen is aimed at the video display screen, the light image can be read by the computer and the coordinates of the point are determined by the system. The coordinate system is translated into a selection displayed on the screen.

Touch Screen

Such a screen works in a similar manner to the light pen. A portion of the screen is touched with a finger to make the selection.

Mouse, Joy Stick, and Trackball

The mouse allows the user to control the screen cursor by moving the mouse on a table surface. When the screen cursor is on a selection, a mouse button is pressed. The coordinates of the cursor are read by the computer and this location is associated with some software option. The joy stick moves the cursor by moving the stick in a specific direction. A trackball is similar to the mouse except that the cursor is moved by rotating a ball mounted in a fixed holder. The cursor moves in the direction of rotation of the ball.

Voice Entry

Data can be entered into the system by using a microphone. Special voice recognition software is required in the system.

Page Scanner

A page scanner can scan an image and translate it into a digital format. The image can be stored and later processed by the computer.

Front End Processors

Front end processors are often employed at the host end of a communication circuit to perform control and processing functions required for the proper operation of a data communication network. Fig. 3-4 illustrates the location of a front end processor in a communication network. The front end processor

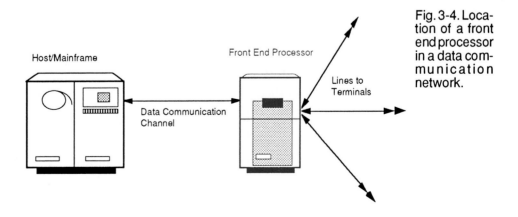

Fig. 3-4. Location of a front end processor in a data communication network.

Host/Mainframe

Front End Processor

Lines to Terminals

Data Communication Channel

provides an interface to the communication circuits. It relieves the host computer of its communication duties, which allows the host to perform the data processing function more effectively.

The typical duties of the front end processor are message processing and message switching. In message processing, it interprets incoming messages to determine the type of information requested. Then it retrieves the information from an on-line storage unit and sends it back to the inquiring terminal without involving the host system. In message switching, the front end processor switches incoming messages to other terminals or systems on a network. It can also store messages and forward them at a later time.

Functions of the Front End Processor

The functions of the front end processor include the following:

1. Circuit polling and addressing terminals. Polling involves asking each terminal if it has a message to send. Addressing involves asking a terminal if it is in condition to receive the message.

2. Answering dial-in calls and automatic dialing of outgoing calls.

3. Converting code from ASCII to EBCDIC or EBCDIC to ASCII.

4. Circuit switching. This allows an incoming circuit to be switched to another circuit.

5. Accommodating circuit speed differences.

6. Protocol conversion, such as asynchronous to synchronous.

7. Multiplexing.

8. Assembling incoming bits into characters.

9. Assembling characters into blocks of data or complete messages.

10. Compressing messages for more efficient communications.

11. Activating remote alarms if errors are detected.

12. Requesting retransmission of blocks of text containing errors.

13. Keeping statistics of network usage.

14. Performing diagnostics on attached terminals.

15. Controlling of editing that includes rerouting messages, modifying data for transmission, etc.

16. Buffering messages before they are passed to the host computer or user terminal.

17. Queuing messages into I/O queues between the front end processor and the host computer.

18. Logging of messages to tape or disk.

19. Identifying trouble or security problems.

There are many vendors of front end processors. Some of the best known models are the IBM 37xx family of communication controllers and the NCR COMTEN 3600 series of front end processors.

Mainframe Computers

Mainframe computers are considered central computer systems that perform data processing functions for a business or industry. In some networks, several mainframe computers can be found sharing the responsibility of processing information as a distributed system. In such systems the hardware, software, processing, and data are normally dispersed over a geographical area. The individual technologies are connected through some type of communication network. As part of this network, mainframe computers can perform networking functions as well as the more traditional processing functions.

A mainframe computer that is built to perform "number crunching" routines may not be suitable to perform communication routines. The type of processing required for communications differs greatly from that required to perform mathematical calculations. For a computer that is built to perform traditional data processing functions, additional or auxiliary hardware is required. The type of auxiliary hardware will depend upon the configuration of the network.

There are three types of configurations, the first of which consists of a computer that is not part of any local or wide area computer network. The circuitry required to handle all communications is built into the machine. Fig. 3-5 shows a typical configuration for this type of centralized system.

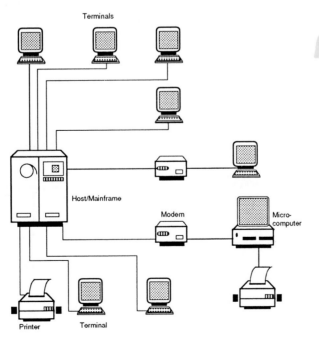

Fig. 3-5. A centralized data communication system.

53

This configuration uses dedicated hardware to handle the interaction between the host system and the data entry terminals.

The mainframe computer can store users' programs as well as the software to handle communication with the users. The type of configuration shown in Fig. 3-5 can be found in manufacturing environments and in dedicated database systems. Even though we refer to the computer as the mainframe computer, this central system is often a minicomputer system.

The second type of configuration is a network that employs microcomputers, minicomputers, and mainframe computers connected through some type of local area network (LAN). Fig. 3-6 depicts this type of system. The network is usually confined to the business office or business complex where the processing is taking place. Users can communicate to the outside world by sending their message to an outside system through the local telephone exchange or some other medium. The local exchange then routes the message through long distance networks until it reaches the local exchange of the receiving system. Finally, the message is routed to the receiving computer or local network. These systems are important, and there are several chapters in this book that further explore the concepts.

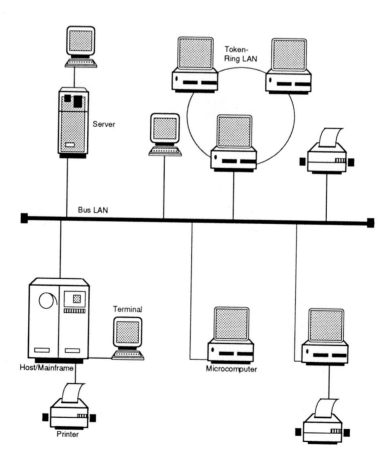

Fig. 3-6. A data communication system using a LAN.

The final type of configuration is one that employs a large general purpose computer along with a front end processor (FEP). Fig. 3-7 shows a diagram of this configuration. The front end processor is known by names such as line controller, communications controller, or transaction processor. The function of the FEP is to interface the main computer to the network where the users' communication equipment resides. It can be a nonprogrammable device that is built to handle a specific situation. Or the front end processor can be programmable and it can handle some processing functions in addition to input/output activities.

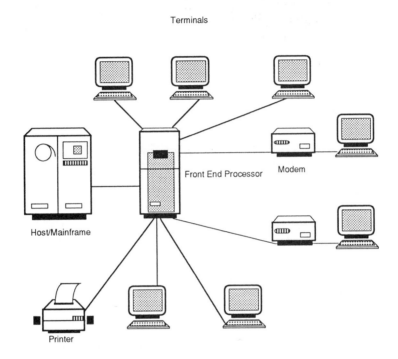

Fig. 3-7. A data communication system using a FEP.

During the past few years, network designers have opted to remove as much processing as possible from the host computer. The idea is to distribute the processing hardware along a network, making the entire system more efficient.

Fig. 3-8 shows an example of this type of network distribution. The front end processor handles the control of all communication functions. The data channel between the front end processor and the host system handles the movement of data into and out of the main processing computer. Remote terminal controllers handle users' terminals. Microcomputers process data locally and later transmit the results to the host system. Telephone exchanges, multiplexers, and other devices are used throughout the network to handle communications efficiently between users and the host computer. Further in this book, chapters on networks and local area networks explain the terminology and concepts in more detail.

Fig. 3-8. A distributed data communication system.

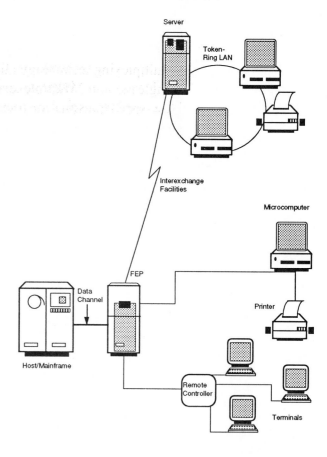

The trend in computer technology is toward faster, smaller, and distributed network systems. However, the central or host system plays an important part in network strategies. The processing and data throughput power of minicomputers and mainframes is superior to that of microcomputer systems. This makes the mainframe or the minicomputer a key component of a successful network configuration. In addition, many network managers rely on a central or host system for security, backup, and maintenance purposes.

Multiplexers

Although modems are used to connect computers over large distances and direct cable is normally employed over short distances, the number of cables required to satisfy all users can at times be overwhelming. In addition, leasing lines from the phone company to communicate between two offices located far away from each other can be expensive. Multiplexers help in solving some of this economic cost by allowing the transmission of multiple data communication sessions over a common wire or medium.

Function

Multiplexing technology allows the transmission of multiple signals over a single medium. Multiplexers (see Fig. 3-9) allow the replacement of multiple low-speed transmission lines with a single high-speed transmission line. The typical configuration includes a multiplexer attached to multiple low-speed lines, a communication line (typically four-wire carrier circuit), and a multiplexer at another site that is also connected to low-speed lines. Fig. 3-10 depicts this configuration. In addition, the figure shows a remote site that is connected to a multiplexer through the use of modems. The remote site contains terminals, microcomputers, modems, and printers attached to a multiplexer. The host site has a multiplexer, FEP, and a host CPU.

Transmission Line

To Terminals

To Computer

Fig. 3-9. Multiplexers help reduce the number of transmission lines.

The operation of the multiplexers, frequently called MUXs, in Fig. 3-10 is transparent to the sending and receiving computers or terminals. The multiplexer does not interrupt the normal flow of data. Multiplexers allow for a significant reduction of the overall cost of connecting remote sites, since the quantity of lines required to connect the sites is decreased.

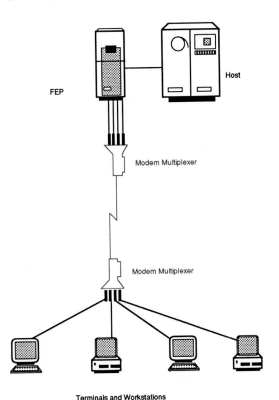

Fig. 3-10. Multiplexer operation is transparent to the operation of the data communication system.

FEP

Host

Modem Multiplexer

Modem Multiplexer

Terminals and Workstations

Techniques

Multiplexing techniques can be divided into frequency division multiplexing (FDM), time division multiplexing (TDM), and statistical time division multiplexing (STDM).

Frequency Division Multiplexing (FDM)

Users of existing voice-grade lines (phone lines) can multiplex low-speed circuits into the standard voice-grade channels by using FDM. In FDM, a modem and a frequency division are used to break down the frequency of available bandwidths of a voice-grade circuit, dividing it into multiple smaller bandwidths. The bandwith is a measure of the amount of data that can be transmitted per unit of time. The bandwidth is determined by the difference between the highest and lowest allowed frequencies in the transmission medium.

As an example, assume that a telephone circuit has a bandwidth of 3100 Hz, and a line capable of carrying 1200 bits per second (bps). Suppose that instead of running a terminal at 1200 bps, it is desired to run three terminals at 300 bps. If three terminals are going to use the same communication line, then some type of separator is required in order to avoid crosstalk (interference of signals from one to another). This separator is called a guardband. For transmission at 300 bps the standard separation is 480 Hz. Therefore, in the above situation, two guardbands of 480 Hz each are required (see Fig. 3-11). Since the guardbands now occupy 960 Hz, and the original line had a bandwidth of 3100 Hz, then the frequency left for the 300 bps transmission is 2140 Hz. If three terminals are required, then 2140 Hz divided by three gives a frequency of 713 Hz to be used per channel.

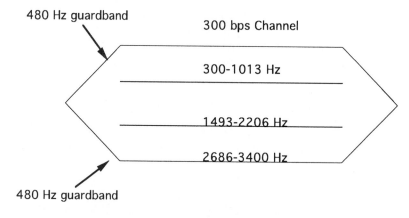

Fig. 3-11. Guardbands in the transmission process.

With FDM it is not necessary for all lines to terminate at a single location. Using multidrop techniques, the terminals can be stationed in different locations within a building or a city.

Time Division Multiplexing (TDM)

Time division multiplexers are digital devices and therefore select incoming bits digitally and place each bit into a high-speed bit stream in equal time intervals. (See Fig. 3-12.) The sending multiplexer will place a bit or byte from each of the incoming lines into a frame. The frames are placed on high-speed transmission lines, and a receiving multiplexer, knowing where each bit or byte is located, outputs the bits or bytes at appropriate speeds.

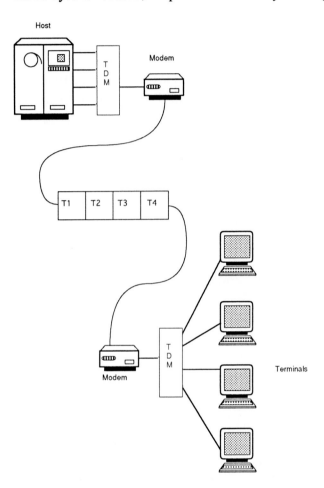

Fig. 3-12. Time division multiplexers in the communication process.

Time division multiplexing is more efficient than frequency division multiplexing, but it requires a separate modem. To the sending and receiving stations it always appears as if a single line is connecting them. All lines for time division multiplexers originate in one location and end in one location. TDMs are easier to operate, less complex, and less expensive than FDMs.

Statistical Time Division Multiplexers (STDM)

In any terminal-host configuration the terminals attached to the host CPU are not always transmitting data. The time during which they are idle is called down time. Statistical time division multiplexers are intelligent devices capable of identifying which terminals are idle and which terminals require transmission, and they allocate line time only when it is required. This means

59

line time is provided only when a terminal is transmitting. This allows the connection of many more devices to the host than is possible with FDMs or TDMs (see Fig. 3-13).

The STDM consists of a microprocessor-based unit that contains all hardware and software required to control both the reception of low-speed data coming in and high-speed data going out. Newer STDM units provide additional capabilities such as data compression, line priorities, mixed-speed lines, host port sharing, network port control, automatic speed detection, internal diagnostics, memory expansion, and integrated modems.

The number of devices that can be multiplexed using STDMs depends on the address field used in an STDM frame. If the field is 4 bits long, there are 16 terminals (2 to the power of 4) that can be connected. If 5 bits are used, 32 terminals can be connected (2 to the power of 5).

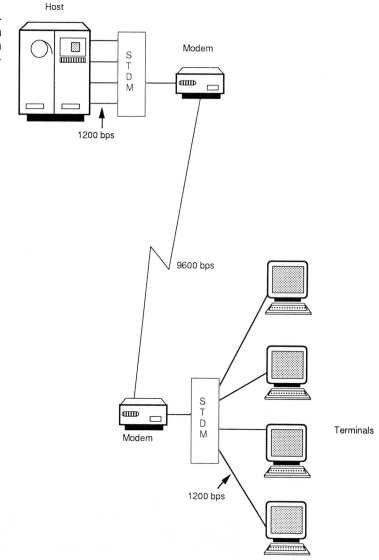

Fig. 3-13. Statistical time division multiplexers in the communication process.

Configurations

Multiplexers can be used in a variety of configurations and combinations. Cascading is a typical configuration used to extend circuits to remote entry points when there are two or more data entry areas. Fig. 3-14 shows an example of cascading multiplexers. In the figure, data entry terminals in a geographical location are multiplexed, and a single carrier sends the data to a temporary receiving location. The data is then demultiplexed and multiplexed by a third multiplexer before being sent to the final destination. Then a multiplexer receives the data and distributes it among the ports of the host system.

The number of ports that a multiplexer can accommodate varies. Commonly there are 4, 8, 16, 32, 48, or 64 ports. The price of a multiplexer will vary with the number of ports in it and the sophistication of the device.

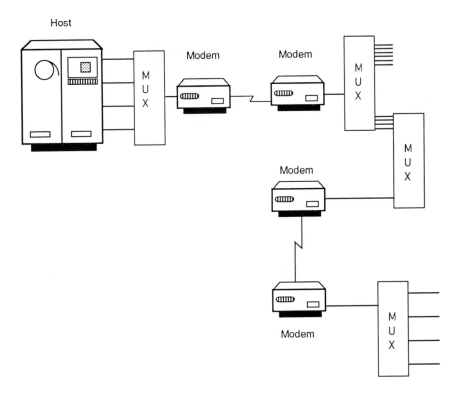

Fig. 3-14. Cascading multiplexing technique.

Types

Newer multiplexers are difficult to define. Some devices have a large array of options and functions that make them work in a specific format under some working conditions. They can be switched to a different type when the conditions change. We will make an attempt to outline some standard types that can be found in the market place. However, keep in mind that some multiplexers can perform the functions of several of the types outlined below.

Inverse Multiplexer

An inverse multiplexer provides a high-speed data path between computers. It takes a high-speed line coming out of a computer and separates it into multiple low-speed lines. The multiple low-speed lines are then recombined by another inverse multiplexer before making connection with the receiving computer.

T-1 Multiplexer

A T-1 multiplexer is a special type of multiplexer combined with a high capacity data service unit that manages the ends of a T-1 link. A T-1 link is a communication link that transmits at 1.544 million bits per seconds. Therefore, T-1 circuits can carry 24 channels of 64,000 bits per second.

Multiport Multiplexer

A multiport multiplexer combines modem and time division multiplexing equipment into a single device. The line entering the modem can be of varying transmission speeds. The multiport multiplexer then combines the data and transmits it over a high-speed link to another receiving multiplexer.

Fiber Optic Multiplexer

A fiber optic multiplexer takes multiple channels of data, with each channel transmitting at 64,000 bits per channel, and multiplexes the channels onto a 14 million bits per second fiber optic line. It is similar in operation to a time division multiplexer, but operates at much higher speeds.

Concentrator

Standard multiplexers are bit- or byte-oriented devices with limited storage capabilities and little computing logic. There are occasions when it is desirable to perform some type of processing on the information traveling through the communication medium for purposes of error detection and editing. In this case, handling the information on a bit-per-bit or byte basis is inadequate. For the processing functions that we are discussing, the information must be handled on a message basis, or on a store-and-forward basis. Store-and-forward means that the message is received at a location, it is validated, and an acknowledgment is sent back to the sender. A device that can perform this type of operation is the concentrator.

A concentrator is a line-sharing device with a primary function that is the same as a multiplexer. It allows multiple devices to share communication circuits. In addition, a concentrator is an intelligent device that sometimes performs data processing functions and has auxiliary storage. Some of the earlier concentrators were statistical multiplexers. That is the reason some vendors call a concentrator a statistical multiplexer or stat mux. In addition to having a CPU, concentrators are used one at a time, whereas multiplexers are used in pairs. Also, a concentrator may vary the number of incoming and outgoing lines, while a multiplexer must use the same number of lines on both ends.

A typical concentrator configuration is depicted in Fig. 3-15. The example shows multiple terminals using a concentrator to access several host systems. Concentrators perform data compression functions, forward error correction, and network-related functions in addition to acting as a line-sharing device. They are considered data processing devices, and newer types of concentrators are built around microcomputers and minicomputers. However, "pure" concentrators don't perform any type of routing of data on a network. They just take data from a central location and distribute it to some remote site and take data from the remote site and send it to the central location. Any routing of data from one terminal to another terminal or from one workstation to another workstation is performed by message switching equipment or front end processors. Above, we use the word "pure" to emphasize that the job of a concentrator does not typically include performing data switching functions. But there are some modern concentrators that do perform switching functions. This is the result of equipment manufacturers trying to cover as much of this market as possible. As the hardware becomes cheaper, equipment manufacturers try to pack as much power in their devices as possible in order to appeal to a larger audience. The result is equipment that performs the duties of multiple devices.

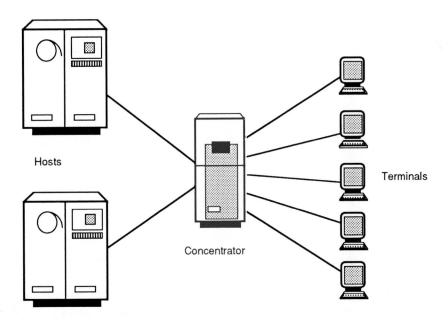

Fig. 3-15. A data communication system using a concentrator.

Cluster Controller

A cluster controller is designed to support several terminals and the functions required to manage the terminals. A modern cluster controller performs many of the functions of a front end processor and is in most cases a smaller version of a front end processor. In addition, it buffers data being transmitted to or from the terminals, performs error detection and correction, and polls terminals (see Fig. 3-16). Polling is a technique by which the controller checks to see which terminals are ready to send data. If a terminal needs to send a packet of data to a host, the cluster controller ensures that the packet gets to its destination. In addition, some cluster controllers can be attached to more than one communication line, allowing one user to have multiple sessions that access multiple computers. Normally, a special key combination switches the user from one host computer to another. Also, not only can a user be attached to multiple computers, but some cluster controllers allow the user to have multiple sessions with the same computer. In this manner, a user can be executing a database query and performing file transfer or some other function in different but simultaneous sessions.

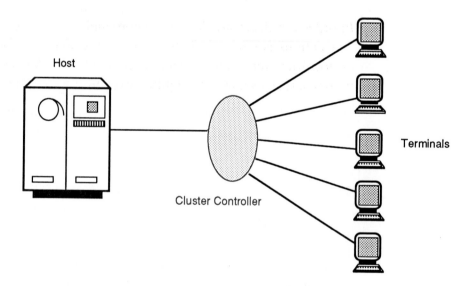

Fig. 3-16. A cluster controller managing several terminals.

Examples of popular cluster controllers are the IBM 3174 and 3274 cluster controllers. These controllers can handle up to 32 terminals and normally interact with 3278/79 terminals or terminal emulators. In the case of the 3174 or 3274, the most common configuration for large scale systems is to attach groups of cluster controllers through a telecommunication line to a front end processor. Common IBM front end processors are the 3705 and 3725. Also, these devices can be nodes in a network, enhancing the capability of the equipment and making their life cycle longer in an era when data communications equipment must coexist with other equipment in network configurations. This concept is explored in later chapters. It is an important point to explore, because of the number of microcomputers being used to communicate with cluster controllers.

Until recently, 3270 or other types of terminals were the main source of communication between users and IBM mainframes. But as the price of microcomputers dropped during the last decade, people used microcomputers with some type of emulation system as a replacement for the communication terminal. Microcomputers gave users the ability to send large amounts of data to the cluster controller that was originally designed to handle short transactions. The end result is an overloading of the cluster controller with the response time increasing in some situations to as much as 20 minutes. This problem is alleviated by using networks and distributing the load of the data communications equipment. The use of the microcomputer as a communicating device between the user and the mainframe also made the protocol converter a popular device.

Protocol Converter

In order for electronic devices to communicate with one another, a set of conventions is required. This set of conventions is called the protocol. A protocol determines the sequence of codes required for data exchange and the bit or character sequences required to control the exchange.

Since computers and other electronic devices sometimes have their own proprietary protocols, protocol converters are used to interconnect two dissimilar computers or terminals so they can talk to each other. As an analogy, imagine a person who speaks only English and another person who speaks only Russian trying to communicate with one another. For the communication to be effective, a translator who understands both languages serves as the bridge between both persons. The protocol converter assumes the role of the translator in the electronic data exchange. Although we discuss only some of the most commonly used protocols in data communications, many more exist. The protocol converter provides an effective means of translating information or packets of data (a message that is subdivided into smaller data units for a more efficient transmission) between dissimilar devices that need to exchange data.

Protocol converters also convert character codes. As mentioned in Chapter 2, two character codes used in the computer environment in the United States are the ASCII and EBCDIC standards. The EBCDIC code is used by IBM in midrange and mainframe systems. The ASCII code is used by virtually every other computer manufacturer. Therefore, to connect an IBM personal computer that uses the ASCII system to an IBM mainframe, an ASCII-to-EBCDIC converter is required (see Fig. 3-17).

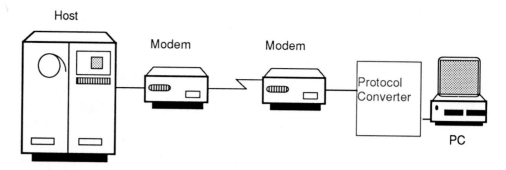

Fig. 3-17. A protocol converter between a PC and a mainframe.

Protocol converters can be hardware or software designed. A hardware protocol converter is treated as a "black box" on the communication line. It performs its function in a manner that is transparent to the system. For example, third party vendors offer asynchronous to synchronous protocol conversion boxes. This allows an inexpensive async terminal to access an IBM mainframe. There are also add-on circuit boards that fit inside microcomputers that perform communications and protocol conversion at the same time. These boards allow a personal computer to emulate a 3278 or 3279 terminal and connect to a 3174 or 3274 controller via a coaxial cable. Some of the cards have the controller built in and can access the mainframe directly.

The other method of protocol conversion is achieved through software. Typically, this software resides in the host system and converts incoming data to the language that the host system can understand. This is an inexpensive manner of achieving protocol conversion. However, it requires attention from the host computer, reducing the amount of time it can apply to other tasks. Whenever possible, hardware protocol converters are used, but be aware that many protocol converters also perform other functions, such as multiplexing and concentrating. Because of these multiple options in a single device, purchasing decisions must be made carefully to avoid duplication or needless acquisition of features. This is especially true as the sophistication of the equipment increases, such as in the PBX.

Private Branch Exchanges (PBX)

A private branch exchange is an electronic switchboard within an organization, with all the telephone lines of the organization connected to it (see Fig 3-18). Normally, several of the telecommunication circuits of the PBX go from this switchboard to the telephone company's main office. These are called trunk lines when they are devoted to voice transmission. If they are used for data communication, they are known as leased lines, dedicated lines, or private lines.

Fig. 3-18. This Northern Telecom PBX is configured for 600 telephone lines. Line cards can be added or removed for smaller or larger configurations. (Courtesy of Northern Telecom, Inc.)

Private branch exchanges, like the centralized switching equipment found at the phone company, are computers that are specially designed to handle voice telephone calls. However, since they are computers, they can also handle data communications in a digital format. Their flexibility in this area, especially when it comes to connecting a terminal or microcomputer to a host system, makes them popular devices used in data communications. But, as we will see shortly, the PBX as a hub for connecting data communication equipment is effective only when the required rate of transmission is low. Before we discuss the capabilities of the private branch exchange, it is important to know some of the history behind the development of the PBX so you may understand the capabilities of any existing PBXs at your site.

PBX History

PBX systems have been in offices for a number of years. As organizations developed and grew, PBX equipment was upgraded and enhanced to meet users' demands. The evolution of PBX equipment can be categorized into several generations.

The first generation of PBXs was placed in service prior to the mid-1970s. They carried only voice and were capable of handling only analog signals. Their design was electromechanical, and they used analog circuitry for switching signals.

The second generation of PBXs was designed between the mid-1970s and the mid-1980s. These were also voice-only PBXs, but they digitized voice signals before transferring them through the switch. This PBX equipment could be modified to carry digital data signals as well as voice. However, the transfer rate for data signals was slow.

The third generation of PBXs has been in existence since the early 1980s. They have the capability to move voice and data at relatively high speeds. Incoming analog signals are converted to digital signals, and therefore offer greater flexibility and capabilities. Most of today's PBXs are from this generation.

The fourth generation of PBXs is characterized by having all voice and data switching capabilities combined in a LAN distribution system. They can serve as voice phone switches, electronic mail, voice mail, and data switches for LANs. However, their implementation has been slow due to the high cost of each line in the system.

Capabilities

Newer digital PBXs, such as the IBM 9751, Northern Telecom's Meridian, and the AT&T System 75 and 85, are designed around 32-bit microprocessor chips that control the entire system. They contain many features, including the following:

1. They can transmit voice and data simultaneously. Obviously, all PBXs can handle voice communications, but most of them have the capability to handle data communications. With this feature, a user with a terminal or a microcomputer can access devices or host computers that are connected to the PBX. In the case of a microcomputer, some type of terminal emulation is normally used to communicate with the host. To access the host, the user dials the number of the site where the host is located. In some systems, system names can be given instead of the number, the PBX's software interprets the name provided and finds the destination

requested. If the host has an available line, the user's microcomputer is connected to the host. When the user is finished with the transmission, the line is made available to another user. In this fashion, other intelligent devices, such as smart facsimile machines and printers, can be made available to users, along with the microcomputer. These facilities can also be made available to users who must dial in from other offices or their homes. Once a line is available to one of these users, he or she has the same capabilities as any user in the office.

2. They can perform protocol conversion, allowing equipment from different vendors to communicate. Modern PBX systems have built-in protocol conversion capabilities that allow microcomputers to connect to host computers with dissimilar protocols without the need of additional equipment. Using an async or sync line provided through the PBX, a microcomputer can be attached to an IBM host, placing the burden of protocol conversion on the PBX instead of the host. Although this type of scenario is not effective when high transmission speeds are required, it is a solution for many users who only need terminal emulation and connection to a host.

3. They can control local area networks from within the switchboard. Private branch exchanges can be used as the connecting hub for several local area networks. In this case, networks that are isolated and need to exchange data with other networks using existing phone wires can use the PBX as a central hub that switches data from one network to another using an available line.

4. They have voice and electronic mail. One of the necessities of the modern office is the need for employees to communicate continuously. Private branch exchanges can provide voice mail for a customer or another user to access the PBX using a telephone, access a private voice mail box by typing a set number of digits from the telephone pad, and then leave a voice message to the owner of the voice mail box. The owner can then retrieve messages in any order, delete messages, forward messages, or save messages.

Additionally, PBXs offer electronic mail. The concept of electronic mail is similar to that of voice mail, but instead of leaving a voice message using a telephone, a terminal or computer is used to leave a written message. The owner of the electronic mail box has the same capabilities as the owner of voice mail boxes in terms of managing the mail stored by the system.

5. Asynchronous and synchronous transmission can be performed simultaneously. With this capability, a corporation can have multiple hosts, some of which may require async data transmission and some that required sync data transmission. The private branch exchange can handle both types of transmission simultaneously, allowing inexpensive async terminals access to their native host in addition to performing the translation required (in some cases) to use an async type terminal on a host requiring sync transmission. Although many PBX systems place the burden of async-to-sync conversion on other devices, they still allow both types of transmission over the same switching lines.

6. Automatic routing is available, ensuring that calls are routed through the least costly communication system. This is an important feature when a long distance call is made and large amounts of data are being transmitted. The ability to find the least costly route can save thousands of dollars annually to corporations that must maintain data lines with remote offices or sites.

7. They can switch digital transmission without the use of modems. Recall that in order for a computer to send data over ordinary telephone lines, a modem is required. When a private branch exchange system is used, any switching of data from one line of the PBX to another of its lines can be done without the need of a modem. The PBX performs all the tasks necessary to ensure that the data gets to its destination. However, you will still need a modem if a call is placed outside the domain of the PBX and a digital trunk line may not be available. In this case, even though the call goes through the PBX, it eventually has to use public phone lines, and the data must be modulated at one end and demodulated at the other end of the communication line. For this task, the modem must be used.

8. They can provide security by requesting and maintaining security access codes. Private branch exchanges can be programmed to request an access code for any person trying to use its services. This provides an added layer of security on what is considered one of the most vulnerable areas of a data communication system.

9. They can connect digital signals to high-speed circuits such as T-1 circuits. Recall that a T-1 line is a high speed line provided by the public telephone system in order to have high efficiency communication between two remote sites. A private branch exchange can be used to provide users with access to this type of communication circuit and, therefore, maximize its use. If a T-1 line is dedicated to a single device, when the device is not using the line, the cost/usage ratio becomes large. A PBX can switch

devices over to the T-1 circuit as the line becomes available, ensuring that the circuit is used as much as possible, thus maximizing the investment in the T-1 line.

10. They allow computer users to select different host computers or destinations without the need to rearrange cables. This is an important benefit of a private branch exchange. Normally, a user would need a cable for each host that he or she needs to access. If only one port is available at the user's terminal, then manual or some other type of switching is necessary when the user logs out of one computer and logs in at another system. This problem is eliminated with the use of a network or a PBX. Since the PBX is an automatic switching device, the user can log out of one computer, and at the same terminal type the code or name of the next host system that needs to be accessed. The PBX will then connect the user, provided that a line is available for the requested host computer. All of these operations are performed from the user's keyboard without the need for the user to physically switch cables or any other type of equipment.

11. They also offer many other features such as call forwarding, call holding, conference calling, and paging.

Besides digital and analog PBX systems, there are other categories into which PBXs can be placed. These are voice only, voice and data, and data only. Even though PBXs offer many advantages for digital data communications, they have limitations in the speed of data transmission. As distance of transmission increases, the rate of transmission decreases. For this reason, a private branch exchange is not normally used as the communication system when large files need to be transmitted frequently or when there is a heavy data transmission requirement with an expectation of small response times. In such cases networks or direct connections are employed.

The private branch exchange or any individual device, including networks, shouldn't be considered as the only solution for the data communication needs of a corporation or institution. Rather, they can be one component of a larger and more complex group of equipment and software that work together to solve the communication needs of the user. No single device will be able to solve all needs, and, in some cases, the solution is too expensive. Each element of a data communication system should be evaluated as an integral part of a much larger solution. Many other devices exist in the market that, although not glamorous or expensive, provide an adequate solution to problems. One such product that has a close relationship with the private branch exchange is the matrix switch.

Matrix Switch

A matrix or data switch is a data and peripheral-sharing facilitator. At its basic level of operations, a matrix switch allows terminals and other electronic devices to access multiple available host processors without the need to physically move any communication line. In this respect, matrix switches operate in a manner similar to early PBXs.

Matrix switches evenly distribute users over multiple processors or devices. If one processor or device becomes overloaded, users can be quickly and efficiently moved to another processor or device. If a line fails, the terminal connected to that line can easily be switched to another available line. Additionally, more terminals can be distributed using matrix switches than using physical wire.

They are effective and relatively inexpensive when compared to local area networks designed to perform the same functions that the matrix switch is designed to perform. Data switches work best when there is a small number of connections that they are responsible for. On the average, eight to twenty-four connections is a normal load for a matrix or data switch. Additionally, they normally use standard serial and parallel connectors to handle the communication with computers and other devices. Using these ports, several computers can be attached to different output devices using the switch as the hub of the operation. When a user needs to send data to a specific device, the switch automatically directs the output of the computer, either through serial or parallel lines, to the right output device.

From the user point of view, the matrix switch is a box that contains several input-ports and several output-ports. A user connects one of the input-ports to the switch through a serial or parallel port depending on the application and the need of the user. Devices or other hosts connect to the output-ports using an available serial or parallel port. Software residing in the switch or the attached computer instructs the device what to do. In addition, many programs are designed to read the settings of the switch, relieving the user from having to set up any parameters manually. Once the software is set up, the user can send print jobs directly to one of the printers attached to the matrix switch. The print job, on many occasions, has embedded commands that provide the switch with the instructions required to perform its duties. In other situations, the software running in the user's computer can send data to the required device without knowing that the switch is present. In this case, the matrix switch handles all communication operations automatically.

The disadvantage of matrix switches is in their lack of power and speed of data transmission. Most matrix switches work in the 19,200 bits per second range, with a few of them transmitting at higher speeds. But their speed is far below the speed of transmission of most local area networks. However, they are simple to install and use without the need for a system administrator. Although matrix switches will never replace true media-sharing local area networks, they are very useful in many data communication situations. If all that is needed is the sharing of devices among several users who are in close proximity, a matrix or data switch should be considered.

Many other devices can be used to extend the capabilities of a data communication system and provide users with an affordable solution to their data communication needs. Some of these additional devices fall under the category of line adapters because they are incorporated directly into the line of communication. These are discussed in the next section.

Line Adapter

A line adapter is a device that is placed in the line of data transmission to perform monitoring functions, extend the range of data transmission, perform security functions, or allow the sharing of a data line. Some of the most commonly used types of line adapters are line monitors, port-sharing devices, line splitters, digital expanders, and security devices such as encryption systems and call-back units. Additional line adapters such as bridges and gateways are discussed in later chapters as a subset of networks. The main purpose of the line adapter is to increase the range and the number of connections possible between users and host systems, especially as distributed systems become more the norm rather than the exception. The first of the line adaptors that we will discuss is the line monitor, and it is used mainly by system administrators as a debugging and management tool.

Line Monitor

A line monitor is used to diagnose problems on a communication line or link. It attaches to a communication circuit, and a digital format of the data flowing through the circuit is displayed on a screen, printed to paper, or stored on an auxiliary device for further analysis.

There are two categories of line monitors, active and passive. Active line monitors can generate data, are interactive, and can emulate various types of monitors. Passive line monitors gather data and store it for analysis at a later time. Modern line monitors provide information about traffic volume, idle status, and errors that take place in the communicating medium. These statistics are normally stored in some secondary storage medium for further analysis and are displayed in a graphical format at the same time that they are being stored.

The hardware monitor is a special type of line monitor. It measures voltage changes in the line and reports changes. Using a hardware monitor, any type of system such as a front end processor, concentrator, and data communication line can be closely monitored. Additional monitors, such as network monitors, are discussed in later chapters, but any monitor of system performance that installs or interfaces between the user's equipment and the data communication line is considered a line monitor.

A typical line monitor can work with data speeds of up to 64,000 bits per second, and has video displays and memory, supports synchronous and asynchronous transmission, has breakout box capabilities (see later section in this chapter), and is capable of being programmed. Using this capability, a system administrator can instruct the line monitor to look for specific signals or to look at the function of individual devices. The purpose is to diagnose problems that a user may report or to find "bottle-necks" in the transmission process in order to improve response time.

Microcomputers can be enhanced to function as line monitors. A PC adapter board, internal RS-232, and software can convert a standard microcomputer into an active and intelligent line monitor and response time analyzer. This is a common procedure in the monitoring of local area networks. Using sophisticated software and an interface card, a personal computer can now perform monitoring functions that expensive line monitors have been performing until recently. In addition, the personal computer can process data as it collects it or store it and process it later.

Channel Extender

A channel extender links remote stations to host facilities. It connects directly to the host system and operates at high speeds. It functions like a small front end processor. In addition to connecting remote work stations and computers to a host, it can support auxiliary devices, including printers, disk drives, and microcomputers. Fig. 3-19 shows the placement of a channel extender in a communication circuit.

Although channel extenders are essentially scaled down front end processors, they are slower and less powerful than FEPs. However, as the cost of hardware decreases and the software in these devices becomes more sophisticated, channel extenders will be competing more directly with front end processors.

Channel extenders provide a method for improving response time and offloading data communication processes from networks, and they provide a less expensive alternative to front end processors. Through the use of channel extenders, the distance limitation of 400 feet between the terminal and mainframe is overcome. This allows for the implementation of distributed processing beyond the basic physical location of the mainframe. This allows

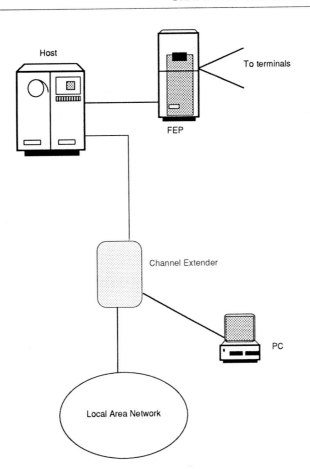

Fig. 3-19. A channel extender in a communication circuit.

several mainframes, minicomputers, and microcomputers to be located many miles apart, yet function as if they were in close proximity. This type of connection can be accomplished by using channel extenders and a T-1 line to connect the computers over long distances. The T-1 line provides the high-speed connection, and the channel extender provides the capability of taking the data signals beyond their 400-feet limit.

Fig. 3-19 shows how distributed processing can be achieved beyond the typical 400-feet limitation for a mainframe data channel interconnection. The mainframe channel can be extended to another mainframe channel by using a channel extender. This device can also connect microcomputers and terminals at remote locations. Moreover, local area networks can be connected to the mainframe channel through a channel extender.

Port-Sharing Device

A port-sharing device allows multiple terminals or stations to use a single port on a front end processor or mainframe system. This type of equipment is used when the capacity of the front end processor or host system needs to be exceeded. For example, it is possible that at a given installation the number of ports available on the host are already used. Therefore, if the host system has 32 ports, then 32 incoming lines may already be attached to devices or allocated to users. What happens if an additional device is required or if new users need to be added to the system? The obvious solution is to expand the system or acquire a bigger system to accommodate all the required devices and users. But what if the processing capabilities of the system are adequate and just the number of ports needs to be increased? Or what if several devices need to share a common port? In this case the solution may be to install a port-sharing device.

For example, if the number of users in the system increases to 48 or if more printers need to be attached, a port-sharing device constitutes a temporary fix until a more appropriate solution is designed. Using a port-sharing device, printers or terminals that are not going to be used simultaneously can be made to share a port and therefore decrease the cost of adding new ports that may be idle during much of the time.

Another example of the use of channel extenders applies to an office or corporation that uses personnel who share a single job. In this case, one or more individuals may perform the same job at different times during the business day or week. However, these individuals may have their own terminals and offices. It seems redundant to equip each employee with a terminal and a line attached to an individual port on the host system. It is a better use of resources to use a port-sharing device or a matrix switch to provide these users with shared access to the resources in the host using a single line or multiple line attached to a port-sharing device. Since only one user will be accessing the host at any given time, this schema will work effectively. In many cases, channel extenders can serve as sophisticated port-sharing devices.

Port Selector

Working along side the port-sharing device, port selectors allow a user to be automatically attached to the first available port on a host system. Where the port-sharing device allows the connection of many terminals to a single port (only one at a time), the port selector may take a single line and can attach this line to any number of ports that are assigned to the port selector (see Fig. 3-20).

Fig. 3-20. Port selector in a data communication system.

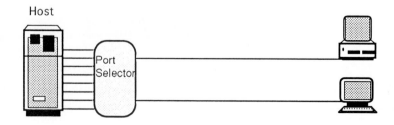

It is normally used in conjunction with dial-up lines where there may be a large number of lines available for connection from the outside, but only a few ports are available for these dial-up users. When a user calls into the system, the port selector searches for an available port on the host. If one is found, the user is connected to that port. If a port is not found, the user is notified of the situation or a busy signal is transmitted back to the user, and he or she is asked to try later.

Modern port selectors can handle incoming calls that use different transmission speeds and different communication protocols such as ASCII and EBCDIC. In addition, they can switch users to dial-up circuits or dedicated lines, perform statistics on the use of the host ports, and provide feedback when a port is not available for the user.

Line Splitter

A line splitter works in similar fashion to a port-sharing device with the difference being the location of the line splitter. A line splitter is normally found at the remote end of a communication line, where the terminal or workstation is located (see Fig. 3-21). Port-sharing devices are normally located at the host end of the communication line.

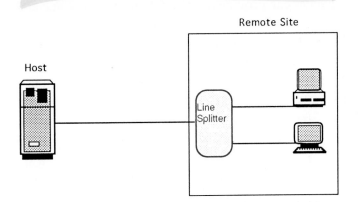

Fig. 3-21. A line splitter at a remote site.

Line splitters act as switches that allow several terminals to connect to a modem to access the host system. Even though multiple terminals are attached to a line splitter, only one communication line exists. Therefore, only one terminal can be communicating with the host at any one time.

As an example of using this technique, assume that four users need access to the host system from a remote location at different times during the working day. One solution is to provide each user with an individual line and a modem in order to access the host system. Therefore, four communication lines and at least five modems are required. Four of the modems are the users' and at least one is needed for the host. This solution, although efficient, could be costly depending on the needs of the users.

Another solution is to use a single line and modem and use a line splitter at the site where the users are located. In this scenario, the line splitter acts as a switch providing one of the users access to the line and modem at any given time. This is a less costly solution than the one mentioned above. However, keep in mind that only one user can access the modem and the data communication line at any given time. The other users must wait for the line and the modem to be given up by the user who is performing the communications before they can transmit data. If a single data communication line must carry the signals of more than one transmission, then another device, the digital line expander, may be used to increase the efficiency of the data line.

Digital Line Expander

A digital line expander allows users to concentrate a larger number of voice and data channels into the bandwidth of a standard communication channel. This is done through the use of hardware and software techniques that make use of the entire bandwidth capability of a standard voice circuit.

For example, if a communication site has only two leased lines between two remotely located terminating points, it can save money by using a line expander to increase the carrying capacity of those lines. One digital line expander can provide up to eight intermixed voice and digital data transmission circuits over a single digital communication circuit. This will obviously reduce the overhead cost of the company and increase the effectiveness of the leased lines. However, as in many other situations, this increase in capacity doesn't come free. If the number of transmissions is increased, the speed of the transmission must be decreased in order to make room for the additional data flowing through the circuit. If a line has a transmission speed of 57,600 bits per second, we couldn't send two transmissions at 57,600 bits per second. But we could send three data signals traveling at a speed of 19,200 bits per second simultaneously by using a digital line expander. Another device that enhances the efficiency of a data communication line is a data compression device.

Data Compression Device

A data compression device can increase the throughput of data over a communication line by compressing the data (see Fig. 3-22). By reducing the amount of memory that a file or message uses, the net throughput of a line can be increased, since more data is being sent per second. This technique is somewhat similar to compression techniques used in expanding the storage capabilities of a hard disk. Compression software, following a specific compression algorithm, intercepts the data that needs to be transmitted and reduces its space requirements. The result is that the same information is packed into a smaller number of bytes and then stored, or in this case sent through the data transmission lines. At some point, the same algorithm must be used again to decompress the data and restore it to its original state.

A data compression device is a microprocessor-controlled device that uses several techniques for data compression. One type of compression technique is to count the number of repeating characters that are in sequence and send this count instead of sending each character. This is called run length encoding.

Another more sophisticated technique is called Huffman encoding. The Huffman encoding algorithm uses tables of the most commonly transmitted characters within a language and adjusts the number of bits needed to transmit each character, based on the relative frequency of the character in the language.

Although a thorough discussion of compression algorithms is beyond the scope of this book, suffice it to say that data compression devices use software techniques to reduce the space requirement of data. Then by sending fewer characters, yet maintaining the integrity of the information, the efficiency of transmission is increased. You may have already seen this type of transmission in a less sophisticated format. Many bulletin boards have their files in compressed format, using one of several popular compressing programs such as PKZIP. The compressed file is then transferred from the host machine, where the bulletin board resides, to the user's computer. Here, using a decompression program such as PKUNZIP, the user decompresses the file, restoring it to its original form. After decompression, the user can use the file the way it was designed to be used. This is a technique commonly employed in the microcomputer communication arena. Fig. 3-23 shows a file before it was compressed by PKZIP and the resulting compressed file and size. As you can see, there is a large decrease in the size of the file after compression. This new compressed file will take less time to transmit than the original file.

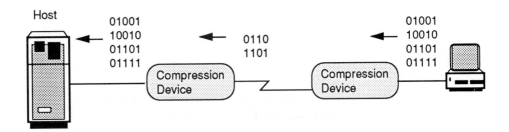

Fig. 3-22. Increasing throughput using data compression.

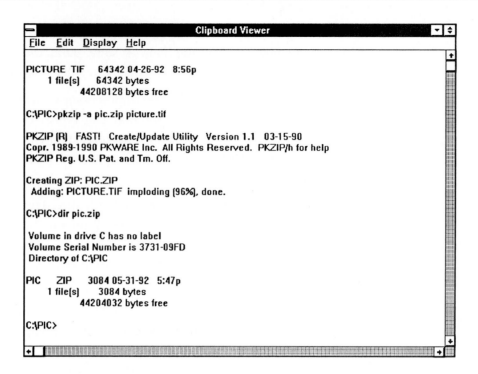

Fig. 3-23. File size before and after software compression.

Security Devices

The concept of sharing resources and files is one of the great appeals of communication networks and centralized computer systems. However, there are times where user access to records and files must be limited to prevent unauthorized access of such items or to prevent inadvertent damage of any critical data. Additionally, data travelling through communication circuits is prone to interception, and the devices attached to these lines are also in danger of intrusion by unauthorized users. Securing these data transmission lines is an important aspect of data communications today. For the purpose of preventing unauthorized access to computing equipment, several pieces of hardware can assist in protecting data flowing through communication circuits. These devices are call-back units and encryption equipment. Additional equipment used in the management and protection of data communication, such as metering software and monitoring equipment, is discussed under the topic of networks.

Call-Back Unit

A call-back unit is a security device that calls back the user after he or she makes a login attempt. After the call is answered, the call-back unit hangs up the phone and the phone number of the originating call is looked up in a table. If the phone that the user is on is an authorized number in the table, then the call-back unit calls the user back and expects the terminal or user's computer to answer the call. If the call is completed properly, the system permits the user to login.

The actual procedure that the call-back unit goes through to secure lines is as follows:

1. A person attempting to access the system makes a connection from a remote terminal or microcomputer using communication software.

2. The person is required to provide an identification number (ID) and a password.

3. The connection is severed after the ID and the password are entered.

4. The ID and password are checked in a table to verify that the user is authorized.

5. If the user is authorized, the call-back unit calls the user's registered phone number. The phone number is stored inside the host and authorized by the company's security personnel.

6. The user's modem is accessed and the session between the terminal and the host begins.

Call-back units provide access only to authorized users, inhibiting access by hackers, unless they are using an authorized phone. However, these units have some problems. First, the host system becomes responsible for the cost of the connection. Second, if a person is on a business trip and tries to access the host system with a portable computer, the computer won't be able to make the connection, since the phone number being used is not registered.

This last problem can be resolved by providing users with a cellular telephone and modem. Using a portable or cellular system, a user can be anywhere the cellular system can receive a signal. Then as long as the portable phone is registered with the system, a call-back unit will be able to locate the user and establish a connection. Several companies, including IBM, make laptop computers that have built in cellular phones and modems for use by sales and executive personnel. These systems are, of course, susceptible to the noise and interference that normally affects cellular equipment.

Another problem with the last solution outlined is that transmission over cellular phones is susceptible to interception by unauthorized users with the proper equipment. If company secrets are transmitted in this manner, there is a good possibility that they could be intercepted and used without the company knowing it. When high security is a necessity, then additional devices such as encryption equipment must be employed.

Encryption Equipment

Some data communication networks, such as those employed by the government and military, require very secure communication. For this purpose, encryption equipment is used to scramble the data at the sending location and reconstruct it at the receiving end. Fig. 3-24 depicts this configuration. Encryption is the transformation of data from meaningful code into a meaningless stream of bits. To make this transformation, the data is sent through an encrypting algorithm with the result being the set of meaningless bits. To see the data in its original format, the scrambled data is sent back through the algorithm which in essence now works in "reverse," restoring the original message. This is somewhat similar to the scrambling that we experience with cable television premium channels. The signal is scrambled as it leaves the broadcasting studio. A descrambler or decoder is necessary to restore the original signal.

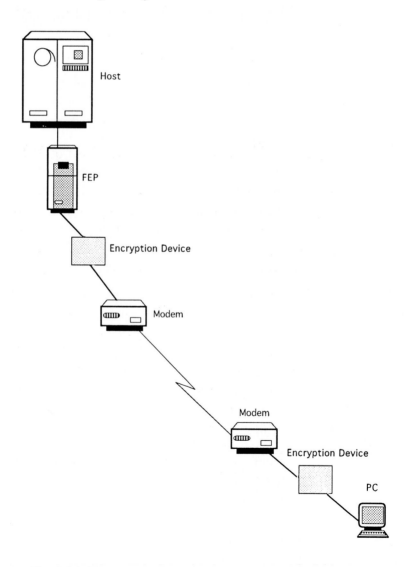

Fig. 3-24. Encrypting devices in a communication system.

Modern encryption devices expect digital information as input, and produce digital information as output. The function of these devices is governed by standards set by the U.S. National Bureau of Standards (NBS). This set of standards is called the Data Encryption Standard (DES), which uses 64 bits to encrypt blocks of 64 bits. Eight of the 64 bits are used for error detection, and a 56-bit pattern is used for the encryption key. This provides 256 possible different key combinations or more than 72 quadrillion possibilities for the key used in encrypting and decrypting the message.

During the transmission of an encrypted message, the same key must be used in the sending and receiving end of the transmission. This means that there must be a mechanism for sending the key to the receiving user. Sometimes the overhead involved during this operation can be costly since expensive and secure lines or some special courier must be used.

Encryption can be achieved through software or hardware implementation. Hardware encryption is faster but less flexible than software encryption. However, there are many chips that implement the DES algorithm that can simply be plugged into a computer and are ready for use. Software encryption is normally used only when there are small amounts of data to be encrypted; otherwise, hardware encryption is employed.

Miscellaneous Equipment

In addition to the data communication devices already mentioned, there are other hardware devices that help in the installation and maintenance of data lines. One of the most common is the breakout box, and it is used to set up the proper cable configurations required in data communications. Although used in several forms of communications, the breakout box is most commonly used to configure pin out configurations in RS-232 ports and serial data communications. Although, the RS-232 is considered a standard, each manufacturer of computing equipment implements one of several versions of the "RS-232 standard." This creates incompatibilities between devices that use the serial port as the main communication device. Some of these cases are terminals and peripherals attached to computers running the UNIX system. In this system, most terminals connect through the RS-232 or serial port, with many of the printers in the system also connected through the serial port. Unfortunately, an RS-232 pin configuration that works for one type of terminal may not work with another terminal from a different configuration. For these reasons, many system technicians make use of the breakout box.

Breakout Box

A breakout box is a passive device that can be attached to a circuit at any connecting point, but it is normally attached at the location of a serial port on a device or computer. It can be programmable or nonprogrammable with the latter being the most commonly used. Once the breakout box is installed it can perform the following functions:

1. Monitor data activity on the circuits. Each line circuit has a light emitting diode (LED) on the breakout box. If there is a signal on the line, the LED lights up.

2. Exchange line connections. One of the major causes of improper communication between devices is crossed lines. Line connections can easily be changed without the need to build a connector for each change.

3. Isolate a circuit. A single line which is suspected of causing the problem can be prevented from transmitting to the receiving device and isolated to see if it is the cause of the errors.

4. Voltage levels can be monitored. Some breakout boxes have voltage meters built in. This allows the user to detect unusual voltages in the circuit.

With the use of a breakout box a user or technician can "quickly" attach a computer to a device and experiment with the pin configuration until the right combination that allows the proper transmission of data without any losses is achieved. Some newer types of breakout boxes claim to be completely automatic. That is, they will automatically detect the right pin configuration for the sending and transmitting devices and adjust themselves to make sure that both devices work properly. Such devices seem to work well in many situations. However, they can't always automatically detect the right configuration. These devices will save a lot of time if they are able to automatically figure out the right cable configuration, but there is a good possibility that you may still have to use a normal breakout box and some trial-and-error techniques before an optimal solution can be found.

Summary

Several types of electronic devices are used in the design and installation of data communication networks. The most commonly used are microcomputers, front end processors, mainframes, concentrators, cluster controllers, PBXs, matrix switches, line adapters, and security devices.

Typical electronic devices used in data communication are microcomputers, terminals, front end procesors, and mainframes. The terminals are used strictly to send and receive data to and from a host computer. There are many variations in terminal attributes. These include keyboards, light pens, touch screens, mice, joy sticks, trackballs, voice entry devices, and page scanners.

Front end processors are employed at the host end of a communication circuit to perform different control and processing functions required for the proper operation of a data communications network.

Mainframe computers are considered central computer systems that perform data processing functions for a business or industry. Mainframe computers are used in networks as host systems or as controllers. There are three types of configurations in which a mainframe can be used. The first is a configuration where the mainframe is a stand-alone system. The second configuration employs minicomputers and microcomputers in a local area network. The third configuration includes a front end processor to help with the communication.

A concentrator is a line-sharing device whose primary function is the same as that of a multiplexer. It allows multiple devices to share communication circuits. Unlike multiplexers, concentrators are intelligent devices that sometimes perform data processing functions and provide auxiliary storage.

Cluster controllers are designed to support several terminals and the functions required to manage those terminals. Also, they buffer data being transmitted to or from the terminals, perform error detection and correction, and poll terminals.

Private branch exchanges are electronic switchboards which connect to all the telephone lines of the organization. They can handle data communications in a digital format. Their flexibility in this area, especially when it comes to connecting a terminal or microcomputer to a host system, makes them a popular device used in data communications.

A matrix switch is similar to a private branch exchange and allows terminals and other electronic devices to access multiple host processors without the need to physically move any communication line. They are less sophisticated than private branch exchanges but are also less costly than PBXs.

Several other devices can be used to expand the communication distance between users and the host system. These devices are called line adapters and they come in different varieties, such as line monitors, channel extenders, line splitters, port-sharing devices, port selectors, digital line expanders, and data compression devices.

Securing data transmission lines is an important aspect of data communication today. Several pieces of hardware can assist in protecting data flowing through communication circuits. These devices include call-back units and encryption equipment.

Another device used in monitoring and improving line channel performance is the breakout box. The breakout box is a passive device that can be attached to a circuit at any connecting point.

Questions

1. Why do we need devices to communicate more than a few hundred feet from a mainframe?
2. What is the main purpose of a matrix switch?
3. Why do we use breakout boxes?
4. What are concentrators?
5. What is the function of a protocol converter?
6. What is the function of a PBX?
7. What is a cluster controller?
8. Describe four different types of line adapters.
9. How does a line monitor work?
10. Why is hardware encryption used?
11. What device(s) could we use to increase the efficiency of a data communication line?
12. What device(s) could be used to increase the use of a data communication line in terms of the amount of data to be transmitted?

Projects

The projects in this chapter are intended to familiarize the student with the basic hardware required to connect computers and printers using standard RS-232 ports. The basic equipment required to perform the projects is outlined in Project 1 of the previous chapter. As an additional challenge, the instructor may provide unknown or lesser known serial printers and instruct the student to design the interface between the printer and a microcomputer.

Project 1. Minimum Interface between a Printer and a Microcomputer

To connect a printer to a computer using the serial port, a minimum null modem eliminator can be used in most cases. The minimum null modem eliminator can be used on devices that support the Xon/Xoff protocol. If your computer and printer support this communication protocol, then pins 4 and 5 can be loop shorted on both systems and also pins 6, 8, and 20 can be shorted. However, all the handshaking must be done through software and not through the hardware. In most cases additional software is not required when printing documents using the interface discussed in this section. The sending software program needs to be instructed that it is communicating with the printer serially and that X-on/X-off should be used in addition to the typical serial parameters .

To construct the minimum null modem eliminator, follow the configuration in Fig. 3-25.

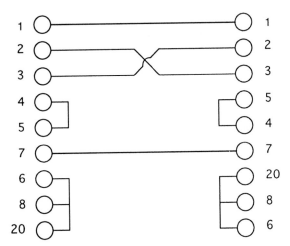

Fig. 3-25. Minimum null modem eliminator.

Project 2. General Interface between a Printer and a Micro-computer

In some situations a minimum null modem eliminator is not sufficient for the printer and the computer to communicate. If the printer seems to "lose" characters or if it prints correctly for a while and then it stops, the configuration in Fig. 3-26 may solve the problem. Some printers require pin 11 (printer ready) to become active by a signal from the union of pins 6 and 8 as in Fig. 3-25.

Fig. 3-26. Connections between a printer and a computer.

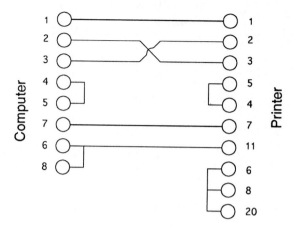

Communication Media

Objectives

After completing this chapter you will

1. Understand the different types of data communication media available in the market place.

2. Be able to make educated decisions about the proper types of transmission media to solve a data communication problem.

3. Understand the selection criteria for the different types of transmission media.

4. Understand different criteria for selecting circuit media.

Key Terms

Bandwidth

Coaxial Cable

Kilobits per Second

Optical Fiber

Twisted Pair

Cellular Radio

Data Channel

Microwave

Satellite

Introduction

All data communication equipment needs some type of transmission medium in order for the transmission to take place. Whether this communication medium is some type of conducting metal, water, air, or vacuum is not as important as recognizing the limitations that the medium imposes on current technology.

The educated data communication manager must understand the limitations and capabilities of all transmission mediums available to perform his or her duties as the person responsible for a successful data communication environment.

Each of the data communication media explored in this chapter has advantages and disadvantages that make it appropriate for some companies and inadequate for other data transmission needs. Although many managers make decisions about the transmission medium based on its data volume capacity and speed of transmission, many other factors affect the overall success of the implementation of a data communication system. The right medium is, of course, a key element in a successful operation. However, speed should not be the sole criterion for determining the appropriate medium.

Additionally, the services offered by common carriers should not be overlooked. These companies have been providing data communication services for many years, and their expertise in this area is often superior to that of company experts. Many companies may benefit from the offerings of such carriers, if for no other reason than the managing of the communication facilities, a task that many small and medium-sized companies tend to overlook.

Therefore, the following chapter should be read with an open mind if a broad understanding of all solutions is to be gained. The chapter presents different types of data transmission media, and then explores some selection criteria for choosing one of these media. Also, the telephone central office is explored along with some of the typical services provided by common carriers.

Circuit Media

The data transmission medium is the physical path that the signal must use in order to travel from the sender to the receiver. There are many types of transmission media to choose from, but they can be classified in general terms into two types:

1. Guided transmission media
2. Unguided transmission media

Guided transmission media include several types of cabling systems that guide the data signals along the cable from one location to another. The other type, unguided transmission media, consists of a means for the signals to travel, but nothing to guide them along a specific path. Examples of these types of transmission media are air and water.

Guided transmission media work by attaching the transmitter directly to the medium. The transmitter can be a microcomputer, terminal, peripheral device, or even a cable television station. The signal travels through the cable and, at the other end, the receiver is also attached directly to the cable.

The cables used in guided transmission are basically wire conductors. Conductors can be classified into four major groups: open wire, twisted pair cable, coaxial cable, and optical fiber cable. Each of these has its own capabilities in terms of data-carrying capacity and speed of transmission. At the low end we can consider the open wire, and at the high end we have optical fiber. Of course, prices increase as the transmission performance of the cable increases.

Unguided media use antennas for the transmission and reception of the data signals. Among the different types of signals that can be transmitted using this format, we have microwave and satellite signals. Although unguided media such as air don't guide the signals along a specific path, the direction of the signal transmitted can be chosen by employing different configurations and arrangement of antennas. In this fashion, a beam of microwaves can be concentrated along a direction where a receiving antenna is expected to be located. The ability to focus a beam of signals in an unguided medium depends on the frequency of the signals being transmitted. The frequency of a signal is the number of cycles per second that signals go through, meaning the number of times the signal varies between two settings in one second. As the frequency gets higher, it is easier to focus the beam in a specific direction.

Although this chapter doesn't discuss all possible types of media configurations, it will discuss the most common types that are found in the marketplace. In most, if not all cases, the different data transmission media described below will satisfy the requirements of any data communication system.

Guided Media

Open Wire

Open wire lines have been around since the inception of the data communication industry. An open wire line consists of copper wire tied to glass insulators, with the insulators attached to wooden arms mounted on utility poles. While still in common use throughout the world, they are quickly being replaced by twisted pair cables and other transmission media. Communication on this medium is susceptible to a large degree of interference, since the cable is open in the atmosphere.

Twisted Pair Cables

Because of the susceptibility of open wire to interference, it is typically wrapped with an insulating plastic coating and twisted together, hence the name twisted pair (see Fig. 4-1). The cables are twisted in pairs because the electrical effect of one current is cancelled by the electrical effect of the other, thereby reducing the amount of interference that the signal is subjected to. In this manner, the signals from one pair of cables are prevented from interfering with the signals of another pair, a type of interference that is sometimes called crosstalk. Twisted pair wiring is a common type of data transmission medium found in homes and buildings. Therefore we need to study it further, along with some of its data communication applications.

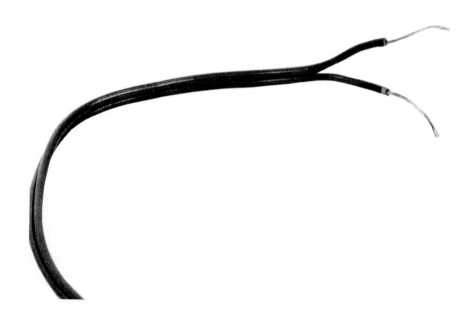

Fig. 4-1. Twisted pair wire.

A twisted pair cable is composed of copper conductors insulated by paper or plastic and twisted into pairs. At the location where the pairs enter a building, a terminating block, also called a punchdown block, is normally found. These pairs are bundled into units and the units are bundled to form the finished cable. Fig. 4-2 shows a terminal connector where twisted pair cables are being used. The terminating block serves several purposes. One of the functions of the terminating block is to act as a distribution panel. From the terminating block wires are distributed to offices or to other distribution panels or blocks located throughout the building. Another function of the terminating block is

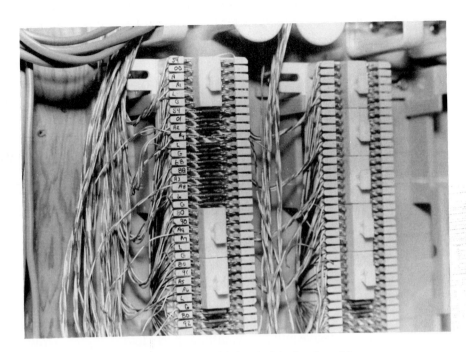

Fig. 4-2. Terminal connector for connecting twisted pair cables.

to act as a demarcation point where the responsibility of the common carrier (the public company who owns the cable) ends and the responsibility of the building owner begins. Any cable that is distributed from the terminating block belongs to private owners and they are responsible for its maintenance and upgrade. This same concept applies to home owners. The phone company owns the twisted pair cable that is used to bring the phone signals up to the house. But the house owner is responsible for the twisted pair phone cable installed throughout the house.

The size of twisted pair cable is measured in gauges, with typical twisted pair cables coming in 26, 24, or 22 gauge. The smaller the gauge number, the bigger the wire. This type of gauge corresponds to thicknesses from 0.0016 to 0.036 inch.

A variation of twisted pair is called the shielded twisted pair or data-grade twisted pair. Shielded twisted pair is twisted cable placed inside a thin metallic shielding of aluminum foil or woven-copper shield and then enclosed in an outer plastic casing. The shielding provides further isolation from the interference caused by the signal-carrying wires. Also, it is less susceptible to interference signals produced by electrical wires or nearby electronic equipment. Additionally, shielded twisted pair cables are less likely to cause interference themselves.

Because of this insulation, shielded twisted pair wire is capable of carrying data signals faster than normal twisted pair wire. However, this type of wire is more expensive and difficult to work with than unshielded twisted pair wire, and it requires custom installation to have a "clean" connection and avoid interference from poorly attached cable. Additionally, the shielding affects the transmission characteristics of the line and reduces the distance over which a signal can be effectively transmitted.

Twisted pair, whether shielded or unshielded, is used to transmit analog and digital signals. If an analog signal is being transmitted, amplifiers are normally required every three or four miles. If digital signals are being transmitted, some type of repeater is required every one or two miles. It has limited distance carrying capabilities, limited bandwidth, and limited data transmission speed. That is, it is very limited in the total amount of data it can transmit per unit of time and has low transmission speeds. Additionally, transmission frequencies can be high for long distances. In this case, electrical interference in the form of crosstalk between adjacent circuits is a problem for twisted pair cables. Even if shielded twisted pair wire is used, the problems above still apply, although to a lesser degree. However, it is inexpensive and commonly available in most offices and buildings. This makes it a popular data transmission medium in data communication systems. To solve some of the problems with twisted pair wire, coaxial cable is employed.

Coaxial Cable

Coaxial cable consists of two conductors. The inner conductor, normally copper or aluminum, is shielded by placing it inside a plastic case or shield. The second conductor is wrapped around the plastic shield of the first conductor. This further shields the inner conductor. Additionally, the second conductor (shield) is covered with plastic or some other protective and insulating cover (see Fig. 4-3).

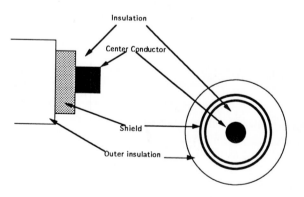

Fig. 4-3. Coaxial cable.

The outer conductor shields the inner conductor from outside electrical signals and reduces the electromagnetic radiations of the inner conductor. The distance between the conductors varies, along with the type of shielding and insulation material used. This difference gives each type of coaxial cable a unique characteristic normally called impedance. The impedance is a measure of the resistance that the conductor has to the flow of electrical signals. Typical diameters of coaxial cables range from 0.4 to 1 inch.

Coaxial cables are sometimes grouped into bundles. Each bundle can carry several thousand voice and/or data transmissions simultaneously. This type of cable has little signal loss, signal distortion, or crosstalk. Therefore, it is a better transmission medium than open wire or twisted pair cables.

It is one of the more versatile transmission media and it has wide acceptance in the communication industry. It is used extensively in television distribution (cable television), local area networks, and long distance phone transmission. We have all seen the coaxial cable that cable companies use in distributing their signals from a distribution building to homes. Today, over half of the residential homes in the United States have cable television, and most of them are connected through coaxial cable.

Coaxial cable is heavier and more expensive than twisted pair wire. It can carry a greater capacity of data over longer distances and it is stronger than twisted pair. This makes it a common choice of data transmission media in factories and other areas where there is a harsh environment. The typical bandwidth of coaxial cable is between 400 Mhz and 600 Mhz. This large bandwidth is what gives coaxial cable its high data-carrying capacity.

It can carry analog and digital signals and, because of its shielded concentric construction, it is less susceptible to interference and crosstalk than twisted pair cable. For transmitting a signal over long distances, repeaters are required every few miles with the number of miles depending on the frequency of the data being transmitted. With higher frequency of data signals, the distance needed between repeaters becomes shorter.

Local area networks have been using coaxial cable as a medium for transmitting data to workstations. Coaxial cable can support large numbers of devices with different data and protocols transmitting over the same cabling system over short and long distances. However, it is important to note that there are many types of coaxial cable with different electrical characteristics. Not all coaxial cable can be used with a particular networking scheme.

Working with coaxial cable takes practice because it is bulkier than twisted pair wire. Therefore, connecting devices using coaxial cable should be done by a professional. One bad connection can render an entire system inoperative. It is wise to invest in good connectors regardless of their price. Additionally, a good crimping tool should be used. Also, invest in good quality coaxial cable. There are many vendors of poor quality coaxial cable that tends to break down after time and corrosion expose the conductors.

Optical Fiber

Optical fiber consists of thin glass fibers that can carry information at frequencies in the visible light spectrum. The data transmission lines made up of optical fibers are joined by connectors that have very little loss of the signal throughout the length of the data line.

At the sending end of a data circuit, data is encoded from electrical signals into light pulses that travel through the lines at high speeds. At the receiving end, the light is converted back into electrical analog or digital signals that are then passed on to the receiving device.

The typical optical fiber consists of a very narrow strand of glass called the core. Around the core is a concentric layer of glass called the cladding (see Fig. 4-4). After the light is inserted into the core it follows a zig-zag path through the core. The advantage of optical fiber is that it can carry large amounts of information at high speeds in very reduced physical spaces with little loss of signal.

Fig. 4-4. Optical fiber compo-nents.

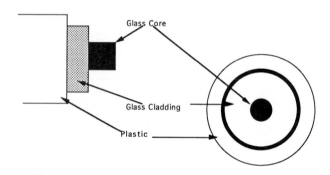

There are three primary types of transmission modes using optical fiber. They are single mode, step index, and graded index (see Fig. 4-5).

Fig. 4-5. Optical fiber transmission modes.

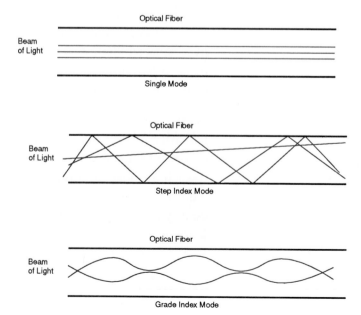

Single mode transmission uses fibers with a core radius of 2.5 to 4 microns. Since the radius of the fiber is so small, light travels through the core with little reflection from the cladding. However, it requires very concentrated light sources to get the signal to travel long distances. This type of mode is typically used for trunk line applications. A trunk line is the cable that carries the signal from a central office to a PBX or building where the signal will then be distributed.

Step index fiber consists of a core of fiber surrounded by a cladding with a lower refractive index for the light. The cable has an approximate radius of 30 to 70 microns. The lower refractive index causes the light pulse to bounce downward back toward the core. In this type of transmission, some of the light pulses travel straight down the core while others bounce off the cladding multiple times before reaching their destination. This mode is used for distances of one kilometer or less.

Graded index fiber has a refractive index that changes gradually as the light travels to the outer edge of the fiber. The cable has a radius of 25 to 60 microns. This gradual refractive index bends the light towards the core instead of just reflecting it. This mode is used for long distance communication.

The promise of optical fiber as one of the best communication media comes from its high bandwidth. Optical fiber has a bandwidth range of about 1014 to 1015 Hz. With a bandwidth much larger than any other type of cable, a single optical fiber can carry the signals of thousands of simultaneous telephone conversations. In addition, optical fiber can carry signals much faster than other cabling schemes without distortion.

In terms of local area networks, the speed of optical fiber is not a good reason to choose it as the data transmission medium. In this situation, fibers carry data at about the same speeds as coaxial cable. However, optical fiber can carry the data longer, more reliably, and more securely than any other type of media. Additionally, fiber has the potential to carry data at higher speeds as the technology develops to take advantage of such a possibility.

Optical fiber can carry digital signals a longer distance than copper wires without the need of repeaters. Additionally, optical fibers don't pick up electrical noise from nearby conductors. On the other hand, copper-based conductors, regardless of the amount of shielding used, always become antennas. The amount of interference in the copper is directly proportional to its length. Since the signal traveling in an optical fiber is not electrical, none of these problems apply.

Optical fiber has additional benefits relating to security. Electrical signals traveling in a coaxial or twisted pair cable can be detected since electromagnetic radiation is emitted. This radiation, with the right equipment, can be used to obtain the original message. Light, on the other hand, doesn't emit electromagnetic radiation. Therefore, it is much more difficult for unauthorized users to pick up the signal in the fiber. Additionally, tapping into an optical fiber, although not impossible, is more difficult than tapping into twisted pair or coaxial cable.

Although more expensive than coaxial cable and twisted pair, optical fiber has the following advantages over them:

1. It has a greater capacity for carrying data due to its large bandwidth.

2. It has the potential for greater speeds of transmission than coaxial or twisted pair cables.

3. It is smaller in size and weight than other conventional cabling systems.

4. It can carry a signal over longer distances than other cabling systems with a smaller attenuation. That is, the signal loss over long distances is less with optical fiber.

5. It is not susceptible to electromagnetic radiation from nearby cables, light fixtures, and motors.

All these features of optical fiber make it a compelling transmission medium. As we move closer to the 21st century, users are demanding more than mere access to text-based data. Newer technologies such as multimedia are becoming standards in the workplace and in education. Multimedia technology incorporates sound, graphics, animation, and full motion video. Documents that incorporate multimedia techniques are being sent through traditional communication media that can handle the massive amount of data that such documents contain. Just a few seconds of full motion video require millions of bytes of information. If companies and institutions expect to move their data communication needs into the future, they will have to design data communication systems that can handle the large amount of information that a multimedia document may require. Electronic mail with voice and video is now available. However, only optical fiber has the bandwidth and speeds of transmission required to manipulate such massive amounts of data effectively and efficiently. By the beginning of the next century, optical fiber will be the dominant data transmission medium for fixed-location applications.

Unguided Media

Microwave

Microwave, or radio transmission as it is sometimes called, is a high frequency radio signal that is transmitted over a direct line-of-sight path between two points. The concept of line-of-sight is important since the earth has a curvature. This necessitates that microwave stations be no more than 30 miles apart with the actual distance varying according to the terrain being crossed. Fig. 4-6 shows a picture of a microwave tower and transmission station.

Fig. 4-6. This microwave tower is located in New Jersey. Both parabolic and horn antennas can be seen. (Courtesy of AT&T Bell Laboratories)

From the picture you can see one of the most common types of microwave antennas, the parabolic antenna or "dish." A normal size for this type of antenna is 10 to 12 feet in diameter and it is fixed to some stationary structure. The function of this antenna is to focus the microwave signals into a narrow beam that is transmitted to a receiving antenna that is directly in the line-of-sight of the sending dish. Microwave antennas are located in high places such as the rooftop of a building and on rigid structures that have a substantial height above the ground.

The primary purpose of microwave towers is to connect computers or communication equipment that are located in different geographical areas. For example, a company with several offices distributed throughout a city could use microwave communications to connect all of their data processing equipment. In this case, the company, if it is a private enterprise, is not allowed to lay its own cabling system across the public right-of-ways (streets and highways). Only common carriers such as AT&T have permission from the local and federal government to perform such actions. However, it is possible for the company in the example to lease lines from a common carrier to connect its distributed offices. Depending on the amount of equipment to be connected and the data communication and processing needs of the company, it may be more cost effective to set up a microwave communication system to solve its communication needs. As long as the microwave antennas are within a line-of-sight of each other, the company in question will be able to connect all of its equipment without the need to lease lines from a common carrier.

But, what happens if the antennas are not in a line-of-sight? Then, in this case, repeating microwave stations must be employed. The typical line-of-sight is about 25 to 30 miles depending on the type of terrain that the microwave tower is located on. Beyond this distance, relay or repeating stations must be employed, otherwise the signal is lost into space (see Fig. 4-7).

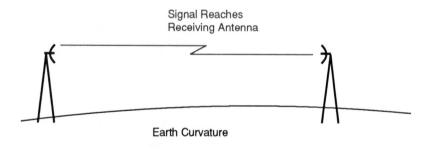

Fig. 4-7. The curvature of the Earth affects the distance between microwave antennas.

A typical microwave system transmits signals with a frequency in the range of 2 to 40 gigahertz. As the frequency increases, so does the bandwidth and therefore the potential for higher carrying loads. Also, as the frequency increases, the data transmission rate increases, but at high frequencies the attenuation of the signals also increases. Therefore, high frequencies are used only for short transmitting distances. These frequencies are subdivided into several types of transmission areas.

Three main groups of radio systems are used for communications lines. They are broadcast, beam, and satellite. Broadcast radio is limited to a unique frequency within the range of the transmitter. Radio beam transmission needs to be repeated if the signal is to travel farther than 30 miles. Normally, radio beam repeaters are found on top of buildings, mountain tops, and radio antennas. Satellite microwave radio is employed to avoid the limitations imposed by the earth's curvature, and it is described in the next section.

Microwave transmission offers speed, cost effectiveness (since there are no cables), and ease of operation. However, it has the potential for interference with other radio waves. This has become more apparent since the popularity of microwave transmission has increased over the last few years. With many microwave systems in place, especially in large cities, the chance of different transmissions overlapping each other and causing interference has increased. Additionally, commercial transmissions can be intercepted by any person with a receiver in the line of transmission, thus creating security risks. Another problem with microwaves is attenuation due to weather conditions. Microwaves tend to be attenuated by the water droplets from rainfall, especially when the transmission frequency is above 10 gigahertz. But even with these problems, microwave technology is a popular solution to data communication problems and needs.

Satellite Transmission

Satellite transmission is similar to microwave radio transmission. But instead of transmitting to an earth-bound receiving station, it will transmit to a satellite several thousand miles out in space (normally approximately 22,300 miles). Fig. 4-8 shows a picture of a transmitting satellite dish antenna.

Fig. 4-8. These satellite dish antennas are about 5 meters in diameter. Other dish antennas are small as 1 meter. (Courtesy of Contel ASC)

The basic components of satellite transmission are an earth station, used for sending and receiving data, and the satellite, sometimes called a transponder. The satellite receives the signals from an earth station (uplink), amplifies or repeats the signal, changes the frequency, and retransmits the data to another receiving earth station (downlink). The frequency is changed so the uplink does not interfere with the downlink (see Fig. 4-9).

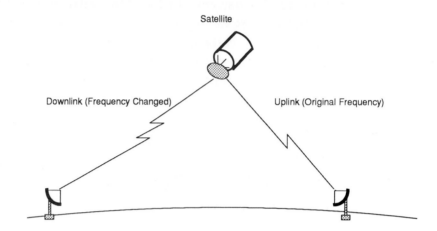

Fig. 4-9. Uplink and downlink satellite transmissions.

In satellite transmission, a delay occurs because the signal needs to travel out into space and back to the earth. Typical delay time is 0.5 second. There is an additional delay due to the time required for the signal to travel through ground stations.

But just as with the earth bound microwave antennas, a satellite must be within a line-of-sight of its earth stations. We use the words line-of-sight to indicate that the earth-based station and the satellite must be in locations that allow for the transmission and reception of a direct beam of microwave signals. Because of this, communication satellites remain stationary with respect to their position over the earth.

Two satellites that use the same frequencies cannot be too close to each other. Otherwise, they will interfere with each other. To avoid this situation, nations that place satellites in orbit around the earth follow a standard that requires them to place satellites with a minimum of 4 degrees of angular spacing as measured from the earth if the satellite transmits in the 4 to 6 gigahertz band. Also, the standard requires a 3 degrees spacing if the satellites transmit in the 12 to 14 gigahertz band. This standard limits the number of satellites that can be placed in orbit.

As stated before, satellites use different frequencies for receiving and transmitting. The frequency ranges are from 4 to 6 gigahertz (GHz), also called the C-band; 12 to 14 GHz, also called the Ku-band; and 20 to 30 GHz. As the value of the frequency decreases, the size of the dish antenna required to receive and transmit the signals needs to increase. The Ku-band is used to transmit television programs between networks and individual television stations. Since signals in the Ku-band have a higher frequency, their wavelength is shortened. This allows receiving and transmitting stations to concentrate the signals and use smaller dish antennas.

One of the most common uses of satellites is in the transmission of television signals. Satellites are being used extensively in the United States and throughout the world for this function. For example, to broadcast a show throughout the continental United States, a television network sends its signal to a satellite that in turn retransmits the signal to a series of receiving stations on the ground. From this station, through microwave or coaxial cable, the signals are relayed to the sets in people's homes.

Satellites are also used extensively for point-to-point trunks between telephone central offices in public telephone networks. Also, they are used by businesses to connect private networks. A user or business leases one or more channels in the satellite. It then connects data processing and communication equipment in a building with similar equipment in a branch or office located thousands of miles away. But, until recently such use of a satellite has been expensive. However, recent developments in the very small aperture terminal (VSAT) system provide low-cost alternatives to expensive traditional satellite transmissions. Using this scheme, several stations are equipped with low-cost antennas. These stations share a satellite transmission capacity for transmission to a central station. The central station exchanges messages with each of the stations and also relays messages between the stations.

Security poses a problem with satellite communications, because it is easy to intercept the transmission as it travels through the air. In some cases, a scrambler is used to distort the signal before it is sent to the satellite, and a descrambler is used in the receiving station to reproduce the original signal. This is the procedure used by several premium cable television channels such as HBO and CINEMAX. A business could employ similar techniques by using some type of software or hardware encryption of the data signal that it needs to transmit.

Cellular Radio

Traditional mobile telephones always had a problem with the availability of channels assigned to communication. It is common to find 20 channels being shared by 2,000 users, making it difficult to obtain a channel to use for communicating with someone else. Cellular radio solves this problem. Cellular radio is a form of high frequency radio transmission where the signals are relayed from antennas that are spaced in strategic locations throughout metropolitan areas.

Each area of service is divided into cells, and each cell has a fixed transmit and receive site. If a person is using a car telephone and moves to the edge of a current cell, the cellular radio system automatically moves the user's communication to another antenna that is closer. In this manner, transmission is not interrupted and the user doesn't have to worry about moving from one cell to another. Additionally, the quality of the transmission is comparable to that found in common hardwired telephone systems.

Cellular radio can be used for voice or computer data communications. A user dials into the cellular system, and the voice or data is transmitted directly from the user's location to the cell antenna. From here it is retransmitted throughout the service area, or in some cases it can be transmitted to a satellite for communications over long distances.

Several laptop and palmtop computers have cellular radio transmission capabilities. This allows a user to be at any location and dial into a central location for the downloading or uploading of data, freeing the sender from locating a telephone outlet and communicating in traditional ways. Many sales personnel, police, or individuals who need access to a central site on demand use cellular radio for their data communication needs.

Circuit Media Selection

With all the different options available for use as a transmission medium, which one is the most efficient and cost effective for a company? The answer to this question may be a single product, but is most likely a combination of products. In any case, many factors influence the decision of choosing a medium for a data communication network. These factors include cost, speed, expandability, security, and distance requirements. Decisions regarding these factors cannot be made independently. Deciding on a cabling scheme depends on the hardware that you have or plan to purchase. Software requirements may indicate a specific cabling system, and the hardware may have to be reconfigured for it.

In addition, data communication system designers will have to contend with two types of designs, one for the communications within the building or campus, and one for the communications to remote locations. Normally, the decisions that apply to communication beyond the immediate premises of the business have broader issues and implications than the decisions required for implementing a data communication system within the immediate business physical environment. This is due to the user not caring about the type of communication medium used by the common carrier providing the transmission media. That is, the user doesn't care that a particular carrier uses one hundred percent optical fiber or coaxial cable. The user is concerned only with the cost and quality of the service that the common carrier provides.

When it comes to providing data communications solutions for in-house needs, many types of issues need to be addressed since the options are wide in terms of cost and the services that they provide. One such crucial decision will involve choosing the right data transmission medium. For pedagogical reasons, each factor will be considered individually.

Cost

The cost of a given communication network will include not only the cost of the medium itself, but also the supporting hardware and software required to manage the network. Installing the cable and supporting hardware and software is just the beginning of the maintenance process. Many managers say the cost of installing the transmission medium is the largest piece of the entire cost of having a data communication system. They are incorrect. The major part of the cost is the personnel required to maintain the system.

The expertise required to maintain a system will increase with the size of the system. At the end of its life cycle, the cost of installing the communication system may be insignificant compared with the cost of personnel required to maintain the system.

In addition, the cost of further expansion must be taken into consideration. For example, a business that is established in Dallas may consider Dallas, Houston, Chicago, and New Orleans as its target cities. To connect its regional offices to its headquarters, this emerging company can use leased lines from a common carrier. However, if it is projected that within five years their contact offices will be in many more cities, a satellite network may be a more cost effective solution than leased lines.

The cost comparisons used in the design and selection of a data communication system must be projected over the expected life of the system and must include at least the following elements:

1. The cost of the transmission medium.
2. The cost of installing the transmission medium and all communication and data processing equipment that will support the system.
3. The cost of personnel to maintain the system.
4. The cost of personnel to train users how to use the system.
5. The cost of upgrades or additions as the needs of the company and users expand.
6. The cost of the software and software upgrades required to keep the system running.

7. The cost of any leased lines or satellite channels leased from common carriers.

Although many more factors also affect the overall cost of a data communication system, the above need to be considered during the feasibility and design phases of the life cycle of the system.

Speed

The transmission speed of data communication systems ranges from a low of 300 bits per second to several million bits per second. Some media, such as twisted pair cable, are less expensive than optical fiber. However, optical fiber can transmit at much higher speeds than twisted pair cable. The cost of increased speed must be balanced against the needs of the data communication system and its users.

Two factors dictate the speed of the data transmission medium: the response time expected by users and the aggregate data rate. The response time is the time it takes from the moment a terminal sends a request to the time the response from the host gets back to the user. A good response time is two seconds or less. However, longer response times may be tolerated to sustain a lower cost of the medium. Also, it is typically better to have a slow response time that is consistent than a response time that is unpredictable. Most users would get frustrated with the data communication system if one day the response time is one second or less and the next day the response time increases to several minutes for no apparent reason.

The aggregate data rate is the amount of information that can be transmitted per unit of time. A company's users may be satisfied with transmission speeds of 9600 bits per second. But at peak processing times, with large files, the speed requirements may range as high as 19,200 bits per second or more. The same communication medium may not work for both speeds.

The planning phase during which the data communication system is designed must consider peak loads in order to have a predictable response time for users. A twisted pair cabling system may be adequate for most types of transmission, but if, during a peak time, speeds of 10 megabits per second or more are required, a different wiring system should be considered.

Additionally, future requirements of the system must be taken into account. For example, if a network is being implemented in an educational institution to satisfy the initial needs of teaching programming languages, designers may choose to implement twisted pair wires. However, as the sophistication of the users increases and technology advances, the rest of the college may decide to use the system and incorporate multimedia concepts into the network. Then the twisted pair scheme will not work. In this case, it would have been better and more cost effective to spend the additional monies and implement the data communication system using optical fiber. Table 4-1 provides the speed of data transmission of the circuit media discussed.

Private and leased lines	300 to 80,000 bits per second
T1-type media	1.5 megabits per second
Coaxial cable	1 to over 500 megabits per second
Optical fiber	over 2 gigabits per second
Microwave	up to 50 megabits per second
Satellite	up to 50 megabits per second

Table 4-1 Data transmission speeds of different media.

Don't forget that the complexity and cost of the transmission medium tends to increase as we move down the elements in this list. Also, cost and speed are just two of the factors that should be considered when choosing the transmission medium for a data communication system. Regardless of the speed of the transmission medium, it may not work for a company unless it has expansion capabilities.

Expandability

Eventually, most data communication systems need to be expanded by adding more devices at a location or by adding new locations. Some transmission media offer more cost effective expandability than others. For example, coaxial cable and satellite-based networks are easier to expand into new locations. If a corporation has headquarters in Dallas, Texas, and opens new offices in London, Great Britain, it may be easier and relatively inexpensive to lease a satellite channel to extend the data communication system from headquarters to the new office. Of course, we say that it may be inexpensive, but the actual costs and savings will depend on the needs and volume of the data transmission requirements imposed on the system.

In many situations, leased telephone lines make expansion into new areas more difficult and costly. The installation of leased lines and the expense of their monthly lease, along with the low data transmission speed, may make using leased lines cost prohibitive. In a situation where high volumes of data must flow constantly between two remote locations, a leased line may not be the best solution. Microwave and other technology should be considered and their costs compared over the life of the systems. This will provide a more accurate picture of the actual costs than just comparing the initial costs of setting up the data communication system.

Future expansions must be considered whenever a data communication network is being designed. For example, a company can install twisted pair cable throughout an entire building. Two or three years after installation it may find that it needs coaxial or optical fiber media. In this case the cost of rewiring the building is larger than it would have been to install it initially. When planning communication systems, both short-range and long-range needs must be considered. This emphasizes the importance of planning when considering a data communication system. Planning must include solutions not only for the immediate needs (short-range goals), but also must include anticipated or future needs that extend beyond three years (long-range goals). Additionally, the planning process must be done according to some type of life cycle development (see Chapter 7). This will ensure that all aspects of the planning process are taken into consideration, as they should be if the project is to be successful.

Security

The lack of security in a data communication network will allow hackers or unauthorized persons to have access to vital data. The data could be used to gain an advantage in the market place, or it could be altered or destroyed, with catastrophic consequences for a business.

Providing a completely sealed network where unauthorized persons can never access the network is impossible. However, some media, such as optical fiber, are more difficult to penetrate than other media, such as coaxial cable or satellite. The most vulnerable medium to the average hacker is switched lines. Once an individual gains access to the switching equipment, this person has good access to the rest of the network. Switching equipment should be protected by using account identification numbers, passwords, and perhaps a call-back unit, as the one described previously in Chapter 3.

Another type of security threat is the invasion of the system by a computer virus. A computer virus could be introduced into the data communication system by an employee of the company. Once inside the system, a computer virus could become an irritation to users or it could destroy data in user computers or host systems. To protect communication systems from this type of security threat, anti-virus or virus scan software can be used to check any disk before it is used in any workstation or to check any file that flows through the system. Monitoring software can also be used to alert system operators to any unusual activities that may be the action of a computer virus.

Not only must a system protect itself against unauthorized users and computer viruses, but it must guard against any physical disaster such as a fire. Many systems have redundant lines and backup systems. Then in case of fire or some other catastrophic event, the critical aspects of the data communication system will continue operation by using alternative equipment and transmission media. Many corporations that use microwaves or satellite communications also have leased lines as backups, in case their primary transmission medium fails.

However, no matter how much backup a system has, it needs a good disaster recovery plan. Security on any data communication system is greatly enhanced by having a proven and well-designed disaster recovery plan as is described in Chapter 7. An effective disaster recovery plan is the result of good management of a data communication system.

Distance Requirements

The distance between a sender and a receiver can determine the type of medium used for data transmission. For example, if two sites that need to be connected are hundreds of miles apart, it is not possible to lay coaxial cable between them. In this case leased lines, satellite, and microwave transmission need to be explored. Don't forget that only common carriers are allowed by law to lay cable across public right-of-ways such as highways. Therefore, if there is a public right-of-way between two locations, even for a short distance, leased lines or microwave communications must be considered since private cable couldn't be used.

Additionally, distance requirements will have to be measured against the volume of data that needs to be transmitted. If two locations are just a few feet apart, but the volume of data to be transmitted is heavy, such as in the use of multimedia technology, optical fiber may be a better solution than twisted pair wire.

Also, distance affects the number of devices that may be served. For short distances twisted pair, coaxial cable, and optical fiber may be used, but even these cabling schemes have limitations in how far they can transmit data without the need of repeaters. The cost of all these devices must be taken into account when designing the data communication system. And, for long distances, the average business may have to rely on local carrier lines, microwave, or satellite media.

Environment

The environment in which a medium must exist will eliminate some options from consideration. For example, local building codes may prohibit a company or educational institution from laying cables under right-of-ways. In this case, microwave radio transmission may need to be used. Another example is a case where phone lines are sharing conduits with electrical wires. This may cause too much interference with digital data transmission.

During the planning stages of a data communication network, the location of the medium and local constraints must be taken into account to avoid costly modifications during installation. For example, if twisted pair wire is used, care must be taken to locate the cable away from electrical motors, fluorescent lights, and other equipment that may cause interference with the data flowing through the medium. Also, some types of communication strategies may not work on all types of cables. A specific strategy may require coaxial cable and may not work with twisted pair wire. Therefore care must be taken to ensure that the communication strategy adopted is compatible with the transmission medium available.

Maintenance

The type of maintenance required for a communication network must also be considered during the planning stage. If a coaxial line or twisted pair wire is broken or becomes defective, it can be repaired easily by finding the troubled section and replacing it. However, if a satellite malfunctions and needs repair, the time required to place it back into normal operation may be lengthy. This is why many communication companies have multiple media backup networks.

Additionally, the personnel requirements to maintain a microwave data communication system are different from the personnel requirements for a local network using twisted pair wires. Even though a data communication strategy may seem the best solution in terms of its capabilities, the maintenance and cost of personnel required to perform such maintenance may render the system too costly to be effective. These economic comparisons must be performed during the planning stages of the system and must be used to find a solution that not only solves the data communication needs of the company but is affordable.

Summary

The data transmission medium is the physical path that the signal must use in order to travel from the sender to the receiver. There are many types of transmission media to choose from, but they can be generally be classified into two types.

1. Guided transmission media.
2. Unguided transmission media.

Guided transmission media include several types of cabling systems that guide the data signals along the cable from one location to another. Examples of this type of transmission media are open wire, twisted pair wires, coaxial cable, and optical fiber cable

The other type, unguided transmission media, consists of a means for the signals to travel but nothing to guide them along a specific path. Examples of this type of media are microwave, satellite transmission, and cellular radio.

Open wire line consists of copper wire tied to glass insulators with the insulators attached to wooden arms mounted on utility poles. Open wire was replaced by twisted pair cables and other transmission media because of the large potential for interference from electrical noise and weather as it lies open in the atmosphere.

Twisted pair cable is composed of copper conductors insulated by paper or plastic and twisted into pairs. At the location where the pairs enter a building, a terminating block, also called a punchdown block, is normally found. These pairs are bundled into units and the units are bundled to form the finished cable.

Coaxial cable consists of two conductors. The inner conductor, normally copper or aluminum, is shielded by placing it inside a plastic case or shield. The second conductor is wrapped around the plastic shield of the first conductor. This further shields the inner conductor. Additionally, the second conductor (shield) is covered with plastic or some other protective and insulating cover.

The last type of guided media covered in the chapter is optical fiber. Optical fiber consists of thin glass fibers that can carry information at frequencies in the visible light spectrum. The data transmission lines made up of optical fibers are joined by connectors that have very little loss of the signal throughout the length of the data line.

In unguided transmission, one common type of transmission is microwave transmission. Microwave, or radio transmission as it is sometimes called, is a high frequency radio signal that is transmitted over a direct line-of-sight path between two points. The concept of a line-of-sight is important since the earth has a curvature. This necessitates that microwave stations be no more than 30 miles apart.

Another type of unguided transmission media is satellite communications. Satellite transmission is similar to microwave radio transmission, except that it transmits to a satellite several thousand miles out in space (normally approximately 22,300 miles) rather than to an earth station.

The last type of unguided transmission media discussed in the chapter is cellular radio. Cellular radio is a form of high frequency radio transmission where the signals are relayed from antennas that are spaced in strategic locations throughout metropolitan areas.

Several criteria can be used to select the appropriate type of transmission media. These criteria are cost, speed, expandability, security, and distance requirements. Decisions regarding these factors cannot be made independently. Deciding on a cabling scheme depends on the hardware that you have or plan to purchase. But software requirements may indicate a specific cabling system, and the hardware may have to be reconfigured for it.

Questions

1. Describe the advantages of twisted pair over coaxial cable.
2. Describe the advantages of coaxial cable over twisted pair.
3. If computer data and video data were to be distributed over the same medium for multimedia purposes, which cabling scheme would you use? Why?
4. How can cellular radio benefit a company?
5. What is a transponder? How does it work?
6. Describe three selection criteria used in deciding the type of transmission media used in data communication.
7. What is a T1 circuit?

Projects

The following are research projects rather than hands-on projects. However, they play an important role in the acquisition and retention of the topics discussed in this chapter. The result of these projects should be a short term paper that follows the criteria established in most technical writing classes. Many students graduate without knowing how to prepare technical documents, and that becomes a handicap in their professional work. These projects will not introduce the student to technical writing topics, but the instructor should emphasize such topics and demand that all work have a professional look and content. For this purpose, the instructor may make available some type of sophisticated word processor with desktop layout capabilities and/or presentation equipment, so the students can begin to appreciate the need for and use of such technology. For this reason, the projects below serve a dual purpose and they should be performed.

Project 1. Comparison of data communication media

Using the local library, find out the cost per foot for the installation and/or leasing of the different transmission media discussed in this chapter. Additionally, research the speed and other technical aspects of the media, and produce a report that outlines their strengths and weaknesses. Compare the cost per megabyte of transmission of each of the media and propose situations or scenarios where one type of media may be more suitable than others. Justify your answers with technical facts or cases.

Project 2. Exploring solutions to data transmission needs.

Find out the data processing capabilities of your institution or choose a specific existing company and perform the same functions. Describe how they implemented the transmission media and how they are using it. Additionally, find future expansion plans and recommend transmission media solutions to such plans. Also, find out how many telephones they are using including outside lines. Find out whether they have their own PBX or if they lease a Centrex system. Find the limitations of their current system and suggest solutions. If they have a PBX, what features does it have? How is it maintained? What is the cost of the system, and does it compare with the cost of having a Centrex system performing the same functions? Always justify your answers with technical facts or cases.

Project 3. Exploring a communication system.

Pick a system to produce a report on:

  a. A cellular system

  b. A voice messaging system

  c. A teleconferencing system

  d. A marine communication system

Produce a two- or three-page report on the capabilities and potential of the system in the data communication field. Always justify any conclusion with technical facts.

Network Basics

Objectives

After completing this chapter you will

1. Understand the benefits of networking.
2. Understand the difference between local area networks and wide area networks.
3. Know the standards that are used in designing networking technology.
4. Know the different types of network topologies.
5. Understand the different devices used for interconnecting networks.
6. Obtain a general overview of design considerations for hybrid networks.

Key Terms

Bridge	Brouter
Bus Network	Gateway
LAN	MAN
Network	OSI Model
PDN	Ring Network
Router	SNA
Software	Star Network
WAN	

Introduction

The concepts explored in previous chapters become the foundation for understanding the importance and functionality of networks. These networks are the basic building blocks of the information age of the 1990s and beyond. The information system industry is being shaped by the use of networks for interconnecting workstations, peripherals, mainframes, and minicomputers. Students in all areas of business need to understand network connectivity issues and the advantages and disadvantages of the different configurations.

This chapter discusses the benefits of having a networked environment and the basics of understanding networks. The difference between wide area networks and local area networks is explained, along with the different types of network topologies that are found in the workplace. Finally, the technologies required to connect dissimilar networks are discussed, along with related design concepts.

The student should read the material in this chapter thoroughly before reading any of the following chapters. Those chapters assume knowledge and understanding of the general networking concepts explored in this chapter. These concepts are crucial in obtaining an educated view of the benefits and problems of designing and interconnecting data communication networks.

Benefits of Networking

The microcomputer, with all of its benefits and usefulness, has serious shortcomings. Initially, microcomputers were designed with a single user in mind. Multiuser systems were delegated to mainframes and minicomputers. This is generally true today, even though many microcomputers have more processing capacity and memory than a large number of the minicomputers in the business market.

Another problem with the microcomputer is that it was not designed to share its resources among other computers. If a printout is required, the personal computer must have its own printer. If a file must be stored on a hard disk, the personal computer must have its own hard disk. To a lesser extent, mainframes and minicomputers have the same problems. Even though a mainframe has many terminals that share disk space and printers, users of other computers within the same corporation may need to share resources in an efficient manner.

For example, assume that a corporation has an IBM AS-400 minicomputer, a Digital Equipment Corporation VAX minicomputer, and many personal computers and terminals. On many occasions the data stored on the AS-400 may be required by users of the VAX minicomputer and vice versa. In addition, some data processed in microcomputers and the resulting information must be shared by users of both minicomputer systems. This scenario creates many different types of information needs that must be resolved in an efficient and cost effective manner. Users should not be expected to duplicate data entry procedures or to master the use of diverse and difficult-to-use systems.

How does a system manager resolve the diverse information needs of users? One solution is to provide two terminals for each user, one for the AS-400, one for the VAX, and a microcomputer for those individuals who need access to software that runs on personal computers. Although this will address the different needs of each user, this solution does not solve the problem of sharing data among the minicomputers.

Another solution is to provide every user a personal computer. Through the microcomputer and with the aide of communication software, each user can access one minicomputer, download the data to a personal computer using the communications program, modify the data locally, and, using a different emulation-communication program, upload the data to the second minicomputer. This solution may eventually work, but it assumes that every user is proficient with both minicomputer systems and the personal computer. In addition, to perform the entire transaction properly, the user must have a good knowledge of microcomputers and communication software. These assumptions typically cannot be made. Statistics show that the majority of users in corporations cannot perform all of the above functions without technical help. Finally, even though a user may accomplish the entire transaction without errors, the method employed is not very efficient.

The isolation of computers described in the example results in duplication of hardware, software, and human resources. Each user must perform duplicate functions in order to transfer the data from one processor to another. These additional functions use time and personnel that could be applied to improve the balance sheet of the corporation.

Another example of the inefficiencies of this approach in a large company would be the implementation of a large number of microcomputers as stand-alone units. If a company has 100 microcomputers and all users need to run a specific package, the company must purchase 100 individual programs if it wishes to remain within the limits of the law. Similarly, each user must be provided with a printer and any other peripherals required to use the software. This duplication of resources is expensive to install and maintain, and space is needed for all the equipment, its containers, and manuals that need to be kept by the company.

Even small companies will find that using computers in an isolated form is inefficient. As an example, imagine a small company that purchases a microcomputer to keep track of inventory. In this scenario, one person keeps the inventory updated, and others occasionally use the microcomputer to check the inventory level and monitor availability of a product. As users find the application beneficial, the demand to use the inventory database increases. The company also grows and expands its product line, adding more inventory items to the database. As the database is used on a continuous basis and the inventory grows, it becomes increasingly difficult to keep the inventory updated, since users monopolize the time during which the computer is accessible. One obvious solution is to purchase more computers and place the database on each of the machines. However, if more computers are purchased to handle the demand, then the complication arises of keeping the database updated on all machines.

The current solution to these problems is to connect all the computers in a network. A computer network can change a group of isolated computers into a coordinated multiuser computer system. A network user can legally share copies of the software with other users, if network versions of the software are purchased. Data can be stored in centralized locations or in different locations that are accessible to all users. Also, printers, scanners, and other peripherals connected to the network are available to all users.

If the inventory system described above was placed on a network with several other computers, the system could be kept updated and could be accessed by many users simultaneously. This is because one of the computers can act as a centralized repository of all software. This computer, normally called a server, will be the only machine that keeps a copy of the database and provides the software to workstations that request it. Since only one copy of the software and data is kept, any user who accesses the database will always have the latest or most current version of the programs and data. Also, having this type of centralized system eliminates the need for additional hardware and software, thus lowering the overall cost to the company.

The method of operating just described has been at the core of companies or departments that have long used minicomputers and mainframes. It is a centralized system that minimizes the expense of purchasing hardware and software, yet it provides shared resources to all users. The network provides all of that, but goes a step beyond in that it provides all the functionality of the centralized system to users who have a computer on their desk. In addition, the network provides all the advantages mentioned above, regardless of the maker of the computer. In this fashion, minicomputers, mainframes, and microcomputers can all be connected to share resources, even though some may be IBM computers, some Apple computers, and others may be made by Digital Corporation.

Hardware Sharing

A network allows users to share different types of hardware devices. The most commonly shared items are hard disks, printers, CD-drives, and communication devices.

Sharing Hard Disks

Today's sophisticated software applications require large amounts of disk space. Software environments such as Microsoft Windows with a word processing package consume in excess of 15 Mbytes of space before any data is saved onto the hard disk. Additionally, as companies require more information about their operation, larger disks are required. A microcomputer database management system such as Paradox or DBase IV managing a corporate database may utilize an additional 20 or 30 Mbytes of storage. If the above software needs to share disk space with some other operating environment such as SCO UNIX, then the storage requirements for a single computer can be in the hundreds of megabytes. Also, if the base machine is not a microcomputer but a minicomputer or mainframe, the disk storage needs are even greater.

Although the price of disk technology has dropped dramatically in recent years, disks with a capacity to store hundreds or billions of bytes are still relatively expensive. In addition, it is not uncommon for microcomputer users to require hard disk capacities of hundreds of megabytes. It would be too expensive to purchase large disk space for all users or all possible situations that may arise within a corporation.

The cost of storage media is just one factor to consider. In addition, the security and backup of storage devices become more difficult to manage when the devices are isolated. If there are many computers in an isolated format, it is difficult to ensure that all important data is properly backed up and safeguarded against possible loss. In addition, the time to perform all the procedures required to safeguard the data is extensive. This requires full-time personnel to perform just those functions. Another problem that arises is making sure that everyone has the most current version of a program on their hard disks. Since there can be many computers, each with the same copy of the program, it becomes difficult to ensure that everyone has the most up-to-date version of a data file or a program.

All of these problems are greatly reduced, and in most cases solved, by using a network that connects all the individual computers. The network backs up the files and software is stored on the hard disks of one or a few central computers. Additionally, since all the software is maintained in one location, everyone is assured of the latest version of data files and software programs.

119

Today's networks are based on the concept of sharing access to disk storage devices. These disks are typically installed on special devices called file servers, which will be discussed in the next chapter. A file server is a computer on a network that provides files and programs to those workstations that request them. As outlined above, sharing disk space has several benefits. The most obvious are costs, integrity of the data, and security.

Costs are reduced by purchasing hard disks to be shared among all users, rather than purchasing one for each user or location. Instead of purchasing a 100 Mbyte hard disk for 100 users, the company can provide smaller hard disks for the users and store the programs required by users on a large centralized hard disk with a server. In addition, if the server's hard disk is large enough, it can also be used to save files that a user may want to store in a location other than his or her workstation. This method of storing data provides users with a "larger" hard disk that has common access. The word "larger" is used in quotations because the user's computer doesn't have the extra hard disk space, but the user does have access to additional storage.

The safety of the data is improved over having it on isolated disks, since a network administrator can make constant backups of all files on the device. This is important when the data manipulated and transmitted through the network is critical to the operation of the company. Remember that it is easier to replace damaged equipment, but some data can't be replaced if lost or damaged. Frequent and consistent backup is one the best ways to ensure that all important data will be available if the main hard disk is damaged and the data is lost. Additionally, having the data in a centralized location on the network safeguards this data from being lost by a user misplacing or damaging floppy disks.

Security of the data is enforced by using the network's built-in security systems. Data on isolated disks is an easy target for anyone who wants to damage it. Network management software can prevent unauthorized users from gaining access to and deleting or destroying important data. Also, many of the network management programs available have computer virus detection capabilities that can prevent these viruses from infecting users' workstations or network servers. Hard disk sharing is only one of the many advantages of networking. Another important device that can be shared through networks is the printer.

Sharing Printers

Printer sharing is common on networks. Printers can be attached to a file server or connected to the network independently of the file server (see Fig. 5-1). Users in the network depicted in Fig. 5-1 can use any of the printers on the system. Instead of each user having a low-cost printer attached to a terminal or microcomputer, a few high-speed, high-quality printers can be

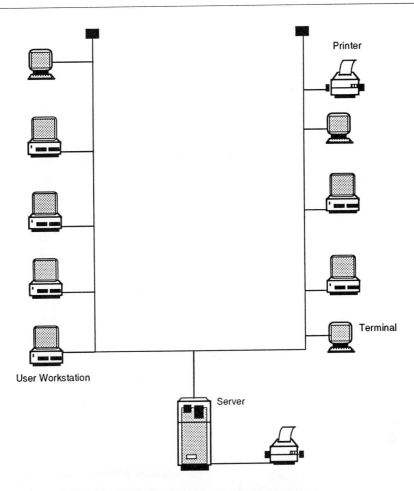

Fig. 5-1. Network showing user stations and file server.

purchased and connected to the network. Any user who needs a fast printout can send the output to the printer nearest to his or her station. This ability to share output devices reduces the cost of the overall system to the company and at the same time allows users to have access to better quality output devices than would otherwise be possible.

Printers are not the only devices that can be shared on a network. Input equipment can be shared along with output devices. Some of these additional devices include facsimile machines, scanners, and plotters. Scanners and facsimile machines have been around the computer industry for a long time. However, they have become popular only during the last few years as their prices have dropped and their quality has improved.

A facsimile machine can be shared as both an input and output device. If the facsimile is an independent machine, it can be attached directly to the network. Then output can be directed to it through the use of specialized software. In the same manner, if the facsimile device and its software are smart enough, any input received can be transmitted and routed to the intended receiver. A facsimile machine can also be shared by attaching it to a workstation and making the workstation act as a gateway or printer server. Also, new facsimile boards that fit inside the computer provide a closer integration of this technology into modern networks and connectivity strategies.

Plotters and other output devices can be shared the same way a typical printer is shared. To the network, a plotter or a printer is simply a logical output device, and they are treated relatively the same. Also, scanners can be shared by attaching the scanner to a workstation and using the workstation to distribute scanned images through the network. Some modern scanners have expansion slots that can be fitted with a network card that provides the scanner with its own identity to the network. This allows the scanner to function on the network without being attached to a specific computer.

Sharing Communication Devices

Personal computer users on a network often need to access remote systems or networks. One possible solution is to provide them with modems and terminal emulation software to access other systems from their individual workstations. This solution is expensive and places a burden on the users who must know all the parameters and communication settings for their particular hardware.

A better solution is to provide users on a network with access to shared modems, gateways, bridges (these devices are more fully discussed in this chapter), and other network and data communication devices without the need to purchase one for each user (see Fig. 5-2). Many companies set up what is called a "modem pool." This is a group of modems that are located in a single place and connected to several communication lines. The modems in the pool are available to users on a "first come, first served" basis. The modems are controlled, in most cases, by a gateway server computer. When a user needs to access another computer at a remote location, the user instructs his or her workstation to connect it to an available modem in the "pool." If a modem is available, the modem is logically given to the workstation for the duration of the communication session. From this point on, the user's workstation utilizes the modem as if it were attached directly to the workstation. After the communication session is over, the modem is returned to the pool, and it is made available to another user who may request it.

In summary, the benefits of sharing hardware on a network are clear. Costs can be reduced by avoiding duplicate hardware, and at the same time users can have access to a variety of devices. Also, data security and safety are improved by having up-to-date backups and enforcing the security measures that are available with each network.

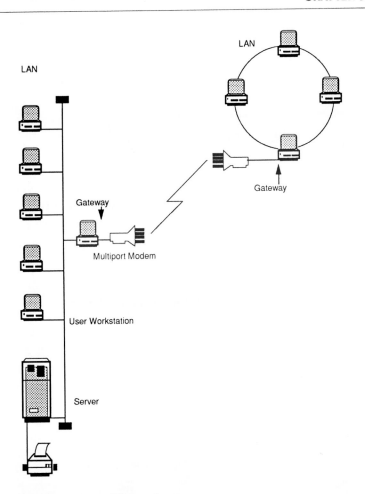

Fig. 5-2. Connecting networks located in different geographical areas.

Software Sharing

Networks also provide benefits in software sharing. Instead of purchasing an individual application program for every user in a company, a network version of the program can be obtained. The software program can be stored on one of the network servers, making the program available to any network authorized user. Also, software designed for networks allows multiple use of the software simultaneously, making a network of personal computers a multiuser system. In this case, users can share the data produced and used by the package at any given time, even though parts of the data files may be in use by another computer.

There are many advantages of sharing software. The most important are cost reduction, legality of the product, sharing data, and having current upgrades. Cost reduction has been explained before. As a further example, imagine purchasing 100 copies of a spreadsheet. Even with group discounts, the price of acquiring all of those packages can be as high as $50,000. Purchasing a network version of the same package for an unlimited number of users will result in a much lower cost. In addition, when an upgrade is available, there is a single cost that is a fraction of the cost of the upgrades for 100 separate copies. Also, software designed for networking places data files in centralized locations that all authorized users can access.

Through the network managing utilities, administrators can enforce security and the legality of all copies used, leaving the user to concentrate on generating and analyzing the data. If a company purchases a license to use 10 copies of a spreadsheet, the number of users that can concurrently access the program can be controlled by the network management system. If all 10 copies of the spreadsheet are being used and another user tries to load a copy of the program, the network management system informs the user that all legal copies are being used and that a current running copy must be closed before a new copy can be loaded into the user's workstation.

As stated previously, backups are also easier to enforce and maintain if all the software resides on one or a few servers. Additionally, some types of networks allow a technician to back up not only the server's hard disks, but also the hard disk of user workstations. Although a network administrator wouldn't want to get into the practice of backing up all users' workstations, the ability to perform centralized and automatic backups enhances the security of the data in case of a disaster.

Networking multiple computers also has an added advantage. The productivity of users can be enhanced by taking advantage of "groupware." Groupware is software that includes electronic mail (e-mail), calendar, appointment, word processing, alarm clock, and other time management software. It allows a user to manage his or her time electronically and communicate this information to other users on the network. It is intended to eliminate much of the inter-office paperwork, making information available to all users faster.

Using groupware, a user can create a memo, mail a copy of it to many other users, check their calendars for an opportune time for a meeting, and schedule the meeting automatically for the people in a given office or department. In addition, electronic alarms can be attached to the calendar to alert users of important events. These and other time management groupware products allow the system to perform the daily operations of the company and keep its employees in contact with each other.

However, even with all the advantages mentioned above, they are expensive and are not problem-free from an administrative and technical point of view. Many companies don't look closely at these problems until it is too late to reverse costly and time-consuming events that are put in motion when a network is implemented. These problems or challenges are explained in the next section.

Challenges of Networking

Although the implementation of a network carries many benefits, as outlined in the beginning of this chapter, its introduction into the work environment presents new challenges and costs that are sometimes not anticipated. These challenges can be summarized as the cost of networking.

The cost of networking includes, but it is not limited to, these factors:

1. The cost of acquiring and installing cables and associated equipment for the transmission of data. Different types of transmission media come with advantages and disadvantages that vary greatly. The cost of the media varies according to the data transmission capacity and speeds of movement through the cable. In addition, it is easier, and therefore cheaper, to install twisted pair wire than it is to install optical fiber. The purchase of transmitting media is just one aspect of this cost.

   Specialized personnel may be required to lay the cable. The cost of contracting a company to perform the "pulling" or layout of the cable will also depend on the number of difficulties that the installers have to overcome as they perform their job. It is cheaper to install cable when a building is being constructed than to have to drill through several feet of concrete after it is built. Also, if the distances are large, additional equipment such as line adapters may be required. The cost of these adapters tends to increase as the sophistication of the media increases.

2. The cost of purchasing the network operating system and network versions of individual software packages. Depending on the type of network being implemented and the number of users, the cost of the software to run the network, the network operating system or NOS, can be several thousand dollars. Even companies with small networks can expect to pay a few thousand dollars for the NOS. Additional modules to the NOS such as network monitoring software and virus protection are not normally included in the basic network operating system package. Depending on the type of network being installed and the number of users, the complete set of software to operate the network can be more expensive than most of the hardware pieces. And, of course, the network operating system alone is not sufficient. Application software must also be acquired.

   Software applications that were running on an individual basis may need to be upgraded in order to obtain network licenses. Additionally, many software programs designed for an individual computer will not execute on a network without modification of

125

the source code. If a company has a heavy investment in software that is not able to run on the network, then the cost of acquiring new software to replace the old can run the cost of the network beyond the fiscal possibilities of the company. And, if the network contains many users and sophisticated applications, someone must maintain the servers and the physical layout of the network itself as people and workstations are relocated.

3. The cost of personnel to manage software installation, expand and reconfigure the network, provide backup, maintenance of hardware and software, and maintenance of the network/user interface. As users become comfortable with the network, their use of it will increase and thus increase the demand for additional network services. Also, people may need to be relocated within an office or building. Someone has to ensure that the network services for these users are not interrupted.

In some cases, the number of users or software used through the system may exceed system resources. Technical personnel will be needed to "tune" and enhance the network to make sure that it works efficiently and effectively. Periodically, passwords may need to be reassigned, backups need to be perfomed, hard disks need to be defragmented, and old accounts need to erased to make room for new accounts. All of these functions require personnel trained and educated in the operation of networks. This is an important point that was mentioned before. Many companies delegate the operation of networks to individuals who don't have any formal training in system design and network operations. These individuals learn as much as possible as they perform their duties, but by the time they learn enough about the network, it may have deteriorated to the point of needing a major and costly overhaul. Technical and network operating personnel must have the formal training that today's sophisticated systems require in order to perform efficiently and effectively.

Finally, as users are added to the network, the security and safekeeping of data becomes critical. Personnel will be required to maintain the network on a full-time basis and to ensure that proper backups are made in a consistent and timely fashion. The network interface will need modification as types and quantities of users change. In most cases, companies should expect that to install a network that serves many users, additional trained personnel need to be hired in conjunction with the purchase of the network itself. A lack of proper personnel is one of the most common factors contributing to a poorly designed system and to the failure of networks.

4. The cost of bridges and gateways to other networks and the software and other equipment required to implement the connection. After the network is implemented, there may be a need to connect it to other communication systems. The equipment used in the networking field to provide connectivity among different network platforms comes in the shape of gateways, routers, brouters, and bridges.

   The technical staff in charge of the network needs to be aware of the differences, capabilities, and cost of these devices. Each was designed for a specific purpose, and using them in the wrong situation or place could disrupt the operation of the network. The cost and challenge of performing this connection are an additional burden to network managers, and additional personnel and training may be required.

5. The cost of training users of the network and the personnel required to manage the network. This is an ongoing and hidden cost due to the turnover of personnel. Many companies don't consider this cost in their design stage. Although the cost of training a network administrator and technical operation staff is in many cases accounted for, the cost of training users is many times ignored. If a user is being trained on how to use the network, the hours spent in training are lost production to the company. Also, if the training is performed off-site, then a replacement may have to be hired during the training period.

   Many administrators claim that these costs are offset by the savings introduced by the employee after the training is completed. Even though an employee may perform his or her duties more efficiently after learning how to use the network, there is a cost associated with training users, and outside consultants or training personnel need to be included in the cost. If the company has a high turnover ratio, this cost will be large.

6. The cost of maintenance, including installation of future software upgrades, correcting incompatibilities between the network operating system and new software upgrades, and correcting hardware problems. As new versions of the network operating system become available, old software programs may not be able to co-exist with the new operating system. In such cases, new versions of application software must be secured. (Of course, if the number of users is large, having a network license can provide substantial savings over purchasing many individual copies of the same program.) The number and frequency of upgrades is a cost that must be scheduled into the system life cycle (see Chapter 7).

7. The cost of hiring a network administrator or specialist to manage the system or to solve problems as they occur. Although many companies use existing personnel to manage new networks, these people will have to give up a minimum of approximately 10 to 20 hours per week to manage and back up the network. Their absence from a task for which they were originally hired will eventually have to be compensated for by hiring assistants or by increasing the salary of such personnel.

8. The cost of network versions of software. Software designed to work on a network is normally more expensive than individual copies of the application. For a network that contains large numbers of users working with a software application, there are cost savings in purchasing a single network version of the program. But for a network with a small number of users, such cost savings may not be realized.

In small companies the task of implementing and managing the network can be performed by one or two persons. However, in large companies, several full-time employees may be needed to perform network management duties. These costs will become a sizable portion of the operational budget of the company. It is important that any implementation of a network follows the rules for system design. Only in such a case will the company be assured that all possible problems and obstacles in the success of the network implementation have been properly addressed and anticipated (see Chapter 7).

Types of Networks

The geographical area covered by a network determines whether the network is called a wide area network (WAN—see Fig. 5-3), metropolitan area network (MAN), or a local area network (LAN). Wide area networks link systems that are too far apart to be included in a small in-house network. Metropolitan area networks connect across distances greater than a few kilometers but no more than 50 kilometers (approximately 30 miles). Local area networks usually connect users in the same office or building. In some cases, adjacent buildings of a corporation or educational institution are connected with the use of LANs. However, the boundaries of a type of network are not as clearly defined in real life as they are in this book. Many companies have networks that encompass hundreds of miles, yet they are still called local area networks. This book will try to differentiate among the three types according to the distance they cover, but keep in mind that their definitions are sometimes altered by the people who implement and manage them.

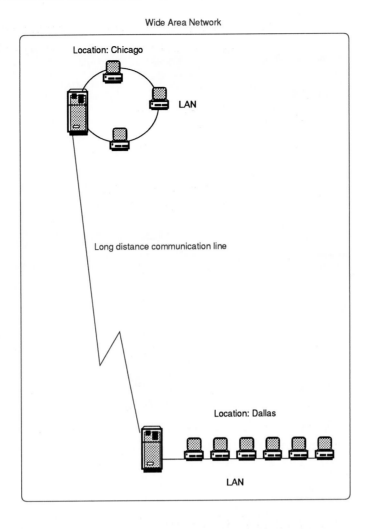

Fig. 5-3. A wide area network.

Wide Area Network (WAN)

Wide area networks cross public right-of-ways such as highways and streets, and most use common carrier circuits for their transmitting medium. They use a combination of the hardware discussed in previous chapters. Wide area networks use a broad range of communication media for interconnection that includes switched and leased lines, private microwave circuits, optical fiber, coaxial cable, and satellite circuits. Basically, a wide area network is any communication network that permits message, voice, image signals, or computer data to be transmitted over a widely dispersed geographical area.

Metropolitan Area Network (MAN)

Metropolitan area networks connect locations that are geographically located from 5 to 50 kilometers apart. They include the transmission of data, voice, and television signals through the use of coaxial cable or optical fiber cable as their primary medium of transmission, although many metropolitan area networks are implemented through the use of microwave technology.

Customers of metropolitan area networks are primarily large companies that need to communicate within a metropolitan area at high speeds. MAN providers normally offer lower prices than the phone companies and faster installation over a diverse routing, and include backup lines in emergency situations.

Local Area Network (LAN)

LANs connect devices within a small area, usually within a building or adjacent buildings. LAN transmission media usually do not cross roads or other public thoroughfares. They are privately controlled and owned with respect to data processing equipment, such as processors and terminals, and with respect to data communication equipment such as media and extenders. Local area networks are covered in detail in the next chapter.

Many local area networks are used to interconnect the computers and peripherals within an office or department. Through specialized hardware and software, each department's LAN is connected to a larger local area network within the company's building. Then, this larger LAN is connected to a metropolitan area network that may interconnect different offices or branches throughout a large city. And finally, the company's MANs may be connected to a wider area network that interconnects the company's regional or international offices.

Each of the types of networks mentioned above has a set of standards that most manufacturers adhere to in order for their equipment to work with equipment manufactured by other companies. This set of standards is a necessity in a computing field that sees equipment manufacturers trying to impose their own standards on customers for the sole purpose of monetary gain. These standards assure customers that, as long as they purchase equipment that follows the established set of criteria for the functioning of communication equipment, they will be able to connect the equipment to their networks and should expect it to work properly. The set of criteria or standards is formulated by country representatives that have grouped together and formed the International Standards Organization for Standardization.

Current Standards

The computer industry is dominated by standards that are the result of several companies forming committees to ensure that the equipment they produce will be compatible. These sets of standards minimize the risk of creating networks that use equipment from different vendors who may follow different protocols. Also, by designing a network with equipment that complies with a set of standards, the users of these networks are assured that they will be able to share information from different sources and over different network schemes.

Additionally, the use of standards in network design and installation helps in managing the system by creating common management processes. At the same time it insulates the network operators from changes at low levels of the standard. Although there are several types of standards in the communication industry, two of the most commonly implemented are those established by the Open Systems Interconnect subcommittee, or OSI, and IBM's System Networking Architecture, or SNA.

Open Systems Interconnect (OSI)

Network evolution has been toward standardized networking and inter-networking technology. One of the most important standards-making bodies is the International Standards Organization or ISO, which makes technical recommendations about data communication interfaces. Standardizing the interfaces and the format of the data flowing through them ensures that, regardless of the equipment manufacturer, the entire network will work as long as the equipment in it adheres to these standards.

History

In 1978, the ISO created the Open Systems Interconnect (OSI) subcommittee, whose task was to develop a framework of standards for computer-to-computer communication. The result of the subcommittee's work is referred to as the OSI Reference Model. It serves as the model around which a series of standard protocols is defined. Using this model, hardware and software companies can develop their products to work within certain parameters that are the guidelines of the model. The resulting product is then able to communicate with other products that follow the same parameters.

The OSI Reference Model is known as a layered protocol, specifying seven layers of interface, wherein each layer has a specific set with functions to perform (see Fig. 5-4). Each layer has standardized interfaces to the layers above it and below it, and it communicates directly with the equivalent layer of another device.

As a result of the OSI Reference Model, the communications industry has concentrated on making products that comply with the interface guidelines, making them OSI compatible. Among the best known customers of OSI products is the federal government, which is committed to purchase large quantities of OSI compatible products through the Government Open System Interconnect Profile or GOSIP. By basing their networks on OSI compatibility, users can discuss product relationships and compatibilities and capabilities in the same working framework.

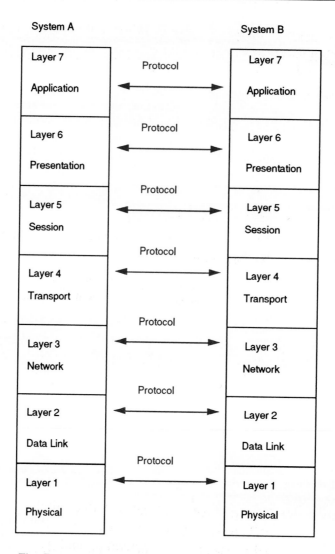

Fig. 5-4. The OSI Reference Model

The OSI Model divides the communication process into seven layered processes. These processes are as follows:

1. The first layer is the physical link control.
2. The second layer is the data link control.
3. The third layer is the network control.
4. The fourth layer is the transport control.
5. The fifth layer is the session control.
6. The sixth layer is the presentation layer.
7. The seventh and final layer is the application layer.

When a company refers to one of its products as working at level two, it means that their product works at the second level of the OSI model and it is "transparent" to any other products that work on layers 3 through 7. The word "transparent" means that the product under discussion will not negatively affect the operation of any other products that work in higher level layers. The lowest level layer is one and the highest level is seven.

Benefits

Having a layered framework, the OSI model offers several benefits:

1. Network hardware and software designers can allocate tasks more effectively among network resources.

2. A network layer can easily be replaced by a layer from another network vendor.

3. Processes from mainframes can be off-loaded into FEPs or other network control devices.

4. Networks can be upgraded more easily by replacing individual layers instead of the entire software system.

The user and network designer are not restricted to using the product of a specific company. If they are not satisfied with the performance or the service of a product provider, they can simply replace the product in question by another of a different company that is OSI compatible and works in a similar manner. To better understand the individual layers, let's take a closer look at the function of each.

Functional Layers

The seven OSI layers define the following standards in the field of data communications.

1. Physical layer. This layer defines all the standards that provide guidelines on how to physically move data bits between modems and perform circuit activation and deactivation. The specifications on this layer define the electrical connections between the transmission medium and the computer. The layer describes how many wires will be used to transmit the signals, the size and shape of connectors, the speed of transmission, and the direction of data transmission.

2. Data link layer. The standards in this layer establish and control the physical path of communication to the next node. This includes detection and correction of errors, handling flow control between modems, and the proper message sequence. This layer is basically responsible for the accuracy of the data transmitted between two locations on the network and the control mechanism for accessing the network.

3. Network layer. The standards defined for this layer provide the necessary control and routing functions to establish, maintain, and terminate communication links between transmitting and receiving nodes.

4. Transport layer. The standards established by this layer are responsible for generating the address of end users and ensuring that all data packets are received. A packet is a block of data that is sent from an originating point to a receiving location.

5. Session layer. It provides the necessary standards to define the interface to manage and support a communication dialog between two separate locations. It establishes a session, manages the session, synchronizes the data flow, and terminates the session.

6. Presentation layer. The standards for this layer define how products may accept data from the application layer and format the data. If there are any data preparation functions, the functions are not embedded into the data; rather, they are performed by this layer. The types of functions that can be performed are data encryption, code conversion, compression, and terminal screen formatting.

7. Application layer. The standards defined by this layer provide guidelines for network services such as file transfer, terminal emulation, and logging into a file server. This layer is functionally defined by the user, and it supports the actual end-user application.

Systems Network Architecture (SNA)

Another standard proprietary to IBM is the Systems Network Architecture or SNA. SNA was introduced in 1974, and today there are over 36,000 SNA compatible network installations. This large installed base warrants the study of SNA and some of the standards established by it.

The SNA strategy is conceptually similar to the OSI model but it is not compatible with it. Like OSI, SNA is divided into seven layers, but these layers are defined differently from those found in the OSI model. In the SNA scheme, the seven layers are as follows:

1. The first layer is the physical layer.

2. The second layer is the data link control layer.

3. The third layer is path control.

4. The fourth layer is transmission control.

5. The fifth layer is data flow control.

6. The sixth layer is the presentation layer.

7. The seventh and final layer is the application layer.

Remember that, although these layers seem compatible to the OSI layers, they are not compatible with each other.

Concepts

The SNA definition divides the network into physical units (PU) and logical units (LU). The physical units constitute the hardware on the network such as printers, terminals, computers, and other processor devices. There are four types of physical units defined as 1, 2, 4, and 5. Presently there isn't a physical unit 3. These four types correspond to the hardware in the following manner:

PU	Hardware
1	Terminals
2	Cluster controllers
4	Front end processors
5	Host computers

The logical units are the users logged onto the network and the application programs running in the system. The logical units or LUs are implemented through software in the network. The communication between users is a communication between logical units called a session. Notice that a physical unit can support many logical units.

The sessions mentioned above need to be established before two LUs can communicate with each other. Sessions occur between terminals and programs, terminals and terminals, and programs and programs. They can also be classified as interactive, batch, and printer sessions with each user having multiple simultaneous sessions, each with its own LU. This provides users of SNA systems the ability to communicate with two or more computers or with two or more programs simultaneously.

The SNA standard specifies that each device uses a 48-bit network address that identifies the LUs and PUs, also called network addressable units or NAU. Each NAU has its own unique address which, due to its 48-bit format, can be a large number, giving SNA compatible networks access to a large number of nodes.

Each of the NAU in an SNA compatible network uses the Synchronous Data Link Control (SDLC) protocol as its primary data link protocol. In addition, SNA can operate with the BISYNC and X.25 protocols. This was implemented in response to a large number of IBM customers requesting access to other networking standards.

SNA networks are normally designed to maximize the network connecting the centralized mainframes that serve as hosts for all data processing activities. The network itself is not as intelligent as other standards in the market. In the SNA architecture, the mainframe is the main processor of data and the network is just an avenue for getting the data to the mainframe.

To manage the SNA network, IBM and other third party vendors provide software to aide in this task. One of these products that is commonly found in many installations is called Netview. Netview becomes an interface between the network administrator and the network itself. This product provides statistics about transmission errors, circuit problems, difficulties with modems, response time, and other network problems. In addition, the Netview product is an "open" product that allows third party manufacturers to create products that interface with it.

Two other common standards in the field of networking and data communications are the X.25 and X.400 standards. The X.25 standard is used for data transmission using a packet switching network and it covers the first three layers of the OSI model. The X.400 standard is used for creating definitions and compatibility in the electronic mail industry.

Network Topology

The configurations used to describe networks are sometimes called network architecture or network topology. Networks can have many different logical and physical configurations. However, regardless of how they are implemented, networks can be placed into one of the following general categories. The most common network topologies are

1. Ring
2. Bus
3. Star
4. Hybrid

Regardless of the configuration used, all networks are made up of the same four basic components:

1. The user workstations that perform a particular operation. In newer implementations, the user workstation comes in the form of a microcomputer.

2. The protocol control that converts the user data into a format that can be transmitted through the network until it reaches the desired location. These are the rules that govern how the data will be moved through the network from the originator of the message to the receiver of it.

3. The interface that is required to generate the electrical signals to be moved on the medium. This interface can be in the form of an RS-232 with its associated signals. In most cases it is handled by an interface board that connects the computer to the transmission media.

4. The physical medium that carries the electrical signals generated by the interface. The physical medium can be twisted pair wire, coaxial cable, optical fiber, microwaves, or some of the other media explored in previous chapters.

In addition to these four categories, networks can be further categorized into narrowband networks and wideband networks. A narrowband is a cable whose characteristics allow transmission of only a small amount of information per unit of time. Larger bandwidth capabilities of a cable mean larger data-carrying capacity. This carrying capacity is controlled and enhanced by the use of different transmission techniques such as multiplexing.

On narrowband networks only one device on the network can be transmitting at any point. This means that only one user can be communicating through the network at any given time. The typical transmission speed for this type of network is up to a maximum of 10 megabits per second. In wideband networks multiple users can be communicating at the same time. Most of the microcomputer networks such as Novell and IBM's PC LAN are considered narrowband where many of the newer wide area networks are wideband networks.

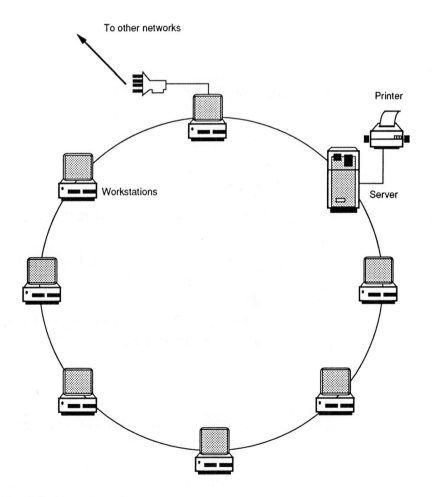

Fig. 5-5. Ring network.

Ring Network

The ring architecture is depicted in Fig. 5-5. This configuration is typical of IBM's Token-Ring network. Each device in the network is connected sequentially in a ring configuration that is shown in Fig. 5-5 as the solid line connecting all devices. The actual physical configuration is such that the beginning and end of the network link are attached so it forms a circle.

In a ring network, each node (receiving/sending station) can be designated as the primary station and the others as secondary stations. Also in this type of network, the wire configuration is a series of loop-type connections from a centralized location called a multistation access unit (MAU). This is done so that if a station on the network malfunctions, the ring will not be broken. The MAU provides a short circuit to ensure the integrity of the network in case of a malfunction in any location on the ring.

In this type of network, data travels around the ring in one direction. Each of the workstations or nodes on the network receives and examines the message transmitted to see if it is for the workstation. If it is, the workstation receives the message and takes appropriate action. If the message is not for the station that is examining it, then it regenerates the signal and sends it through the network again. The time required for the data to travel around the ring is called the walk time. The message knows the destination because each workstation in the ring network has a unique address.

Reliability is high in ring networks, assuming that the integrity of the ring is not broken. Also, expanding a ring network is easy to achieve by removing one node and replacing it with two new ones. Finally, the cost of the ring network is usually less than that of the star and hybrid networks.

Bus Network

A network based on the bus topology (also called a tree topology) connects all networked devices to a single cable (called the bus) running the length of the network. Fig. 5-6 depicts this configuration. Cables running between devices directly connect them to the bus. Therefore, data may pass directly from one device to another without the need of a central hub, as in the star configuration. With some applications, however, the data must first be moved in and out of a central controlling station, as in the case of a Novell network.

In the typical implementation of the bus configuration, all nodes on the bus have equal control. One end of the bus is called the head end. The two ends of the cable or bus are carefully terminated so the data can be absorbed, preventing it from traveling the opposite direction and interfering with other

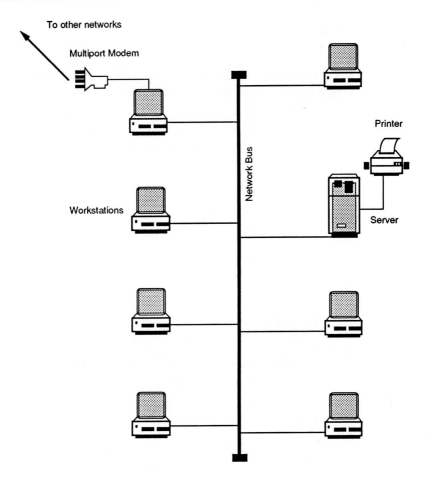

Fig. 5-6. Bus network.

signals traveling through the bus. Without these terminations the data moving through the bus could be lost when interference from incoming reflected waves cancels the electromagnetic waves that carry the signal.

Bus networks are, in essence, multipoint networks, in that a single cable extends through the length of the network with many nodes or stations attached to the bus at different locations. This type of network topology is very popular in PC-based networks. However, the distance that one of these networks can encompass is limited. This is because each time a node taps into the bus, some of the signal is lost on the cable. Because of this signal loss, typical cable distances are 2,500 meters and the practical number of nodes is 100 as in the case of Ethernet.

The reliability of bus networks is good unless the bus itself malfunctions. Losing one node does not have an effect on the rest of the network. But expandability is the strength of the bus topology. A new node can be added by simply connecting it to the bus. Because of the number of nodes and travel distance limitations, bus networks are normally limited to local area network installations.

Star Network

In a star network (sometimes called a hub topology), all devices on the network are connected to a central device that controls the entire network (see Fig. 5-7). The central location receives messages from a sending node and forwards them to the destination node. This central location becomes a hub that controls all the communication in the network.

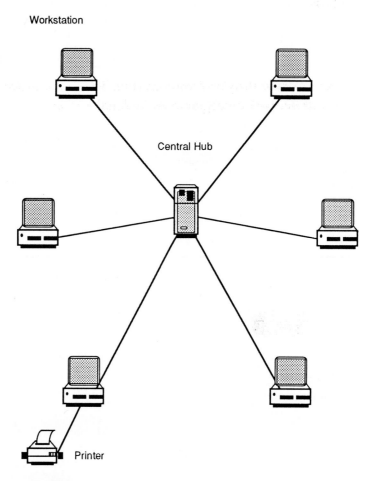

Fig. 5-7. Star network.

The star topology is a traditional approach to interconnecting equipment in which each device is linked by a separate circuit through a central device such as a PBX. In this case the PBX receives a message from a workstation and switches it to a receiving station.

Star networks have several advantages. They provide the shortest path between nodes in the network. Messages traveling on the network must pass through one hub to reach their destination. Therefore, the time required to get a message from the source to its destination is short. A star network also provides the user with a high degree of network control. Since all messages must pass through a central location, this station can log traffic on the network, produce error messages, tabulate network statistics, and perform recovery procedures.

Expanding a star network is relatively easy. To add a new node, a communication link is attached between the new node and the central device, and the network table on other nodes is updated. However, the reliability of star networks is low. If the central station malfunctions, then the entire network fails. This type of topology is common among networks designed by AT&T.

Hybrid Networks

A network with hybrid topology (Fig. 5-8) contains elements of more than one of the network configurations outlined above. For example, a bus network may have a ring network as one of its links. Another type of hybrid topology is a star network that has a bus network as one of its links, where a workstation is normally found.

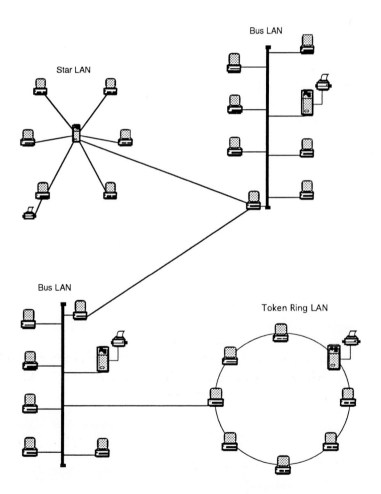

Fig. 5-8. Hybrid network.

This type of network is becoming more common in the workplace due to the ability of many protocols to interact with each other. In addition, the creation of standards promotes the design of multiple topology networks, since one topology may be more efficient or effective in a given situation than the other topologies. Yet, at some point in time, the different network topologies need to allow their users access to each other's resources.

Packet Data Networks (PDNs)

Packet switching is a widely used technique for exchanging data between computers over local area networks that may be in diverse geographical locations. Networks using these techniques are called packet data networks, or PDNs. Packet switching is a store-and-forward data transmission technique in which messages are split into small segments called packets.

A packet is a logical container in which messages are transported from one originating location to their destination. Each packet is assembled at a workstation by a packet assemble/dissassemble facility or PAD. Then it is transmitted through the network independently of other packets, whether or not the other packets are part of the same transaction. The packets belonging to different messages travel through the same communication channel. When the packets that contain a message arrive at their destination, the PAD facility examines them and assembles the data contained in them into the original message.

Each packet in the network has a predetermined length that ranges from a few hundred bits to several thousand bits. This length is determined by the data transmission characteristics of the network through which the packets are moving. If a message is longer than the number of bits that the packet can store, several packets are sent, each identified with a sequence number. The communicating terminals or workstations that send the packets are connected via what is called a virtual circuit.

Virtual Circuits

A virtual circuit is a communication path that lasts only long enough to transmit a specific message. Virtual circuits are controlled by software that connects two nodes as if they were on a physical circuit. The address of the destination node is contained in the packet of data. When a workstation begins to send packets of data, the network is responsible for ensuring that the packets arrive at their destination. By knowing the originating and destination addresses of the packet, the network establishes the virtual circuit. When all the packets are sent, the virtual connection is broken. This avoids hardware problems that arise due to data speed mismatches and helps in retransmitting the packet in case of errors.

Example of a PDN

To better understand how these packets move through a network, let's follow a message as it is sent from a terminal to its destination address using a virtual switched connection (see Fig. 5-9).

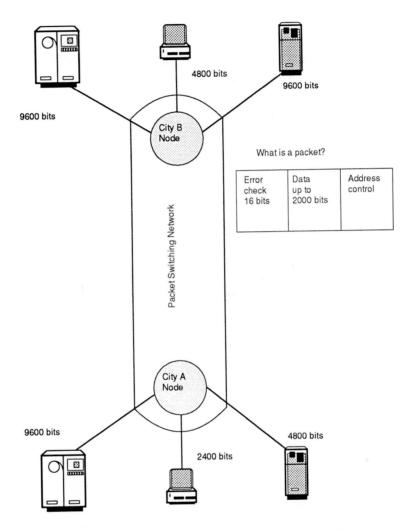

Fig. 5-9. A message sent using a virtual switched connection.

The first step is for the user to connect to a packet switching network. After the physical connection is made, the login procedure takes place. After the login procedure, the address of the receiving node is provided. The PDN then performs a call request packet from the sending node to the receiving node. The call request is delivered to the receiver as an incoming call packet. If the receiver accepts the call, it sends a call accepted packet that the sender node receives as a call connected message. Then the data exchange begins.

After the data is transmitted, either node can transmit a clear request to the other node. The receiver of the request acknowledges the disconnect with a clear confirmation control packet and the transmission is completed.

During data exchange, the process of splitting messages into individual packets is called packetizing. Packets are assembled and disassembled either at the sender's terminal or the receiver's terminal, or sometimes by the packet assembly/disassembly (PAD) facility mentioned above. In either case, packetizing is performed almost instantaneously, and data is transmitted in a virtually uninterrupted stream.

By using PDNs, users are only charged for the amount of data transmitted and not for the amount of connection time. In addition, PDNs provide access to many different locations without the cost of traditional switched connections. However, since PDNs are usually shared networks, users must compete for access. Therefore, it is possible for traffic from other users to block the transmission of a message. Also, if the number of data packets to be transferred is large, the cost of using a PDN can exceed that of leased lines.

Network Interconnectivity

As networks proliferate in the workplace, homogeneous networks are no longer the rule, but rather the exception. Heterogeneous or hybrid networks have become prominent in the workplace. They are composed of several network segments that may differ in topology, protocol, or operating system. For example, some networks contain a mixture of personal computers running on a bus network using Novell's NetWare, UNIX workstations using Ethernet on a token ring, and minicomputers running any of the several large-platform protocols.

During the first years of networking and data communications, these systems were designed to communicate with devices using the same topology and protocol on a homogeneous networked environment. Modern design strategies may include many different topologies in a communications solution that encompasses large geographical areas. To network these types of topologies into a single seamless environment is not an easy task, yet there are many combinations of hardware and software that can provide solutions for connecting hybrid network designs.

Connecting Hybrid Networks

Before any attempt is made to connect a mixture of network configurations, some basic network characteristics need to be understood. One of these characteristics is the network topology. The network topology is the way a network is configured. Different topologies were outlined previously in this chapter.

Another network characteristic is the protocol. Recall that the protocol is a set of conventions or rules for communication that includes a format for the data being transferred and the procedures for its transfer. When connecting networks, the protocol, as well as the topology, must be considered. Two networks that use the same topology but different protocols cannot effectively communicate without help. We call these heterogeneous networks.

Heterogeneous networks can be thought of as being made of building blocks connected by "black boxes." The building blocks are self-contained local area networks with their own workstations, servers, and peripherals. Each consists of a single topology and a single protocol.

To connect two of these boxes, a boundary must be crossed. A connection must be established between both boxes either by a physical cabling scheme or by radio waves. The device that makes the connection, the black box, does not change either interconnecting network. It simply transfers packets of data between the networks. It not only satisfies all the physical requirements of both networks, but also transfers the data safely and securely from one network to the other.

The ability to connect two heterogeneous networks depends on two requirements. The first requirement is that the topologies must be able to be interconnected. Second, there must be a way to transfer information between dissimilar systems of communication (protocols). This means that at some point a common protocol must be employed. There are several ways to accomplish this. Most solutions use high-level protocols for moving data and employ tools for inter-networking such as bridges, routers, brouters, and gateways. Each of these devices has distinct characteristics and specific applications.

The type of device used in connecting dissimilar networks will depend on the amount of transparency desired and the cost that a company is willing to pay for such devices. A rule of thumb is that the more sophistication a device has, the higher the transparency will be to the users and networks and the more expensive the equipment will be. With this in mind, let's take a closer look at some of these interconnectivity devices.

Bridges

Bridges are normally employed to connect similar networks. Both interconnecting networks should have the same protocol. The result is a single logical network (see Fig. 5-10). A bridge can also be employed to connect networks that have different physical media. For example, a bridge may be used between an optical fiber-based network and a coaxial cable-based network.

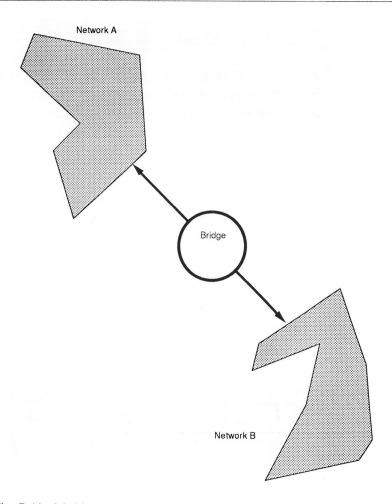

Fig. 5-10. A bridge connecting two networks.

Bridges may also be used to connect networks that use different low-level communication protocols. Therefore, under the right circumstances, a bridge may be used to connect a token ring network and a star network running different communication protocol software.

Bridges feature high-level protocol transparency. They can move traffic between two networks over a third network that may exist in the middle of the others and that does not understand the data passing through it. To the bridge, the intermediate network exists only for the purpose of passing data.

Bridges are intelligent devices. They learn the destination address of traffic passing on them and direct it to its destination. They are also employed in partitioning networks. For example, assume that a network is being slowed down by excessive traffic between two of its parts. The network can be divided into two or more smaller ones, using bridges to connect them. However, since bridges must learn addresses, examine data packets, and forward messages, processing is slowed down by these functions.

Routers

Routers don't have the learning abilities of the bridge, but they can determine the most efficient data path between two networks. They operate at the third layer of the OSI model (see Fig. 5-11).

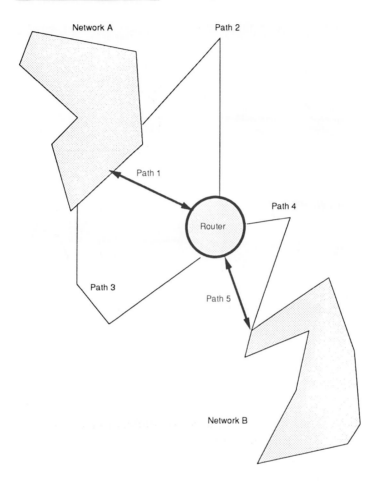

Fig. 5-11. Networks connected by a router.

Routers ignore the topologies and access levels used by networks. Since they operate at the network layer, they are unconstrained by the communication medium or communication protocols. Bridges know the final destination of data packets, but routers know only where the next router is located. They are typically used to connect networks that use the same high-level protocol.

When a data packet arrives at the router, it determines the best route for the packet by checking a router table. The router sees only the packets sent to it by a previous router, where bridges must examine all packets passing through the network. The most common use of routers is to connect networks that have similar protocols but use different packet sizes. Depending on the source,

147

routers are sometimes described as bridges and sometimes as gateways. Most large inter-networks can make good use of routers as long as the same high-level protocol is used.

Brouters

Brouters are hybrid devices that incorporate bridge and router technology. Often they are improperly referred to as multiprotocol routers. In fact, they provide more sophistication than true multiprotocol routers. Brouters provide the advantages of routers and bridges for complex networks. Brouters make decisions on whether a data packet uses a protocol that is routable. Then they route those that can be routed and bridge the rest.

Gateways

Gateways are devices that provide either six- or seven-layer support for the OSI protocol structure. They are the most sophisticated method of connecting networks to networks and networks to hosts (see Fig. 5-12). Gateways can connect networks of totally different architectures. With a gateway, it is possible to connect a Novell PC-based network with an SNA network and make the sharing of resources transparent to the user.

Fig. 5-12. Networks connected by a gateway.

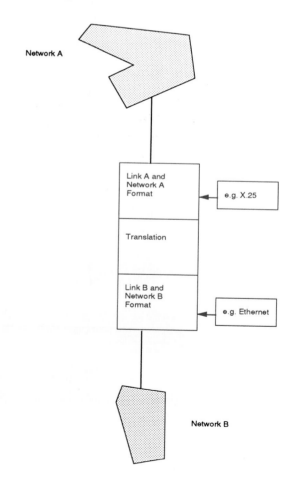

Gateways do not route data packets within networks. They simply deliver their packets so the network can read them. When a gateway receives a packet from a network, it translates it and routes the packet to a distant-end gateway. Here the packet is retranslated and delivered to the destination network. A gateway is the most sophisticated method for interconnecting wide-area networks.

Planning a Hybrid Network

Even though previous chapters in this book dealt with the different concepts of network design, this section provides a general overview of planning a heterogeneous network. For an in-depth view of network design fundamentals, read Chapter 7.

Typically a network administrator or designer does not plan a network from scratch, but inherits one. However, if one can be planned from the beginning, several issues should be considered. The first of these issues is to decide on the objectives for the new system.

These objectives normally include connecting different work situations with different needs. Therefore, it is a good idea to start by defining the individual needs of the users of the network. Each department that is going to be affected by the network will have different requirements that may be solved by different types of technologies. Instead of deciding at this point on how to interconnect networks, it is better to understand the expectations of the department that will use them.

Once the needs of the individual users have been established, the commonalities can be identified. This can be done by considering how an individual topology, or set of topologies, and a single protocol may be used throughout the system. If possible, a single network topology and protocol will reduce the number of potential problems that may arise in the operation of the network. Additionally, the required technical knowledge of maintenance personnel is reduced, along with the amount of maintenance time required to keep the system operational.

After the individual workgroup and its related needs have been established, the designer must consider how best to incorporate the workgroups into individual local area networks or network segments. Once each of these segments is designed, the next step is to incorporate the individual network segments into a network at each location.

After individual segments are successfully connected into a single network, the interconnectivity needs of the different buildings in the office complex or campus should be considered. In this case the network designer must deal with traffic flow. Managing traffic flow includes two main issues. One issue is the speed of data transmission between locations. The other is the amount of congestion on the routes between locations.

Data speed problems can be addressed by employing a fast communication medium such as optical fiber, if the distance between buildings is short. Otherwise, high-speed dedicated links, such as T-1 lines, may need to be considered since private companies don't have the rights to extend their own cables across thoroughfares or public right-of-ways.

Congestion of traffic in the lines becomes a concern when public data communication circuits are used. Since these lines may be shared by many devices, it is easier to exceed the capacity of the transmission medium, causing a slowdown in the overall speed of transmission. Alternative methods of traffic routing need to be considered. For example, if the network spans an area from Chicago to Dallas, alternate routes such as through Kansas City or Memphis are possible paths if the main route becomes congested.

Traffic problems are addressed by some companies by using a technique called the spanning tree algorithm. Using this technique, bridges can be placed between long haul locations. Under the control of the spanning tree algorithm, the bridges making up the alternative routes, let's say, between Chicago and Dallas, conduct tests to determine the best communication path at any given time. The one with the best path becomes the forwarding bridge, and the others stay in a holding pattern. If the communication link begins to deteriorate, the other bridge starts forwarding messages and the original bridge stays on hold. This technique can also be used between buildings that are short distances from each other in order to have a consistent throughput efficiency in the communication circuit.

Managing Hybrid Networks

Today's network managers have a large array of sophisticated tools to manage and correct problems in homogeneous and heterogeneous networks. The type of management tools utilized fall into three general levels of sophistication and flexibility of usage.

The first level consists of simple performance monitors. Performance monitors provide information on data throughput, node errors, and other occurrences. A product that falls into this category is Novell's LANtern. LANtern offers a cost effective way of monitoring individual networks or network segments and reporting the existence of problems. This solution is good for small to medium-sized networks.

The second level consists of devices or software that perform network analysis. These add meaning to the data generated by the network monitor. An example of a network analyzer is Novell's LAN analyzer. Network analyzers provide a large amount of information about the network operation, but require skillful and knowledgeable network operators to interpret the data. Also, network analyzers are very expensive.

The third level of network management tool is designed for wide area hybrid networks. These tools come in two different types. One is a new array of global network management tools that allow a network administrator to obtain a global and sometimes graphical view of the operations on the entire network. The other type of management tool comes in the form of two emerging standards called The Simple Network Management Protocol (SNMP) and the Common Management Information Protocol (CMIP). Both techniques have the same goal, that is, to move information across a network so the network manager can find problems in the system. Even though these techniques have different designs and reporting options, they will play an important role in future management of wide area hybrid networks.

Summary

A computer network can change a group of isolated computers into a coordinated multiuser computer system. A network user can legally share copies of the software with other users. Data can be deposited in centralized locations or in different locations that are accessible to all users. Printers, scanners, and other peripherals connected to the network are available to all users. Additionally, a network allows users to share many different types of hardware devices. The most commonly shared devices are hard disks, printers, and communication devices.

Software designed for networks allows multiple users to access programs simultaneously and share the data produced and used by the application. The advantages of software sharing are many. The most important are cost reduction, legality of sharing the product, sharing data, and up-to-date upgrades.

The geographical area covered by the network determines whether the network is called a wide area network (WAN) or a local area network (LAN). Wide area networks link systems that are too far apart to be included in a small in-house network. They can be in the same city or in different countries. Local area networks connect devices within a small local area, usually within a building or adjacent buildings.

Network evolution has been in the direction of standardized networking and inter-networking technology. One of the most important standards-making bodies is the International Organization for Standardization (ISO), which makes technical recommendations about data communication interfaces. The

151

OSI Reference Model, created by the ISO, is known as a layered protocol, specifying seven layers of interface, where each layer has a specific set of functions to perform.

The configurations used to describe networks are sometimes called network topology. Networks can take on many different logical and physical configurations. However, regardless of how they are implemented, networks can be placed into one of four general categories. The most common network topologies are ring, bus, star, and hybrid.

One commonly used technique that networks use to transmit data to users' workstations is called packet switching. Packet switching is a store-and-forward data transmission technique in which messages are split into small segments called packets. Each packet is switched and transmitted through the network, independently of other packets belonging to the same transaction or other transactions. The packets belonging to different messages travel through the same communication channel. The communicating terminals or workstations are connected via a virtual circuit.

As networks proliferate in the workplace, homogeneous networks are no longer the rule, but rather the exception. Heterogeneous or hybrid networks are prevalent. They include several network segments that may differ in topology, protocol, or operating system. The ability to connect two heterogeneous networks rests with two requirements. First, the topologies must be capable of being interconnected. Second, there must be a way to transfer information between dissimilar systems of communication (protocols). This means that at some point a common protocol must be employed. There are several ways to accomplish this. Most use high-level protocols for moving data and employ tools for inter-networking such as bridges, routers, brouters, and gateways.

Questions

1. Why should individual microcomputers be connected into a network within an organization?

2. What is a local area network?

3. What is a wide area network?

4. What are the most common network topologies?

5. Describe the bus network topology.

6. What is a gateway?

7. What is a bridge?

8. What is a router?

9. What is packetizing?

10. Describe the operation of a PDN.

11. What is a hybrid network?

12. What tools are available to manage a hybrid network?

13. What is a communication protocol?

14. What is the first consideration in designing a hybrid network?

15. What is OSI?

16. What are the different layers of OSI?

Projects

Objective

This project will familiarize the student with the software techniques required to transfer files and establish a two-way serial communication between computers using different operating systems but the same communication protocol. It is important that the student understand the individual concepts of basic file transfer and communication between two microcomputers using a direct serial or a modem connection. If two different computers are not available, then the project can easily be modified to accommodate two computers of the same type. In this case the student should be instructed that the process for dissimilar systems is the same and the process of file transfer among different systems will be simulated.

Project 1. Communication between a Macintosh and an MS-DOS-Based PC through the Serial Port

Several methods allow you to connect a Macintosh and an MS-DOS-based PC or compatible through the serial port to provide file transfer capabilities. One of these methods is to purchase a commercial product specifically designed for this purpose, such as Maclink PC, and follow the instructions in the manual to perform file transfers. This package comes with all the cables and software required to perform the connection.

Another method is to use your existing communication software to perform the connection and the transfer. In addition, you will need to make a cable to physically connect the two machines. In this section we will take the second approach.

The cable can be constructed in two phases. The first step is to purchase a Mac to modem cable from your local computer store. This is done because of the small serial interface on the Macintosh side. The cable costs approximately $5.00, making this a simpler approach than working with the small Mac interface.

The serial cable will not work by itself. A null modem will be required to complete the circuit. To build a null modem refer to Chapter 2 projects. Connect the serial cable and the null modem and then connect one end of the serial cable to the Mac and the free end of the null modem to the PC (see Fig. 5-13).

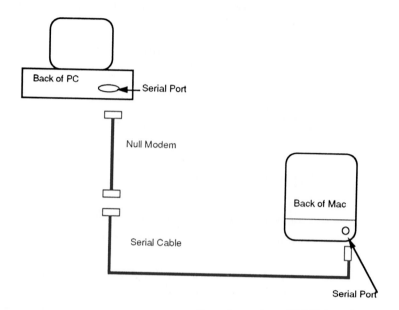

Fig. 5-13. Connecting a Macintosh and an IBM PC.

Now you are ready to establish the connection using whatever communication software is available. For this example, use the communication tool in Microsoft Works for the Macintosh and Microsoft Works for the MS-DOS-based PC. We have chosen Works on the Mac and the MS-DOS-based PC due to their popularity and availability. If your system does not have these two software products, use any type of communication software for both systems. The screens will look different depending on your communication software, but the procedures are basically the same.

Before the communications link can be established, both systems must have the same communications settings. Fig. 5-14 shows the communication settings that will be used for this project.

To set the right parameters on the Macintosh you will need to perform the following general steps:

1. Launch the Microsoft Works program (or your communication software).
2. Select New and choose the communications tool.
3. You will see a screen like the one shown in Fig. 5-15.
4. Click on the Communications menu and select Settings.

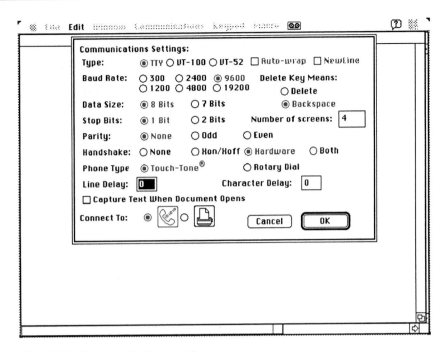

Fig. 5-14. Communication settings.

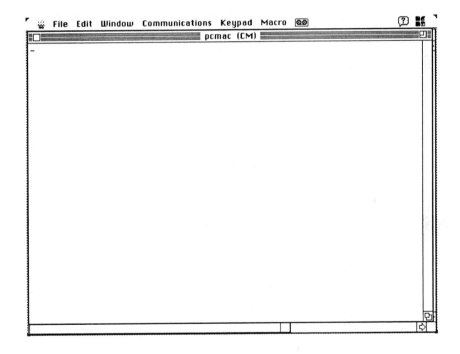

Fig. 5-15. Main terminal screen.

5. You should have a screen similar to the one shown in Fig. 5-14. At this point make sure that your screen has the same settings as those found in Fig. 5-14, regardless of your communication program.

On the IBM side you will need to perform the following steps:

1. Run the Works program or your communication application.

2. Select Create New File and then choose New Communications from the opening menu and press the ENTER key.

3. You should now have a screen like the one shown in Fig. 5-16. Press the ENTER key.

4. Type 9600 for the Baud rate, and set the other parameters the same as those in Fig. 5-14 Now you are ready to establish communications.

5. Select the Options pull-down menu and choose Terminal. Here move the cursor to Local echo and press the ENTER key to place a check mark.

6. On the IBM PC side select the Connect pull-down menu and choose Connect.

7. Type the following on the MS-DOS-based PC side: "Now is the time for all good men to come to the aid of their country."

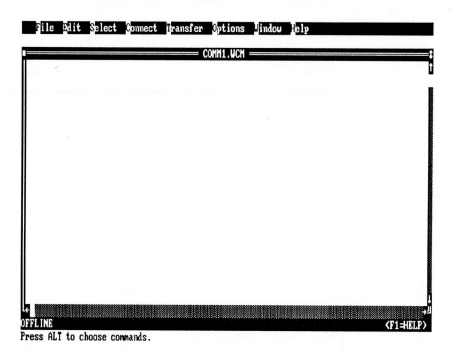

Fig. 5-16. Communication screen for the IBM PC.

You should see the same text you typed on the MS-DOS-based PC side displayed on the Macintosh side as you type. This is a successful connection.

Now we will transfer a file from the PC to the Macintosh. The file to be transferred can be of any type you desire. For this exercise we will transfer the file created by typing the following text using the word processing tool in Works for the PC and then save it as LETTER.WPS.

To whom it may concern,

This is a sample data file to test the communication capabilities of the Works program. Files can be transferred with any type of communications program that supports uploading and downloading of text and binary files.

We are copying the same paragraph again below this one.

This is a sample data file to test the communication capabilities of the Works program. Files can be transferred with any type of communications program that supports uploading and downloading of text and binary files.

To transfer this file from the PC to the Mac, follow these instructions:

1. Click on the Communications pull-down menu on the Mac and select Receive File. You should get a screen like the one in Fig. 5-17. Make sure that you select Xmodem Data.

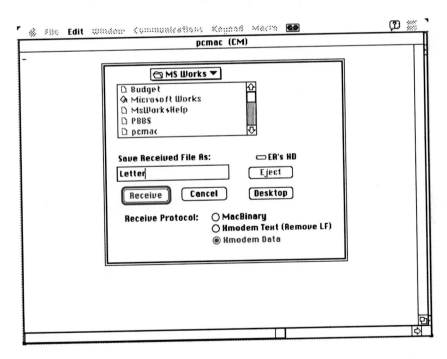

Fig. 5-17. Data receive dialog.

2. Type the name of the file that is going to receive the transferred data. Type LETTER for the name of the file and press the ENTER key.

3. On the MS-DOS-based PC side select the Transfer pull-down menu and choose Send File.

4. Type the name of the file to be sent. In this case it is LETTER.WPS. Then press the ENTER key.

5. The Mac screen will look like the one in Fig. 5-18 and will indicate the number of characters received. The MS-DOS-based PC side will transmit and the Mac will receive the transmission, storing the data in a file labeled LETTER.

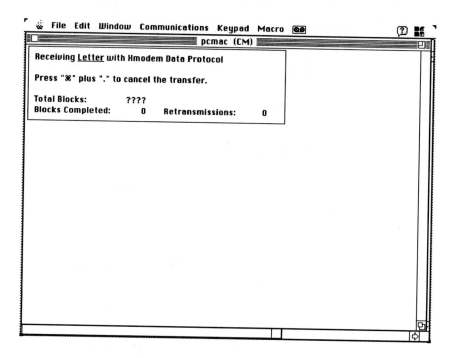

Fig. 5-18. Transmission screen for the Macintosh.

After the transmission is completed, the Mac will sound a short beep to indicate the end of transmission and you will have a file called LETTER in the Works folder on the Mac. The same process can be repeated in reverse order to transfer files from the Mac to the PC.

To transfer files using a modem, the process is virtually the same, except that a modem connection must be made. The serial cable developed in Chapter 3 can be used to connect the modem to the computers. One of the computers will be the host, and its modem will be set to answer mode. This can be done by activating a switch on the modem. The software on the host will be indicated to receive and the sender will transmit using the procedure outlined above. Even though we used a Mac and an MS-DOS-based PC in the example above, the same procedure can be used to connect any types of microcomputers.

Local Area Networks

Objectives

After completing this chapter you will

1. Understand the importance of a local area network.
2. Understand the function of a local area network.
3. Have a general view of the types of applications running on a local area network.
4. Understand the hardware and software components of a local area network.
5. Understand the different topologies of local area networks.
6. Understand the standards that guide the design of local area networks and their protocols.

Key Terms

Bus Topology	CAD
CSMA/CD	File Server
Local Area Network	Network Operating System
Novell	Office Automation
Protocol	Ring Topology
Star Topology	Wide Area Network
Workstation	

Introduction

The rapid acceptance of local area networks has made networking a common event in the workplace, especially in education. The local area network allows individuals to share resources and offset some of the high costs of automating processes. An individual at any computer on a local area network can create a document and send it to another computer on the network for editing or printing purposes. The access provided by local area networks is controlled and, to some extent, secure.

These concepts, as well as some of the inner workings of the hardware that make up the local area network, are explored in this chapter. Additionally, the most commonly used protocols and the standards set up by the IEEE are defined, along with their impact on local area network design.

Local Area Networks

Definition

One of the largest growth segments of the communication industry since the early 1980s is local area network (LAN) technology. This growth has resulted in lower prices for the hardware and software required to implement a local area network. The lower prices of hardware components have translated into less expensive microcomputers, which have replaced terminals as the main hardware interface to the user. In addition, the increase in power of the processors that control the microcomputer has made the microcomputer a powerful workhorse that in many instances has replaced the minicomputer. That is the reason most LAN workstations today are microcomputers. Not all LANs are composed of microcomputers, for many LANs contain a mixture of microcomputers, minicomputers, and mainframes. However, the microcomputer is well suited to be an active participant in local area networks. If we compare only numbers, the majority of the computing devices in local area networks are microcomputers.

Local area networks connect devices that are confined to a small geographical area. The actual distance that a LAN spans depends on specific implementations. A LAN covers a clearly defined local area such as an office suite, a building, or a group of buildings. To better understand LANs, it is important to know their uses.

Benefits

Most LANs are implemented so that users in the network can transfer data and share resources. A LAN implementation can provide high-speed data transfer capability to all users without needing a system operator to facilitate the transmission process. Even when connecting a LAN to a wider area network that covers thousands of miles, data transfer between users of the network is time effective and in most cases problem free.

Another reason for implementing a LAN is to share hardware and software resources among users of the network. Even though the price of microcomputers and their peripherals has dropped in recent years, it is still expensive to provide every user with a hard disk, printers, CD drives, scanners, plotters, and many of the other devices that are common in today's personal computers. Although the cost of some of these items is relatively inexpensive, it is not cost effective to purchase ten laser printers for ten workers in an office where the distance between workers is small, because the printers will often be idle. Since not all workers will be printing at the same time and all the time, it is more practical to implement a local area network so all users can share one or two printers (see Fig. 6-1).

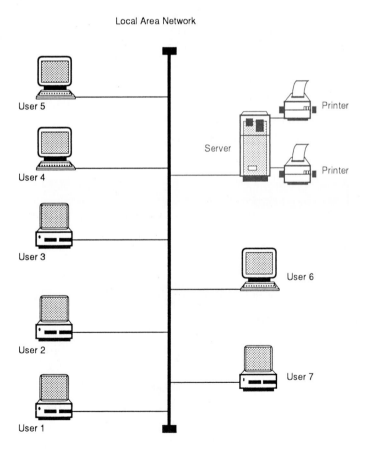

Fig. 6-1. Users sharing printers over a network.

LANs also allow users to share software and the data produced by the software. Software for which a site license has been obtained can be placed on a shared hard disk drive. The software can then be downloaded to the individual workstation, provided that license agreements are observed. This type of sharing is efficient and has the additional benefit of facilitating backups of network-installed software and the installation of software upgrades as they become available.

In addition to the benefits outlined above, local area networks encourage security of data and software from physical disasters as well as computer viruses. Since all the workstations on the LAN are connected to each other and in most cases the bulk of the data and software resides on a file server, it is easier to perform frequent and complete backups of all important data and programs. Additionally, modern network monitoring software has sophisticated virus detection mechanisms that help prevent the invasion of computer viruses into the workstations and servers.

Some of the more compelling reasons for installing a LAN are:

1. Sharing of software
2. Sharing of data
3. Sharing system resources
4. Security and backups
5. Easier maintenance and upgrades

Sharing Software

Imagine an office that has 20 employees, all using personal computers with word processing, spreadsheet, and database software. If each user is to have individual copies of software, there must be a legally purchased copy of each package for each user.

Another solution is to purchase network versions of all software products and install a single copy of each on a local area network connecting all users. Purchasing a network version of a software product is, in many situations, less expensive than buying individual copies for each user.

Additionally, there isn't the need to keep track of 20 copies of the same software product. Only one copy needs to be administered.

Sharing Data

With network copies of software programs, the data generated by one user can be used by others in a "transparent" mode. That is, all users can work with the same data file as if it were their own. With individual copies of software, data generated on one workstation must be physically moved from one machine to another. Data for sales, inventory, and other departments must be moved often to keep it current, requiring additional processing and duplication of files.

Sharing System Resources

Network versions of software also save on hard disk space. Instead of using space on multiple users' hard disks, the software can be placed on the network server's hard disk. This allows the software and data to be shared by everyone on a local area network.

Security and Backup

Individual copies of software on multiple workstations are difficult to safeguard from unauthorized individuals. It is relatively easy to go to a person's desk and damage or change data files.

Using the security resources of a network, software can be safeguarded by installing passwords, trustee rights, and file attributes. This enhances the safety of data files and programs in a manner that is almost impossible with individual software.

With multiple users working with stand-alone programs, backing up software becomes a difficult task. Users are not always prompt when it comes to backing up important software and data. Using the network resources, software and data can be backed up from a single location with minimal effort. This also enhances security since the latest copy of a file is assured when using the latter method.

Easy Maintenance and Upgrades

In many situations, users of a particular package do not have the latest updates or modifications. Sometimes this is due to a lack of time to install software upgrades, and other times there is a lack of funding to purchase the latest release of a product.

If network software is used, only one upgrade copy of the software needs to be installed and/or modified to get the latest features. Also, in large corporations with many users, the cost of upgrading a network version of a software product can be substantially less than purchasing individual copies of the same program.

Applications

Not only are local area networks a good mechanism for sharing hardware and enforcing security, but they promote the sharing of application programs that, in many cases, take advantage of the capabilities of the LAN to enhance the flexibility and usefulness of the programs. There are many of these LAN applications. Some of the more common types of applications are office automation, factory automation, education, computer-aided design, and computer-aided manufacturing.

Office Automation

Microcomputers have provided office workers the ability to automate their processing needs. The local processing power of the microcomputer, coupled with software such as electronic mail, calendar automation, shared databases, and document exchange, have changed the way offices conduct business. Offices connected by a local area network can now exchange documents electronically, schedule meetings electronically by finding the best hours that workers can meet, and share high-quality output devices such as laser printers at a fraction of the cost of stand-alone systems.

A LAN can provide office workers with the following capabilities:

1. Memo and document distribution to recipients using electronic mail.

2. Automatic meeting scheduling with electronic calendars. The scheduler can automatically find commonly available times and schedule the participants.

3. Downloading of software from a file server at speeds comparable to that of local hard disks.

4. Multiple user access to printers, plotters, facsimile machines, CD drives, and scanners.

5. Multiple user access to documents for editing purposes and for sharing among other users.

6. Centralized backup of all documents by the network administrator. This ensures workers that, in case of a disaster, their work and files are recoverable and safe.

7. Enhanced security of files and data by allowing the LAN to safeguard files residing on the file server.

8. Extracting data from a centralized database and manipulating the data locally on a microcomputer.

9. Composing parts of a document or project and submitting them to a centralized location for integration with other parts of the document produced by other workers on the network.

10. Entering transactions to be processed on other LANs.

11. Sending data from the LAN to other users on a WAN or other LANs.

Education

Educational institutions have found LANs to be an invaluable tool in the education process. Colleges and universities use LANs to provide students access to a centralized server from which they can communicate with faculty or other students through electronic mail, access software required for class assignments, and place assignments on a centralized disk for faculty retrieval and review.

Research faculty and students have access through LANs to the local library and through gateways to electronic libraries throughout the world. In addition, the academic community has access to information located in large geographical areas through wide area networks such as Bitnet.

CAD

Computer-aided design (CAD) software allows users to have a workstation to create drawings, architectural blueprints, and electronic maps without the need of pencil and paper. A LAN used to connect CAD stations allows designers to place notes and instructions to drafters on a centralized server. Each drafter can retrieve the information, ask for further clarification, and complete a portion of the drawing. Then the drawing can be sent to other workers on the LAN for completion and then to a plotter. In most cases, many engineers work on portions of a single project collectively. A LAN enables them to quickly exchange and share information in order to complete the project. CAD systems are used extensively by car manufacturers, aerospace workers, and computer corporations.

CAM

Computer-aided manufacturing (CAM) systems are used to control assembly lines, manufacturing plants, and machinery. A LAN in a computer-aided manufacturing environment allows the automatic control of scheduling, inventory, and ordering systems. Errors that are found by the individual system in the manufacturing process can be transmitted by the LAN to a centralized location for analysis and correction. Instructions can then be transmitted through the LAN to correct the problem and continue the manufacturing process.

All of the above application categories demonstrate the extensive and various uses of local area networks. However, it is important to understand that LAN applications fall into three categories. Most software that needs to be used in a LAN can be divided into the categories of network incompatible, network compatible, and network aware.

Network incompatible software cannot be used at all on a normal LAN while it is stored on a file server. Usually the problem involves the program's use of low-level operations to control the disk drive or access its own files. These low-level operations access the hardware of the computer directly, rather than using the operating system function calls that network operating systems normally employ to access the resources managed by the file server.

Other problems can arise when the program is simply incompatible with the resident network driver programs (programs that allow the computer hardware and operating system to take advantage of network functions), although this situation is rare. In this case the program cannot be run on a computer that is attached to the network. When the software can be run with the network drivers loaded in main memory, but not on the network, it is necessary to install it on the workstation's hard disk. This makes the program an individual software application on the user's workstation and not a networked application.

Network compatible software includes all programs that can be run on the network, even though they might not be network specific versions. Many programs have no install options that indicate which logical hard disk they are running on. These programs can simply be copied to a network directory. Others, such as older versions of WordStar, can be installed on any of the network server's hard drives using the appropriate install procedures. This is often the easiest type of program for the network supervisor to install. Still others may be programmed to always look on a certain disk drive for their files, for instance on drive C. In this case, the network operating system will typically have some types of commands or functions that can be used to direct drive letter C of the workstation to the appropriate network directory or location where the files to be executed are located. The programs in this category must be handled very carefully in regard to federal copyright laws. Under almost all license agreements accompanying the software, one copy of the software must be owned for each user accessing the program.

Network aware programs have been written to detect and sometimes take advantage of a network. Many programs released in the last few years are designed specifically to detect that they are running on a network and to allow only one user to access them. This prevents users from illegally using more copies of the software than they own. Usually, special multiuser versions of such programs are available that allow five, ten, or some other number of users to access the software simultaneously. The multiuser versions are always more expensive than single-user versions. But they are less expensive than an equal number of single-user copies. Other programs are written to take advantage of the network environment. These programs offer electronic mail, quick messages, easy use of network printers, or network use of a common database.

As can be seen from this discussion, the number of applications that can run on a network are many. However, it is important to be aware of the different types of programs available in the market and how they can interact with the network. Many of the newer applications in the market are network compatible products. Additionally, companies that produce individual applications for single-user computers also have multiuser and network compatible versions of their programs.

LAN Characteristics

Today's local area networks have a number of characteristics that are common among most of the topologies that form their configurations. When a LAN is purchased, the following characteristics should be considered. LANs can provide users with:

1. Flexibility
2. Speed
3. Reliability
4. Hardware and software sharing
5. Transparent interface
6. Adaptability
7. Access to other LANs and WANs
8. Security
9. Centralized management
10. Private ownership of the LAN

Flexibility

Many different hardware devices such as plotters, printers, and computers can be attached to a local area network. A station or node on a local area network can be a terminal, a microcomputer, a printer, a facsimile machine, or a minicomputer. In addition, individual local area networks can be connected to form a bigger data communication system than the individual LANs by themselves. In most cases, adding or removing one of these devices to or from the LAN is simply a matter or attaching or removing a cable from the device to the transmission medium. Afterwards, software takes care of the rest of the functions required to make the new device available to the system or to remove it from its "inventory."

In addition to the network operating system, which is required, other types of software applications can also reside on file servers on the LAN. In an automated office, as one person is using electronic mail, another can be accessing a database, while another may be manipulating data in a spreadsheet and sending output to a shared laser printer.

Also, local area networks can handle applications with different processing and data transfer capabilities. As an example, some users may be transferring text files through the network at the same time other users are transmitting high resolution images from a CAD system. This flexibility is inherent on most types of LANs and is one of the reasons for their success.

167

Speed

LANs can have high-speed data transfer. This speed is required because of the large number of bytes that must be downloaded when a workstation requests a software application. A good rule of thumb is to have a LAN that downloads files at a speed comparable to the transfer rate from a hard disk to the memory of a microcomputer.

Speeds of local area networks range from a few hundred thousand bits per second for the inexpensive, parallel port-based, local area networks to several million bits per second. The cost and complexity of the local area network tends to increase according to the speed of transmission and the volume of data that it can handle.

Reliability

A LAN must work continuously and consistently. For a LAN to be considered reliable, all stations must have access to the network according to the privileges established by the network administrator. A single station shouldn't monopolize the capacity of the LAN, since that would inhibit access by other users and increase the response time experienced by network users.

Also, local area networks should be able to recover from a system failure without losing jobs or files located on the server. If a station malfunctions, the rest of the network should continue operating without problems.

Hardware and Software Sharing

Sometimes there is a specialized device called a server to facilitate sharing. A server is a computer on the LAN that can be accessed by all users of the network. The server contains a resource that it "serves" to the LAN users. The most common type of server is the file server. Using the office automation example, imagine that there is a node located in one of the offices where a file server resides. The file server can contain software applications and data files, and it may have printers, plotters, and other devices attached to it. Other users on the network access the application software and data files stored on the file server. When a user's workstation requests a file, the server "serves" the file to the user's workstation (also called the client).

Servers can provide users other services besides files or programs. Some servers, in addition to being file servers, are also printer servers. These servers have printers, plotters, or some other output device attached to them that can be used by any users on the LAN to send a document for output. In many cases, servers are used as printer servers only, leaving other computers to perform the tasks of file servers. When a document from a user needs to be printed on one of the printers attached to the file server, the document is printed from the user's workstation in much the same manner as if the printer were attached locally. The document reaches the file server and it is transformed into a file that is then "served" to the printer.

Additionally, when software upgrades become available, the upgrades can be placed on the server. When a user requests the software, the user automatically receives the latest release of the product. In this manner, file servers become repositories for software applications.

The software residing on the server consists of software products with a site license for a predetermined number of users. For example, a company may decide that, of their 200 employees, only 50 will be using a word processor at any given time. Therefore, instead of buying 200 copies of the same program, it can purchase one copy with a site license for 50 simultaneous users. The one copy of the software is placed on the file server and downloaded to a user workstation whenever it is requested. This avoids the need to pass diskettes or to keep large inventories of application software and hardware.

Transparent Interface

Having a transparent interface implies that network access for users should be no more complicated than accessing the same facilities using a different interface. A user should not be expected to learn a series of complicated commands to print a file. Instead, the system should use the same commands or similar commands to the ones that he or she used when the workstation was not attached to the LAN. For example, if an application is invoked from a local hard disk by typing its name and then pressing the ENTER key, the same procedure should work when requesting the application from a file server.

Adaptability

A well-designed LAN has the ability to accommodate a variety of hardware and can be reconfigured easily. If a new device such as a plotter or a facsimile machine needs to be added to the network, it should be done without disruption to the users. Additionally, if a node needs to be removed, added, or moved to another location, the network should allow any of these changes without affecting existing users. A LAN should also be capable of expansion without regard to the number of users. That is, the number of users should not inhibit the need for expanding the services of the LAN.

Access to Other LANs and WANs

In many situations a LAN is just a small component of a much larger network distributed through the corporation facilities. A large corporation may have LANs of different topologies and use different protocols, including packet switching and wide area networks. A LAN should allow user access to the global facilities in the corporation by connecting the local area network to the wide area network facilities using some type of gateway. This connection should also be transparent to the user.

Security

Connectivity and flexibility of a local area network should not be accomplished at the expense of security. If data and user communication are allowed to be accidentally or intentionally disrupted, then the LAN loses its integrity.

The LAN should have provisions for ID and password security mechanisms. File security should be enforced with the use of read, read-write, execute, and delete attributes. These attributes act on files and directories to prevent the unauthorized copying, deletion, or modification of data. Many operating systems, such as UNIX, already have these types of attributes as part of their security mechanisms. LANs also implement them, and in many cases, take security a few levels higher than the methods employed by the operating system.

Additionally, virus detection mechanisms should always be in place. As users are added to the network and dial-in lines are made available, the potential for the introduction of a computer virus into the network increases. In many cases, the viruses act on the individual workstations and leave the servers alone, mainly because of the protection mechanisms available to the server through the network. However, other viruses replicate themselves through the network, creating an overload of traffic and shutting down practical implementation of the network.

Security should also be extended to hardware devices attached to the network. The LAN should be able to restrict access to hardware devices to only those users who have proper authorization. This can be accomplished through the use of software, mostly the network operating system, and hardware such as call-back units.

Centralized Management

Most LAN installations are intended to reduce costs and promote ease of use. A LAN should minimize operator intervention and contain several management tools that provide a synopsis of the operation of the network to the network operator. Additionally, the network operator should be able to perform backups of the entire system from a centralized station.

The network operating system has management utilities that enable the local area network operator to obtain a synopsis, at any given time, of the performance of the network and of traffic that flows through it. However, in this case, many LAN administrators find that such monitoring and management utilities are not enough to get a complete "picture" of the network and where some of the problems may be located. For this purpose, many third party vendors offer management and monitoring equipment and software that enhance the software available with the LAN.

Private Ownership

The hardware, software, and data-carrying medium are normally owned by the corporation or institution that purchased the LAN. This is in contrast to wide area networks in which the hardware is owned by the corporation but the medium belongs to a public carrier. All repairs, maintenance, and new connections are the responsibility of the owner of the LAN.

In conclusion, the above characteristics of local area networks are those that the industry perceives as the qualities of a "good LAN." They can also serve as a comparison list when deciding on the type and configuration of the local area network that needs to be installed at a particular location. However, to obtain a better idea of the involvement required to install a local area network, its components must be understood.

LAN Components

Two major items must be considered when planning or installing a LAN: the network hardware components and the network software. Three major categories of devices make up the hardware components of a local area network (see Fig. 6-2). These are the server, the LAN communication system, and the workstations.

Fig. 6-2. LAN hardware components.

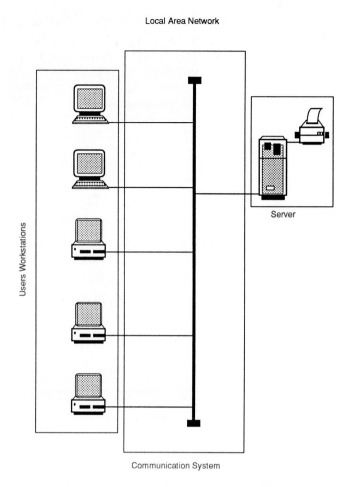

Local Area Network

Server

Users Workstations

Communication System

Servers

As stated before, servers are computers on the network that are accessible to network users. They contain resources that they "serve" to users who request the services. The most common type of server is a file server. Most LANs have at least one file server, and they often have multiple file servers. The file server contains software applications and data files that are provided to users upon request. For example, if a user needs a spreadsheet, a request for a specific spreadsheet package is sent to the file server. The server finds the requested application on its disk and downloads a copy of it to the requesting workstation. As far as the user is concerned, the spreadsheet behaves as if it were stored on a local disk.

The file server is simply a computer with one or more large-capacity hard disk drives. Normally it is composed of a minicomputer or a fast microcomputer. This is done since many users will be accessing the server at the same time, requiring a high performance machine with fast hard disks.

If a LAN relies on the server for all of its functions, this technique is called a dedicated server approach. Other LANs do not require a distinction between a user workstation and the file server. This approach is called a peer-to-peer network. In a peer-to-peer network any microcomputer can function as the file server and user at the same time (sometimes called a nondedicated server).

File servers are not the only type of server that can be present on a network. Any computer that has a sharable resource is considered a server. For example, if users of a LAN need to have access to modems, it is possible to have a computer that contains several modems for user access. This is called a modem server. A gateway is also a type of server, a gateway server. Also, a network can have compact disk (CD) servers. These consist of an array (2 to 14) of CD drives attached to a microcomputer. Users can then access any of the CD disks on the server from their workstations.

As mentioned above, file servers can be nondedicated or dedicated. If a file server is dedicated, it can only be used as a file server and not as a workstation. This is typical when a LAN has many users. For small local area networks, a file server may function in a nondedicated fashion as a file server and as a user workstation.

Choosing Servers

If the network consists of only one server, the choice of where to install shared software is easy. However, if multiple servers are available, a decision must be made as to which server will hold the shared software.

There are several possibilities for multiple server networks. Assume that a network consists of two servers. One possibility is to purchase two copies of the software and install one on each server. Another possibility is to purchase a third server and place all shared software on it. A third option is to install the software on one of the servers and let users of the other servers attach themselves to that one. (see Fig. 6.3).

Each of these approaches has its pros and cons. If a copy is purchased for each server, the expense of the extra copy may be more than having a network version of the software and a license for all possible users. Additionally, there is the need to keep security and maintenance of the same software product on multiple servers.

Placing all shared software on a single server may prove to be too much for a computer acting as the server. Too many users can slow the response time of the server to unacceptable levels. In addition, hard disk space is quickly consumed by the large amount of software in the server, adding to the degradation of the response time of the system.

Acquiring a third server to place all shared software on and putting the data on the others is probably the most elegant solution. However, in many situations this is not economically feasible.

173

Fig. 6-3. Possible server configuration.

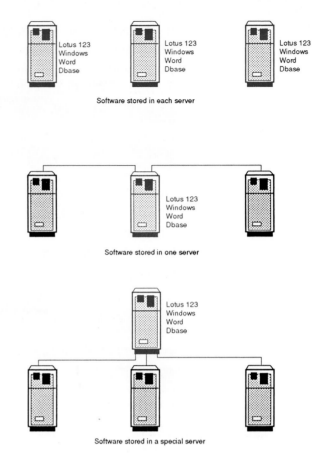

A final possibility is to spread all shared software among the available servers. This allows the purchase of a single network version of a software product, along with a license for the number of users involved. This method also allows the load created by the shared software to be spread evenly among all available servers (see Fig. 6-4).

Fig. 6-4. Distributing software among servers is an efficient way to maximize the hardware.

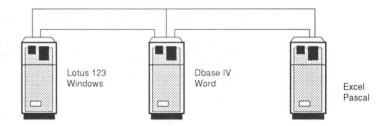

Workstations

The typical LAN workstation is a microcomputer. For the remainder of this book it is assumed that file servers and workstations consist of some type of microcomputer. Terminals can also be used to communicate on a LAN, but the cost of a personal computer is usually low enough to be justifiable, since a complete computer is obtained.

Once the microcomputer is connected to a LAN, it is used in similar fashion to a microcomputer in stand-alone mode. The LAN just replaces the locations from which files are retrieved. Some LANs, such as those that use Novell NetWare, can have workstations from different vendors, such as IBM and Apple. Users of NetWare can attach an IBM PC or clone and a Macintosh and use their machines the same way they used them in their stand-alone configuration.

The responsibility of the PC workstation is to execute the application served by the LAN file server. On most LANs the workstation typically does the processing. On distributed LAN networks, the file server and the workstation can share the processing duties. This scenario is typically found on LANs dedicated to database functions.

After an application is served to the PC workstation, the application begins execution. During the execution of the program, the user may want to store a file or print a file. At this point the user has two options. To save a copy of the file, the user can save it on a hard disk or floppy disk local to the workstation that he or she is using. The other option is to save it on the file server's hard disk. In the latter case, the file could be made available to all other users on the LAN, or kept for private use by using file security attributes. If the user decides to print the file, it can be sent to a printer attached to the server, or printed locally if the workstation has a printer attached to it.

All workstations and the server must be connected through some type of transmission medium. We call this the local area network communication system, and, as explained in previous chapters, it can consist of twisted pair wire, coaxial cable, optical fiber, and other types of communication media.

The LAN Communication System

When two or more computers are connected on a network, a special cable and a network interface board or card (NIC) are required in each computer and server. The cable is used to connect the network interface board to the LAN transmission medium. Most microcomputers are not equipped with an interface port that can be connected to a second microcomputer for networking purposes (except the Macintosh computer that has a built-in AppleTalk port). Although some networks are implemented through the parallel port or the serial port of personal computers, these networks operate at very low speeds making them unusable for most companies or situations where large volumes of data need to be transmitted. As a result, a network interface card (NIC) (see Fig. 6-5) or network adapter must be installed in the microcomputer. There are many different types and brands of NICs, but each performs the same function. It allows the microcomputer to be connected to a cabling system and transmits data between computers attached to the data transmission media at high speeds.

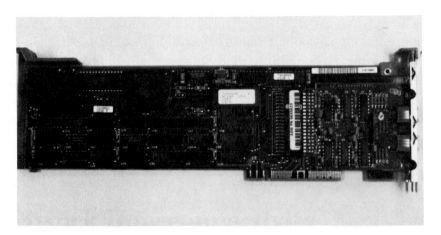

Fig. 6-5. Network interface card.

The speed of transmission will depend on the type of medium, the capabilities of the NIC, and the computer that the NIC is attached to. Typical speed ranges for LANs are from 1 to 16 megabits per second and a few are even higher. However, since the workstations on the LAN are connected by a cable, the geographic range the LAN can cover is limited to buildings or campuses where the cable can be laid.

Data is transmitted from a workstation to a file server and vice versa by packetizing it. When a file is requested from the file server, the NIC translates this file into data packets. Normally, the data packets are of fixed size, although they could be different sizes. Most adapters use packets of 500 to 2,000 bytes. The file server's NIC places the data packets on the network data transmission medium, where they are transmitted to the workstation NIC. Here the data packets are reassembled into the original data file and given to the workstation.

Each data packet contains the address of the workstation on the network that is to receive the data packet (see Fig. 6-6). The address of each node in the LAN is provided by the NIC. This address can be set with switches on the NIC when it is installed, although some NICs already have the address set at the factory before they are shipped to a customer.

Fig. 6-6. A data packet.

Error check 16 bits	Data up to 2000 bits	Address control

The NIC address uses a combination of 8 bits, and therefore can have a value of from 1 to 256. This limits the number of users on the LAN to 256. Large LANs can be created by joining two or more LANs into a single network using one of the network interconnecting devices explained in previous chapters. Some new network adapters, such as 16-bit cards, have larger addresses by using more bytes to form the address. However, many LANs still use the system just outlined.

LAN Software

The processes that take place on the hardware devices of a LAN must be controlled by software. The software is the network operating system. One of the most widely used network operating systems is NetWare by Novell, Inc.

The network operating system controls the operation of the file server, and it makes the network resources accessible and easy to use. It manages server security and provides the network administrators with the tools to control user access to the network and to manage the file structure of the network disks.

The network operating system controls which files a user can access, as well as how the user accesses the files. For example, a user may have access to a word processor file, but it can only be read and not modified. At the same time, another user may have access to the same file and be able to modify it.

In most cases, the network operating system is an extension of the PC workstation operating system. The same commands used to retrieve, store, and print files on the microcomputer are used to perform these functions on the network. The network operating system also provides extensions to the PC operating system to do some functions more efficiently.

Choosing a Directory for Shared Software

In addition to choosing the server where the shared software is to reside, the directory structure of this server must also be decided. There are several possibilities. One is to place all shared programs under the main or root directory. The other possible solution is to create a directory under the root directory and name this subdirectory SHARESOF, PROGRAMS, or something that indicates its purpose (see Fig. 6-7 for two such subdirectories).

The first solution may not be the best approach. One problem is that the root directory may become cluttered as new programs are added to the server. This makes the task of maintenance and backup more difficult, since each shared program name must be identified during backups.

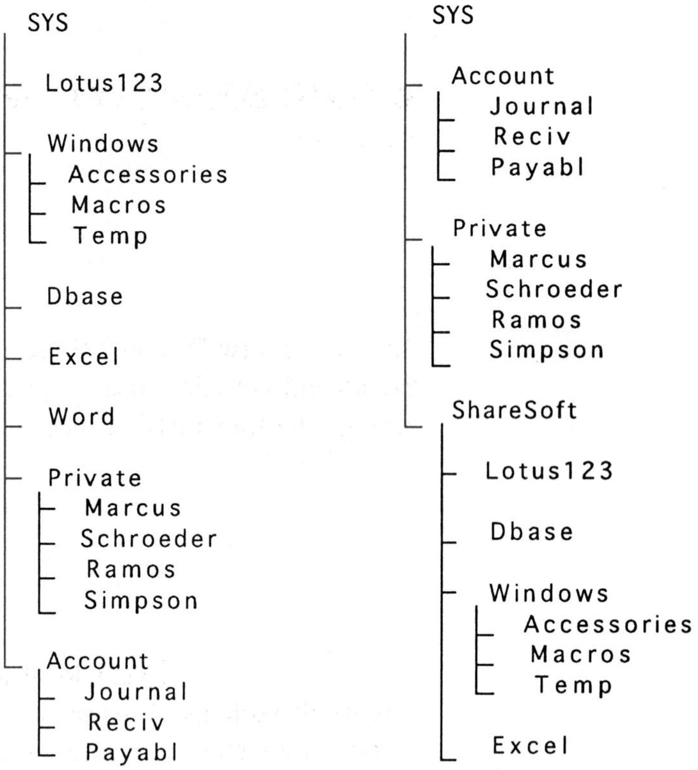

Fig. 6-7. Possible network subdirectories where applications can reside.

```
SYS
 |
 |- Lotus123
 |
 |- Windows
 |    |- Accessories
 |    |- Macros
 |    |- Temp
 |
 |- Dbase
 |
 |- Excel
 |
 |- Word
 |
 |- Private
 |    |- Marcus
 |    |- Schroeder
 |    |- Ramos
 |    |- Simpson
 |
 |- Account
      |- Journal
      |- Reciv
      |- Payabl
```

```
SYS
 |
 |- Account
 |    |- Journal
 |    |- Reciv
 |    |- Payabl
 |
 |- Private
 |    |- Marcus
 |    |- Schroeder
 |    |- Ramos
 |    |- Simpson
 |
 |- ShareSoft
      |- Lotus123
      |
      |- Dbase
      |
      |- Windows
      |    |- Accessories
      |    |- Macros
      |    |- Temp
      |
      |- Excel
```

The second method is the better one. During backup procedures the entire shared software subdirectory can be backed up with a single command. Additionally, establishing security rights over one subdirectory is easier than over multiple subdirectories.

A more complex task is when some software is supposed to be "public domain" and other software is to be secured. The words "public domain" mean that all programs or data in the subdirectory are available to all users for downloading to their workstation, and there are no restrictions imposed on how they use it. Even though such software is shared, it should not share a parent directory with programs and data that require large measures of security.

LAN Configurations

Network topologies were introduced in Chapter 5. Three of these topologies, the bus, ring, and star are used extensively in LAN implementations. However, regardless of the topology used in the physical layout of the LAN, most LANs can be divided into baseband and broadband networks.

Baseband vs Broadband

Baseband local area networks are capable of carrying only one signal at any given time. The signal is the data that is carried by the media utilized to connect the different nodes in the network. Since only one signal travels through the transmission medium, the entire bandwidth of this medium is used to move the digital bit that is part of the message from one node to another in the LAN.

Broadband networks don't suffer from the limitations of baseband networks. Broadband networks use frequency multiplexing techniques to send data through the transmission medium. The multiplexing techniques allow the network to divide the frequencies available in the cabling medium to create different paths or channels that can be used to deliver the data to the nodes. This allows the network to support many different information paths using the same cabling system.

Although broadband networks provide more capacity and flexibility to organizations, the typical local area network tends to be baseband. The reasons for such decisions are several, but cost, complexity, and the potential for failure are the most commonly cited.

Broadband networks, because of their larger size and the different signals they carry, are more complex to operate and maintain than baseband networks. This complexity also increases their cost. Additionally, assume that data and video signals travel through the same LAN. If the LAN fails, then not only are the data signals lost, but also the video signals. This increases the impact of a failure on the entire organization.

Broadband and baseband are terms used to classify the networks. However, within these two configurations, the physical layout of the network is also used to distinguish one system from another. This physical layout was described in previous chapters when the general network was considered. But, the same physical layout or topology can be applied to local area networks.

Topologies

Bus Topology

As mentioned in previous chapters, in the bus topology the microcomputer workstations are connected to a single cable that runs the entire length of the network. Data travels through the cable, also called a bus, directly from the sending node to the destination node.

The bus topology is the most widely used of all LAN configurations. The reason for its success is the early popularity of protocols, such as Ethernet, that used this configuration.

Ring Topology

A ring configuration uses a token passing protocol (see next section). It is the second most popular type of configuration. The ring topology connects all nodes with one continuous loop. Data travels in only one direction within the ring, making a complete circle through the loop.

Star Topology

The third major topology is the star. In a star configuration, each node is connected to a central server. Data flows back and forth between the central server and the nodes in the network.

LAN Protocols

Local area networks have a variety of configurations. However, regardless of the LAN configuration, every message transmitted contains within it the address of the destination node. In addition, each node in the network looks for its address in each message. If the address is present, the station picks up the message. Otherwise the message is allowed to circulate through the transmission medium. But, for this process to take place, the different hardware in the network must communicate under the control of some type of software.

The software that allows the network hardware to communicate is called the protocol. The protocol is necessary so that all stations on the system can communicate with each other, whether they are from the same vendor or not. The protocol consists of the set of rules by which two machines talk to each other. It must be present, along with the LAN hardware and the network operating system. Some communication protocols were discussed in previous chapters.

Other common protocols used in LANs are the logical link control (LLC) protocol established by the Institute of Electrical and Electronic Engineers (IEEE) 802 Standards Committee, the carrier sense multiple access/collision detection (CSMA/CD) protocol, and the token passing protocol.

LLC Protocol

The most important aspect of LAN protocols is the logical link control or LLC. This is a data link protocol that is bit oriented. An LLC's frame, also called a protocol data unit, contains the format shown in Fig. 6-8. The destination address identifies the workstation to which the information field is delivered, and the source address identifies the workstation that sent the message. The control field has commands, responses, and number sequences that control the data link. The information field is composed of any combination of bytes.

Header (size is variable)	Destination Address (8 bits)	Source Address (8 bits)	Control Field (8 or 16 bits)	Data (8 x n bits)	Trailer (size is variable)

Fig. 6-8. Format of LLC packet.

CSMA/CD Protocol

The carrier sense multiple access with collision detect (CSMA/CD) is a commonly used protocol that anticipates conflicts between nodes trying to use a communication channel at the same time. CSMA/CD was designed to deal with signal collisions inside the transmission media and resolve the conflicts that arise from such collisions. One of the older networking standards, Ethernet, uses this protocol as its controlling standard.

To understand how the CSMA/CD protocol works, let's look at an example of two nodes sending messages through the network transmission medium. If one of the nodes of the network sends a message and no other node is transmiting a signal, then the first node will sense that the communication channel has no "carrier" and that it is free. In this case, the node places the message on the communication media, and the message is allowed to travel through the network to its destination.

If two nodes transmit a signal at the same time, the signals collide, raising the energy level on the communication channel. This signals that the messages or data being transmitted are interfering with each other. In this case, both nodes stop transmission and wait a random amount of time before the transmission starts again. Since each node waits a random period of time, they will begin transmitting at different times, with one of the nodes gaining access to the communication channel before the other node, and therefore sending its message. After the first message is sent, the second node will sense when the communication medium is free and transmit its message.

The CSMA/CD uses frames as its basic data format. The header of the frame, also called the preamble, synchronizes the transmitter and receiver. A control field is used to indicate the type of data being transmitted. In addition, a 32-bit CRC field is used to prevent errors from getting through the system, providing good error detection capability.

Ethernet, AT&T's Starlan, and IBM's PC Network are three networking products that use the CSMA/CD protocol. Ethernet was one of the first commercially popular LAN protocols. Ethernet was developed by XEROX corporation in the early 1970s and has become one of the most widely used networking systems in the design and implementation of LANs. One corporation that uses Ethernet as its main networking solution to connect its terminals and microcomputers to its servers is Digital Equipment Corporation.

Token Passing Protocol

The token protocol is based on a message (token) being placed on the communication circuit of a LAN. Here it circulates until acquired by a station that wishes to send a message. The station changes the token status from "free" to "busy" and attaches the message to the token.

In the network, the token moves from station to station, with each station examining the address contained in the token. When the message arrives at the receiving station, the station copies it. The receiving station passes an acknowledgment to the sending station. The sending station accepts the acknowledgment and changes the token status from "busy" to "free." At this stage, the other stations or nodes in the network know that they can send messages. The token then continues looping on the circuit until another station places a message in it to be delivered to another node in the network.

LAN Standards

As in the general discussion of networks, the type of protocol and access method used depends on which LAN standard a specific vendor follows. The standards used in the design of local area networks are set by the Institute of Electrical and Electronic Engineers (IEEE) 802 Standards Committee. These standards have the headings of the subcommittee that created them. As such, the most important of these are as follows:

1. 802.1
2. 802.2: LLC Protocol
3. 802.3: CSMA/CD Baseband Bus
4. 802.4: Token Passing Bus
5. 802.5: Token Passing Ring
6. 802.6: MAN

These standards are used by equipment manufacturers to ensure that their equipment is compatible with any other equipment that is manufactured by other vendors, but follows the standards. In addition, it gives LAN implementors a frame of reference from which to work as they use different vendors to build their networks.

802.1

The 802.1 is known as the highest-level interface standard. This specification is the least well defined because it involves a lot of interfacing with other networks and some of the specifications are still under consideration.

802.2: LLC Protocol

The 802.2, or LLC Protocol, is equivalent to the second layer of the OSI model and was described previously in this chapter. It provides point-to-point link control between devices at the protocol level. Many of the applications designed for data on LANs use the 802.2 standard so that they can interface with the other layers of the OSI model.

802.3: CSMA/CD Baseband Bus

The 802.3 is known as the carrier sense multiple access/collision detection (CSMA/CD) baseband bus. It describes the techniques by which any device on a bus can transmit when the medium interface determines that no other device is already transmitting.

This type of LAN uses coaxial cable or twisted pair wire as the transmission medium. At the physical level, this standard also defines the types of connectors and media that can be used.

The 802.3 standard is based on research originally done by the Xerox Corporation. Xerox called this type of local area network Ethernet. It is among the most popular and is widely used.

802.4: Token Passing Bus

The 802.4, or token passing bus, describes a method of operation where each device on a bus topology transmits only when it receives a token. The token is passed in a user-predetermined sequence and guarantees network access to all users. Since the bus topology does not provide a natural sequence of stations, each node is assigned a sequence number, and the token is passed from one station to another following the sequence numbers assigned to the stations.

802.5: Token Passing Ring

The 802.5, or token passing ring, is the mechanism utilized on IBM's Token-Ring LAN. It uses a token to pass messages between workstations as outlined previously. Several types of cables can be used for token ring LANs, but twisted pair and coaxial cable are the most commonly used.

802.6: MAN

The 802.6, or MAN, is the metropolitan area network standard. The specifications were developed to create standards for networks whose stations were more than five kilometers apart. The criteria include standards for transmitting data, voice, and video.

General Installation of a LAN

Once the topology and vendor of the local area network are selected and the network distribution is designed, the next step in the LAN evolution is the installation (see next chapter). The type and amount of personnel required for the installation of the LAN depend on the size, type, and scope of the LAN itself. However, they all share some common characteristics. Some of these characteristics are as follows:

1. Most LANs use a personal computer as the basic client.

2. Most LANs use one or several fast computers as dedicated servers.

3. All clients have to be provided with an interface card that allows the client computer to become an active member of the network.

4. All hardware in the LAN needs to be protected.

5. Although each LAN operating system is different in how it works and is installed, they all require a network profile to be created and maintained.

6. All users must log in to the network to have access to networking services.

7. All networks have legal issues regarding the use of software that must be dealt with.

These characteristics are the same for all LAN implementations. Therefore, the next section covers the LAN installation process in a general format, in order to be applicable to as many LAN configurations as possible. The student is reminded that, although the processes outlined below may seem simplistic, network installation is a complex task that requires thorough preparation prior to installation. Therefore, before installation of the network takes place, the installers will need to follow a system development cycle or approach using systems analysis and design techniques as they are explained in the next chapter. Failure to follow these guidelines will most likely result in a network with poor performance or many other anomalies that will make the LAN unsuccessful.

Installing the LAN Hardware

Most LANs have what is called a LAN kit. It consists of the network interface cards, communication medium cables, and LAN operating system. Assuming that a complete LAN kit is available, the first step is to install the NIC in each microcomputer that is going to be part of the LAN. The NIC is installed in one of the expansion slots inside the machine. The NIC will be responsible for all the network communications between the client computer and the rest of the system. For this purpose, it has a unique address that identifies the client system to any other devices that are part of the LAN.

In many cases the NIC already has a unique address "burned in" by its manufacturer. If the NIC's address was set at the factory, the NIC can be installed as is. Otherwise, a set of dip switches on the NIC must be set to a combination that has not already been used on the LAN. It is suggested that each NIC on the network follow a sequence. Then if something goes wrong during the operation of the network it will be easier to identify problems.

After the NIC is installed, each microcomputer must be connected to other microcomputers on the LAN. The most common way of doing this is to connect each microcomputer in a daisy chain configuration but this will vary according to the type of topology chosen. The first and the last of the microcomputers are given an ending plug called a terminator. This indicates to the network that there are no more nodes in the network beyond these points. The cable used to connect the microcomputers can be optical fiber, coaxial, or twisted pair cable, depending on the requirements of the LAN and anticipated upgrades.

In a general format, that is all the basic hardware installation requirements. Of course, the level of difficulty in performing the above installation will depend on the wiring system layout and the distances involved. But, regardless of the neatness of the cable arrangement, once the NIC is installed properly and each NIC is connected with the right cabling system, the network is ready to accept the software. However, one important aspect that shouldn't be ignored is the protection of the hardware that has just been installed.

Protecting the Hardware

Electronic equipment is succeptible to power sags, power surges, and electrical noise. As described in previous chapters, a power surge is a sudden increase in power, which in many cases can destroy the microchips that make up the computer circuitry. A power sag is a loss of electrical power, and it can force a computer reset or a network shutdown. Information stored in RAM prior to a power sag is lost, and, in some situations, a network can't automatically rebuild itself to continue operating. Electronic noise is interference from other types of electrical devices such as air conditioners, transformers, lights, and other electrical equipment.

Several devices can protect computers against the problems just outlined. These are power surge protectors, power line conditioners (PLCs), and uninterruptible power supplies (UPSs). The type of device used depends on the equipment to protect, the importance of the data stored in the equipment, and economics.

Power surge protectors are the least expensive of all protecting devices. They range in price from a few dollars to approximately $150. They protect equipment from short duration electrical surges (called transients) and from voltage spikes. Their price depends on the type of materials used to make up the device and how fast these components react to a power surge. Devices with faster reaction time are generally more expensive. Whenever possible, the protector with the fastest reaction time should be purchased. Power surge protectors are normally found at the users' workstations.

Power line conditioners (PLCs) are more expensive than surge protectors. They protect equipment against electrical noise and interference from other equipment. Most PLCs also protect against surges and sags in electrical power. They tend to filter out electrical noise while maintaining power within acceptable levels for the computer to operate. Many user workstations and servers use PLCs to guard against temporary and very short duration power spikes and sags.

Uninterruptible power supplies allow a system to continue functioning for several minutes even when there is a total loss of power. Normally, the additional running time provided by the UPS is enough to safely shut the system or network down; on many occasions, the time is long enough that power is restored without having to shut the system down. They should be used by all servers to protect users' data and the network from a sudden and unexpected loss of power. Additionally, a UPS protects against power surges and electrical noise.

All network servers should be protected by a UPS, and at a minimum, each workstation should have a power surge protector. This will prevent the most common network problems associated with disruptions in the power required to keep the network operational. Once the hardware is installed and properly protected, the next step is to install the LAN software.

Installing the LAN Software

To install the LAN software, the network operating system must be installed, a station profile for each microcomputer needs to be created, and a profile for each microcomputer logging onto the LAN also needs to be created. The process required to install the network operating system varies according to the type and size of the LAN.

On networks such as Novell's, the network operating system replaces the workstation's native operating system. This involves reformatting the hard disk of the computer that is going to act as the file server. In this case, installing the network operating system consists of following instructions displayed on the screen after placing the network system disk in the drive and turning the computer on. The procedure consists of loading the LAN kit disks in the sequence requested by the installation module. The entire process is normally self-explanatory after the first instructions are displayed on the screen.

On smaller networks, the network operating system is loaded when the user turns on the microcomputer, or it is done automatically by using a batch file that is executed automatically. The network operating system manuals that come with the LAN kit indicate which files must be placed in batch files and which files must reside on the file server.

The Network Profile

A network profile must be established for each microcomputer on the LAN. The profile indicates the microcomputer's resources that are available for other network users. This profile is set up once when the network is installed, but it can be changed later if necessary.

The profile contains information about user access privileges and password requirements. Additionally, it indicates which devices are printers, which hard disks are shared, and the access mechanisms for these. For example, if a user has a hard disk called C: and it is not included in the network profile, this disk is not accessible to other users.

Also, each user has a profile which adds security to the LAN. Each device has a name code and each user has a name code. During normal execution of the network operating system, only users with the correct codes and security access can use specific devices.

Login to the Network

The last step in installing the local area network software is the login process. Assuming there are no hardware problems, each microcomputer on the LAN has, in its autoexecutable batch file, a copy of the network files required to incorporate the microcomputer into the LAN. When the computer is booted, these files take over the operation of the microcomputer hardware and make a connection to the file server through the NIC and the network cable.

The first network request found by the user is a login ID that is unique to each user, and then a password which may or may not be unique to each user. In some set-ups, the password may be requested from each user. If the user profile software on the server acknowledges an authorized user, the microcomputer becomes active on the network and can perform any functions authorized for the specific machine.

Remote LAN Software

Remote software offers microcomputer users the ability to operate programs and access peripherals on a remote system by using a modem. In addition, remote LAN software allows users to have node-to-node communications so users can share networked applications.

This type of software can be used for technical support, group conferencing, and training. Also, network managers can control network functions from locations other than a network station or the file server. Additionally, technicians at remote locations can access a LAN experiencing problems. This is done to conduct diagnostic tests and software repairs.

Legal Issues

Software installed on a LAN needs to meet certain legal criteria. Some network administrators feel that a single legally purchased copy of an application can be placed on a file server and made available to all users. This is illegal. An application software program can be used on a LAN only when a site license exists for the package. Furthermore, the number of users accessing the application program needs to be limited to the number of users stipulated in the licensing agreement. Honesty and integrity are the best paths to follow in this area.

Several management tools are available to aid network managers in enforcing the proper and legal use of software on the network. Among these, metering software is the most widely used. Metering software can be used to monitor the number of users who are running a specific application. The network manager can instruct the software to lock out of the application any users who will create a potential legal conflict. When a user releases the application back into the system, a new user can be added to the total number that have access to the program. Many of the metering programs can perform this process automatically. Additionally, many network aware programs have this type of capability built in.

The Network Server

Since most LANs that use PCs as the basic client use some type of server to provide networking functions to users, it is important to discuss some of the characteristics that make a good server. As mentioned before, in many LANs the server is another microcomputer that contains large hard disk storage and a fast CPU. But the configuration of the server shouldn't be left to chance or given low priority. A poorly configured server can slow the response time of the network or require excessive maintenance.

Server Hardware

The primary function of a server is to provide a service to network users. Servers can provide files to users, printing, and communication services as well as other services. The most important server in a LAN is the file server. Because in most LANs all requests must be processed through the file server, it has a much higher workload than that of a typical stand-alone microcomputer. The stand-alone PC takes care of the needs of a single user. The file server takes care of the needs of all users on the network. Therefore, careful consideration must be given to the hardware that constitutes the file server.

First, a network designer needs to decide whether a dedicated or nondedicated file server is going to be used. Since a nondedicated server functions as a file server and as a user workstation, a dedicated server will outperform a nondedicated server. For example, assume that an MS-DOS-based PC is being considered as the server, and NetWare is the operating system. If the clone is not 100 percent compatible with the IBM PC, interrupts used by NetWare may conflict with the software.

For large networks, the file server should be a dedicated server, and the fastest and most efficient hardware should be considered. Also, to avoid execution problems, a new dedicated server should be compatible with the network software.

Since the file server is just a computer with some added hardware and software, the main components of the server that will affect speed are the central processing unit, the hard disk and controller, RAM caching, hard disk caching, and the random access memory installed on the server.

The Central Processing Unit (CPU)

The central processing unit performs the calculations and logical operations required of all computers. All programs running on a computer system must be executed by the CPU.

In the personal computer market, the CPU classifies the computer. In the IBM market area, the original IBM PC had a CPU that consisted of 16 bits with a bus consisting of 8 bits. This meant that 16 bits were used to perform the calculations, and data moved inside the computer 8 bits at a time. The processor used in the original IBM PC was the Intel 8088. When the IBM AT was introduced, it had a 32-bit CPU with a bus of 16 bits. Today, the fastest IBM microcomputers and compatibles use a CPU and data bus, both of which process 32 bits. Today, the processors of choice are the 80386 and the 80486, but recently announced faster Intel processors may change user choices in the future. One good alternative for a server is one where the processor can be upgraded in the future. This provides the best solution for the money at present, but preserves the investment in the hardware by providing an upgrade path.

The main difference between the CPUs in the market is the speed of processing that they are capable of. The size of the data bus and the CPU's clock speed govern the speed of a microcomputer. The bus is the pathway that connects the CPU with the network interface card and other peripherals attached to the microcomputer. The size of the bus determines how much data can be transmitted in each cycle of the CPU's clock. A larger bus size can move data faster and provide better performance.

The CPU's clock speed is the other factor that affects performance. The clock speed determines how frequently cycles occur inside the computer, and therefore how fast data can be transmitted. The clock speed is measured in cycles-per-second or Hertz (Hz). The original IBM PC had a clock speed of 4.77 MHz. Recently produced microcomputers have clock speeds of 50 MHz and higher.

Whenever installing a new file server, a computer with a faster CPU clock and the largest possible data bus should be utilized. Of course, the computer with the faster CPU and the larger bus is going to be more costly. For small networks, clock speeds of 8 to 20 MHz and a data bus of 16 to 32 bits should be considered. For large networks, clock speeds of 25 MHz or more and a data bus of 32 bits should be considered. However, with the price of high-end CPUs dropping all the time, even small networks will eventually be able to utilize servers with CPU speeds of 50 MHz at the price of yesterday's 20 MHz CPUs.

The Hard Disk and Controller

A fast computer with a slow hard disk will deteriorate the performance of a LAN. The hard disk is a mechanical device that contains metal platters where data is stored for later retrieval. The hard disk controller is a circuit board that directs the operation of the hard disk.

As data moves inside the server at speeds of up to 10 million bits per second, data moves to and from the hard disk at speeds of approximately 1/20th of that in the best of situations. This can create a bottleneck that slows the LAN for all of its users. A fast hard disk and controller are essential to the performance of a LAN.

The average time required for the disk to find and read a unit of information is called the access speed. Most drives today have access speeds that range from a low of 9 milliseconds to a high of 80 milliseconds.

Hard disk controllers come in four different categories with varying performance, and they vary in the size of hard disk that can be attached. These are the categories:

1. ST506. Standard on most IBM ATs and compatibles. This drive controller has a transfer rate of approximately 7 megabits per second and supports a maximum of two drives, each with a size up to 150 megabytes.

2. ESDI. Enhanced Small Device Interface. This is standard on many 80386 based computers. The controller has a transfer rate of 10 megabits per second and supports a maximum of four disk drives. Typical drives have 300 megabytes.

3. SCSI. Small Computer System Interface. This controller has data transfers of approximately 10 megabits per second and supports up to 32 disk drives. This type of controller supports drives having a capacity of 700 megabytes and more.

4. IDE. Intelligent Drive Electronics. IDE controllers combine features of the other three interfaces and add additional benefits. They are fast like ESDI drives, intelligent like SCSI drives, and look like standard AT ST506 interfaces to the system. With capacities of up to 300 megabytes and even larger disks, this type of controller is becoming increasingly popular. They suffer from a lack of standardization, but there are new proposals in the market that attempt to create a better standard for this type of drive.

In addition to considering the speed of the hard disk and the hard disk controller, drives with enough size to support future upgrades and expansion should be considered.

Random Access Memory

Random access memory (RAM) is used by the file server to store information for the CPU. The speed of the RAM installed in the CPU determines how fast data is transferred to the CPU when it makes a request from RAM. If the speed of RAM is too slow for the type of CPU in use, problems will arise and LAN deterioration will take place. Care should always be taken to match the speed of RAM to the speed of the CPU clock for optimum performance.

Some network operating systems, such as NetWare, use RAM as buffer areas for print jobs and for disk caching. Disk caching is a method by which the computer will hold in memory the most frequently and recently used portions of files, increasing the efficiency of the input/output process.

If a file server has only the minimum amount of RAM to run the network operating system, performance will deteriorate as users are added to the LAN, due to the increased access to the hard disk by the file server. Adding extra memory will increase the performance of the network by increasing the efficiency of the input/output operations.

Server Software

To effectively provide file-sharing services, the software that controls the file server must provide security, concurrent access controls, access optimizing, reliability, transparent access to the file server and peripherals attached to the server, and interfaces to other networks.

The file server software should provide user access to those elements necessary to perform job functions, while restricting access to items for which a user does not have access privileges. This means that some users do not know that more files exist. Other users are allowed to read them, and still others are allowed to delete or modify them.

Concurrent access controls allow users to access files in a prioritized fashion using volume, file, and record locking. These controls allow a file to be changed before another user reads the information. Otherwise, a user may be reading data that is no longer current.

Access optimization is achieved by having administrative tools in the LAN that allow for the fine tuning of the network. This provides users with the best possible response time while safeguarding the contents of users' files. Some of these tools are fault tolerance, file recovery, LAN to mainframe communications, disk caching, and multiple disk channels.

The software in the file server and the server itself need to have a continuous and consistent mode of operation if users are to trust the network. In some situations, multiple servers offer each other backup services and increase the reliability of the LAN.

Transparent access means that using the LAN should be a natural extension of the user knowledge of the individual computer system. LAN users are typically not computer experts. Access to the file server should be no more difficult than accessing a stand-alone computer. This includes accessing peripheral devices such as printers, plotters, and scanners. Additionally, often the LAN needs to interface with other LANs. The server software should have extensions that allow this to take place.

LAN Security

As the network grows in size and importance, security will become one of the major concerns for the network administrator. The threats that can affect the LAN come from unauthorized users gaining access to sensitive volumes or data files, computer viruses corrupting users' files and programs, accidental erasure of data and programs by authorized users, power failures during an important transaction, breakdown of storage media, and others. Although security mechanisms are explored in other sections of this book, the following is a general overview of some security measures that are common practice for many network administrators.

Volume Security

One of the most important functions of LAN software is the security of the network against accidental or unauthorized access. One methodology is to split the file server's hard disk into sections, or volumes. Each volume can be given public, private, or shared status. If a volume is made public, then everyone on the network has access to its contents. Private volumes can be accessed only by single users for read or write functions. Finally, shared volumes allow all authorized users to have read and write access to the contents of the volume. This type of security is set up by the network manager using network management tools and then it is enforced by the network operating system or NOS, every time a user logs into the network. Additionally, the use of script or login files can help in establishing better security controls. These types of files are executed every time a user logs into the network. They contain a combination of commands that takes the user to a specific path and locks him or her out of other areas of the network. Some file servers have more sophisticated security levels than the ones mentioned above. Network operating systems, such as Novell's NetWare, allow not only volume security attributes, but extend the security attributes to individual files on any volume.

Locking

Another type of security employed by LANs is volume, file, and record locking. Volume locking is a technique by which a user can lock all other users out of a volume until he or she is through with the volume. Some networks allow locking to be placed at the file level. Others allow locking at the record level. Record locking is preferred under normal circumstances, since a user can control one record while other users have access to the rest of the records and the rest of the network files.

Others

Additional types of security that LANs can provide are data encryption, password protection to volumes and files, and physical or electronic keys that must be inserted into a network security device to gain access. Also, antivirus protection software and network management programs provide network managers with additional resources to help protect users and network files.

Summary

Local area networks are networks that connect devices that are confined to a small geographical area. The actual distance that a LAN spans depends on specific implementations. LANs are implemented in order to transfer data among users in the network or to share resources among users.

A LAN implementation can provide high-speed data transfer capability to all users, without a system operator to facilitate the transmission process. Even when connecting a LAN to a wide area network that covers thousands of miles, data transfer between users of the network is time effective and, in most cases, problem free. The other reason for implementing a LAN is to share hardware and software resources among users of the network.

There are many LAN applications. Some of the more common types of applications are office automation, factory automation, education, computer-aided design, and computer-aided manufacturing.

When a LAN is purchased, the following characteristics should be kept in mind. LANs can provide the user with

1. Flexibility
2. Speed
3. Reliability
4. Hardware and software sharing
5. Transparent interface
6. Adaptability
7. Access to other LANs and WANs
8. Security
9. Centralized management
10. Private ownership of the LAN

Two major items must be considered when planning or installing a LAN: the network hardware components and the network software. There are three major categories of devices that make up the hardware components of a local area network. These are the server, the LAN communication system, and the workstations.

A file server is a computer with some added hardware and software. The main components of the server that will affect speed are the central processing unit, the hard disk and disk controller, and the random access memory installed in the server.

To effectively provide file-sharing services, the software that controls the file server must provide security, concurrent access controls, access optimizing, reliability, transparent access to the file server and peripherals attached to the server, and interfaces to other networks.

LAN servers are computers on the network that are accessible to network users. They contain resources that they "serve" to users who request the service. The most common type of server is the file server. Most LANs have at least one file server, and many have multiple file servers. The file server contains software applications and data files that are provided to users upon request.

When two or more computers are connected on a network, a special cable and a network interface board are required in each computer. Connect the server to the cable and then connect the cable to the board. Most microcomputers are not equipped with an interface port that can be connected to a second microcomputer for networking purposes (except the Macintosh). As a result, a network interface board (NIC) or network adapter must be installed in the microcomputer.

The processes that take place in the hardware devices of a LAN must be controlled by software. The software comes in the form of the network operating system. One of the most widely used network operating systems is NetWare, which is provided by Novell, Inc.

The network operating system controls the operation of the file server, and it makes the network resources accessible and easy to use. It manages server security and provides the network administrators with the tools to control user access to the network and file structure.

Network topologies come in many different configurations. The bus, ring, and star topologies are used extensively in LAN implementations.

The LAN protocol is the set of rules by which two machines talk to each other. It must be present in addition to the LAN hardware and the network operating system. Some communication protocols used in LANs are the logical link control (LLC) protocol established by the Institute of Electrical and Electronic Engineers (IEEE) 802 Standards Committee, the carrier sense multiple access/collision detection (CSMA/CD) protocol, and the token passing protocol. The type of protocol and access methodology used depends on which LAN standard a specific vendor decides to follow.

Questions

1. What is a LAN?
2. What types of applications can be found on most LANs?
3. Describe the major characteristics of LANs.
4. What is a file server?
5. What is the function of the network interface card (NIC)?
6. What is the purpose of the network operating system?
7. What are protocols?
8. What is the LAN communication system?
9. Briefly explain two different LAN topologies.
10. What is the 802.2 IEEE standard?
11. What is token passing?
12. Describe three characteristics that affect file server efficiency.
13. Describe four characteristics of server software.
14. Why is it important to have a fast hard disk and controller on a file server?

Projects

Objective

This project provides hands-on knowledge of software that allows remote access of a personal computer from another personal computer. This type of software is becoming more common in the workplace to provide assistance to users from remote locations. It also helps users run programs that reside in computers located at remote sites. It can also be used to transfer files between computers that have incompatible disk drives.

Project 1. Remote Access to a PC

There are situations in the workplace in which, for instructional or error-checking needs, it would be desirable to control the functions of one personal computer (host) from another personal computer (remote). The remote computer can be located next to the host computer or miles away in a different geographical location.

To perform the operation, the host and remote computers need to run special software that allows the host to become a "slave" or extension of the remote system. Several commercial programs are available to perform such functions. One of these programs is a shareware program called The TANDEM Remote System (TTRS).

The TANDEM Remote System is shareware software. It can be acquired free of charge in most cases from local user groups or dealers who sell public domain software at nominal prices. The software can be tried, and, if found satisfactory, the user is expected to send a contribution back to the author of the program. In return, the author provides, in most cases, program documentation and enhancements to the software.

The main components of TTRS are two programs, TANDEM.EXE and TMODEM.EXE. TANDEM.EXE is the host program and TMODEM.EXE is the remote program. The function of the system varies slightly depending on whether the remote and host systems are connected directly with a null modem or through telephone lines.

Direct Connection. Before the remote computer can access the host system, the proper hardware must be connected to both computers using the standard RS-232 port. Follow these steps to see if you have all the required items:

1. Write down the port number (COM1 or COM2) that you are going to use on the host computer.

2. Write down the port number (COM1 or COM2) that you are going to use on the remote computer.

3. Using a null modem cable (see Chapter 3 projects), connect the two computers using serial port 1 (COM1).

4. Boot up both systems.

5. Make two copies of the original software. One copy will be used in the remote system and the other in the host computer.

With the TTRS diskettes in the computers' A drives or installed on their hard disks you will need to launch the TMODEM program in the remote computer and TANDEM in the host computer. The command lines are as follows.

For the remote computer the command line is

d:>TMODEM port, baud-rate, , D

> d:> is the drive where the program is located
>
> port is the serial port
>
> baud-rate is the baud rate of the serial port
>
> D indicates that the two computers are connected directly

For the host computer the command line is

> d:>TANDEM port, baud-rate, , D
>
> d:> is the drive where the program is located
>
> port is the serial port
>
> baud-rate is the baud rate of the serial port
>
> D indicates that the two computers are connected directly

6. In the host computer type TANDEM 1, 9600, , D
7. In the remote computer type TMODEM 1, 9600, , D

At this point a password will be required. The passwords available are in a file called PASSWRDS.DAT that is on the original distribution disks.

8. Type any of the passwords provided on the original disk.

Telephone line access. To access the host computer through the telephone lines, a modem must be present at the host site and at the remote computer. You may want to refer to projects in previous chapters that show you how to connect a modem to a microcomputer.

1. Write down the port number (COM1 or COM2) that you are going to use on the host computer.
2. Write down the port number (COM1 or COM2) that you are going to use on the remote computer.
3. Make sure that the host system is attached to a modem set in the "answer" mode, and that the modem is connected to a telephone line.
4. Make sure that the remote system is attached to a modem set in the "originate" mode, and that the modem is connected to a telephone line.
5. Boot up both systems.
6. Make two copies of the original software. One copy will be used on the remote system and the other on the host computer.

With the TTRS diskettes in the computers' A drives or installed on their hard disks, you will need to launch the TMODEM program in the remote computer and TANDEM in the host computer. The command lines are as follows.

For the remote computer the command line is

> d:>TMODEM port, baud-rate

d:> is the drive where the program is located

port is the serial port

baud-rate is the baud rate of the serial port

For the host computer the command line is

d:>TANDEM port, baud-rate

d:> is the drive where the program is located

port is the serial port

baud-rate is the baud rate of the serial port

7. Assuming that the host's modem is connected to COM1 and that your modem can transmit with a speed of 1200 baud, in the host computer type TANDEM 1, 1200.

8. Assuming that the remote's modem is connected to COM1 and that your modem can transmit with a speed of 1200 baud, in the remote computer type TMODEM 1, 1200.

9. The remote modem program will ask you to enter the phone number of the host modem. Type the number correctly without spaces or extra characters. If the connection is successful you will see a CONNECT message on the screen.

For Both Cases. At this point a password will be required. The passwords available are in a file called PASSWRDS.DAT that is on the original distribution disks.

10. Type any of the passwords provided on the original disk.

At this point the two computers should be connected. Under the TTRS control several commands can be used to control the host system, run programs on the host from the remote computer, and transfer files. These commands are as follows:

CLS. Clears the screen.

DIR. Displays directories of the host computer. It uses the same specifications as the DOS DIR.

DOS. Takes you to the operating system. This allows the remote computer to run programs that reside on the host computer.

BYE. Hangs up the phone and waits for the next call.

SHUTDOWN. Terminates TANDEM on the host computer from a remote location.

CHAT. Provides a clear screen so that the remote computer can communicate with someone at the host computer.

SEND. Transfers files between the host and the remote computers.

To transfer files between the host and the remote, the command line is as follows:

TANDEM:>SEND direction d:FILE.EXT [d:FILE.EXT]

The direction parameter uses the symbol ">" to indicate "to" or the symbol "<" to indicate "from." In addition, the words "HOST" and "REMOTE" are used to establish the direction in which the file is to be transmitted. For example, if a file named DATA.DAT resides on the host main directory and it needs to be transferred to the remote computer and placed in a subdirectory named C:\DATAFILE, the command line is as follows:

11. TANDEM:>SEND   >REMOTE   C:\DATA.DAT
     C:\DATAFILE\DATA.DAT

This procedure can be used to transfer files between desktop computers and portable computers.

To run a program from the remote computer that resides on the host computer the process is as follows:

12. Type DOS and press the ENTER key.

You will be taken to DOS and any DOS commands you type will affect the host system but will be displayed on the remote computer.

13. Type the name of the program that you wish to run and press the ENTER key.

14. When you are ready to return to the TANDEM environment, exit the program. Type EXIT, and press the ENTER key.

The TANDEM Remote System is useful in many situations in the work environment. It can be used to run demonstrations simultaneously on two computers, to run programs that reside at the office from home, and to provide assistance to users at remote locations.

Network Design Fundamentals

Objectives

After completing this chapter you will
1. Be familiar with the life cycle of network design and implementation.
3. Understand the importance of response time, network modeling, message analysis, and geographic location in network design.
4. Know the different types of security threats to a data communication network.
5. Know some standard controls for unauthorized access to a network by users and by computer viruses.
6. Understand the basic principles for developing a disaster recovery plan.
7. Understand the basic principles for developing a network management plan.

Key Terms

Computer Virus	Disaster Plan
Encryption	Feasibility Study
Life Cycle	Network Management
Network Modeling	Network Security
Password/ID	Response Time

Introduction

Designing or upgrading a network is a complex and time consuming task that must follow standard system analysis methods. The typical planning methodology includes following the system life cycle and its inherent phases. Although the phases are not always followed in the sequence provided, it is important that network designers follow the life cycle process if the result is to be successful. This chapter describes the different phases of system analysis and network design. Also, some specialized topics of network design, such as response time and network modeling, are explored.

The introduction of computer processing, centralized storage, and communication networks has increased the need for securing data stored in these systems. This emphasis manifests itself in the increase of available techniques and methods for detecting and deterring intrusions into the network by unauthorized users. Several types of network security enforcement techniques are explained. Additionally, a discussion of viruses is presented.

An additional measure of network security is the implementation of a network disaster recovery plan. The plan must be implemented within the framework of the system analysis approach. Several ideas on how to design a recovery plan are presented in the chapter.

The Life Cycle of a Network

The life cycle of a network is an important planning consideration because of inevitable technological changes that will have to be dealt with during the development and operation of a network system. Each network is a representation of the technology at the time of its design and implementation. Eventually, the network will become obsolete. New technologies and services will emerge, making it cost effective to replace outdated equipment and software with newer, more powerful, and less expensive technology.

During its life cycle, a network passes through the phases outlined in Fig. 7-1:

1. The feasibility study involves the subphases of problem definition and investigation. The problem definition attempts to find the problems that exist in the organization that caused management to initiate the study. The investigation subphase involves gathering input data to develop a precise definition of the present data communication conditions and to uncover problems.

2. The analysis phase uses the data gathered in the feasibility study to identify the requirements that the network must meet in order to have a successful implementation.

3. During the design phase, all components of the network are defined so their acquisition can be made.

4. The implementation phase consists of the installation of the hardware and software that make up the network system. Additionally, during this phase all documentation and training materials are developed.

5. During the maintenance and the upgrade phase, the network is kept operational and fine-tuned by network operations personnel. Additionally, updates of software and hardware are performed to keep the network operating efficiently and effectively.

The life cycle concept can be applied to network design as a whole or in part. As a network moves through these phases, the planner becomes more constrained in the alternatives available for increasing data capacity, in the applications available, and in dealing with operational problems that may arise. These restrictions are the result of increased costs and the difficulty in changing the operational procedures of the network. In addition, although the phases of the life cycle are presented here as a series of steps, the designer may have to go back through one or more phases of the design process. This feedback mechanism is important in order to incorporate concepts or ideas that may surface during the design and installation of the network.

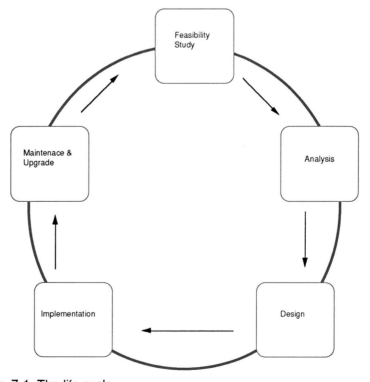

Fig. 7-1. The life cycle.

The Feasibility Study

The feasibility study is performed in order to define the existing problem clearly and to determine whether a network is operationally feasible for the type of organization that it plans to serve. This is not the place to determine the type of network that may be implemented. Rather, the designer needs to fully understand the problem or problems that are perceived by the management personnel who initiated the request for the study. This phase of the life cycle can be subdivided into problem definition, problem analysis, and solution determination.

Problem definition is the first step in the feasibility study. It is important to distinguish between problems and solutions. If a solution is made part of the problem definition, analysis of alternative solutions becomes handicapped. The problems need to be analyzed to determine whether and how they may point to the formulation of a new network or the upgrade of an existing network. The investigation of the current system takes place by gathering input data from the personnel involved in the use of the network and from the personal observations of the designer.

Interviews with users help to develop a precise definition of current data processing needs and to identify current problems. This process emphasizes only the information that is relevant to the network planning and design process. Additionally, interviews involve personnel in the network design process, therefore facilitating its acceptance when the final product is implemented. This data-gathering process concentrates on terminal or workstation location, the current type of communication facilities and host computer systems, and the future data processing and communication requirements that network users expect.

Aside from the interviews with current or potential network users, technical reports and documents can provide insight into the operation of an existing network. Research can provide exact locations of workstations, multiplexers, gateways, transmission speeds, codes, and current network service and cost. This information complements the interviews of personnel. It is essential in order to determine where potential problems may arise and to provide an effective solution to the corporation.

When extensive on-site interviews and surveys are not economically feasible, questionnaires can be used to gather information. Questionnaires and survey techniques can be combined with follow-up interviews to gather and validate data about the existing network. This helps ensure the success of the final design. Field personnel must always be encouraged to participate fully in developing accurate and complete data and in providing ideas and insights that cannot be provided in questionnaires.

The third aspect of the feasibility study is to examine possible solutions to the problem definition, identify the best solution, and determine if it's realistic based on the gathered data. This analysis provides a "best-scenario" solution, the one that provides the best all-around method for dealing with the problem.

At the end of the feasibility study, a report is produced for management. The report should contain the following items:

1. Findings of the feasibility study

2. Alternative solutions in addition to the best possible solution

3. Reasons for continuing to the next phase of the process

4. If a realistic solution was not found, recommendations for another study and the methodology to follow in order to arrive at a feasible solution

Analysis

This phase encompasses the analysis of all data gathered during the investigative stage of the feasibility phase. The end result is a set of requirements for the final product. These requirements are approved by management and implemented by the designer or designers of the network.

The formulated requirements must relate computer applications and information systems to the needs for terminals, workstations, communication hardware and software, common-carrier services, data input/output locations, data generation, training, and how the data will be processed and used. As a result, the formulated requirements identify the work activities that will be automated and networked. They relate the activities to the information input/output, the medium of transmission, where and how the data resides, and the geographic location where the information must be generated and processed.

Since data communication networks serve many types of applications, the volume of information for all applications must be combined to determine the final network design. Analyzing the raw data acquired in the investigation section of the feasibility study helps identify the total data volume that must be moved by the network.

The final product of this phase is another document, sometimes called a functional specifications report, which includes the functions that must be performed by the network after it is implemented. The report can include the following sections:

1. Network identification and description

2. Benefits of proposed network

3. Current status of the organization and existing networks

4. Network operational description

5. Data security requirements

6. Applications available for this network

7. Response time

8. Anticipated reliability

9. Data communications load that the network will support

10. Geographic distribution of nodes

11. Documentation

12. Training

13. Network expected life

14. Reference materials used in preparing the report

Many other requirements besides these can be incorporated into the report, but they provide a good basis to work from. The number and complexity of the requirements will vary according to the type and size of network being recommended.

Design

The design phase of the life cycle is one of the longest phases. The outcome of this phase depends on the expectations of management and the economics of the corporation. At a minimum it will include a set of internal and external specifications. The internal specifications are the "blue-prints" of how the network operates, including modules used for building the network. The external specifications are the interfaces that the user will see when using the network. Both of these specifications may include data flow diagrams, logic diagrams, product models, prototypes, and results from network modeling.

At this point, designers should have a detailed description of all network requirements. These requirements should now be prioritized by dividing them into mandatory requirements, desirable requirements, and wish list requirements.

The mandatory requirements are those that must be present if the network is to be operational and effective. The desirable requirements are items that can improve the effectiveness of the network and the work of the users, but can be deferred until later if other priorities warrant it. The wish list requirements are those provided by workers who feel that such items could help them increase their individual productivity. However, when implementing wish list requirements, the network designer needs to be careful. Small increases in productivity might require a large cost, and the money might be expended more effectively in other areas.

The design phase will also indicate how the individual network components will be procured and will outline the procedures for installation and testing of the network. The final document produced during this phase will become the "blueprint" for the remaining phases of the life cycle. Several items that network designers will have to address during this phase are response time, a network model, geographic scope of the network, message analysis, and some software and hardware considerations.

Response Time

One of the most important requirements in network design is response time. Response time is the time that expires between sending an inquiry from a workstation or terminal and receiving the response back at the workstation. The total response time of a network is comprised of delay times that occur at the workstation end when transmitting a message, the time required for the message to get to a host, the host processing time, the transmission back from the host to the workstation, and finally the time required for the workstation to display the information to the user. Usually, a shorter response time requirement will dictate a larger cost of the system. A typical cost versus response time curve is found in Fig. 7-2. The graph shows that the cost of a network is exponentially proportional to the average response time required.

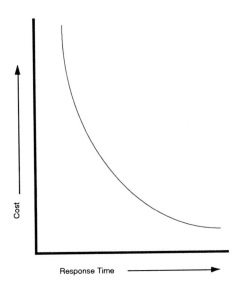

Fig. 7-2. Cost vs response time graph.

To find the response time for a network that has yet to be implemented, the designers should look at statistics from other operating networks with similar work loads, a comparable number of users, and similar applications being run. Although the scenario may be difficult to find, comparing similar networks will provide statistics with approximate average response times and some indication of pitfalls for the network being designed. In situations where a similar network is not available, predicting techniques must be used. These techniques are based on network modeling and simulation methods.

Simulation is a technique for modeling the behavior of the network. The response time is viewed as an average of the time elapsed for certain discrete events. (Fig. 7-3 depicts some of the causes for increasing response times.)

Fig. 7-3. Reasons for increasing response time.

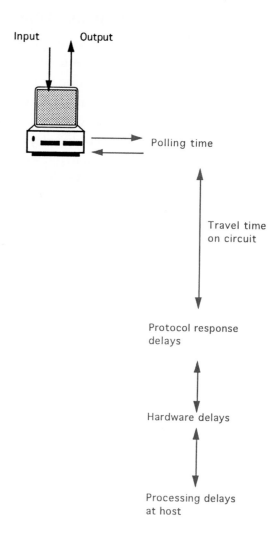

Simulation programs are written to emulate a series of real-life events, and the elapsed time for each event is added up to provide a measure of the response time and behavior of the network.

Network Modeling

One of the major uses of the data-gathering process is in developing a network topology. The load (the number of messages that need to be transmitted) and site data are used as input for network modeling programs. Network modeling programs use mathematical models that simulate a network.

The network design alternatives are mathematically modeled for performance and then for cost, using public network tariffs and the geographically distributed peak loads found during the investigation step of the feasibility study. The data that makes up the model can be placed in several commercially available software programs to better understand the behavior of the network under certain conditions. The model created, along with the simulation tool, provides an overall performance capacity and cost analysis for each network alternative. However, simulating a network is a complex task that requires a thorough understanding of networks and of the simulation program and its limitations. The advantage of having a model that can be manipulated electronically is that "What if" questions can be asked of the model, and the effect of any changes can be visualized and understood before any money and effort are spent in setting up the network. A good model will allow designers to find weaknesses in the design plan and to anticipate any problems that may appear during installation or operation of the network.

The output from the model is the basis for recommendations of a particular network design to be implemented. All aspects of the network should be included in these recommendations. Some of these factors are least-cost alternative, short response time, technical feasibility, maintainability, and reliability.

Once the overall network topology has been determined, the model is manually fine-tuned to achieve the levels of operational performance required. The modeled network may place hardware in locations where it is not cost effective, due to the time and cost of maintaining such equipment. In this case it would be better to incur the additional cost and place the items in a location where they are more accessible for maintenance purposes.

Network modeling tools are limited in their abilities to analyze the different data communication requirements. They normally model one aspect of the system, such as the speed link between workstations and servers. To model the other aspects of the network, subsequent iterations of the model are performed. The results of each analysis are combined to produce a final network configuration.

Geographic Scope

To better understand the geographical scope of the network, several maps may need to be generated. The geographic maps of the scope of the network should be prepared after the model is created and tuned. The geographic scope of the network can be local, city-wide, national, or international. Normally, a map is prepared showing the location of individual nodes. The individual items that connect each node, such as gateways and concentrators, do not have to be indicated on the map (see Fig. 7-4).

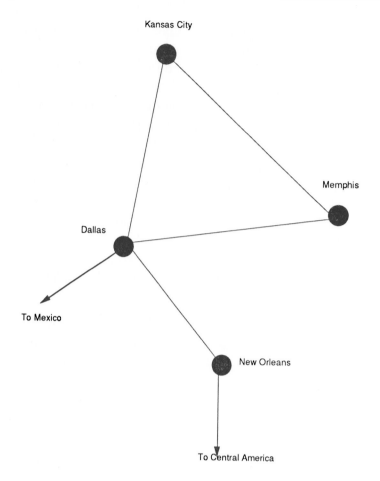

Fig. 7-4. Geographic scope of the network

The next map to be prepared indicates the location of nodes within the boundaries of the country. It needs to show the different states or provinces that will be connected, and a line must show each connection from state to state.

The third type of map that may be required shows the location of the individual cities that are part of the network. The map should contain lines that connect each city in the network in the same logical fashion that the actual communication lines are distributed.

The last map shows the local facilities and the terminal or workstation location. It can be as wide as the boundaries of a city or as specific as the individual buildings and offices that are part of the network. Individual network connectivity items such as concentrators and multiplexers are not required to be displayed on the map. It is possible that, at this stage, the location of these items is not yet determined.

Message Analysis

Message analysis involves identifying the message type that will be transmitted or received at each terminal or workstation. The message attributes are also identified, including the number of bytes for each message. Message length and message volume identification are critical to determine the volume of messages that will be transmitted through the network.

The daily traffic volume is sometimes segmented into hourly traffic to provide the designers with the peak traffic hours. This information is used to identify problems with data traffic during peak hours.

It is important to note that most networks are designed based on average traffic volumes instead of traffic volume during peak hours. For most organizations it is not cost effective to purchase a network based solely on volume during peak hours.

Software/Hardware Considerations

The type of software purchased for the network will determine the operation of the network. It will specify whether the network will perform asynchronous or synchronous communications, full-duplex or half-duplex communications, and the speed of transmissions. Additionally, the software will determine the types of networks that can be accessed by the network being designed.

The network designer should select a protocol that is compatible with the OSI seven-layer model and one that can grow as the network grows within the organization. The protocol is a crucial element of the overall design, since the server architecture must interface with it. If the protocol follows accepted standards, the addition or replacement of multiple platform servers can be accomplished without many difficulties.

The pieces of hardware that are part of a network are

1. Terminals
2. Microcomputers and network interface cards
3. File servers
4. Terminal controllers
5. Multiplexers
6. Concentrators
7. Line-sharing devices
8. Protocol converters
9. Hardware encrypting devices
10. Switches
11. PBX switchboards

12. Communication circuits

13. FEPs

14. Port-sharing devices

15. Host computers

16. Channel extenders

17. Testing equipment

18. Surge protectors, power conditioners, and uninterruptible power supplies

Each of these devices has a unique graphical representation that varies slightly according to the designer (see Fig. 7-5). He or she should prepare a graphical representation of the network hardware using the symbols outlined in Fig. 7-5 or similar ones.

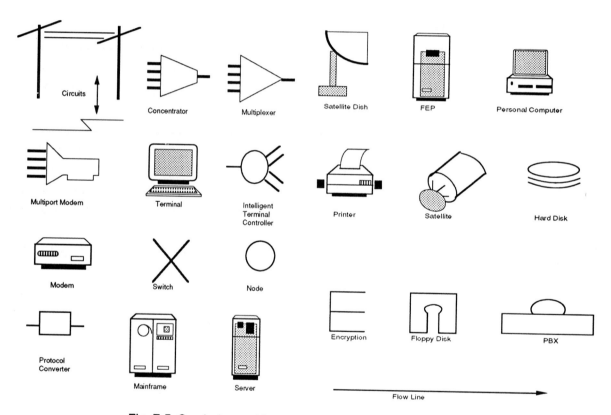

Fig. 7-5. Symbols used in network design.

The final hardware configuration needs to take into account the software protocol and network operating system that are going to be implemented in the network. The results should be the least-cost alternative that meets all the organization's requirements. Additionally, before ordering any hardware, the designers should decide how to handle diagnostics, troubleshooting, and network repair. Most new network hardware has built-in diagnostics and testing capabilities.

Finally, selecting hardware and software involves selecting more than just a system. It involves selecting a vendor. The vendor's ability to maintain, upgrade, and expand the network components will determine the overall success of the network.

Implementation

During the implementation phase the individual components of the network are purchased and installed. This phase can be divided into

1. Software acquisition. If a new network is being implemented, the necessary network operating system, application software, managing software, and communication protocols must be procured. A useful tool in software and hardware procurement is a request for proposal (RFP). The RFP is based on the network requirements produced in the investigation step of the feasibility study. Bids come from potential vendors in response to the RFP. The bids are evaluated, using specified criteria, and one is selected.

2. Hardware acquisition. Hardware procurement can be done from the same software vendor or a third party vendor may be used. Some software can run on a multitude of computer hardware configurations (sometimes called platforms). Deciding on the software first helps narrow the selection of a hardware vendor.

3. Installation. During or after the hardware and software acquisition, the individual components need to be assembled into what will become the network. The final product of this phase is an operational network system.

4. Testing. Testing should be conducted in an integrated fashion. That is, hardware and software should be tested simultaneously as they are implemented, trying to process maximum work loads whenever possible. This will provide statistics that indicate the best and worst possibilities of network efficiency. It will also provide feedback for fine-tuning the network before it becomes fully operational. Integrated testing ensures that all parts of the system will function together properly.

   Testing should be performed using test plans developed during the design phase of the life cycle. There must be a complete and extensive test plan that produces predictable test results reflecting the operation of the network under real-life situations. These results are necessary if management is to trust and accept the network.

5. Documentation. Even though documentation is placed in the life cycle at this stage, it should be an integral part of each phase in network design. Reports that document every aspect of the net-

work, from its conception until final implementation, must be present for audit trail purposes and must always accompany the network. These documents can take the form of reference manuals, maintenance manuals, operational and user manuals, and all the reference materials used in the feasibility study.

6. Switch-over. The switch-over step consists of moving all transactions from the old system to the new system. The final product of this step is the active working network. The switch-over plan must include milestones to be reached during the transition period and contingency plans in case the new system does not meet operational guidelines.

The Request for Proposals

Once the network has been designed, but before implementation can proceed, the specific vendors must be selected. A formal approach is to send a request for proposal (RFP) to prospective vendors. The RFP is a document that asks each vendor to prepare a price quotation for the configuration described in the RFP. Some RFPs give vendors great latitude in how the proposed system should be implemented. Others are very specific and expect detailed technical data in response from the vendor.

The format of an RFP can vary in terms of specificity. However, as a general rule, an RFP contains the following topics:

o   Title page. This identifies the originating organization and title of the project.

o   Table of contents. Any lengthy document should have a table of contents to provide a quick reference to specific topics.

o   Introduction. This is a brief introduction that includes an overview of the organization for which the final product is intended, the problem to be solved, schedule for the response to the RFP, evaluation and selection criteria, installation schedules, and operation schedules.

o   RFP response guidelines. The RFP guidelines for responding to it establish the schedule for the selection process, the format of the proposal, how proposals are evaluated, the time and place of proposal submission, when presentations are made, and the time for the announcement of the winner or winners.

o   Deadlines. The deadline and place for submitting responses to the RFP must be stated clearly throughout the proposal. The deadlines should also include equipment delivery dates and the date to commence operations.

o   Response format. The format of the response to the RFP depends on the user. Normally, responses come in two separate documents. One document contains the specific technical details of the proposed system. The other document has the financial and contractual details.

o   Evaluation criteria. The RFP needs to describe for the vendors how the responses will be evaluated. It should include a prioritized list indicating the items that are the most important. This allows the vendors to provide further information on these items in their responses.

Typically, vendor responses include the following items:

1. System design
2. System features
3. Upgrade capabilities
4. Installation methods
5. Installation schedule
6. Testing methods
7. Maintenance agreements
8. Cost of items
9. Payment schedule
10. System support
11. Warranty coverage
12. Training options

This is the largest portion of the RFP. It describes the problems that need to be solved. Solutions to these problems should not be included in this section. Rather, the vendors should be allowed to propose their own solutions.

Maintenance and Upgrade

The last phase in the life cycle of the network is the maintenance and upgrade of the components of the network. During the maintenance and upgrade period the system is kept operational and fine-tuned to keep adequate performance levels and fix system problems.

The products of this phase are change and upgrade requests, updates to existing documentation to reflect changes in the network, and reports and statistics from the monitoring and control functions of the network.

At some point in the life of the system, the new network in its own turn will be replaced or phased out. This final stage in the life cycle leads to the beginning of a new life cycle as the organization goes through the same process to find a replacement or upgrade to the existing system.

Network Security

An important responsibility of network managers is maintaining control over the security of the network and the data stored and transmitted by it. The major goals of security are to prevent computer crime and data loss.

Detection of security problems in a network is compounded by the nature of information processing, storage, and the transmission system in the network. For example:

1. Data is stored on media not easily readable by people.
2. Data can be erased or modified without leaving evidence.
3. Computerized records do not have signatures to verify authenticity or distinguish copies from originals.
4. Data can be accessed and manipulated from remote stations.
5. Transactions are performed at high speeds and often without human monitoring.

The threat of the loss of the data stored in the network is sufficient reason for implementing methods and techniques to detect and prevent loss. It is important to incorporate the security methods during the design phase of the life cycle rather than add them later. Although no system is completely sealed from outside interference, the following methodologies will help in preventing a breach in network security.

Physical Security

The main emphasis of physical security is to prevent unauthorized access to the communications room, network control center, or communications equipment. This could result in damage to the network equipment or tapping into the circuits by unauthorized personnel.

The room or building that houses network communication equipment should be locked, and access should be restricted by network managers. Terminals should be equipped with locks that deactivate the screen and keyboard switch. In some situations, instead of keys and locks, a programmable plastic card can be used. The locking mechanism that accepts the card may be programmed to accept passwords, in addition to the magnetic code in the card.

Encryption

With many networks using satellite and microwave relays for transmitting data, anyone with an antenna can pick up the transmission and have access to the data being transmitted. One method to safeguard the information transmitted through the airwaves, and even data transmitted through wires, is called encryption or ciphering.

Encryption involves substituting or transposing bits that represent a known data message. The level of encrypting can be of any complexity, and it is usually judged by a work factor. A higher work factor indicates a more complex cipher or encryption.

As shown in Fig. 7-6, an encrypting system (also called a cryptosystem) between a sender and a receiver consists of the following elements:

1. A message to be transmitted and protected.

2. A large set of invertible cryptographic transformations (ciphers) applied to the message to produce ciphertext and later to recover the original message by applying the inverse of the cipher to the ciphertext.

3. The key of the cryptosystem that selects one specific transformation from the set of possible transformations.

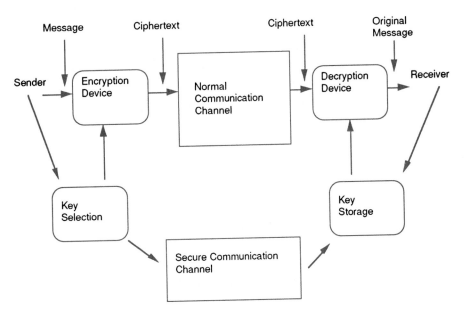

Fig. 7-6. Encrypting system

A cryptosystem is effective only if the key is kept secret. Also the set of ciphers must be large enough that the correct key could not be guessed or determined by trial-and-error techniques.

The National Bureau of Standards has set a data encrypting standard (DES). The DES effectiveness derives from its complexity, the large number of possible keys, and the security of the keys used. The DES transformation is an iterative nonlinear block product cipher that uses 64-bit data blocks. It is implemented on special purpose microcircuits that have been developed for DES and are available commercially. The DES encrypting algorithm is used in reverse for decrypting the ciphertext. The key is also a 64-bit word, 8 of which are parity bits. Therefore, the effective key length is 56 bits (see hardware encrypting in Chapter 3).

The suitability of a type of encrypting algorithm for applications in a data network depends on the relevant characteristics of the applications running in the system, the characteristics of the chosen algorithm, and the technical aspects of the network. Even though the purpose of encrypting is to secure data, the effect of the cryptosystem on the network is equally important. A cryptosystem that provides excellent security may deteriorate the performance of the network to unacceptable levels.

User Identification and Passwords

User identification (ID) and passwords are the most common security systems employed in networks, and at times the easiest to break. The user ID is provided by the network manager when the user profile is added to the network. The password is normally at the user's discretion. Unfortunately, many users choose passwords that are too simple and that can be easily guessed by trial and error, such as their last name.

Some systems provide the generation of passwords for users. This technique is more effective than allowing users to define their own passwords. The user must keep the password available, but protect it from being accessible by others.

User IDs and passwords by themselves are not an effective security technique. When combined with call-back units (see Chapters 2 and 3), encrypting devices, and network physical security, they provide an effective deterrent to unauthorized users.

Time and Location Controls

The time and location of user access to the network can be controlled by software and hardware mechanisms. Some users may be allowed to access the system only during specific times of the day and on specified days of the week. Other users may only access the system from specified terminals. Although such measures are an inconvenience to users, they help in managing data flow and in monitoring the network usage.

Time controls are performed on individuals by having a user profile in the network that determines the day and time intervals during which the user can access the system. Location controls are enforced by having a terminal profile. The terminal profile identifies the terminal and sets up specific paths that the terminal can follow to access selected data. No matter who the user is on the terminal, the terminal profile can be given a higher priority to override the user profile.

Switched Port and Dialing Access

The most vulnerable security point on a network is switched ports that allow dial-in access. They are a security risk because they allow any person with a telephone and terminal to access the system. To enhance the security of switched ports with dial-in access, they should be operational only during the time when transactions are allowed, instead of 24 hours per day. A call-back unit (see Chapter 3) can be used to deter unauthorized calls and to ensure that calls are made only from authorized locations.

The telephone numbers of the switch should be safeguarded and only be available to personnel who must have access to them. User identification and password enforcement take on a higher priority with dial-in access. In systems that contain critical data, a person-to-person authentication as well as application-to-user authentication should be used.

Audit Logs

Transaction logs are an important aspect of network security. Every login attempt should be logged, including date and time of attempt, user ID and password used, location, and number of unsuccessful attempts. In some situations, after a number of unsuccessful login attempts are made, the data described above may be displayed on an operator console for immediate action.

Many of the above methods can be incorporated into a system including extensive audit trails that collect the necessary information required to determine who is accessing the system. However, audit trails are worthless unless network managers study them and monitor the network.

Viruses

A computer virus is an executable computer program that propagates itself, using other programs as carriers, and sometimes modifies itself during or after replication. It is intended to perform some unwanted function on the computer system attached to the network.

Some viruses perform simple annoying functions such as popping up in the middle of an application to demonstrate they are there. Other viruses are more destructive and erase or modify portions of programs or critical data. They are typically introduced into network computers by floppy disk based software that was purchased or copied. Many of the known viruses enter networks through programs or data downloaded from electronic bulletin boards. Some are deposited on networks by the creator of the virus. Other viruses migrate from network to network through gateways and other interconnecting hardware.

Viruses can be monitored and eliminated at the user level with the use of antivirus software. This type of application program searches files and looks for known computer viruses, alerting users of their presence. At this point, the user has the option to eliminate the virus or take some other security action. This process can take place on a stand-alone machine before introducing the application in the network. Additionally, the user can also run a virus scanning program from a directory in the network. The program will then scan the user's floppy disk and report any suspicious files.

At the system manager level, virus protection can be accomplished by using a network statistical program with a virus detection component that is designed to run as the network operating system is active. This type of application watches for signs of a virus and alerts the LAN manager at the first symptom. The program warns the LAN manager when application or data files show any change from the original. An example of this type of application is TGR Software's SCUA Plus.

It is important to note that antivirus software does not identify all viruses circulating. This type of software can only work on known viruses and offers little protection against new or unknown viruses. On a regular basis, the makers of antivirus software provide upgrades that contain protection against new computer viruses, introduced since the last release of the virus protection program.

Disaster Recovery Planning

The increased use of computer systems and data communication networks has expanded the need for a realistic disaster plan. The network manager needs to be involved in such planning and should have knowledge in the areas that follow:

1. The need for disaster planning
2. Computer backup approaches
3. Network backup approaches
4. The characteristics of a disaster backup strategy

5. Planning processes of the organization

6. The impact of a data network disaster on the organization

Planning for a disaster is much like planning for a new system. It requires goals, objectives, design, implementation, testing, documentation, and maintenance. Producing a good disaster plan requires significant organizational skills. However, LAN developers and LAN managers should also concentrate on disaster prevention measures. Good prevention measures may allow the disaster recovery plan not to be used. Some of the measures below and others will make the recovery process easier and protect users' information.

1. Adequate surge protectors. All computers in the network should be protected with surge protectors that can react to a large voltage spike in as little as one or two nanoseconds. This type of device normally costs about $100, so it can be expensive to outfit a network with many workstations. However, when compared with the cost of a workstation, it is worth the price.

2. Servers must be protected with a UPS. A UPS protects against voltage surges and drops. In many networks, the server contains invaluable data that a company needs to function. Protecting the data is one of the most important functions of the LAN manager. Additionally, the UPS allows the proper shutdown of the network in case of a loss of power.

3. Communication line protectors and filters. Computers connected to modems and telephone lines also need protection from incoming noise and surges that may travel through the phone lines.

4. Protect cables. All cabling must be protected and placed in locations where a user cannot accidentally tamper with the line.

5. Adequate backups. Continuous and comprehensive backups will ensure that all data and programs are safeguarded. If possible, during a period of network inactivity, the backup and recovery plans outlined below should be rehearsed.

Characteristics of the Disaster Recovery Plan

A disaster plan must meet certain criteria, including:

1. Reliability

2. Operability

3. Response time to activate the plan

4. Cost effectiveness

Reliability

Whatever the strategy taken to safeguard the network and the data stored on it, the organization must be confident that, in case of a disaster, the plan will work. Confidence can be achieved by using proven techniques to replace network media in case of a failure.

The best plans are those that are kept simple. The plan needs to be tested in order to ensure that the information in the system is secured. Any disaster plan is suspect without proper testing.

Operability

The methods used for recovering from a disaster should be consistent with the normal methods of backup and restore that are used in the routine management of the network. This ensures that, in case of failure, trained personnel will be able to restore the system quickly and without errors. Additionally, the plan should be well documented and distributed to appropriate personnel.

Response Time to Activate the Plan

The recovery plan must be capable of being activated within the time constraints imposed by the network. In some cases, backup networks are activated on a temporary basis until the stricken facility is restored to an acceptable operational level. The network design must be flexible to allow for time-sensitive considerations.

Cost Effectiveness

The recovery plan must be cost effective since it will be idle for most of the network life. However, in a disaster, the backup system must also be flexible enough for long-term use, if necessary.

Disaster Recovery Methodologies

Extensive planning and research are required to produce an effective disaster recovery plan. Some of the concerns that a manager may want to address in preparing a recovery plan follow:

1. Create a list of the critical applications. This will require involvement from top management. The items on the list should be prioritized, and their impact on the firm should be analyzed.

2. Determine the required recovery time for the organization.

3. Determine the critical nodes in the network.

4. Analyze the critical work load for each node, and create a transaction profile for it.

5. Analyze the use of shared communication facilities and alternate methods of information transfer.

6. Obtain best vendor and carrier lead-time estimates for a backup network.

7. Identify facilities that exceed the recovery time. That is, these facilities are critical and the recovery time exceeds the allowable down time. These must be restored first.

8. Determine costs.

9. Have the vendor develop a plan to connect users with planned backup networks.

10. List all cable and front end requirements.

11. Make a list of equipment that can be shared, such as modems.

12. List all facilities that can be provided at the recovery site in case of a prolonged down time.

13. List all support personnel available for recovery.

14. List all dial-up facilities at the recovery site.

The Planning Process

The disaster recovery plan may be divided into strategic and implementation sections. The strategic section lists the goals, design objectives, and strategies for network recovery. The implementation section describes the steps to take during the recovery process. Some of the major items to be included in the plan are provided below.

1. List all assumptions, objectives, and the methodology for implementing the objectives.

2. List all tasks to be performed before, during, and after a disaster.

3. Put together a technical description of any backup networks.

4. List all personnel involved in the recovery phase and their responsibilities.

5. Describe how the recovery site will be employed.

6. Make a list of critical nodes and their profiles.

7. Make a list of vendors and carriers who will supply facilities and backup.

8. Make a list of alternate sources of equipment and supplies.

9. Create all necessary network diagrams.

10. Make a list of all required software, manuals, testing, and operational procedures of backup networks.

11. Diagram all backup circuits.

12. Describe procedures for updating the recovery plan.

A commitment to an effective disaster recovery plan must have the support of top management. They must be aware of the consequences of the failure of such a plan. A team consisting of a coordinator and representatives from management is required to continually upgrade the plan as facilities are added and modified, if the firm is to be protected.

Network Management

For a network to be effective and efficient over a long period of time, a good network management plan must be created. The network management plan must have two goals:

1. The plan should prevent problems where possible.
2. The plan should prepare for problems that will most likely occur.

A comprehensive plan needs to include the following duties:

1. Monitor and control hard disk space.
2. Monitor network work load and performance.
3. Add to and maintain user login information and workstation information.
4. Monitor and reset network devices.
5. Perform regular maintenance on software and data files stored in the servers.
6. Make regular backups of data and programs stored in the servers.

Managing Hard Disk Space

The server's hard disk is one of the network's primary commodities. Files for network-based programs are stored on the hard disk. Print jobs that are sent from workstations to network printers are stored on the hard disk in a queue before they are printed. And in some networks, personal files and data are stored on the network hard disk.

If the hard disk space fills up, then print jobs can't be printed and users can't save their data files. Data files may also be corrupted since data manipulation can't be accomplished.

Disk space must be available at all times for legitimate users of the network. The hard disk space must be checked every day. Growth of users' files should be controlled to ensure that a single user doesn't monopolize the hard disk. Unwanted files must be deleted, and when heavy disk fragmentation occurs, all files could be backed up and the disk reformatted. This will allow defragmentation of files on the hard disk and provide for more efficient access to data on the server's hard disk. Some networks allow the use of software to repack files on the hard disk and eliminate file fragmentation. When possible, such tools should be used. However, all files should be backed up before using a defragmentation software application, in case something goes wrong.

Monitoring Server Performance

The performance of the LAN's server will determine how quickly the server can deliver data to the user. The servers must be monitored to ensure that they are performing at their peak.

Several factors determine the response of a server. One of these factors is the number of users that are attached to the system. Working with more users will slow the server response time. If a specific application has a large number of users, the server that contains the application could be dedicated to serve only such a program. Other servers could be used to distribute the load of other programs on the system.

Additionally, the server's main memory (RAM) should be monitored to make sure that it is used efficiently. Many servers use RAM as disk buffers. These buffers cannot function if there isn't sufficient memory to run the network operating system and the buffers. If a server has to reduce the number of buffers required for I/O, the overall performance of the network will suffer.

Most networks provide tools that show statistical data about the use of the network and outline potential problems. An experienced network administrator uses these statistics to ensure that the network operates at its peak level at all times.

Maintaining User and Workstation Information

Network users have network identification numbers that can be used to monitor security and the growth of the network. A network manager must keep a log of information about the network users such as login ID, node address, network address, and some personal information such as phone, name, and address. Also, network cabling, workstation type, configuration, and purpose of use should be kept in records. This information can be stored in a database. It can be used to detect problems with data delivery, make changes to users' profiles, workstation profiles, accounts, and support other tasks.

Monitoring and Resetting Network Devices

A network consists not only of servers and workstations but also of printers, input devices such as scanners, and other machines. Some devices may need to be reset daily (such as some types of gateways), while other devices require periodic maintenance. Some types of electronic mail routers may need to be monitored hourly to make sure they are working properly. In either case, all devices should be monitored periodically, and a schedule of reset and maintenance should be created to ensure that all network devices work when a user requests them.

Maintaining Software

Software applications, especially database applications, need regular maintenance to rebuild files and reclaim space left empty by deleted records. Space not used must be made available to the system, and in many cases index files will have to be rebuilt.

Additionally, as new software upgrades become available, they need to be placed in the network. After an upgrade is placed in the network, file cleanup may have to take place. Also, any incompatibilities between the new software and the network will need to be resolved.

Old e-mail messages will have to be deleted and the space they occupy made available to the system. The same type of procedure will have to be performed as users are added to or deleted from the network.

Making Regular Backups

Backups of user information and data must be made on a periodic basis. If a server's hard disk fails, a major problem could occur if backups are inadequate.

Backups of server information are normally placed on tapes or cartridges. Tapes and cartridges offer an inexpensive solution to backup needs and can hold large amounts of information. Their capacity ranges from 20 megabytes to as much as 2,200 megabytes.

Writing information from the server's hard disk to a tape or cartridge is a slow process. Network managers should have automated backup procedures and a tape system that offers 1 to 3 megabytes of transfer speed per minute.

Summary

The life cycle of a network is an important planning consideration. One significant aspect is the technological changes that will have to be dealt with during the useful life of the network. Each network is a representation of the technology at the time of its design and implementation.

During the course of its life cycle, a network passes through the following phases:

1. The feasibility study involves the subphases of problem definition and investigation. The problem definition attempts to find the problems that exist in the organization that caused management to initiate the study. The investigation subphase involves gathering input data to develop a precise definition of the present data communication conditions and to uncover problems.

2. The analysis phase uses the data gathered in step 1 to identify the requirements that the network must meet if it is to be a successful implementation.

3. During the design phase, all the components that will comprise the network are developed.

4. The implementation phase consists of the installation of the hardware and software that make up the network system. Also, during this phase, all training and documentation materials are developed.

5. During the maintenance and upgrade phase the network is kept operational and fine-tuned by network operations personnel. Additionally, updates of software and hardware are performed to keep the network operating efficiently and effectively.

One of the most important requirements in network design is response time. Response time is the total time that expires between sending an inquiry from a workstation or terminal and receiving the response back at the workstation.

One of the major uses of the data gathering process is in developing a network topology. The load and site data collected are used as input for network modeling programs. These programs use mathematical models to simulate a network.

The network operating system and the protocols that the host can handle limit the number and types of application software programs that can be used on a network. These limitations can be overcome with the acquisition of protocol converters and FEPs.

The type of software purchased for the network will determine whether the network uses asynchronous or synchronous communication, full-duplex or half-duplex communication, and the speed of transmission. Additionally, the limitations imposed by the software will determine the types of other networks that can be interfaced with. The network designer should select a protocol that is compatible with the ISO seven-layer model and one that can grow as the network grows. The protocol is a crucial element of the overall design, since the server architecture must interface with it.

Once the network has been designed, the specific vendors must be selected. A formal approach is to send a request for proposal (RFP) to prospective vendors. The RFP is a document that asks each vendor to prepare specifications and a price quotation for the configuration described in the RFP.

An important responsibility of network managers is maintaining control over the security of the network and the data on it. The major goals of security measures are to prevent computer crime and data loss. Some of the data losses can be the result of computer viruses. A computer virus is an executable computer program that propagates itself, using other programs as carriers, and sometimes modifies itself during or after replication. It is intended to perform some unwanted function on the computer system attached to the network. Viruses can be monitored and eliminated with the use of antivirus software.

Another method to safeguard the information transmitted is called encrypting or ciphering. User IDs and passwords by themselves are not an effective security technique. When combined with call-back units, encrypting devices, and network physical security, they provide an effective deterrent to unauthorized users.

The time and location of user access to the network can be controlled by software and hardware mechanisms. Although such measures are an inconvenience to users, they help in providing access to data by monitoring communication sessions and access during critical times. The most vulnerable security point on a network is switched ports that allow dial-in access. To enhance the security of switched ports with dial-in access, they should be operational only during the time when transactions are allowed. A call-back unit can be used to ensure that calls are made only from authorized locations.

The increasing use of computer systems and data communication networks requires that managers need a realistic disaster plan. The network manager needs to be involved in the planning and should have knowledge in

1. The need for disaster planning
2. Computer backup approaches
3. Network backup approaches
4. The characteristics of a disaster backup strategy
5. Planning processes of the organization
6. The impact of a data network disaster on the organization

Planning a disaster recovery system requires goals, objectives, design, implementation, testing, documentation, and maintenance. A disaster plan must meet certain criteria:

1. Reliability
2. Operability

3. Response time to activate the plan

4. Cost-effectiveness

For networks to be effective and efficient over a long period of time, a good network management plan is needed. The network management plan must have two goals:

1. The plan should prevent problems where possible.

2. The plan should prepare for problems that will most likely occur.

A comprehensive plan needs to address the following tasks:

1. Monitor and control hard disk space.

2. Monitor network work load and performance.

3. Add to and maintain user login information and workstation information.

4. Monitor and reset network devices.

5. Perform regular maintenance on software and data files stored on the servers.

6. Make regular backups of data and programs stored on the servers.

Questions

1. Briefly describe the life cycle phases for network design.

2. Name four items that should be included in the report produced at the end of the feasibility study.

3. Why is network response time important?

4. What is network modeling?

5. What is the purpose of message analysis?

6. Name ten hardware items that are part of a network.

7. What are the steps of the implementation phase?

8. What are the major sections of an RFP?

9. Briefly describe encryption.

10. Why are passwords and user IDs not enough security for a network?

11. What is a virus? How can it be detected?

12. Why should there be a disaster recovery plan for a data communications network?

13. Name four characteristics of a disaster recovery plan.

14. Name four major items that should be included in the recovery plan.

Projects

Objective

There are two different projects in this section. The first project provides some general guidelines for troubleshooting a small local area network. Before expensive testing methods are used to find problems with LANs, the guidelines provided below may find and correct a problem in a more efficient manner. The second project is the study of the design and installation of a local area network for the computer laboratory.

Project 1. Troubleshooting a LAN

Troubleshooting a LAN is accomplished by using an established methodology of problem determination and recovery through event login and report techniques. Some troubleshooting techniques will be explained in later chapters in this book. However, sometimes the best planned approach does not work. The following suggestions may accomplish what the scientific methods can't do. Try to follow them in the order they are listed.

1. If the problem appears to be on the network, try turning the power to network devices off and on in a systematic manner. Turn off the power to routers, gateways, and network modems. After turning the power off, wait approximately 30 seconds and turn the power back on. Sometimes a device gets "hung-up" because of an electrical malfunction or an instruction that it cannot execute.

2. If the problem appears to be in your workstation, turn the machine off and reboot the computer.

3. Check for viruses on the file server and your workstation.

4. Reload the network software and any other software that controls devices such as gateways.

5. Swap out devices, cables, connectors, and network interface cards on your machine and then across the network.

6. Reconfigure the user profile in the network server.

7. Add more memory to the file server.

If the above suggestions do not work and the LAN manuals do not offer any other possibilities, call the LAN vendor.

Project 2. Study of a Local Area Network

Go to the school's data processing center or any other site where a local area network may be in operation. Carefully document the following topics by questioning network managers and by observing the LAN in operation.

1. Describe the hardware that constitutes the LAN. Use the following checklist as a guide.

   a. Is the network a peer-to-peer network or a dedicated file server network?

   b. What models of server(s) are available?

   c. What is the internal configuration of the server(s) (i.e., amount of RAM, disk space, processor speed, coprocessor speed, number of floppy drives and types, etc.)?

   d. What models of workstations are available?

   e. What is the internal configuration of the workstations (i.e., amount of RAM, disk space, processor speed, coprocessor speed, number of floppy drives and types, etc.)?

   f. What make, model, and type of network interface card is being used?

   g. What is the network configuration? Why was this type chosen?

   h. What models and types of printers are available to network users?

   i. Are there any gateways to other networks? If yes, what type and models are available?

   j. What are the physical limitations of the network (i.e., number of users, maximum distance of transmission)?

   k. What type of transmission medium is being used? Why was this type chosen?

2. What network operating system is in place? Why was this type chosen?

3. How do the users interact with the software stored on the network?

4. What type of work is normally accomplished by the workstations?

5. How do users perform network operations such as printing, copying files, and so forth?

6. What are the maintenance policies?

7. Are there any support fees? If yes, what type and amount?

8. What is the cost of adding stations?

9. What is the cost of adding a server?

10. What are the system management procedures in place and their cost?

11. How are software licensing agreements handled?

12. What types of upgrades or modifications are planned for the next three years?

After all the material is compiled, create a report indicating your findings about the status of the local area network. The report should consist of at least five pages, but it will probably be much longer.

After completing the report on the actual LAN, provide suggestions for improving the system without increasing the current costs. For each suggestion, provide evidence in the form of interviews, data compiled from magazines, or vendor specification sheets. Is there a way to provide a better service and lower the costs? What problems do you anticipate with this network during the next three years? How can a solution be in place before serious interruption of LAN services takes place?

Introduction to Novell NetWare

Objectives

After completing this chapter you will

1. Understand the basic hardware components required to install NetWare.
2. Obtain an overview of the software components of NetWare.
3. Understand Novell's shell.
4. Understand the concept of volumes and drive mappings.
5. Understand the concept of trustee and trustee's rights.

Key Terms

Client Computer

Login Script

Network Interface Card

Server Computer

Trustee Rights

Volume

Drive Mapping

NetWare

Search Drive

Trustee

User Environment

Introduction

This chapter introduces a network operating system known as Novell Net-Ware. It will introduce concepts that will be more thoroughly discussed in later chapters. Originally designed for computers running the CP/M operating system, Novell quickly adapted NetWare for use on the IBM PC. This move ensured NetWare's success.

NetWare's major components are

1. Software:

   NetWare Operating System on a shared computer called the file server

   The shell, a set of memory resident programs which run on the PC which is known as the client, node, or workstation

2. Hardware:

   Network Interface Card in all nodes and in the file server which, together with the cable connecting the NICs, provides the network hardware interface

The NetWare Operating System, which is installed on the file server, allows the file server to act as a "traffic cop" which manages access by clients to the files stored on the file server's hard disk.

The NIC physically connects the client (user's) computer to a file server where data can be shared by all the users on the network.

The shell allows the user to treat the file server as if it were a disk drive attached to his client computer. Ordinary DOS commands can be used on the file server, and several additional functions are available. The user can create drive mappings and search drives to make more effective use of the data and programs on the file server. The data and programs can be protected by assigning the proper trustee rights to the other users on the network.

Overview of NetWare

Little remains constant in the world of networking. Network operating systems, hardware components, and topologies have changed rapidly over the last several years to keep pace with advancing technology and consumer demand. Novell, Inc. has performed better than most at maintaining a saleable product and a share of the market. Novell's original network product, however, did not do well. The system was a file server and network operating system software, with serial cables to connect to client computers running the CP/M operating system. The product line was expanded somewhat, but the company went bankrupt. Novell's reorganization, however, took place at an opportune point in history. The introduction of the IBM PC gave Novell an entirely new market. Novell's operating system was eventually rewritten to allow the IBM PC to be used as both the file server and the client. Novell has introduced many software and hardware products since then. It now controls the largest single share of the local area networking market with Novell NetWare. "NetWare" refers to all of Novell's network operating system products.

Novell NetWare was originally designed around hardware using a star topology to communicate with a single file server. The file server simply allowed client computers to store and share files. This structure has influenced all of Novell's products to date. NetWare has become largely hardware independent, allowing many topologies and file servers to be used simultaneously, but communication on the network is still handled almost entirely through a primary file server. Two client computers may be connected directly to each other by a network cable, but for a file to be transferred from one to the other, that file must first be sent to the file server, then to the target client computer. Of course, the network provides many other functions, but they are generally centered around the idea of a client computer connected to a file server.

By far, the most common client on a Novell network is an IBM PC or PC-compatible computer running DOS, although Macintosh and OS/2 clients are also now used. DOS is the software that handles all of the low-level functions of the computer such as reading and writing to the disk drives, loading and executing application programs, and handling input from the keyboard. When running an application program such as a word processor, DOS allocates memory, reads the program from the disk drive and then allows the program to begin. The application program can then use the resources of the computer through what are known as DOS function calls. For instance, there are many different types of printers and dozens of companies manufacturing them. To the application program, this is irrelevant. It will simply make a DOS function call to write data to the printer, and DOS will handle the output to the device.

Since even DOS can't "know" the details of every peripheral device one might attach to a computer, including a network, programs known as drivers are often used to help DOS provide a common environment for application programs to work in. Attaching a Novell network to a computer is a good example of this and essentially involves two components: the network interface card or NIC, and the network driver programs. Novell offers a variety of programs that serve as the drivers depending on the configuration of the workstation.

The NIC is the hardware that is physically connected to the network, much like a telephone is the piece of hardware that is physically connected to the telephone network. It generates the proper electrical signal to communicate on the particular type of network being used. It may use pulses of light or radio waves to send signals across the network.

The network drivers used on a particular workstation must consist of an appropriate combination of the programs needed to perform three functions: provide a hardware dependent driver for the network card, provide the appropriate communications protocol to be used on the network and provide an interface for the user.

Novell's long-used system of providing the hardware dependent driver and the communications protocol is to use a program called IPX.COM. It must be generated at the time NetWare is installed because it is actually built out of two components. One component is the hardware dependent NIC driver and the other is the IPX protocol driver. The resulting IPX.COM program (IPX stands for Internetwork Packet eXchange) is then unique to the type of NIC it will run on.

More recently, Novell has changed the focus of its efforts to a standard called Open Data-Link Interface. The two functions of the NIC driver and IPX protocol driver have been spread out over three programs. The first program is called LSL.COM (LSL stands for Link Support Layer). It allows multiple protocols, which are loaded later, to be run on the same NIC. The second program is strictly a NIC driver program and is given a name that indicates which brand of NIC it supports. IBM PC Network II cards, for instance, use a program called PCN2L.COM. A network card called the SMC EtherCard PLUS Elite10T/A uses a program called SMCPLUS.COM. These programs are packaged with the NIC, and Novell also provides them for major brands of network interface cards. The third program is the protocol driver, IPXODI.COM. As its name indicates, it is an Internetwork Packet Exchange protocol driver that conforms to the Open Data-Link Interface standard.

The third function, that of a user interface, is provided by one of three different versions of essentially the same program: NETX.COM, XMSNETX.EXE or EMSNETX.EXE. The three different versions of this program are needed to take advantage of different memory configurations of the workstation. NETX.COM uses conventional memory, XMSNETX.EXE uses extended memory and EMSNETX.EXE uses expanded memory. The different memory configurations will be discussed in more detail in later chapters. The letter "X" appears before the extension (.EXE or .COM) in each of these names to indicate that they can be used with any DOS version. Prior to the release of DOS version 5.0, Novell supplied the rather cumbersome collection of NET2, NET3, NET4, XMSNET2, XMSNET3, XMSNET4, EMSNET2, EMS-

NET3, and EMSNET4 for use with DOS 2.x, DOS 3.x, and DOS 4.x respectively. Using the ODI approach for IPX, one must merely include the following in one's AUTOEXEC.BAT:

LSL

NIC driver such as PCN2L

IPXODI

NETX (or XMSNETX or EMSNETX)

Together, the network drivers make up the NetWare shell which is a complete interface between DOS and NetWare. The word "shell" refers to an interface provided to users to allow them to interact with the computer in a transparent or natural manner. This shields users from the complex low-level operations of the computer and the network. Therefore, the network shell protects the user from having to know how to interact directly with the network.

The User Environment

Network Volumes and Drives

The highest level in the NetWare directory structure is the NetWare volume. All file servers must have a volume called SYS:, and a file server may have a total of up to 64 volumes. Volumes may span physical disk drives, or they may divide a physical disk drive. In either case, volumes are specified during installation. Volumes are divided into directories.

The NetWare shell allows DOS and the user to treat the file server as a disk drive attached to the client computer. DOS assigns a drive letter to each of the disk drives physically attached to the computer. A and B designate floppy disk drives while C, D, and E usually represent user hard disk drives. On a typical system, with two floppy disk drives and a hard disk drive, DOS would assign A, B, and C to the those disk drives. When the NetWare shell programs are loaded, another drive letter is made available to the user. Typically, F is used to designate the first network drive and is often used to designate the SYS: volume. In this textbook, all references to the F: drive assume that F designates the entire SYS: volume.

Ordinary DOS commands like DIR (which displays a list of the files on the disk) and CHDIR (which moves access to a different area of the disk) can be used on the network drive F. In addition, application programs can make ordinary DOS function calls to carry out their functions on the network drive as if it were a hard disk attached to the computer. The network drive is the hard disk on the file server, the same hard disk accessed by every other user on the network.

Fig. 8-1 shows three computers, a file server and two client computers. The first client has local disk drives A, B, and C. It also has access to drive F, which is actually on the file server. The second client has only one local disk drive, but can also access drive F.

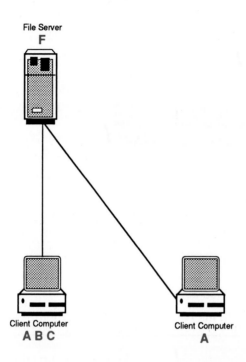

Fig. 8-1. Client computers network to a server.

DOS Directories

In DOS you can create directories to organize the data on a disk. A directory contains files grouped together on the disk. Every disk has what is called the root directory even though it is not referred to it as "root" in any DOS command. Since a "\" (a backslash) is used to separate directory names, a backslash with no name is considered the root directory.

Fig. 8-2 shows how a hard disk might be organized. The files in the root directory could be listed by typing the DIR command. The DIR command lists the files in the current directory. In this case DIR C: would list the files COMMAND.COM, LSL.COM, PCN2L.COM, IPXODI.COM, NETX.COM

Fig. 8-2. Possible hard disk organization.

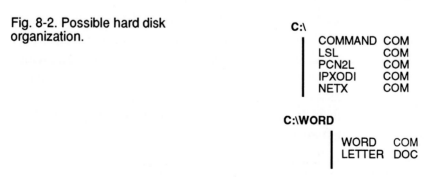

and a directory called WORD. The files in the directory WORD could be displayed by typing DIR C:\WORD and pressing the ENTER key. WORD.COM and LETTER.DOC would be listed. Another way to view the list of files in the WORD directory would be to use the CHDIR command. CHDIR stands for change directory and can be abbreviated further by using only CD. If you were to type CD C:\WORD, the current directory would be changed to the WORD directory and DIR C: would list the files WORD.COM and LETTER.DOC. In this way the drive letter C moves around the disk drive pointing to different areas. Just as the root directory contains a directory called WORD, the WORD directory could contain another directory and so on.

The same commands can be used on the network drive F. In Fig. 8-1 the first computer could create a directory called F:\HISFILES by using the MKDIR command. MKDIR stands for make directory and can be abbreviated further by using only MD. By typing the command MD F:\HISFILES, the first user can create a place to store files on the file server. The user at the second computer could type MD F:\HERFILES. Now, if either computer user typed DIR F:, both directory names would be listed.

Drive Mappings

With directories containing directories and every user on the network creating directories, the directory structure can become quite complex.

Suppose a user on the network needed quick and easy access to files in both the F:\HISFILES directory and the F:\HERFILES directory. Rather than constantly using the CHDIR command to move drive F to the other area, he could use the NetWare MAP command to create a drive letter for one of the directories. Fig. 8-3 shows the result of the first user typing MAP G:=F:\HERFILES. This creates drive letter G which points to the HERFILES directory on the same physical drive as F:\HISFILES.

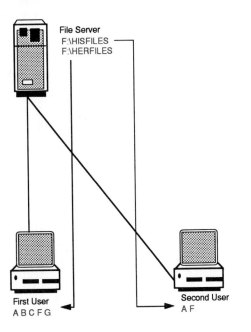

File Server
F:\HISFILES
F:\HERFILES

First User
A B C F G

Second User
A F

Fig. 8-3. Paths for different network users.

This arrangement does not affect the second user. Drive mappings pertain only to the client computer where the MAP command was issued. Each user still has access to the HERFILES directory through drive letter F. The first user simply has the choice of using drive letter F or drive letter G.

Paths and Search Drives

Drive mappings allow users to access data easily without worrying about the directory names. The DOS PATH statement allows the user to completely ignore the current directory when running programs. NetWare combines these functions in the search drive. Ordinarily, to execute a program, it must reside in the current directory or the full path must be used when referring to the program. The "path" is the complete directory name where the program resides. Referring to Fig. 8-3, the first user may have a program in the HISFILES directory called WORD.COM. If the current directory is F:\HERFILES, he would have to type F:\HISFILES\WORD to execute the WORD program. DOS provides a means to shorten this in the PATH command. The PATH command tells the computer where to look for a program if it can't be found in the current directory. If the first user types PATH F:\HISFILES he can use all the programs in the HISFILES directory without typing the entire path. He could simply type WORD and the computer would look in the current directory first, then look in the HISFILES directory and find, and then execute, the program. Multiple directories can be included in the PATH command to instruct the computer to search several areas for the program. The command PATH F:\HERFILES;F:\HISFILES would tell the computer to search the current directory first (as it always does), then the F:\HERFILES directory, and lastly the F:\HISFILES directory. A NetWare search drive is a drive mapping that is automatically inserted in the PATH.

In Fig. 8-4, the second user has typed the command MAP S1:=F:\HISFILES. This NetWare command automatically chooses a drive letter starting from the

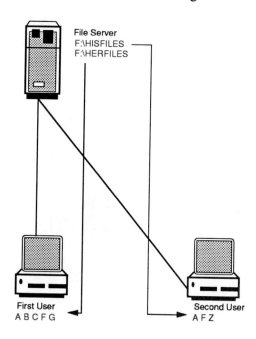

Fig. 8-4. New paths of users after MAP command

File Server
F:\HISFILES
F:\HERFILES

First User
A B C F G

Second User
A F Z

end of the alphabet and maps it to the directory indicated. But the drive letter is more than the pointer used in the other drive letters, it is also a PATH to the directory. The second user can use drive letter Z as she would any other drive letter, but if she is using drive A, for instance, she needs only to type WORD to run the program contained in the F:\HISFILES directory.

Trustee Rights

NetWare allows users to share data or to restrict access to data. Trustee rights allow access to specific directories on the file server. Without trustee rights to a certain directory, a user cannot access the data in that directory. Trustee rights are composed of several permissions a user may have to a specific directory or file. These permissions include Supervisory, Read, Write, Create, Erase, Modify, File Scan and Access Control. Each of these permissions may be granted or denied to a user. The meanings of these permissions or rights with respect to a directory are listed below:

* **Supervisory.** The user has all other rights in the directory even if the directory does not allow certain rights.

* **Read.** The user can open and read files in the directory. The File Scan right is usually also given with the Read right so that the user can see the directory's directory listing.

* **Write.** The user can write to existing files in the directory.

* **Create.** The user can create new files in the directory.

* **Erase.** The user can erase files in the directory.

* **Modify.** The user can modify the Attribute flags of the files in the directory. The Attribute of a file indicates what access all users have to a file.

* **File Scan.** The user can see what files and subdirectories are listed in the directory.

* **Access Control.** The user can grant rights to other users in the directory.

Fig. 8-5 shows the trustee rights each of the users has to the file server using the first letter of the above listed rights. The first user has all rights except Supervisory and Access Control to the F:\HISFILES directory. He can use all

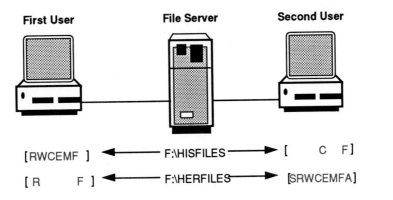

First User   **File Server**   **Second User**

Fig. 8-5.
Trustee rights
for users.

[RWCEMF] ◄─── F:\HISFILES ───► [C F]

[R   F] ◄─── F:\HERFILES ───► [SRWCEMFA]

241

of the files there any way he wants, but he cannot grant those rights to any other users. He only has Read, and File Scan rights in the F:\HERFILES directory. This means he can only read from the data there, not change it or add to it. The second user has all rights to the F:\HERFILES directory. She could even grant additional rights in that directory to the first user. Her access to the F:\HISFILES directory is restricted to Create and File scan. This allows her to create new files in the directory but not to read or change the files already there.

Batch Files and Login Scripts

Many of the commands described above could become quite tedious if you had to type them every time you used the computer. This is why DOS provides a means for storing these commands in a file known as a batch file. A batch file is a list of commands that can be executed by entering the file name.

For instance, if a user needed to execute the commands listed in Fig. 8-6, those commands could be stored in a file called START.BAT. The ".BAT" portion of the name is called the extension and, in this case, indicates that the file is a batch file. With this file in the current directory the user only needs to type Start. The computer will read the file and execute the commands listed in it.

```
MAP G= F\HERFILES
CHDIR F:\HISFILES
PATH G:
WORD
```

Fig. 8-6. Commands for the batch file START.BAT.

NetWare provides a similar function in the form of login scripts. Login scripts are lists of commands that are executed when a user logs into NetWare. Logging in identifies the user to the network so trustee rights can be established. A user might type LOGIN USER1, then a password. NetWare would verify the password is correct, establish the trustee rights for the user, execute the System Login Script, and then execute the login script for that user. Each user may have a different login script, and the login script may execute batch files.

Together, batch files and login scripts free the user from a great deal of typing each time she or he starts working on the computer. Additionally, the user may not need to know many of the DOS and NetWare commands if the login scripts and batch files are already installed.

A Novell Network Example

As outlined before, a local area network links two or more computers and other peripherals together for the purpose of sharing data and equipment. A Novell NetWare-based local area network normally is considered a dedicated file server network. That is, the network has at least one computer whose job is to act as a central data storage system.

Novell networks can consist of one or more file servers, each with dozens of workstations, multiple shared printers, and other devices that can be attached to the file server or workstations.

A small office network or a teaching laboratory can be established easily by creating one for the first time or by using existing networks. The basic components are as follows:

1. A file server (An IBM-compatible computer with a 80836sx or faster processor) with at least 4 megabytes of RAM and a hard disk (preferably with a minimum of 80 megabytes of storage).
2. Network interface cards (NICs) for the server and the workstations.
3. Transmission media (twisted pair, coaxial, or other type according to the type of NICs used).
4. Novell NetWare 3.11 or higher.
5. A printer should also be added to the network (preferably more than one).

If a Novell NetWare-based network is not already available, the process for installing one is outlined in previous chapters. (The following list provides a general review of the process.)

1. Find a location for the server.
2. Find a location for the workstations.
3. Configure each NIC to contain a unique network address.
4. Install the NIC in each of the workstations and servers that will make up the nodes of the network.
5. Connect each node with the medium chosen.
6. Write down all the hardware that makes up the network.
7. Install the NetWare network operating system and use the data from item 6 to answer NetWare's requests.

Fig. 8-7 displays a possible configuration for such a laboratory or work environment. If the network is used to provide instructions on the use of commands and network management, a program called LANSKOOL from Lan Fan Technologies, Inc. may be a good addition to the system. This

243

program allows the instructor to project his or her workstation screen on the screen of other users for the purpose of answering questions or for instructional needs.

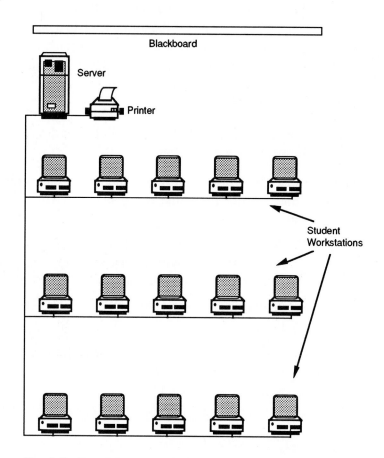

Fig. 8-7. Possible network configuration for training users

The other scenario consists of a Novell network that already exists. It is costly to purchase additional workstations, materials, and space if all that is required is a laboratory or room for providing training to users. If a current network is in place with user's workstations available, all that is needed is an additional server that can function as a training server for the users. This server can be connected to the existing wiring and, after NetWare is installed in it, training can be conducted using existing workstations. Fig. 8-8 shows this scenario. The equipment required for this situation is as follows:

1. A file server (An IBM-compatible computer with an 80386sx or faster processor) with at least 4 megabytes of RAM and a hard disk (preferably with a minimum of 80 megabytes of storage).

2. A network interface card (NIC) for the server.

3. Novell NetWare 3.11 or higher.

4. A cable to connect the new server to existing network cable.

Main Servers

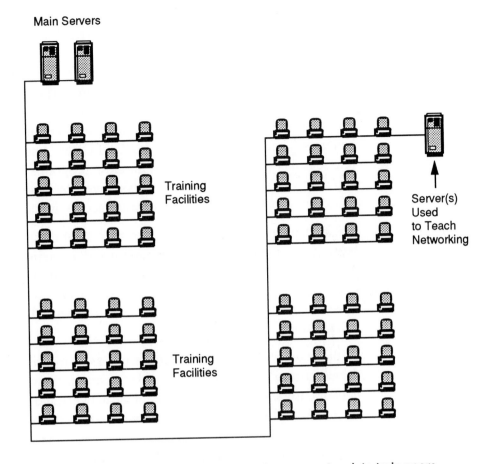

Training Facilities

Server(s) Used to Teach Networking

Training Facilities

Fig. 8-8. Additional configuration for setting up a network to train users

The process to install the server is as follows:

1. Find a location for the server. If it is going to be used for training, then probably the classroom is a good place.

2. Install the NIC in the server and, if required, provide a unique address.

3. Connect the server to existing network transmission media.

4. Install NetWare on the server and provide a unique server name.

The process of installing NetWare is provided in the next chapter in this book. After the server goes on line, users who need training will simply attach their workstation to the server. Any commands issued and any modifications to the environment stay in the training server without affecting the rest of the users and file servers. The server can be configured so that users can attached themselves to other servers.

Summary

NetWare provides access to a file server by many client computers through the hardware and software on each computer. The hardware consists of a network interface card or NIC. Under DOS, using the ODI concept, the NIC is controlled by LSL.COM, a program named to represent the brand of NIC being used and a program called IPXODI.COM. Another program, NETX, provides the interface to DOS. With these programs loaded, the file server appears to the client computer as a disk drive attached to the client computer. DOS commands can be used to create and access directories on the file server.

The four programs make up the NetWare shell that serves as the interface between the computer operating system and the network operating system. The NetWare shell allows DOS and the user to treat file servers as a disk drive attached to the client computer. This protects the user from having to learn new commands and makes using the network a natural extension of the user's workstation.

With the use of batch files, login scripts, drive mappings, paths, and search drives, a user's environment can be customized without affecting other network users. In addition, security of the network and user files are enhanced by the use of Login IDs and passwords and trustee rights. The LOGIN ID/Password combination controls physical access to the network. Trustee rights determine the specific type of access privileges that each user possesses.

Questions

1. What does DOS stand for?

2. What are the three components needed for attaching a computer to a Novell network?

3. Under DOS, files may be stored in different areas on the same disk. What are these areas called?

4. What does CHDIR stand for?

5. What NetWare command changes the assignment of drive letters?

6. What does the PATH command tell the computer?

7. A user on a Novell network must have a set of permissions to use a directory on the file server. What are these permissions called?

8. If a user has Read and File scan rights in a directory, can the user store data there? Why or why not?

9. DOS allows a list of commands to be entered in a file. What is this type of file called?

10. A user executes his login script once only in a session. When?

Project

Objective

Before NetWare can be installed on a system, a listing of hardware, users, and other resources must be recorded. Also, all steps taken during the installation process must to be recorded in case something goes wrong and an audit needs to occur.

Additionally, knowing the applications, directories, users, and workstations on the network will help in maintaining the network and in performing future upgrades or expansions that may be required.

Creating a Novell NetWare Log Book

A typical log book contains the information outlined below. One should be created for each server.

Name of the server.

Type of hardware.

Date of installation.

Name of installer.

Operating system:

> Name and version of the operating system in use.
>
> Installation date of the operating system.
>
> Name of the operating system installer.

Server:

> Purchase date of the server.
>
> Server's network address.
>
> Location of the server.

Volume:

> Volume(s) name(s) in the server.
>
> Volume disk number.
>
> Volume(s) size(s).

Users' workstations:

> Users' names.
>
> Users' locations.
>
> Users' network addresses.

Users' workstation types.

Users' workstation RAM.

Users' workstation disk options.

Users' workstation graphics boards and monitors.

Users' workstation hardware options (other).

Applications:

Name of the applications in use.

Application's vendor.

Application's purchase date.

Application's version number.

Application's memory requirements.

Application's disk space requirements.

Additional log information.

Using a word processor and the preceding list as a guide, create a NetWare log book and fill in the information requested for the network that you will be installing during the hands-on portion of this class. Make sure that all information is correct because once the network is set up, it is difficult and time consuming to correct major errors or omissions in the setup process.

NetWare Installation

Objectives

After completing this chapter you will

1. Understand the use of NetWare utility menus.
2. Understand the STARTUP.NCF and AUTOEXEC.NCF files.
3. Be able to load a valid NetWare shell.
4. Understand NetWare Loadable Modules.
5. Be able to configure and install NetWare.

Key Terms

AUTOEXEC.NCF

Hard Disk

NetWare Loadable Module

Network Card

STARTUP.NCF

Workstation

File Server

Hard Disk Controller

NetWare Shell

RAM

Tape Backup

Introduction

In Chapter 8 some of the fundamental concepts of Novell NetWare were introduced. This chapter will begin to demonstrate the concepts with hands-on exercises in NetWare installation and maintenance. First, one must select the right version of NetWare from NetWare Lite through NetWare version 4.0.

NetWare Version 3.11 represents more than just improvements on the original. NetWare versions through 2.2 are designed to operate on an IBM-PC compatible with an 80286 or faster central processing unit (CPU). The 80286 CPU is the microprocessor chip that controls the operation of the computer. Beginning with version 3, NetWare has required a more powerful CPU. NetWare version 3 was originally called NetWare 386 because it required a machine based on the Intel 80386 CPU. What once was Novell Netware 386 now runs on other computers such as 80486 and is now called Netware Version 3. Even though each version must be written for each type of computer it is to be run on, Novell wanted to show that the network operating system was not limited to an 80386 processor. Many versions are now available from Novell which cover a variety of hardware platforms and user needs.

One significantly different version is the System Fault Tolerant version or SFT version. It includes features to ensure data integrity that previous versions did not have. The three most important features are Disk Mirroring, Disk Duplexing, and Transaction Tracking.

Disk Mirroring uses two hard disks attached to the same hard disk controller. All the data is written to both hard disks in exactly the same way. If one of the hard disks should fail, the other contains all the data, and normal operation continues until the LAN administrator or other maintenance person can replace the failed drive.

Another method for ensuring the data on the hard disk remains intact is called Disk Duplexing. It uses two controller cards and two hard disks. Again the data is duplicated on the second hard disk, but it is sent to it separately so failures in the controller card will not damage the data on both hard drives.

Transaction Tracking helps ensure data accuracy by keeping an ongoing record of past changes to the data on the disk. If a user is in the process of making several changes to a database when, for instance, there is a power failure, the changes can be "rewound" so they can be verified.

For IBM-compatible computers, the least expensive and least functional system is NetWare Lite. It is intended for very small networks with limited ability. Novell's latest release is NetWare Version 4.0, a full-featured version of NetWare which is primarily targeted for very large networking environments. NetWare Version 3.11 is widely used and very functional for most requirements. It provides a broad range of functions including connectivity to other types of networks. It is also available in versions that provide the same functions with a smaller number of workstations attached. At the writing of this book, Novell had condensed its offerings by selling NetWare versions 2.2, 3.11, 4.0 and NetWare Lite only.

Novell NetWare 3.11 will be the model for the remainder of this text. Many of the commands available in NetWare 3.11 are also available in version 2.2. Although the most significant difference (for the purposes of this text) is the installation process, a statistical comparison of Version 2.2 and 3.11 is shown in Table 9-1.

	Version 2.2	Version 3.11
Logical simultaneous connections on each file server	100	250
Concurrent open files per file server	1,000	100,000
Maximum files concurrently using TTS	200	10,000
Volumes per file server	32	64
Hard disks per volume	1	32
Hard disks per file server	32	2,048
Directory entries per volume	10,240	2,097,152
Maximum addressable RAM memory	15.6 MB	4 GB
Maximum addressable disk storage	2 GB	32 TB
Maximum file size	256 MB	4 GB
Maximum volume size	256 MB	32 TB

Table 9-1 NetWare Version 2.2 and 3.11 compared.

Installing NetWare

Novell has worked very hard to provide the installer with a menu-driven interface that allows easy selection of important options or a relatively simple default installation in which the NetWare installation program determines how NetWare should be installed. Both methods require the installer to have some information and experience.

The installer must have a complete list of the hardware on the file server, including information on the type of hard disk and the type of network card to be used. NetWare's control of the file server depends on its being able to communicate with each peripheral device accurately.

Communication with most devices depends on three pieces of information, the base memory address, the base I/O address, and the interrupt number. The computer's memory is arranged so it can be accessed through use of an address. Memory at the base memory address is often used by the Network Interface Card as a buffer. This buffer stores information the NIC sends to the processor before it is ready to process it. The base I/O address is the address of an I/O port that defines the way the processor communicates with a device. The base memory and base I/O addresses of each peripheral must be known by NetWare, and therefore the installer.

The CPU spends most of its time reading from memory and executing the instructions it finds there. Some devices, however, must interrupt this process so the CPU can perform some special, critical task. A network interface card, for example, must interrupt the CPU so incoming data can be dealt with. Each device needing access is assigned an Interrupt Request Line number. The number and the base memory and base I/O addresses are often selectable on the device so the person installing the equipment can make sure that each device does not use another's address or interrupt number. The Interrupt Request Line number used in each peripheral must also be recorded for use during installation.

Often the equipment on the file server will require special drivers supplied by the manufacturer. A driver is a program written to control a specific peripheral such as a tape drive. Novell may not have supplied the driver for a particular unit. If it is intended to be used with NetWare, the manufacturer of the tape drive must supply the driver on diskettes. These drivers must be available at the time of installation. Similar information for each type of workstation on the network will also be needed. The following are items that the network administrator needs to be concerned with before installing NetWare. Use the list below to collect and record this information.

For the file server the information required is as follows.

1. File server. The make and model type of the computer that will be used as a file server.

2. Hard disk type. Manufacturers and model numbers of all hard disks attached to the file server.

3. Hard disk controller type. Manufacturers and model numbers of the controller cards used with the hard disks, including RAM and ROM addresses and Interrupt Request Lines used.

4. Network card type. Manufacturers and model numbers of the network interface cards used, including RAM and ROM addresses and Interrupt Request Lines used.

5. Tape backup type, if tape is to be attached directly to the file server. Manufacturers and model numbers of the tape drive units installed, including RAM and ROM addresses and Interrupt Request Lines used.

6. Types of printers attached to file server. Manufacturers and model numbers of the printers that will be attached to the file server and the ports, LPT or COM, that will be used with each.

For the workstation the information required is as follows:

1. Workstation manufacturer and model. The make and model type of the computer that will be used as a workstation.

2. Amount of Random access memory (RAM). Amount of conventional memory. Conventional memory is the memory below 640K. The installer also needs to know the amount of extended or expanded memory. Extended memory and expanded memory are different conventions for using memory above 640K. If the workstation has 1 megabyte of RAM the memory between 640K and 1 megabyte is extended memory and not normally addressable by DOS. Some programs, including NetWare, can use this memory. If the workstation has more than 1 megabyte of RAM it might be extended or expanded. The expanded memory conventions allow programs to switch blocks of data back and forth between the expanded memory region and the conventional memory region below 640K.

3. DOS version. The DOS versions used on all workstations to be attached to the network.

4. IBM or compatible. Some of the installable options in NetWare are specific to IBM computers.

5. Interrupt Request setting, I/O address setting, and Memory address setting on the network interface card.

The installer should be familiar with DOS. Much of the setup after installation of the file server requires a complete understanding of DOS directories, commands, and batch files.

Installation Preparation

Before installing any program, including a network operating system, backup copies of the distribution diskettes should be made. NetWare is not copy protected, so DOS commands can be used to make copies.

To make the copies, have the number of original disks plus two or three extras. They must be the same type of disks as the NetWare distribution disks. NetWare is shipped on either 3 1/2- or 5 1/4-inch disks, each size now being high density. The extra disks may be needed if some of the new disks do not format correctly.

Attach the label stickers to the blank disks if needed, and set the write protect tabs on the original disks. When a disk is write protected, the computer cannot write to or change any information on the disk. On 3 1/2-inch disks, the write protect tab is the small sliding tab on the corner of the disk. It should be set in the open position so the hole goes through the disk. On a 5 1/4-inch disk, the write protect tab is a small sticker that covers the hole in the side of the disk; the disk is protected when the tab is on. The procedures to make the backup copies is the same as for ordinary DOS files. Step by step instructions are provided in the hands-on section of this chapter.

NetWare Menus

All NetWare utility menus are designed around a few relatively simple rules of operation. Understanding how these menus work is essential since many of them change as you use them. In some utilities, completing an option makes another option available. Also, the menus may include different items depending on how the utility was started.

Fig. 9-1 shows an example of the opening menu of the NetWare System Configuration utility SYSCON. Along the top is a box that indicates the name and version of the utility and may also display the date and time. No information in this box can be changed by the user.

Notice that some boxes are drawn with a single line while others are drawn using double lines. Single-line boxes in NetWare menu utilities usually contain information that the user cannot change. The box in the middle of the screen shows main menu for this utility. It consists of a bright double line with various options inside. To select an item, use the arrow keys to move the highlighted bar to the option desired. Then press the ENTER key.

If there are more items than can fit in the box, a small arrow pointing down will appear in the lower left of the box. Another method for selecting options from a list is to begin typing the name of the option. The highlighted bar will move to the appropriate option as you type.

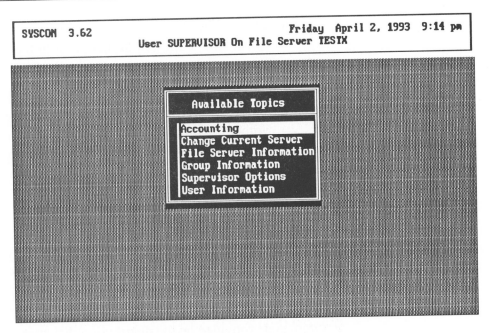

SYSCON 3.62   Friday April 2, 1993 9:14 pm
                    User SUPERVISOR On File Server TESTX

Available Topics

Accounting
Change Current Server
File Server Information
Group Information
Supervisor Options
User Information

Fig. 9-1. Screen displaying the System Configuration utility.

The NetWare menus often use Novell's names for the keys rather than the commonly accepted name for the key. For example, the SELECT key is the ENTER key on the keyboard. The following list shows the Novell names for certain keys and their functions.

1. Select. The ENTER or RETURN key. The select key is used to choose an item from a list.

2. Help. The F1 key. This key will provide information on the options currently available to the user. Pressing F1 twice shows the uses of all the function keys.

3. Modify. The F3 key. Some highlighted options can be changed by pressing the F3 key. If an option can be changed this way, a new box will appear for the user to put the new information in.

4. Mark. The F5 key. Some menu commands can be executed on multiple items. The F5 key marks the items in a list so the next command will affect them all.

5. Accept. The ESCAPE key. This is the most unusual feature of the NetWare menus, because it seems backwards from computer conventions. After making selections in a menu, the user presses the ESCAPE key to return to the previous menu. Rather than discarding the changes the user made, this choice accepts and saves them.

6. Cancel. The F7 key. This key returns to the previous menu without saving the options selected.

7. Insert. The INSERT key. This key is used to insert a new item in a list. If it is allowed at that point in the menu, the user will be prompted for an item to place in the list.

8. Delete. The DELETE key. This key will delete an item from a list.

9. Exit. ALT/F10. This key combination exits the menu utility without saving any pending information and without prompting the user with "Are you sure?" (Often, however, changes are saved as they are made.)

Creating a NetWare Shell

In previous versions of Novell NetWare, an appropriate network shell had to be created for each workstation, specific to the type of NIC in the workstation. As discussed earlier, the shell is the software interface to the rest of the network. NetWare built the shell programs by combining the IPX shell program code provided on the distribution diskettes with the drivers for the particular network card being used. This type of network shell is known as a dedicated IPX. NetWare still ships with drivers for many different brands of network cards, using standards such as Ethernet and Token-Ring. Drivers are also included for many nonstandard or proprietary cards. NetWare Version 3.11 still provides a program called WSGEN which can, for most network interface cards, still generate a dedicated IPX. If you desire to create a dedicated IPX, you are referred to the NetWare Manuals for information on creating such an IPX.

In the latest releases of NetWare, however, a new type of network shell is used. It is called the Open Data Link Interface or ODI.

The ODI drivers are complete programs for specific network cards that do not need any special linking. Additionally, the IPXODI approach to the shell allows the same network interface card to support two protocols at once, for example, NE2000 Ethernet for IPX and IP drivers for TCP/IP.

In either case, ODI or dedicated IPX, the shell programs are usually loaded onto a bootable disk to make access to the network as easy as possible. A bootable disk is a disk that the DOS system files have been previously loaded onto. The disk may also be known as a boot disk. To create a NetWare boot disk you will need the copies of the NetWare disks, a DOS disk, a blank disk, and any special driver disk that your network interface card may require. You will need a blank disk for each type of computer you intend to make a boot disk for.

Installing NetWare on the File Server

Installation and loading procedures for NetWare 3.11 are significantly different from those used for the 2.X versions of NetWare. In the 2.X version, the network operating system had to be configured and then linked prior to installation on the file server. Then, if one or more of the configuration parameters had to be changed, the entire configuration, linking, and installation process had to be repeated.

NetWare version 3.11 is dynamic and uses NetWare Loadable Modules (NLM's) to supply drivers and other software needed to control the network. Drivers can be unloaded and reloaded with different configurations without downing the file server.

As with other versions of NetWare, it is still a good idea to choose hardware components which are on Novell's approved list. Also, even though NetWare is fully configurable from NLM's, it is still very important that the installer write down hardware details such as memory addresses, interrupts, and I/O addresses as though configuring a 2.X version of NetWare. Verify that interrupt numbers are not duplicated and that I/O addresses and memory addresses do not overlap within a driver or across drivers.

Like some earlier versions of NetWare, NetWare 3.11 requires some extended memory to operate. It is also a good idea to make sure that you have enough extended memory to support your operation prior to the initial installation process. In general the amount of memory needed is the greater of 4 MB or the result of multiplying the size of the hard drive in megabytes by .023 and then dividing by block size in kilobytes plus 2 MB for the operating system. For example, assuming a block size of 4KB and a hard disk size of 200 MB, $(200 \times 0.023)/4 + 2 = 3.15$. Therefore, the amount of memory needed is 4 MB. If the volume has added name space, the formula is the same, but instead of multiplying by 0.023, multiply by 0.032.

Logging onto an Existing File Server

Assuming the file server is up and running and the cabling system is complete, a workstation should now be able to login to the server.

To login, a workstation needs to be booted with the NetWare boot disk created earlier, and the workstation's AUTOEXEC.BAT should be modified to include

> LSL
>
> NIC driver (such as PCN2L)
>
> IPXODI
>
> NETX (or XMSNETX or EMSNETX)

Note that all four programs are on the WSGEN diskette distributed with NetWare 3.11. If the network interface card uses the default interrupt, I/O address, or Memory settings, no further action is needed. Otherwise, one must enter the actual settings into a text file called SHELL.CFG which must be in the same directory as IPXODI.COM.

If the user is successful in communicating with the network via the above four programs, the entry of the DIR F: command will show the LOGIN directory on the file server. The LOGIN directory is where users are placed when they are connected but not logged into the file server.

If the installer is the first user to login to this file server, the only user names available are SUPERVISOR and GUEST. Since GUEST has very few rights, it is the supervisor that creates all other user names allowed to login to the server.

Logging in as the supervisor is achieved by typing LOGIN SUPERVISOR and pressing the ENTER key. A prompt by the LOGIN program to enter a password will appear. Pressing ENTER indicates that the installer does not have a password.

Typing DIR F:\ and pressing the ENTER key shows that even though this is a new file server, it is not an empty one. NetWare has created four directories called SYSTEM, LOGIN, MAIL, and PUBLIC. The SYSTEM directory contains the NetWare program files that actually run the network. The LOGIN directory contains the LOGIN program and other programs or data files a user might need before logging into the network. The MAIL directory contains a directory for each user with the user's login script in it. Each of those directories contains files that are used by NetWare to maintain the user's account. The fourth directory created by NetWare is the PUBLIC directory. It contains all the NetWare utilities that users, including the supervisor, use to manage their accounts and files. In the following chapters those utilities will be further explored.

Before leaving any network terminal, a user, especially the supervisor, should logout. Making this a habit is an important component of network security. The LOGOUT program is used to close the user's account on the file server, but it does not completely disconnect the workstation.

To logout, the command LOGOUT is typed at the F> prompt and the ENTER key is pressed. At this stage, workstations can access the LOGIN directory and its contents, but not actually be logged in. The workstation can be turned off without fear of leaving files open on the server.

Typically a network file server is left turned on all the time. This is because the most stressful part of the operation of any computer equipment is turning it on or off. If it is necessary to turn the server off, the DOWN command must be entered at the file server keyboard. It ensures that all files the workstations might have left open are closed and that any files the server was using are closed. The DOWN command also informs workstations and other servers on the network that the server is no longer available. The file server can be safely turned off after it has responded to the DOWN command.

Hands-on NetWare Installation

Installation Preparation

Making Backup Copies with a Dual Disk Drive Computer — Two Disk Drives of the Same Type

If the computer being used to make the backup copies has two disk drives of the same type specified as A and B (e.g., two 3 1/2-inch drives or two 5 1/4-inch drives), follow the instructions below. If the computer has only one disk drive, skip to the Single Disk Drive instructions.

1. Boot the computer with a DOS disk. The DOS disk should be write protected to help protect against computer viruses.

2. Type **DISKCOPY A: B:** and press the ENTER key.

The DISKCOPY program will instruct you to insert the source disk in drive A: and the target disk in drive B:. The original NetWare disk is the source disk and one of the blank disks is the target.

3. Press the ENTER key when the disks are inserted and the copy process will begin.

When the copy has been successfully made, the DISKCOPY program will ask you if you would like to copy another.

4. Answer Yes by pressing Y and pressing the ENTER key. You will be prompted to insert source and target disks again.

5. Remove the two disks you started with and write the name of the original on the copy. Insert the second source disk and another blank disk. Continue this process with all of the NetWare distribution disks.

Making Backup Copies with a Single Disk Drive Computer

A single disk drive computer will probably have a hard disk installed and will only need to be turned on to be booted with DOS.

1. Type **DISKCOPY A: A:** and press the ENTER key.

2. The computer will ask you to insert the source disk in drive A. Press the ENTER key when ready.

The computer will read the disk and then ask for the target disk to be put in Drive A. It then writes to the target disk and may ask for the source disk again. This process continues until the copy is complete. Copying disks with a single disk drive takes a little longer because you may have to change the diskette several times to make one copy. Copy all the NetWare disks, writing the name of each original on its copy.

Installation

Boot the file server with DOS to prove that the computer is operating properly as a DOS machine. Then, create a bootable DOS or C drive partition on the system disk using FDISK and DOS version 3.1, 3.3x, 5.0, or 6.0. (According to Novell, there are potential problems in using DOS versions 3.2 and 4.0.) The partition is needed so that the file server can boot from its hard drive without the requirement of a special boot diskette.

1. Follow the DOS instructions for partitioning the hard drive, and allow 3MB to 5MB for the DOS partition. Make this partition active.

2. Format the DOS partition using FORMAT C:/S so that the system is transferred. This allows the server, once installed, to boot or come up without a diskette in the A: drive.

3. Copy the NETWARE SYSTEM-1 and SYSTEM-2 diskettes to this DOS partition.

4. Boot your computer by pressing CONTROL, ALT, and DELETE keys simultaneously to verify that your C: partition is actually bootable.

The rest of the hard disk can be used for NetWare. If you do not create a DOS partition on the hard drive, you must always boot the file server from the special boot diskette. This disk is created by formatting it with the /S format option and performing step 3 above to the disk.

In earlier versions of NetWare, the remainder of the hard drive had to be low-level formatted prior to proceeding with installation. This step is no longer necessary.

Do note, though, that if either the FDISK or the formatting step fails, there is a hardware problem that must be corrected prior to proceeding with the installation.

5. Assuming all steps to this point have been completed success-fully, you may now load SERVER by typing **SERVER** and then pressing the ENTER key.

6. NetWare then asks for a file server name. Type in a desired name between 2 and 47 characters long. (Be aware that many commands reference the file server name; therefore, the name should not be unnecessarily long.)

7. Then, NetWare asks for a hexadecimal number (one to eight digits and greater than 00000000) for the internal network number. This number must be unique among the file servers which are connected to one another. This number is used by the NLMs for communication.

8. NetWare then displays the NetWare Version number and the user count. Verify this information against what you purchased.

You should then see a colon, the normal prompt for the file server console.

9. You are now ready to load the driver for the hard disk. Novell supplies five standard drivers: ISADISK, DCB, PS2ESDI, PS2MFM, and PS2SCSI. If your hard drive is not among the supplied drivers, your supplier must supply the hard disk driver, and you must load it. To load a Novell-supplied hard disk driver or one your supplier has provided, type the following and then press <Enter>.

   LOAD XXX (where XXX is the name of the driver, including the path name if the driver is to be loaded from diskette)

10. Now that the file server recognizes itself as a file server, and now that it recognizes its own hard drive, you are ready to load and run the INSTALL program by typing the following and then pressing ENTER.

    LOAD C:INSTALL

    NetWare will then prompt you through the remaining steps of the installation process.

11. First, the main screen appears (see Fig. 9-2). This screen allows you to specify

    Disk Options

    Volume Options

    System Options

    Product Options

    or to EXIT.

Each of these options can be selected and configured

12. Choose Disk Options by pressing ENTER. With the exception of the Partition Tables option, the options in this submenu are usually needed for diagnostic purposes in the event that the hard disk drive's performance becomes suspicious.

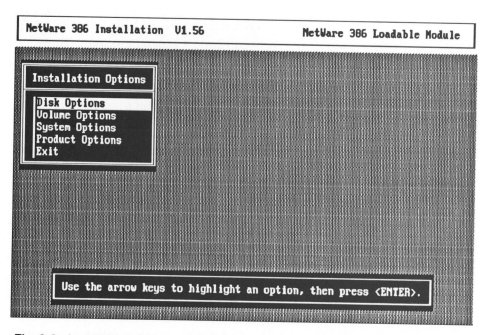

Fig. 9-2. Installation Options Menu for NetWare Version 3.11.

13. Partition Tables must be selected during initial installation to assign the NetWare partition. Select this option by highlighting Partition Tables and pressing the ENTER key.

When you select this option, NetWare will display a partition type screen and the Partition Options submenu will be displayed. See Fig. 9-3. Prior to creating the NetWare Partition, only the DOS partition and Free Space should

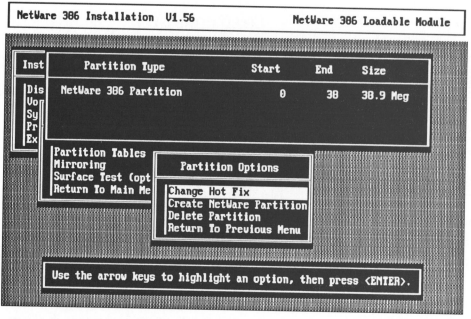

Fig. 9-3. Partition Type Table.

appear in the list of drives which are attached to the controller. If no drives or the wrong type of drives appear in this display, stop immediately. If no drives appear, then check connections and retry this option. If the wrong types of drives appear, escape out of this menu back to the : prompt and repeat all file server installation steps. When the correct list of disk drive(s) is displayed continue.

14. Cursor down to the Create NetWare Partition option and press ENTER. This selection allows you to create a NetWare partition from the remainder of the hard disk drive.

Note that you can change the size of the "Hot Fix" area on the hard drive. While it is not a good idea to reduce the size of the Hot Fix area, it may be advisable to increase the size of the hot fix table if the hard disk drive already has many spared sectors upon initial installation. By enlarging the hot fix area, you allow more space for redirection in the event a bad block is discovered during processing.

15. Press ESC, then Y and ENTER to create the NetWare partition.

16. Press ESC twice to go back to the Installation Options menu. (Refer to Fig. 9.2)

17. Volume Options on Installation Options Menu. This option allows you to choose the volume configuration for the file server. Select this option by highlighting it and then pressing the ENTER key. Press INSERT to create the first volume (See Fig. 9-4)

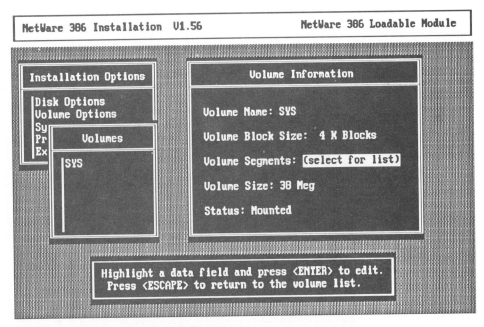

Fig. 9-4. Volume Information Screen.

263

As mentioned earlier in the text, the first volume of the hard drive must be named SYS:. The default block size is 4K. To use the entire remainder of the hard drive and the default block size, press the ESC key, the Y key, and ENTER to create the SYS: volume.

To reset the block size and/or to create additional volumes, first assign the desired number of volume segments to the SYS volume. The number of volume segments can be calculated by taking the size in megabytes of the desired volume and then dividing that number by the block size. For example, to assign 70 MB to the SYS: volume, the volume segment size would be (70 x 1024)/4 = 17920 blocks. When entries are complete, press the ESC, Y, and ENTER keys to return to the Volume list.

To insert an additional volume, press <Ins> while on the Volume list. NetWare will prompt you for the volume name, block size, and volume segments.

Note that while 4K is the default block size, you can adjust the block size to 8K, 16K, 32K, or 64K. The block size indicates the number of bytes which are read or written at one time to the disk. It is usually a good idea to use the default unless you specifically know that a different block size would function better.

18. Press ESC to return to the Installation Options Menu.

19. The System Options item on the Installation Options Menu allows you to load additional software and drivers so that the file server can function and so that it can automatically boot as a file server. (See Fig. 9-5). Choose this option by highlighting System Options and then pressing the ENTER key.

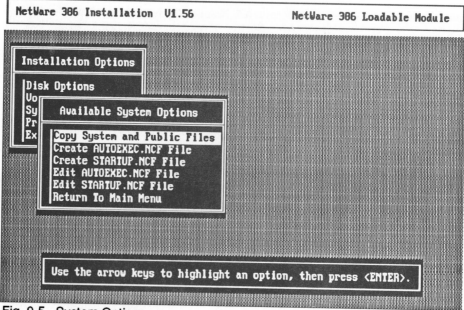

Fig. 9-5. System Options.

20. You must first copy System and Public files from the distribution diskettes to the file server NetWare Partition. To do this, highlight Copy System and Public Files and press ENTER. Since you haven't mounted the volume, you are now prompted to do so. From this point, follow the prompt to copy these diskettes to the file server.

21. After the System and Public diskettes have been copied to the file server, you must create STARTUP.NCF. Highlight this option and press the ENTER key. The option lets you create the file needed to automatically load the disk driver and set the operating environment for the file server. The STARTUP.NCF file is stored on the bootable DOS drive (C: if your server will boot from the hard drive). When selected, this option should display the suggested STARTUP.NCF file based on the disk driver already loaded. To save this STARTUP.NCF file, press the ESC key and then select Yes to save the configuration. To modify the STARTUP.NCF, edit the file and then press the ESC key and select Yes to save the configuration.

22. Press the ESC key to go back to the Installation Options menu.

23. The Product Options selection is used to load such things as the NLM for Macintosh.

24. Press the ALT and ESC keys simultaneously to proceed without selecting product options.

At this point, you should be back to the : prompt on the file server monitor, but the Install program is still running. You are now ready to load the LAN drivers, the drivers which will control the operation of the NICs. You must load each driver and then bind it to the IPX protocol.

25. To load a LAN driver, type

    LOAD XXX and press the ENTER key.

    Here XXX is the complete path name and file name for the LAN driver. If you are in doubt as to the LAN driver's name, consult the documentation for the network interface card you are using.

    NetWare will then prompt you for the port and interrupt number for the NIC. Again, refer to the documentation for your NIC for this information and for the jumper settings on the NIC itself.

26. Bind the LAN driver to the IPX protocol by typing **BIND IPX to YYY** and pressing the ENTER key.

    Here YYY is the name of the LAN driver without the complete path name.

For example, if your network interface cards were NE2000 Ethernet cards, which you wish to use with IPX, you would type:

LOAD NE2000 and press the ENTER key.

Here, you can accept the default or type in the correct one and press the ENTER key. Then type BIND IPX to NE2000 and press the ENTER key.

The driver must be loaded for each NIC in the file server.

27. You will be prompted to enter a network number. This number is a unique 8-digit hexadecimal number greater than zero to be assigned to the cable segment to which the network is attached. This is not the internal network address for the file server, and it must not be the same as the internal network address. If the cable segment already has been assigned a network number (i.e., if the cabling connects an operating network), the same network number must be used.

28. Return to the Install utility by pressing the ALT and ESC keys simultaneously.

29. Highlight the System Options and press ENTER. On the system options submenu, highlight Create AUTOEXEC.NCF and press the ENTER key.

The system will then display all of the commands you have entered as part of the installation process and show them as the potential AUTOEXEC.NCF. This file is similar to the AUTOEXEC.BAT file in that it executes when the file server is booted and will automatically load and bind the drivers you have selected individually in the installation process. Make sure the AUTOEXEC.NCF file is correct and edit it to fix anything that is incorrect before saving it by pressing the ESC key and then selecting Yes to save the file. (See Fig. 9-6).

30. Exit Install by pressing the ESC key twice and selecting Yes. You should be back to the : prompt.

31. The installation process is now complete. To check to see if your installation process worked, down the file server by typing **DOWN** and press the ENTER key.

32. Wait for the prompt which instructs you to type in EXIT to return to DOS. Type in **EXIT**, and turn off the file server. Turn it back on. Your file server should automatically boot. Type **SERVER** (or create an AUTOEXEC.BAT to execute SERVER).

Fig. 9-6. A sample AUTOEXEC.NCF.

Creating the Workstation Boot Disk

The last step in the installation process is to create a workstation boot disk. The most straightforward way of doing this is to format the disk with the /S option.

1. Boot the computer with the DOS diskette

2. Type **FORMAT A: /S** and press the ENTER key. The format program will prompt you to insert a new diskette.

3. Insert the blank disk in drive A: and press the ENTER key when ready.

The new disk will be formatted and the DOS system files will be placed on the diskette so it is bootable. When the format process is complete, label the disk NetWare Boot Disk. We will now place on this disk the NetWare files required to boot the machine and attach it to the network.

Copying the Open Data-Link Shell to the Bootable Diskette in a System with a Hard Drive and a Single Floppy Drive

1. Boot your computer

2. Type **MD C:\TEMPFILE**

3. Insert a copy of the WSGEN diskette from the NetWare distribution diskettes into the A: floppy drive.

4. Type **COPY   A:\DOSODI*.*   C:\TEMPFILE*.***

5. Type **COPY   A:NET*.*   C:\TEMPFILE*.***

6. Remove the WSGEN diskette from the A: drive

7. Insert the bootable diskette created above into the A: drive

8. Type **COPY   C:\TEMPFILE\LSL.COM   A:** and press the ENTER key

9. Type **COPY C:\TEMPFILE\IPXODI.COM   A:** and press the ENTER key

10. Type **COPY C:\TEMPFILE*****.COM   A:** where ***** is the driver for the type of network interface card in your workstation and press the ENTER key (PCN2L.COM for IBM PC II network cards).

11. Type **COPY   C:\TEMPFILE\NET*.COM   A:** and press the ENTER key.

12. Type **COPY CON: A:AUTOEXEC.BAT** and press the ENTER key

13. Type **LSL** and press the ENTER key.

14. Type ***** and press the ENTER key where ***** is the network interface card driver mentioned above.

15. Type **IPXODI** and press the ENTER key.

16. Type **NETX** and press the ENTER key.

17. Press F6 and the ENTER to save the AUTOEXEC.BAT file.

Two Diskette Drives of the Same Type

With two disk drives of the same type, the following instructions can be used to copy the network shell files to your boot disk.

With the WSGEN disk in drive A: and the your boot disk in drive B:

1. Type **COPY A:\DOSODI\LSL.COM B:** and press the ENTER key.

2. Type **COPY A:\DOSODI*****.COM B:** and press the ENTER key where ***** is the name of the driver for the type of network interface card in your workstation

3. Type **COPY A:\DOSODI\IPXODI.COM B:** and press the ENTER key.

4. Type **COPY A:NET*.* B:** and press the ENTER key.

5. Type **COPY CON: A:AUTOEXEC.BAT** and press the ENTER key

6. Type **LSL** and press the ENTER key.

7. Type ***** and press the ENTER key where ***** is the network interface card driver mentioned above.

8. Type **IPXODI** and press the ENTER key.

9. Type **NETX** and press the ENTER key.

10. Press the CTRL key and the Z key at the same time to save the AUTOEXEC.BAT file.

Testing the New Boot Diskette

1. Insert the boot diskette with the AUTOEXEC.BAT just created into the A: drive.

2. Press the CONTROL, ALT, and DELETE keys simultaneously to boot your workstation.

3. Type **F:** and press the ENTER key.

4. Type **LOGIN XXXXX\SUPERVISOR** where XXXXX is the name of the file server which you wish to log in and press the ENTER key .

5. Type the SUPERVISOR'S password, if one has been assigned.

Note that the files copied to the disk can be copied to the workstation's hard disk. The commands in the AUTOEXEC.BAT above can be incorporated into the workstation's AUTOEXEC.BAT file so the workstation will boot up to the network. The last line could be F: to get to the login prompt automatically.

Summary

NetWare must be installed for both the workstation and the file server. Using NetWare Version 3.11, the shell can be created by executing a series of programs via the AUTOEXEC.BAT file on the workstation without need for configuration. That program is then placed on a bootable disk with the appropriate NETX program. The version of NETX used depends on the version of DOS used and whether the workstation has expanded or extended memory.

The file server is prepared with the installation process. Through use of the INSTALL NetWare Loadable Module, files called STARTUP.NCF and AUTOEXEC.NCF are created so that the file server can automatically boot with the configuration selected during the INSTALL process.

With the file server completely installed and running, a user can login by running the AUTOEXEC.BAT on the workstation boot diskette which automatically runs the Open Data-Link version of the IPXODI program and the appropriate NETX program.

Questions

1. In a NetWare utility menu, can the user change data in a box made with a double line?

2. In most NetWare menus, what key is pressed to accept the selections and return to the previous menu?

3. Does a NetWare boot disk need DOS on it in addition to the NetWare shell programs?

4. How is the Open Data-Link version of IPX different from earlier versions of IPX?

5. Is 00000001 a valid network address?

6. Is FILESERVER a valid server name?

7. What are the four directories created on the file server during the installation process?

8. What is a NetWare Loadable Module?

9. What must be done to change a Network Interface Card Driver on a file server which has already been installed?

10. How much memory is needed for a file server with a single 255 MB volume?

Projects

Objective

The following projects are designed to familiarize you with the process of booting a workstation, logging into the network, and using the help facility available in NetWare.

Project 1. Logging into NetWare

1. Boot a workstation with the appropriate disk.

2. The AUTOEXEC.BAT should cause you to be attached to a file server.

3. Type **DIR F:** and notice the number of bytes free listed at the bottom of the screen.

4. Login as the SUPERVISOR. Press SHIFT PRINT SCREEN to record the results.

5. Type **DIR F:** and notice the number of bytes free listed at the bottom of the screen. Why is this figure larger than the one shown earlier?

Project 2. Using the NetWare's Help Facility

NetWare contains a help facility that contains extensive information about NetWare commands, concepts, utilities, and messages.

1. Login as the user GUEST.
2. Type **HELP** and press the ENTER key.

To navigate in any of the help screens use the TAB key.

3. Press the TAB key until the cursor is under the triangle marker at the left of Network Concepts and press the ENTER key.
4. Press the TAB key until the cursor moves to Ip--M and press the ENTER key.
5. Move the cursor to Log in and press the ENTER key.

Read about the login procedure and make any notes that you deem necessary.

6. Press the ESC and the DOWN ARROW keys until the cursor reaches Login Scripts and press the ENTER key.

Read about the login scripts and make any notes that you deem necessary.

7. When you finish reading the information, press the ESC key several times until the NetWare OS screen is displayed.
8. Type **HELP LOGIN** and press the ENTER key.

You will see the earlier login help screen.

9. Practice viewing and reading several other NetWare commands.

The SYSCON Utility and Login Scripts

Objectives

After completing this chapter you will

1. Understand the importance of the System Configuration utility, SYSCON.
2. Understand the functions of each of the main menu selections in SYSCON.
3. Understand the purpose of a login script.
4. Understand login script commands.
5. Understand how to use login script variables.
6. Be able to login and logout of a file server.
7. Be able to create a user with appropriate Login Script using SYSCON.

Key Terms

Account Balance   File Server

Groups   Login Script

Passwords   Rights

SYSCON   Trustees

Introduction

In the last chapter, Novell NetWare was installed on the file server and the workstation was booted with the network shell. That arrangement allowed the user supervisor to login to the file server and view the files listed there. Now the file server must be set up to allow other users to login and easily manage their files and directories.

The NetWare System Configuration utility SYSCON is used to accomplish this. With it the supervisor can create user accounts and groups of user accounts. Each account or group can have different access rights, legal login times, and other attributes. Many of the controls used to set up the user's environment are executed when the user logs in through the use of a login script. It can set the user's drive mappings, check various conditions at the time the user logs in, and write messages to the screen.

SYSCON

Introduction

SYSCON allows the network supervisors to create, change, and delete users and groups of users in addition to enabling many other functions. It is by far the most important utility Novell provides with NetWare since it used to set up the most fundamental aspects of the network. As with many NetWare utilities, some menu options only appear for the supervisor. Users can choose other limited menu options themselves to view and change their own accounts.

Fig. 10-1 shows SYSCON's main menu, which is labeled Available Topics. These topics comprise the essentials of managing the network as a whole. Starting from the top of the menu, SYSCON's primary functions are

1. Accounting
2. Change Current Server
3. File Server Information
4. Group Information
5. Supervisor Options
6. User Information

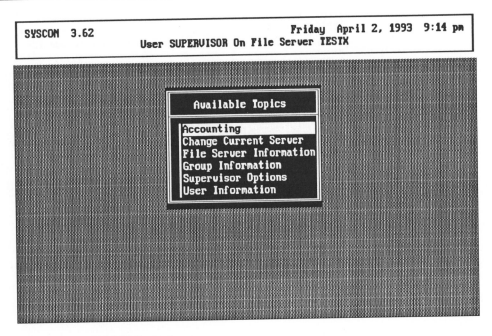

```
SYSCON  3.62                          Friday  April 2, 1993  9:14 pm
                       User SUPERVISOR On File Server TESTX
```

```
                        ┌─────────────────────────┐
                        │     Available Topics     │
                        ├─────────────────────────┤
                        │ Accounting               │
                        │ Change Current Server    │
                        │ File Server Information  │
                        │ Group Information        │
                        │ Supervisor Options       │
                        │ User Information         │
                        └─────────────────────────┘
```

Fig. 10-1. SYSCON's main menu.

The SYSCON Options

Accounting

NetWare is capable of tracking how much each user uses the network. The supervisor can set up each account to be charged a certain rate for various functions of the network. This process is referred to as accounting because it is often used by companies who want to charge each department for its use of the network.

Change Current Server

With the SYSCON program, the supervisor can manage up to eight file servers. He or she can perform all of the functions provided by SYSCON on each of the file servers attached to the network but not simultaneously. Through NetWare Version 3.11, the supervisor must select the file server to be used, then create users or make other changes to each individual file server. Some other networks, most notably Banyan VINES, allow the supervisor to create users and groups that can login to any server attached to the network. NetWare Version 4.0 also provides for a user to be set up as a network user, not just a user on a particular file server.

File Server Information

This option displays a list of information about the file server currently selected. Fig. 10-2 shows a typical File Server Information box. Note that it is a single line box, which means that the information in it cannot be changed.

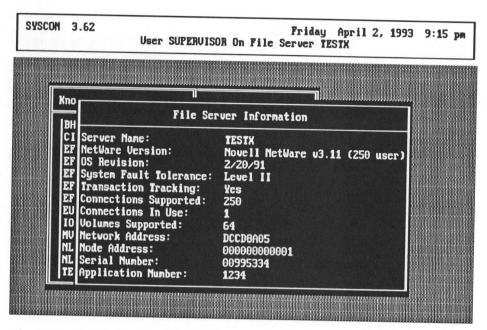

Fig. 10-2. File Server Information box.

Group Information

This selection displays a list of groups of users on this server. Each group name in the list can be selected to display a list of options available. The options are very similar to those available for individual users. Using carefully arranged groups, the supervisor can avoid many details when creating individual accounts and can make changes to the characteristics of many users by making changes to the groups to which they belong. Fig. 10-3 shows the list of groups on the left and the options available after a group has been selected on the right. Notice that create and delete a group are not listed as options. As in most of the NetWare utilities, creating a new item is accomplished by pressing the INSERT key and deleting an item is accomplished by highlighting it and pressing the DELETE key.

Supervisor Options

Not all the information for setting up a user account needs to be entered for each user or even each group. The supervisor has several options that can be used to establish defaults that will be in effect for each new user created. For instance, if the supervisor wanted login time restrictions for all of the new users, he or she could set those defaults from the Supervisor Options menu shown in Fig. 10-4. The defaults set in this menu do not affect existing users. Only users created after the default values have been saved are affected. Even then, characteristics of all users created using the default parameters can be manually reconfigured by the supervisor.

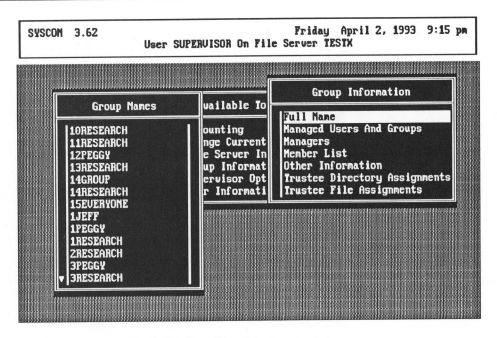

Fig. 10-3. Group information for a file server.

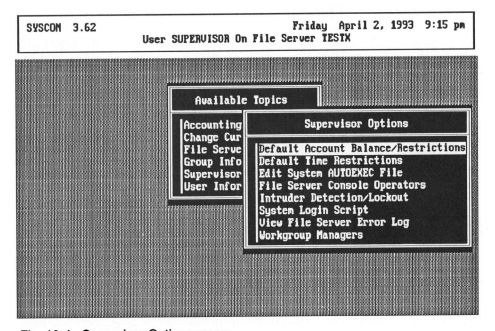

Fig. 10-4. Supervisor Options menu.

User Information

As in Group Information, the User Information option displays a list of existing user names. The supervisor can press INSERT to create a new user, press DELETE to delete a listed user, or highlight a user name and press the ENTER key to select it. Pressing ENTER on a highlighted user name brings up the User Information menu, as shown in Fig. 10-5. This menu provides the most important options for running the network. From here the supervisor controls the most fundamental options a user has.

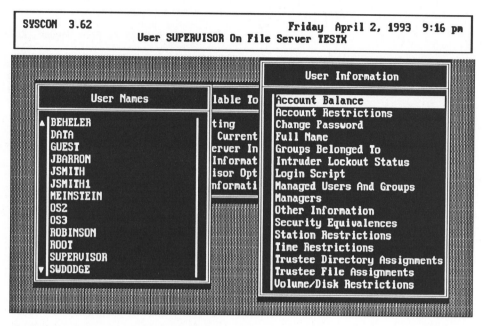

Fig. 10-5. The User Information Menu.

The User Information Options

The User Information menu allows the supervisor to set up individual accounts and assign different attributes to each. The options available in this menu are:

1. Account Balance (appears only if Accounting is enabled)
2. Account Restrictions
3. Change Password
4. Full Name
5. Groups Belonged To
6. Intruder Lockout Status
7. Login Script
8. Managed Users and Groups
9. Managers
10. Other Information
11. Security Equivalences
12. Station Restrictions
13. Time Restrictions
14. Trustee Directory Assignments
15. Trustee File Assignments
16. Volume/Disk Restrictions

Account Balance

This Option allows Supervisors to initialize and monitor a user's account balance. This option does not appear if Accounting has not been enabled on a given file server.

Account Restrictions

There are many separate options that can be set from the Account Restrictions menu as seen in Fig. 10-6. All of these options except Account Disabled can be set under the Supervisor Options as Default Account Balance/Restrictions (see Fig. 10-4). These options include the ability to restrict an account to a certain period of time, limit the number of people that can be logged in under a single user name, and limit the use of a password. The user can be forced to use a password or allowed to log in without one. With a password he or she may or may not be allowed to change it, or may be forced to change it at specified intervals.

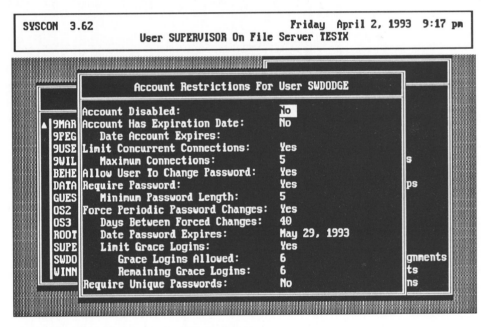

Fig. 10-6. The Account Restrictions menu.

Change Password

An important part of network security is the ability to frequently change the user's password. The user can change it (if the proper rights are provided to the user) or the supervisor can change it using this option. Note that neither the user nor the supervisor can view an existing password, but can only change it.

Full Name

For accounting purposes a Full Name can be assigned to each user name. While a user name may be something like JSMITH the full name might be JOHN MAXIMILIAN SMITH.

279

Groups Belonged To

Each user may belong to several groups or to no groups at all. When selected, this option displays a list of all the groups a user belongs to on the right. Fig. 10-7 shows how a particular user's groups might stack up.

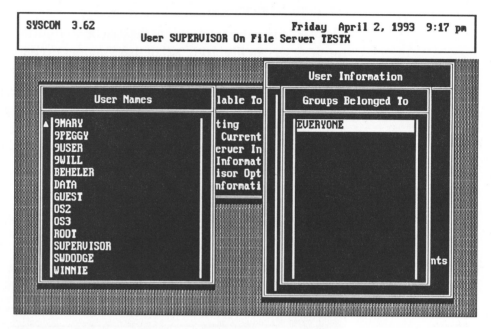

Fig. 10-7. Screen displaying a particular user's groups.

Intruder Lockout Status

This option shows whether or not an account has been locked out due to Intruder Detection. The supervisor can reenable a locked account using this selection.

Login Script

NetWare allows each user name to have a login script which establishes much of the user's environment each time he or she logs in. Fig. 10-8 shows the login script editor. SYSCON provides the supervisor with a simple editor for creating and modifying the login script. This login script performs several mapping operations such as mapping the \SOFTWARE\DATA directory to appear as the root directory of drive I. A message is displayed to the user, and finally the EXIT command sends a command to DOS to display a directory listing. All of these commands are executed each time the user GUEST logs in. NetWare does not require each user to have a login script since the supervisor can set a System Login Script in the Supervisor Options menu. However, it is usually important that each user be given a login script for security reasons.

Earlier versions of NetWare were distributed with a mail package of questionable value. The existence of this mail package has influenced the directory structure of NetWare to this day. A weakness in NetWare is in its handling of login scripts and user mail. Specifically, they are both stored in the same directory, a subdirectory under the MAIL directory. Since every other user on the network must have create access to the mail directory in order to leave mail, those other users could conceivably create a login script and copy it to any user who did not already have a login script.

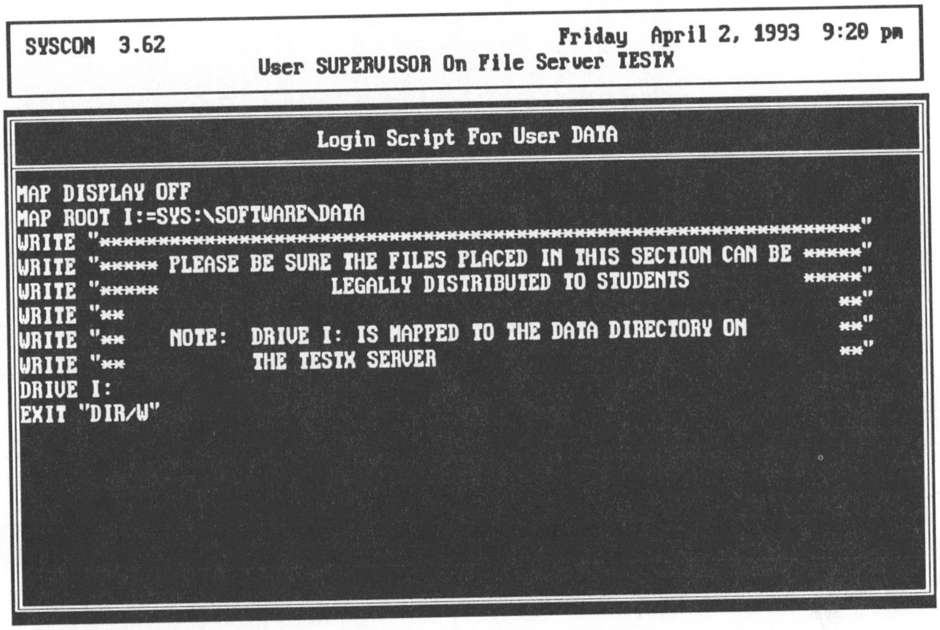

```
SYSCON  3.62                              Friday  April 2, 1993  9:20 pm
                       User SUPERVISOR On File Server TESTX

                        Login Script For User DATA

MAP DISPLAY OFF
MAP ROOT I:=SYS:\SOFTWARE\DATA
WRITE "********************************************************************"
WRITE "***** PLEASE BE SURE THE FILES PLACED IN THIS SECTION CAN BE *****"
WRITE "*****                LEGALLY DISTRIBUTED TO STUDENTS          *****"
WRITE "**                                                              **"
WRITE "**    NOTE:   DRIVE I: IS MAPPED TO THE DATA DIRECTORY ON       **"
WRITE "**                   THE TESTX SERVER                           **"
DRIVE I:
EXIT "DIR/W"
```

Fig. 10-8. A typical login script.

Managed Users and Groups

Fig. 10-9 shows a box that lists the users and groups which are managed by this user. The screen is blank indicating no users, but if there was a listing, it would display those users and groups to which the user can grant and revoke rights. The users and groups which are designated as Direct are specifically assigned to this user to manage. Those users and groups marked as Indirect are users or groups created by NetWare but which are managed by this user.

Managers

This option specifies the managers of the user. Modifications to this list are limited to those who are managers.

Other Information

This option displays information such as the date the user last logged in, disk space usage information, and the user ID number (the object ID for the user). The Object ID identifies the users to the NetWare bindery and also identifies the subdirectory under the SYS:MAIL directory where the user's login script is stored.

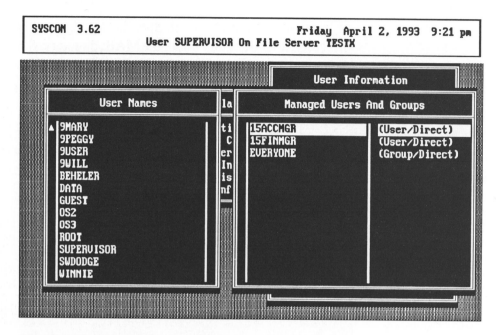

Fig. 10-9. Managed Users and Groups.

Security Equivalences

After assigning all the directory rights and groups for one user, the supervisor may wish to duplicate those rights for another user. To do this, the supervisor can select Security Equivalences after creating the new user. From there the supervisor simply selects the name of an existing user or group from a list. This feature is commonly used to make users' security equivalent to the supervisor.

Station Restrictions

Each network interface card on the network has a unique number consisting of the network number and the node number. Together they are known as the network address. The supervisor can restrict a user to logging in only at specific network addresses, which effectively means only at specific computers. This restriction should be used sparingly because it limits a user's ability to work on another station when his or her own machine is unavailable.

Time Restrictions

In addition to restricting a user to specific computers, the supervisor can also restrict a user to certain times of the day on certain days of the week. Fig. 10-10 shows the chart used by the supervisor to assign these times. Each asterisk represents a half hour interval. Here, user SWDODGE is given access to the network every day from 3:30 a.m. until 12:00 midnight.

Trustee Directory and File Assignments

When a user is given any access to a directory on the file server he or she is known as a trustee of that directory. The supervisor must assign the user as a trustee to each directory he or she will need to access. The supervisor must also assign which rights the user will have in each directory. This is the most

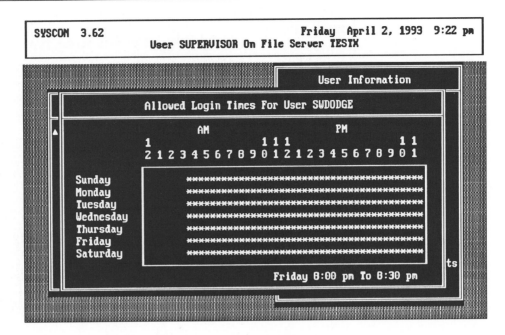

Fig. 10-10. Chart used to assign time restrictions.

direct way of making a user a trustee of a directory, but there are two other ways. First, the user could be a member of a group that is a trustee. Second, the user could be made a Security Equivalent to a user with access to a certain directory. Either way, a user must be given access to a directory to have any rights there. From a documentation point of view, it is better to give a user explicit rights to a directory rather than rely on security equivalences to obtain those rights.

Fig. 10-11 shows user GUEST's trustee assignments. It does not show trustee assignments that GUEST may have from being a member of a group or from being a Security Equivalent to another user. From the screen in Fig. 10-11 the supervisor has four options. First, by selecting a directory listed and pressing ENTER the supervisor can modify the rights user GUEST has to one of those directories. Second, the supervisor can press DELETE on a directory to completely remove the user as a trustee. Third, the INSERT key can be used to add a new directory to the list. And fourth, the ESCAPE key accepts any changes made, and SYSCON returns to the User Information menu.

Trustee File Assignments give rights to specific files rather than to all files in a directory. Explicit rights to a file override any earlier limitations in Trustee Directory assignments.

Volume/Disk Restrictions

This option enables supervisors to limit the disk space a user may use on each volume of the file server. It also displays the amount of space a user has used on each volume. (See Fig. 10-12.)

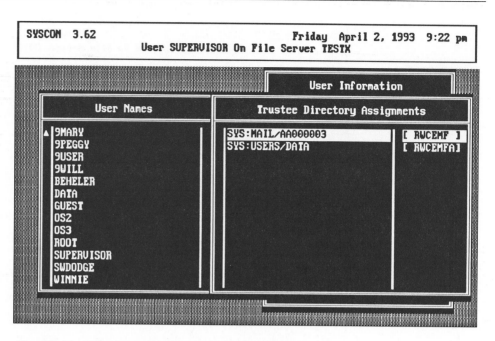

Fig. 10-11. Trustee assignments for user GUEST.

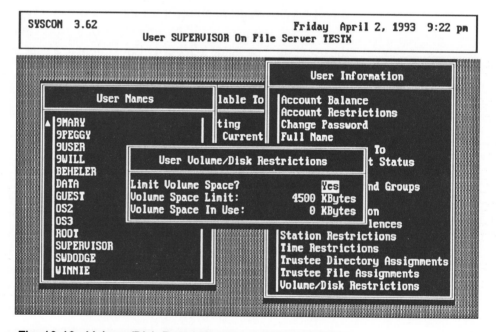

Fig. 10-12. Volume/Disk Restrictions.

Login Scripts

As mentioned earlier, every time a user logs in, NetWare is capable of running a login script. Its function is to issue all the commands needed to set up the user's environment. The environment, in this case, refers primarily to the drive mappings created for the user, but there are many other commands available in login scripts for customizing the login.

The login script is essentially a program that the supervisor writes using a strict set of rules and commands available. A user might type LOGIN JSMITH at the F> prompt after loading the appropriate network drivers. The LOGIN program checks the user name given and executes the system login script set up by the supervisor using SYSCON (see Fig. 10-4), and then executes the user's login script. Many of the commands that can be used in a login script can also be used from the command line. In other words, if the appropriate PATHs have been established, a user can issue several of the commands by typing the name of the command at the F> prompt. The ATTACH command is a good example. The ATTACH command can be used in a login script, and a program called ATTACH.EXE resides in the F:\PUBLIC directory. ATTACH.EXE performs exactly the same function as the ATTACH command in a login script.

The following is a list of login script commands and their uses. Items listed in parentheses are options that may be used. Notice the /user name option in the ATTACH command listed first. Since this option is shown inside the parentheses for the file server name option it can be used only if the file server name option is used and cannot be used by itself. Similarly, the ;password option is shown inside the parentheses for the /user name option, which indicates the ;password option cannot be used unless the /user name option in used. The "|" symbol between two options means one or the other may be used, but not both. Some commands require a parameter. In these cases the parameters are not shown in parentheses. In addition, some commands have several other forms. In such cases, the optional form or forms of the command are displayed following the default syntax.

1. ATTACH (file server name (/user name (;password)))
2. BREAK ON | OFF
3. COMSPEC = drive:(\)file name

   COMSPEC = *n:(\)file name

   COMSPEC = Sn:(\)file name
4. DISPLAY file name

   FDISPLAY file name
5. DOS BREAK ON | OFF
6. (DOS) SET name="value"
7. DOS VERIFY ON | OFF
8. DRIVE drive letter:

   DRIVE *drive number:
9. EXIT ("file name")

10. #program name with command line options
11. FIRE PHASERS number TIMES
12. IF condition (AND condition) THEN command
    IF condition (AND condition) THEN BEGIN
    commands
    END
13. INCLUDE file name
14. MACHINE = "name"
    MACHINE NAME = "name"
15. MAP
16. PAUSE
    WAIT
17. PCCOMPATIBLE
    COMPATIBLE
18. REMARK remark statement
    REM, *, or ; are all remark statements
19. WRITE "comment to be displayed"

Commands

ATTACH

Ordinarily a user logs in to a single file server using the LOGIN command. The ATTACH command in a login script attaches the user to another file server that may be on the same network. This command can also be executed from the command line. Suppose user JSMITH has an account with the same password on two file servers on the network called FS_ONE and FS_TWO. JSMITH's workstation is normally connected to FS_ONE but he usually needs access to FS_TWO also. An ATTACH command could be placed in the login script of his account on FS_ONE that reads

    ATTACH FS_TWO

The LOGIN program will execute the ATTACH command and login JSMITH to FS_TWO using the same user name and password that was used on FS_ONE. The system and user login scripts on FS_TWO are not executed when access to FS_TWO is via the ATTACH command.

Another possibility is that JSMITH might log into any one of many workstations that may be connected to either file server, and he needs access to both servers. If he logs in at a workstation that is already connected to FS_ONE he would need to use the ATTACH command to log into FS_TWO. Likewise, if the workstation is already connected to FS_TWO, he would ATTACH to

FS_ONE. In this case an ATTACH command would exist in the login scripts for both of the accounts. Each would ATTACH to the other file server. On FS_ONE the login script would read

> ATTACH FS_TWO

And on FS_TWO the login script command would be

> ATTACH FS_ONE

The other options of the ATTACH command are used only if the user name or password is different on the other file server. If user JSMITH's supervisor changed her mind about how much access he should have to FS_TWO, she could remove his account there and insist that he use another account for such purposes called STAFF with a password of PICNIC. JSMITH's login script on FS_ONE would now read

> ATTACH FS_TWO/STAFF;PICNIC

The login script for the STAFF account would not need an ATTACH command.

Note that although the syntax of the ATTACH command allows for a password to be explicitly coded in the login script, it is not usually a good idea to do so because it limits the ability to change the password regularly without changing the login script.

BREAK

The BREAK command controls how the keyboard responds during execution of the login script. If the command BREAK ON is used, the login script can be halted by holding down the CONTROL key and pressing BREAK. The BREAK key may also be labeled SCROLL LOCK. If the command is in the form BREAK OFF, the execution of the login script cannot be stopped with CONTROL-BREAK. Note that this command affects only the execution of the Login Script.

COMSPEC

The COMSPEC command can be very important to the proper operation of the workstation. DOS always keeps a pointer (called the COMSPEC environment variable) to the file containing the command processor program. The command processor provided with every version of DOS is a program called COMMAND.COM. DOS must be told where this file is located because it must often be reloaded into memory after the execution of a program. Ordinarily when a computer is booted the COMSPEC variable is set to point to the COMMAND.COM that was used to boot the computer. If the computer was booted from floppy disk drive A:, the COMSPEC variable would probably read

> COMSPEC=A:\COMMAND.COM.

But if the boot disk was then removed, COMMAND.COM would no longer reside where the COMSPEC variable points to. If this computer were on a network, the COMSPEC variable could be set to point to a copy of COMMAND.COM on a network drive where it cannot be removed.

The COMSPEC login script command allows the variable to be set automatically when the user logs in. In its simplest form, the command COMSPEC = drive:(\)file name sets the COMSPEC variable to a value such as

COMSPEC = F:COMMAND.COM

where F: has already been mapped to a directory containing a copy of COMMAND.COM. The drive option can indicate any drive letter that exists at the time the COMSPEC command is executed.

The two other forms of the command allow the COMSPEC variable to be set to a value that is indicated at the time the login script is executed. An "*n:" indicates a drive number that might be used in the login script. The command might read

COMSPEC = *2:COMMAND.COM

The result is to set the COMSPEC variable to point to a copy of COMMAND.COM in a directory on the second network drive, already mapped to whatever the drive letter may be.

The "Sn:" in the third form of the command indicates a search drive number. Under NetWare, a special type of drive mapping called a search drive can be made to allow the computer to automatically search a directory for a program that is not in the current directory. When mapping such a search drive, the user maps a search drive number such as S1: or S2:. NetWare designates the associated drive letter by starting at the end of the alphabet, so S1: becomes drive letter Z: and S2: becomes Y: unless those letters are already in use. By using a command such as

COMSPEC = S1:COMMAND.COM

the supervisor can ensure that the COMSPEC variable points to the first search drive already assigned, without knowing what drive letter it is using.

In any of the three forms of this command, the drive letter used should point to the directory containing the COMMAND.COM program, because the command accepts only twelve characters after the drive specification. With this restriction a command such as

COMSPEC = S1:\DOS\COMMAND.COM

would not be legal. The path \DOS\COMMAND.COM is too long.

DISPLAY

Using the DISPLAY command, a message can be displayed on the screen each time a user logs in. The message is contained in a file represented by the file name option in the command. The file name can include a complete directory path such as

DISPLAY F:\PUBLIC\MESSAGE.TXT

DISPLAY is used when the file contains only the ASCII characters that are to be displayed. FDISPLAY is used when the file contains control characters placed there by a word processing program that are not intended to be displayed. FDISPLAY will filter out these characters before printing the message on the screen.

(DOS) BREAK

DOS also has a BREAK command. This login script command sets the DOS environment variable to BREAK ON or BREAK OFF.

(DOS) SET

The SET command is used to set any DOS environment variable to any value. These values can be checked later by other login script commands, batch file commands, or other programs. This command is identical in function to the DOS command SET. The only differences are the optional word DOS and the use of quotation marks around the value in the login script command. Some examples are

DOS SET USER="JANE"

SET ROOM="D229"

SET PROMPT="PG"

Several login script variables can be used to place special values in an environment variable. These variables will be discussed later.

DOS VERIFY

The DOS VERIFY flag can be set so that each time a file is copied DOS will read the newly created copy and compare it with the original to ensure it is correct. The login script command DOS VERIFY can be used to turn this feature on or off.

DRIVE

The drive command is used to set the default drive. Normally the default drive is the first network drive, usually drive F. With the DRIVE drive letter: command it can be set to any valid local or network drive letter. The DRIVE *drive number: form of the command is used to set the default drive to a number indicating the order in which the drive was mapped. For instance, the command

DRIVE *1:

would set the default drive to the first network drive letter, which might be F.

The command

DRIVE C:

could be used to set the default drive to be the local hard disk drive C:

EXIT

The EXIT command is used to terminate a login script and to start another program. It is often necessary to start another program, usually a menu program, at the conclusion of the login script. When the LOGIN.EXE program finishes processing the login script, it can pass control on to any executable program named in the parameter "file name". For example, if user JSMITH needed a menu program called MENU.EXE executed each time he logged in, the last line in his login script might be

EXIT "F:MENU"

The item in quotes can actually be any DOS command as long as it is fourteen characters or less in length. Therefore, in addition to any executable program, any batch file or DOS internal command can be used. For example, suppose a user simply needed a directory listing each time he logged in. The last line in the login script would be

EXIT "DIR /W"

The login script for user GUEST in Fig. 10-8 uses the EXIT command in this way. Since the option in quotes is sent directly to DOS, drive numbers cannot be used. Also, programs that terminate and stay resident should not be used.

#Program name with command line options

The "#" symbol is known as the External Program Execution command. This command tells the LOGIN program to temporarily suspend its operations to load and run the program named. When the program is finished, control is returned to the LOGIN program and the login script resumes execution at the next line. The program called by the External Program Execution command must have either an .EXE or .COM extension, but it can be called from any directory with any command line options it needs. The login script command

#F:\APPS\LOTUS\LOTUS COLOR.SET

loads and executes a program called LOTUS from the F:\APPS\LOTUS directory and passes the command line parameter COLOR.SET to it. As with the EXIT command, terminate and stay resident programs are excluded.

The example above, however, would be a very unusual case since after the user exited the LOTUS program, control would return to the LOGIN program and the rest of the login script would be executed.

FIRE PHASERS

The FIRE PHASERS command is used to catch the user's attention by generating a science fiction like sound. The "number" parameter tells the login script how many times to make the sound. The command

FIRE PHASERS 3 TIMES

would cause the alarm to sound three times. This command should be used judiciously, especially if it is placed in the System Login Script which is executed by all users. Execution of this command must totally complete prior to the login script's continuing.

IF Statement

This command structure allows the login script to test conditions and execute different commands based on the result. The command executed as a result of the comparison can be any valid login script command. In the diagram of the IF THEN structure, the "condition" represents a true or false comparison of two items. The comparison will always be in the form

ITEM OPERATOR ITEM

where the operator tests the relationship between the two items. In the first form of the command, a single command is executed as the result of any number of comparisons, if they are all true. In the second form of the command, the key word BEGIN is used to start a list of commands to be executed. The key word END is used to indicate the end of the list of commands. Between the BEGIN and END may be any number of commands that will be executed only if all the conditions are true. It is important to note that the IF THEN statement must be allowed to wrap naturally when it extends beyond one line of the screen. Also, the IF THEN with the BEGIN and END option must be allowed to wrap naturally until the BEGIN has been entered. Then, each additional command should wrap naturally with the ENTER key being pressed at the end of each command.

The IF THEN command will accept many different operators in the testing of the two items, as shown below:

To represent equal	To represent not equal
IS	IS NOT
=	!=
==	<>
EQUALS	#
	DOES NOT EQUAL
	NOT EQUAL TO

Four more relationships can be tested using the following operators. Either the symbols on the right or the words on the left may be used in the IF THEN command.

IS GREATER THAN	>
IS LESS THAN	<
IS GREATER THAN OR EQUAL TO	>=
IS LESS THAN OR EQUAL TO	<=

Several pairs of items can be compared using the AND operator. Also, the AND operator may be replaced with a comma. Comparisons such as these are possible:

IF DAY_OF_WEEK IS "Monday" AND HOUR >= "09"
THEN SET NOW="*"

This command tests whether a variable DAY_OF_WEEK is equal to Monday and checks whether a variable HOUR is greater than or equal to 9. If both conditions are true a DOS environment variable NOW is given a value of "*".

IF DAY > THAN "15", DAY_OF_WEEK IS NOT "Sunday"
THEN BEGIN

FIRE PHASERS 2 TIMES

DOS SET REMIND="Pay the bills today!"

END

This command checks to see if the day of the month is greater than 15 and makes sure the day of the week is not Sunday. If those conditions are met, the alarm will sound two times and a DOS environment variable is set to the string "Pay the bills today!"

The variables DAY, DAY_OF_WEEK, and HOUR are login script variables that are set before execution of the login script. Many more such variables are available for use in the IF THEN command as well as other commands. The following is a complete list of the login script identifier variables available. (Note that all are character variables and, as such, must be compared to constant values in double quotes.)

Variable	Possible Values
AM_PM	(am or pm)
DAY	(01 - 31)
DAY_OF_WEEK	(Sunday - Saturday)
ERROR_LEVEL	(0 - 255)
FULL_NAME	(The user's full name recorded in SYSCON)
GREETING_TIME	(Morning, Afternoon, Evening)

HOUR	(1 - 12)
HOUR24	(00 - 24)
LOGIN_NAME	(The user's login name)
MACHINE	(The name of the workstation type of computer)
MEMBER OF	(The MEMBER OF variable is a special case in that it is not used with a comparison operator. It is used to check if the user is a member of a given group.)
MINUTE	(00 - 59)
MONTH	(01 - 12)
MONTH_NAME	(January - December)
NDAY_OF_WEEK	(1 - 7 where Sunday is 1 and Saturday is 7)
NEW_MAIL	(YES or NO indicating whether new mail is waiting for the user)
OS	(The operating system running on the users' workstation)
OS_VERSION	(The version number of a DOS workstation)
P_STATION	(The physical node number of the workstation)
SECOND	(00 - 59)
SHELL_TYPE	(A code number indicating the type of network shell running on the user's workstation)
SHORT_YEAR	(The last two digits of the year)
SMACHINE	(A shortened name for the workstation type)
STATION	(The connection number assigned to the workstation)
YEAR	(The year)

INCLUDE

This login script command tells the login script to pull in a second file as a part of the currently executing login script. When the commands are finished executing in the second login script, control is returned to the calling login script. Each script file can call other script files to a maximum of ten login scripts.

Nesting login scripts in this way can be very helpful if many different users need a section of their login script to be the same, but heavy nesting is not recommended because it makes documenting a user's actual login script unneccesarily difficult.

MACHINE

The MACHINE command sets the MACHINE variable to a name intended to represent the type of workstation computer being used. The two forms of the command are equivalent.

MAP

The MAP command is used to display or set the drive mappings of the workstation. It assigns drive letters to directories on the file server or drives on the local workstation or displays those assignments. There are fourteen separate forms of this command, each requiring a complete description. This command is another in which the login script variables can be used. Directory names used in the MAP command can contain login script variables preceded by a "%".

Suppose that F: is mapped to volume SYS:\ and that a directory has been created for each user with the user's name being the name of the directory. For user JSMITH the directory would be F:\JSMITH. A directory for each user is usually referred to as a user's home directory. Each user might need a drive letter assigned to his or her home directory in the login script. To do this a MAP command could be placed in each user's login script that includes the login script variable LOGIN_NAME.

> MAP H:=F:\%LOGIN_NAME

When LOGIN.EXE executes this command it will replace the %LOGIN_NAME with the individual user's name and, in the case of user JSMITH, the result would be

> MAP H:=F:\JSMITH

giving the user a new drive letter H: that points to the F:\JSMITH directory.

In its simplest form, the MAP command alone displays all drive letter assignments, including the drive letters assigned to local disk drives. The command

> MAP drive:

displays the directory or local drive that the drive letter listed points to.

MAP drive:=directory

sets the drive letter listed to point to the directory listed. The directory may contain the volume name.

MAP drive:=directory ; drive:=directory ; ...

shows that multiple drive letter assignments may be made following a single MAP command. Each assignment is separated by a semicolon.

MAP directory

changes the current drive letter to point to the directory listed. The directory may contain a volume name.

MAP drive:=

assigns the drive letter listed to point to the current directory.

MAP drive:=drive:

assigns the drive letter on the left to point to the directory pointed to by the drive letter on the right.

MAP INSERT search drive:=directory

creates a new search drive pointing to the directory listed.

MAP DEL drive:

deletes the drive letter assignment.

MAP REM drive:

removes the drive letter assignment, exactly the same as the MAP DEL command.

MAP DISPLAY OFF

instructs LOGIN.EXE not to display the drive mappings made when the user logs in. Ordinarily the drive mappings are displayed.

MAP DISPLAY ON

explicitly tells the LOGIN.EXE program to display the drive mappings when the user logs in.

MAP ERRORS OFF

instructs LOGIN.EXE not to display any error messages that may be generated as a result of an incorrect MAP command in the login script. Ordinarily all errors would be displayed.

MAP ERRORS ON

explicitly tells the LOGIN.EXE program to display all error messages concerning MAP commands in the login script.

PAUSE

The login script command PAUSE works exactly the same as the DOS batch file command of the same name. It halts execution of the login script and displays the message "Strike a key when ready...". After the user presses a key the login script is resumed at the next command. The word WAIT may be used for the same function.

PCCOMPATIBLE

This command is only necessary when the workstation has been set to identify itself incorrectly as not being an IBM PC-compatible computer. It allows other commands in the login script to treat the workstation as compatible, even though the login script variables MACHINE and SMACHINE may indicate a different type of computer. The two forms of the command, PCCOMPATIBLE and COMPATIBLE are, of course, completely compatible.

REMARK

Often the supervisor will wish to place remarks or comments in the text of the login script that are not intended to be executed. These might include explanations of a particularly complex IF THEN structure, the need for various drive mappings, or a message for future supervisors. Either of the four forms of the REMARK command will prevent LOGIN.EXE from attempting to execute the remark statement following it.

WRITE

The WRITE command is roughly equivalent to the PRINT command in the BASIC programming language or the ECHO command in a batch file. It displays the text following it on the user's screen at the time it is executed. The easiest way to use the WRITE command is to simply put a message in quotes.

> WRITE "Welcome to file server FS_ONE."

The WRITE command above would tell the user which file server he or she just logged in to. But WRITE commands can be much more flexible. The text to be displayed can use the same login script variables that the IF THEN command can use. As in the MAP command the variable is preceded by a "%" to tell the LOGIN.EXE program to convert it to the value it represents. In the command

> WRITE "Welcome %LOGIN_NAME, to file server FS_ONE."

the %LOGIN_NAME would be converted to the user name. In the case of user JSMITH, the message displayed would read;

> Welcome JSMITH, to file server FS_ONE.

The login script variables can also be used outside the quotes without the preceding "%". The command

WRITE "Welcome ";LOGIN_NAME;", to file server
FS_ONE."

is exactly equivalent to the write command above. Notice that a semicolon is used to separate the components of the text when a variable is used outside the quotes and without the "%". Also note that identifier variables must be in upper case in most instances, so it is a good idea to use upper case all the time.

In addition to the login script variables, there are four special symbols that may be used within the quotes to control the format of the text printed on the screen. They appear in Table 10-1.

Symbol	Description
\r	Carriage return. Causes the cursor to return to column one on the same line of the screen.
\n	New line. Causes the cursor to go to the first column of the next line. The cursor will automatically go to a new line at the end of a WRITE command.
\"	Embedded quotation mark. Must be used to display a quotation.
\7	ASCII character seven. Causes a beep sound to be generated.

Table 10-1. Format symbols.

The WRITE command below shows the effects of some of these symbols.

WRITE "HAPPY\n   \"BIRTHDAY\"\n   ";LOGIN_NAME

For user JSMITH, the output on the screen would look like this:

HAPPY

"BIRTHDAY"

JSMITH

The login script commands listed above give the supervisor a very powerful language to meet the user's needs. With them a user's environment can be constructed to allow him or her to use the network freely or to take the user directly into an application. The possibilities are endless.

In the next section of this chapter, SYSCON will be used to create users, assign them trustee rights, and create login scripts.

Hands-on NetWare

In the previous chapter, Novell NetWare was completely installed on a file server. However, the installation of the NetWare software was only a small part of creating a usable network. The structure of the directories, the creation of user accounts, the setting up of network printers, and many other tasks will require much more work and thought. A network's supervisor is the one who must consider how the network will be used and determine how best to serve each user, while maintaining overall system continuity and security.

When NetWare is installed, a user account is automatically created called SUPERVISOR. It has complete trustee rights over the entire server and permission to use all menus in each of the NetWare utilities. Originally the account has no password, so the first thing that should be done on any newly installed Novell network is to give the user SUPERVISOR a password. To do this, the file server must be running, and a workstation must be booted with the proper network drivers. In this section you will prepare the server and workstation for operation, login to the network, start the SYSCON utility, and give the account SUPERVISOR a password of FIRST. All commands shown here are written in upper case characters for clarity. However, they can be entered as either upper or lower case.

Preparing the Network for Operation

1. Prepare the server for operation by simply turning it on. A message saying that the LAN is initializing and the volumes are being mounted should appear.

2. At a network workstation, boot the workstation with the appropriate DOS boot disk. To do this, insert the workstation boot disk created in Chapter 9 into drive A. If the computer is off, simply turn it on. If the computer is on, hold down the CTRL and ALT keys and press the DEL key. The computer should read the disk and display a message showing the DOS version being used. An A> prompt should be at the left of the screen.

If you are using the IPXODI version, your AUTOEXEC.BAT should already be modified to load the shell. Otherwise, you must do steps 3 through 6.

3. Type **LSL** and press ENTER

4. Type the name of your NIC driver and press ENTER

5. The network drivers must now be loaded into memory. Type **IPXODI** and press the ENTER key. A message should appear confirming that the IPXODI program has successfully loaded.

6. Type the name of the appropriate NET# program needed. The "#" symbol here represents the number of the DOS version being used. Your screen should say what version the computer was just booted with. If the version is 2.x, type NET2 and press the ENTER key. If the version is 3.x, type NET3 and press the ENTER key. If the version is 5.0, type NET5. Note also that you may type NETX for any version of DOS.

If the workstation booted successfully and the network drivers were loaded successfully, the screen should appear similar to the one in Fig. 10-13. The DOS version, the version and type of IPXODI, and the version of the NET# program may all be different. The "A>" prompt shows the default drive is still the local drive A:. To perform any network operations it is necessary to access the network drive. The network drivers automatically assign the first drive letter to the network drive based on the next letter available after the letters reserved by the workstation for local drives. DOS reserves drive letters A - E unless the DOS LASTDRIVE command is used or there are more than five disk drives on the workstation. The next drive letter available on almost all DOS workstations is then F.

Logging In

Once the network drivers have been loaded, the workstation is attached to the file server, but no one is logged in. Logging in tells the file server who the user is and how much access that user has.

1. Type **F:** and press the ENTER key. At this point no user is logged in, so the workstation has only limited access to the server.

2. Type **DIR** and press the ENTER key. The files available to all workstations, whether a user is logged in or not, should be displayed on the screen or scroll by depending on how many files are stored in the system. They are stored in a directory already created by NetWare called F:\LOGIN.

3. Type **LOGIN SUPERVISOR** and press the ENTER key.

If the system asks for a password, type the password for SUPERVISOR and press ENTER.

Starting the SYSCON Utility

The SYSCON utility is a program on the file server stored in a directory called F:\PUBLIC. It is used for much of the setup and maintenance a supervisor must do.

1. Type **CD\PUBLIC** and press the ENTER key.

2. Type **DIR** and press the ENTER key. This step is included to familiarize you with the environment of the file server. A directory listing of all the files the NetWare installation program has placed in the PUBLIC directory should scroll by. The list is quite long and represents all the NetWare utilities a general user might need. The SYSCON utility is here because a user can view or modify many of his or her own attributes.

3. Type **SYSCON** and press the ENTER key. SYSCON's main menu should appear, similar to the screen in Fig. 10-14.

```
C>ipxodi
NetWare IPX/SPX Protocol  v1.10 (910625)
(C) Copyright 1991 Novell, Inc.  All Rights Reserved.

IPX protocol bound to WDPLUS MLID Board #1.

C>netx

NetWare V3.22 - Workstation Shell (910731)
(C) Copyright 1991 Novell, Inc.  All Rights Reserved.

Running on DOS V5.00

Using configuration file NET.CFG
FILE HANDLES 60
SHOW DOTS ON

Attached to server TESTX
04-29-93    11:35:27 am
```

Fig. 10-13. Screen displaying a successful load of network drivers.

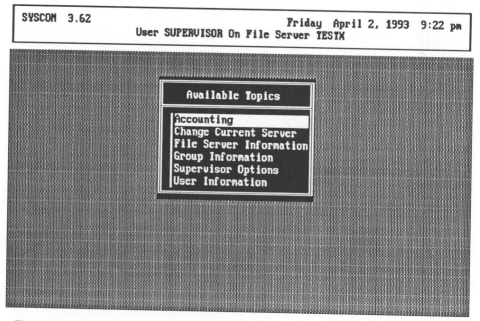

Fig. 10-14. The SYSCON main menu.

Changing a User Password

Each user account on a NetWare file server can be given a password. The password is intended to be kept secret so that only a certain person or set of people can access the account. The user's name is intended to be public so everyone on the network can interact with the user through electronic mail or other network services. The supervisor's account is a special case in two respects. It is absolutely important that unauthorized people do not use the supervisor account, and it is absolutely critical that the supervisor does. If a user forgets his password the supervisor can change it to a new one. But, if the supervisor forgets his or her own password and has not created a supervisor-equivalent user, NetWare must be reinstalled. A good idea is to write down the supervisor password and place it in a sealed envelope. Then, place the envelope in a secure place such as a locked cabinet or vault.

Remember that, in a NetWare utility, an item can be highlighted by moving the cursor or by typing the name of the item to be selected. A list of users on a large network can be quite long, so the easiest way to find the supervisor account is to type SUPERVISOR. The cursor will move to the first occurrence of the letters typed. For instance, when "S" is typed the alphabetically first user name that begins with "S" will be highlighted. If the only other name that began with "S" was SUE, it would stay highlighted until the "P" in the word supervisor was typed.

1. Move the cursor down to User Information and press the ENTER key. The list of user accounts should appear.

2. Press the ENTER key when the user name SUPERVISOR has been highlighted and the User Information box will be displayed on the right side of the screen.

Notice that there are now three menu boxes on the screen. Only one menu is active at any one time, and SYSCON tells the user which one by highlighting the border of the active box.

3. Move the cursor down to the option Change Password and then press the ENTER key. Another box will appear at the bottom of the screen as shown in Fig. 10-15.

The Change Password option will not display the old password; it only prompts for a new one. In fact, there is no method for finding out what a current password is. Even as a password is typed, it is not displayed on the screen. When ENTER is pressed after typing a password, the password box flickers away for an instant and returns. The password must be typed a second time for verification. If the two entries do not match, the user must start over.

4. In either upper or lower case letters, type the word **FIRST** and press the ENTER key.

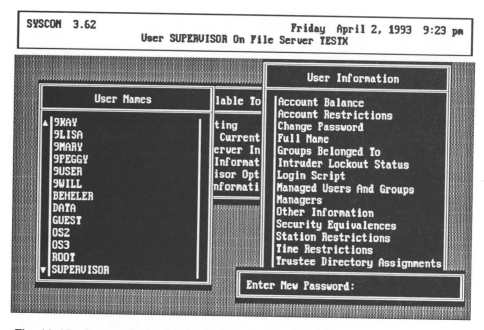

Fig. 10-15. Screen displaying dialog box to change the password.

5. Type **FIRST** again to verify and press the ENTER key. When this operation has been completed, the cursor will return to the User Information menu.

Testing the Password

Presumably, the password has been set to the word FIRST, but, as with any complex system, nothing can be believed until it has been tested. In some situations the supervisor will create all user passwords and not allow any changes. In others, the supervisor only creates an initial password. After the user has logged in, he or she may be allowed to change it. In either case, a good supervisor will test everything possible. To test a password, the user must log out of the network, then log back in.

1. Press the ESC key several times until you see the SYSCON final menu box, as shown in Fig. 10-16.

2. Select Yes to exit SYSCON by pressing Y and the ENTER key.

3. At the F> prompt type **LOGOUT** and press the ENTER key. A message should appear saying what time user SUPERVISOR logged out, from which station, and from which server.

4. At this point the workstation is still attached to the file server. Type **DIR** and the listing of the F:\LOGIN directory should be displayed on the screen or scroll by as it did earlier in the Logging In section.

5. Type **LOGIN SUPERVISOR** and press the ENTER key.

6. Type **FIRST** at the password prompt and press the ENTER key.

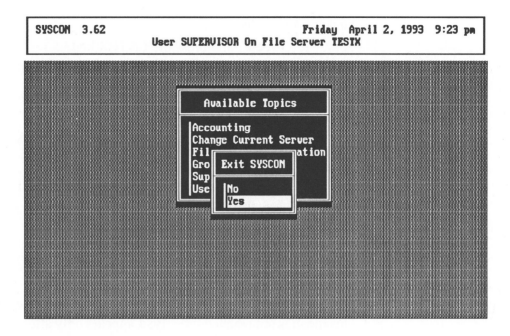

Fig. 10-16. Exit option from the SYSCON utility.

The word FIRST will not appear on the screen as it is typed. If you were able to login successfully, the password was correctly entered in SYSCON twice and in the LOGIN program once. As a general rule, after changing a password, if you cannot login using the password, try variations of misspellings of the word.

> 7. To complete the exercise, type **LOGOUT** again and press the ENTER key.

After installing NetWare and giving the account SUPERVISOR a suitable password, the system supervisor should use the actual SUPERVISOR account as little as possible. For maximum security, new user accounts should be created that allow the supervisor to perform the tasks required of him or her at lower security levels. The supervisor account is simply too important and powerful to use frequently. In the next section a new user will be created. This user will be able to perform all supervisor tasks needed for the rest of the exercises in this book.

Creating a User Account

Only the supervisor, a supervisor equivalent, or a workgroup manager can create accounts. The last section ended by giving the supervisor account the password FIRST. That account and password must be used again to create supervisor equivalent accounts to be used for the exercises after this chapter. The file server and the workstation must be running, and the network drivers should be loaded on the workstation for the following steps.

To enter SYSCON

1. Type **F:** and press the ENTER key.
2. Type **LOGIN SUPERVISOR** and press the ENTER key.
3. Type **FIRST** at the password prompt and press the ENTER key. The word FIRST will not appear on the screen as it is typed.
4. Type **CD\PUBLIC** and press the ENTER key.
5. Type **SYSCON** and press the ENTER key.
6. Highlight Accounting and press the ENTER key.
7. If an Install Accounting? message appears, press Y and press the ENTER key.
8. Press the ESC key.

The User Information Menu

Creating a new user in SYSCON involves using the User Information Menu. This menu is not reached directly; it appears only after a user name has been selected. If the user name does not yet exist, it must be inserted into the list of user names. When the User Information option is selected from the SYSCON main menu, the list of names appears first. After a name has been selected or inserted, the User Information menu allows the supervisor to establish the users' attributes such as trustee rights, group status, and login scripts.

1. Move the cursor to the User Information line and press the ENTER key. The list of users should appear on the left of the screen.
2. Press the INSERT key. A box asking for a new user name should appear in the center of the screen.
3. To establish a unique user name for each student on the network, type in your first initial and last name, then press the ENTER key. A message could appear informing you that name already exists. If it does, try a different form of your name.
4. Press the ENTER key. A box appears giving a suggested name for a directory to be created for the user's home directory.
5. Press ESC to reject.
6. Press ENTER on the highlighted new user name.

When a user name has been successfully entered, the user's name should be in the list of users on the left and the User Information menu should be on the right. In the following sections, most of the options in the User Information menu will be used.

Checking the Account Balance

Depending on how other options may have been set, this user may be charged for connect time. By setting charge rates and account balances the supervisor can limit the time a user is connected to the network or how many of the network services a user can access without checking with the supervisor. When creating a new user, it is important to ensure that the account balance allows the user to login.

1. From the SYSCON opening menu, Available Topics, highlight User Information and press ENTER.

2. Press ENTER on your name, the user created in the last section.

3. Highlight the Account Balance line in the User Information menu and press the ENTER key. A small box similar to the one in Fig. 10-17 should appear.

4. Move the cursor to the line that reads Allow Unlimited Credit.

5. Press the Y and ENTER keys.

6. Press the ESC key to accept the changes and return to the User Information menu.

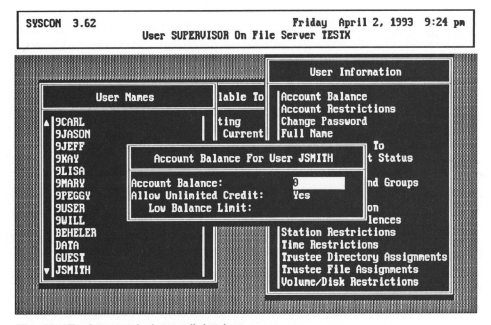

Fig. 10-17. Account balance dialog box.

The Account Restrictions Menu

This screen allows you to change many of the fundamental attributes of the account. The cursor can be moved up or down the list of account restrictions. When an item is highlighted, a new value can be simply typed in. The ESCAPE key is used to accept the changes after all modifications have been made. Follow the instructions below to ensure that all of the values are correct. Move the highlighted area to the appropriate field by pressing the up or down cursor keys.

Before proceeding make sure the Accounting feature is turned on for this server.

1. From the SYSCON Available topics menu, highlight Accounting.

2. Press ENTER.

3. Press Y to answer Yes to Install Accounting (this will show up if Accounting is off).

4. Press the ESC key to exit the Accounting menu options.

Now you are ready to proceed with the Account Restrictions menu.

1. Move the cursor to the Account Restrictions line of the User Information menu and press the ENTER key. A large box should appear with the title Account Restrictions For User USERNAME. (Here, USERNAME is a generic term that represents the user that your account has and you are working with.)

2. The field at the end of the Account Disabled line should now be highlighted and should say No.

3. Account Has Expiration Date should say No. Without an expiration date, the cursor will skip to the Limit Concurrent Connections field when the down cursor key is pressed. Move the cursor to this option.

4. Press the Y and ENTER keys. The cursor should move to the Maximum Connections field.

5. Press the 1 and ENTER keys. With a one in this field only one workstation can be logged in under this user name.

6. With the cursor on the Allow User To Change Password field, press the Y and ENTER keys.

7. With the cursor on the Require Password field, press the Y and ENTER keys.

8. With the cursor on the Minimum Password Length field, press the 4 key and press the ENTER key.

9. With the cursor on the Force Periodic Password Changes field, press the N and ENTER keys.

10. With the cursor on the Require Unique Passwords field, press the N and ENTER keys.

11. Press the ESC key to return to the SYSCON User Information menu.

Creating a Password

This account will need to be password protected just as the supervisor account is. Ordinarily a password should be unusual and not associated with the user in any way.

1. Highlight the Change Password option on the User Information menu and press the ENTER key.

2. Type the word **NEWPASS** in the box provided and press the ENTER key. The word will not show on the screen as it is typed.

3. For verification the password must be entered again. Type the word **NEWPASS** and press the ENTER key.

Creating a Login Script

To facilitate this user's access to the network, a login script can be created which maps search drives to frequently used directories. The directories that would be helpful are F:\PUBLIC, F:\SYSTEM and F:\LOGIN. Other information may be put in a login script that displays a message when the user logs in.

The following steps create a login script that maps the proper search drives and displays an interesting message.

1. Select the Login Script option from the User Information menu by highlighting Login Script and pressing the ENTER key.

Since this user does not have a login script, SYSCON offers to make a copy of another login script. A Copy Login Script From box appears to allow you to type in the name of another user with a login script.

2. Press the ENTER key to indicate that no other login script is to be used. A blank screen similar to the one in Fig. 10-18 should appear.

At this point, any login script can be typed in. Like most word processors, the cursor keys move only where characters or spaces have been typed. The login script can be any length because the screen inside the box will scroll as it is filled up. Also, the INSERT and DELETE keys function much as they would in any full screen editor.

3. Type **MAP S1:=SYS:\PUBLIC** and press the ENTER key.

4. Type **MAP S2:=SYS:\SYSTEM** and press the ENTER key.

5. Type **MAP S3:=SYS:\LOGIN** and press the ENTER key.

6. Type **IF DAY_OF_WEEK IS "Monday" WRITE "Monday Again!"** (all in one sentence) and press the ENTER key.

7. Type **WRITE "Another %DAY_OF_WEEK %GREETING_TIME."** (all in one sentence) and press the ENTER key.

8. Press the ESC key. A box will appear asking you if you want to save the changes.

9. Press the Y and ENTER keys. The User Information menu should reappear.

The SYS: in the above login script commands specifies a volume on the file server. Volumes are major divisions of the file server's hard disk.

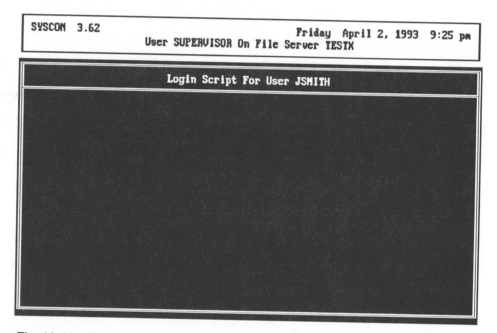

Fig. 10-18. Data entry screen for creating login scripts.

Setting the Security Equivalences

On any NetWare network, there should be at least one account that has a security equivalence to user SUPERVISOR. That other account should be used most of the time that supervisor maintenance is required. In this exercise the user account will be given supervisor security equivalence.

1. Highlight the Security Equivalences option in the User Information menu and press the ENTER key. A list of current security equivalences for this user will appear on the right side of the screen as it does in Fig. 10-19.

2. Press the INSERT key.

3. Highlight the word SUPERVISOR. As the word SUPERVISOR is typed the highlighted bar will move along a list of users and groups of users until user SUPERVISOR is marked.

4. Press the ENTER key on the user SUPERVISOR. SUPERVISOR will be added to the list of security equivalences.

5. Press the ESC key to accept the changes and return to the User Information menu.

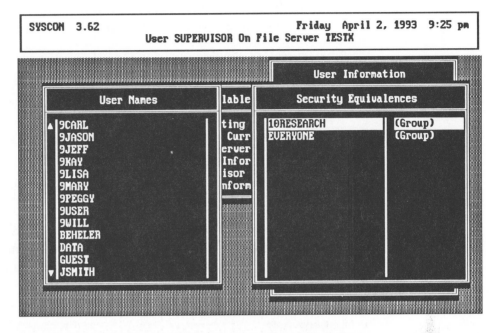

Fig. 10-19. Screen displaying security equivalences for a user.

Setting Trustee Directory Assignments

Directory access rights are called Trustee Directory Assignments in Net-Ware. Each user with privileges in a certain directory is said to be a trustee of that directory. In this example the user being created is equivalent to user SUPERVISOR and so is automatically given trustee rights in all directories. However, most users will not be given such rights. The following steps demonstrate the process of modifying the trustee privileges of a user.

1. Highlight the Trustee Directory Assignments option of the User Information menu and press the ENTER key. The current Trustee Assignments for this user will be displayed on the right of the screen.

2. To add a trustee assignment to this list, press the INSERT key twice.

A long box labeled Directory In Which Trustee Should Be Added will appear near the top of the screen when you press INSERT the first time. The complete directory name could be typed in at this point, but SYSCON allows you to select from the available directories also if you press INSERT again.

3. Press the ENTER key on the file server name.

309

4. With volume SYS highlighted, press the ENTER key. A list of directories should appear.

5. Move the cursor to the SYSTEM directory and press the ENTER key.

6. Press the ESC key to accept the directory as it is shown in the long box along the top of the screen and press the ENTER key.

A new directory should now be in the list of trustee assignments. But when an assignment is made, the default values for access rights are only Read and File Scan as denoted by the [R   F] after the directory name.

7. Highlight the SYS:SYSTEM directory in the Trustee Assignments box and press the ENTER key. The Trustee Rights Granted box will appear on the left of the screen.

8. Press the INSERT key and a Trustee Rights Not Granted box will appear on the right.

Fig. 10-20 shows the two boxes. Each right that needs to be granted to this user can be selected individually or a number of them can be marked and granted all at once. Most of the time a block of rights will need to be given to a user, so that is what will be done in this case.

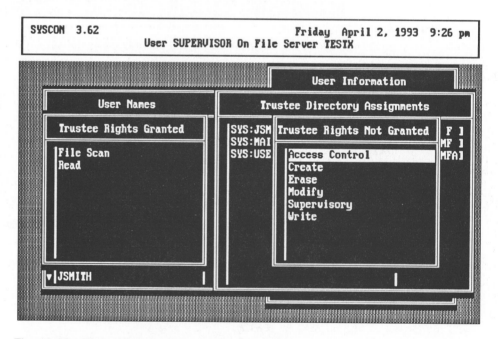

Fig. 10-20. Dialog box to assign rights to trustees.

9. Press the F5 function key. This marks the rights to be added to the user.

10. Press the DOWN ARROW key to move the highlighted bar to the next trustee right not granted.

11. Press F5 again.

12. Continue marking the trustee rights not granted until they are all marked.

13. Press the ENTER key. The rights not granted should move to the rights granted box.

14. Press the ESC key twice and the User Information menu should reappear.

Limiting Disk Space

1. Highlight the Volume/Disk Restrictions option on the User Information menu and press ENTER.

2. Press ENTER on SYS.

3. With the cursor on the Limit Volume Space field, press the Y and ENTER keys.

4. With the cursor on the Volume Space Limit (in KB) field, type the numbers 1024 and press the ENTER key.

5. The User Volume/Disk Restrictions menu should now look similar to the one shown in Fig. 10-21. Press the ESC key to accept these changes and return to the User Information menu.

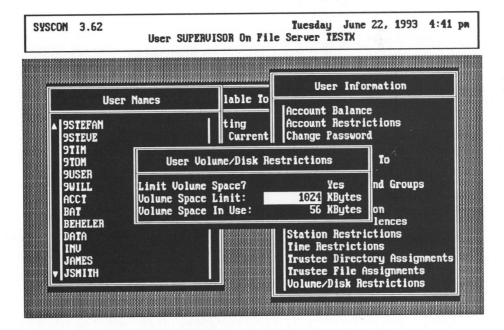

Fig. 10-21. Account restriction dialog box.

Testing the New Account

This user should now be set up to be able to perform any task the supervisor might need to do. But again, the job is not finished until it has been tested. To do this the current user, SUPERVISOR, must logout and the new user must login.

1. Press the ESC key three times until the Exit SYSCON? box appears.

2. Press the Y and ENTER keys.

3. Type **LOGOUT** and press the ENTER key.

4. Type **LOGIN** and the name you gave to the user just created on the same line and press the ENTER key.

5. Type the password given to the user just created, and press the ENTER key.

For now it will be assumed that if the user can log in, the account has been set up correctly.

6. Type **LOGOUT** and press the ENTER key.

Summary

The most important aspect of managing a network involves the creation of user accounts. These accounts control how and when the user will be able to use the network. With the System Configuration utility, SYSCON, the supervisor can create accounts that allow users to do the work they need to do and provide them with login scripts that set up helpful environments. The login script commands and variables available allow the supervisor to create very complex programs that can take different actions based on who the user is, the time of day, and other factors.

When creating a user, the supervisor can specify user equivalences. The new user can be given security equivalence to any user or group already on the server, including the supervisor.

Questions

1. How can a supervisor record how much time a user spends on the network?

2. How can a supervisor save time when creating individual user accounts and also be able to easily make changes to collections of users?

3. In a network with many file servers running NetWare version 3.11, can the supervisor update the user accounts on all the file servers simultaneously?

4. Under which of SYSCON's main menu options can the supervisor set default values for all users created in the future?

5. How can the supervisor affect the user's environment each time the user logs in?

6. What can the supervisor do if a user forgets his password?

7. What should the supervisor do to ensure the security of the SUPERVISOR account?

8. Explain the function of the following lines in a login script:

   IF DAY IS EQUAL TO "29" AND MONTH = "02" THEN BEGIN

   WRITE "Today is special!"

   END.

Projects

Objective

The following projects will provide additional practice on how to create a user and login scripts. Login scripts provide a mechanism by which the system manager can customize the network and thereby make using the system easier for users.

Project 1. Using the SYSCON Utility

1. Use the SYSCON utility to create a new user. Use your initials as the name of the user.

2. Give the new user Read and File Scan rights to the SYS:\LOGIN, SYS:\SYSTEM, and SYS:\PUBLIC directories. Leave the default Trustee rights for the Mail directory.

3. Create a login script for the user that maps the drive letters F:, G:, and H: to the directories listed above.

4. Add statements to the login script that print the message "Today is the first day of the rest of your life" only if the user logs in on today's date.

5. Using SHIFT/PRINT SCREEN, print the login script just created.

6. Login as the new user. Use the SHIFT/PRINT SCREEN keys to record the results of the login script.

7. While still logged in as the new user, start the SYSCON utility and attempt to create another user.

8. Exit the SYSCON utility and login under the supervisor equivalent account.

9. Start the SYSCON utility and delete the new user.

10. Exit the SYSCON utility.

Project 2. More Login Scripts

1. Using the SYSCON utility create two new users, US1 and US2.

2. Give them the same rights as GUEST and assign US1 to a new group named DATABASE. US2 should not be a member of the DATABASE group.

The rest of the exercise would normally be created from the SYSCON utility under the Supervisor Options/System Login Script options. However, since this is a student exercise and since the System login script would affect all users, you must create the same login script for both US1 and US2. DO NOT MODIFY THE SYSTEM LOGIN SCRIPT!

3. Turn off the map display.

4. Type the basic login script commands. (MAP a search drive to the PUBLIC directory, and set up COMSPEC.)

5. Type all mappings to the basic applications installed on your file server.

6. Make sure that everyone's first network drive is mapped to his or her home directory.

7. Type a greeting to be displayed when a user logs in.

8. Type the commands necessary to display the type and version of the operating system.

9. Type the commands necessary to display the current date and time of day.

10. Type the commands needed to display "USER IS A MEMBER OF DATABASE".

11. Type the commands necessary to remind all users of a meeting that begins at 12:00 noon every day of the week.

12. Turn the map display on and display the mappings at the end of the script.

13. Login as both new users (one at a time) and test the scripts. Print the results of each login using SHIFT/ PRINT SCREEN.

14. Print both login scripts.

Security, Organization, and Management

Objectives

After completing this chapter you will

1. Understand the need for organization in the network.
2. Know the advantages of organizing users into groups.
3. Recognize the available trustee rights.
4. Understand the available file attributes.
5. Understand the main menu functions of the FCONSOLE program.
6. Be familiar with the four levels of security.
7. Know how to assign restrictions to a user's account.
8. Know how to create groups.
9. Know how to use FCONSOLE to observe network activity.

Key Terms

Data Organization

FCONSOLE

Groups

Levels of Security

Trustee Rights

Directory Rights

File Attributes

Group Hierarchy

Passwords

Introduction

A network may have many functions. It may have electronic mail, shared printers, or shared modems. But all of these functions are usually secondary to providing users with shared disk space for programs and data. In addition to the shared space, most users will need to be able to store data in a private area.

Creating a structure in which users can access the shared data they need and protect their private data is the supervisor's most challenging task. Usually programs and data must be placed in different areas with different access rights. Different users will have many different needs, and normally several groups of users will have similar needs. Under NetWare, the supervisor can grant trustee rights to these groups and still be able to customize the accounts of each user. The principle of allowing some users access to data while restricting other users is known as network security. NetWare establishes security at four levels, through passwords, trustee directory and file rights, directory rights, and file attributes. This multilevel approach allows the supervisor to customize the security requirements to fit any need.

Careful management of the users and their data must involve backing up the data. Backing up the data on the file server is important to preserve both the application software and the NetWare files. In addition to managing file software, the supervisor must maintain control over the network as a whole. Part of this can be done using the File Server Console program FCONSOLE.EXE.

Levels of Security

There are four main levels of security:

1. Passwords
2. Trustee Directory and File rights
3. Directory rights
4. File attributes

Passwords

Each NetWare account can be given a password. The password is a string of characters that the user types in when he or she logs in. The LOGIN.EXE program compares the login name and password to those stored by NetWare.

If they match, the user is allowed access to the account. The login name is intended to be known by everyone while the password is kept secret by the user.

The supervisor can give the user a password or allow the user to choose one the first time he or she logs in. After it has been entered, neither the user nor the supervisor can view it. If it is forgotten, the only way to access the account is for the supervisor to change the password. In the System Configuration program, SYSCON.EXE, the supervisor can set defaults concerning passwords for all new accounts. Fig. 11-1 shows the Supervisor Options menu in SYSCON. By selecting Default Account Balance/Restrictions, the supervisor can access the menu shown in Fig. 11-2. This menu is almost identical to the Account Restrictions menu that can be accessed for each user. It shows the restrictions that can be placed on the user's password.

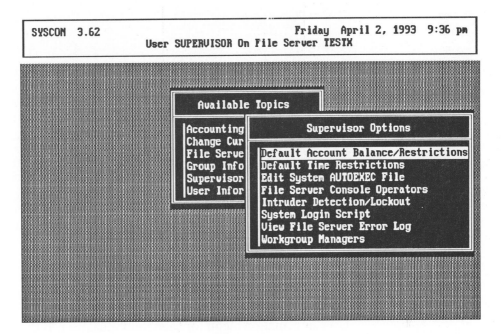

Fig. 11-1. Supervisor options menu in SYSCON.

Minimum Password Length

The account can be required to have a password or not required to. If it does have a password, a minimum length can be set. The default minimum password length is 5 characters; the maximum is 128 characters.

Force Periodic Password Changes

A password is effective only if it is secret. If the same password is used for a very long time, the opportunity for an unauthorized person to discover it may be increased. This is why the account can be set to periodically force the user to change the password. If this feature is set, after the specified number of days has passed, LOGIN.EXE will automatically prompt the user for a new password when he or she logs in. The account can be set to allow a certain number of grace logins that prompt the user for a new password but do not require one. If the Require Unique Passwords option is set to YES the user must enter a different password each time. NetWare remembers the last eight passwords so one could begin repeating passwords after the eighth password is used. While using the same password for too long may allow someone to discover it, forcing the user to change it too frequently may also force the user to write it down too often or to use obvious words.

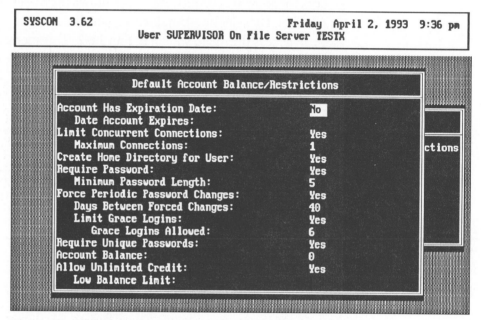

Fig. 11-2. Default account balance and restrictions dialog box.

User Password Changes

One account restriction that cannot be set in the Default Account Restrictions/Balances menu is Allow User to Change Password. This can only be set in the User Information menu for each individual user. If the option Allow User to Change Password is set to No, the supervisor must enter a password for each user and accept responsibility for changing it.

Trustee Rights

Each user must be given trustee rights through his or her individual account or through a group to have any access to the server at all. In NetWare Version 3.11, both Trustee Directory and Trustee File assignments are possible. When a user is given some access to a directory, he or she is said to be a trustee of that directory. Fig. 11-3 shows the trustee rights for user DATA in a directory called SYS:GATE\GW. The column on the right of the Trustee

Directory Assignments shows all of the rights given to the user in each directory. The Trustee Rights Granted box on the left is really a menu allowing the supervisor to insert new rights or delete existing ones.

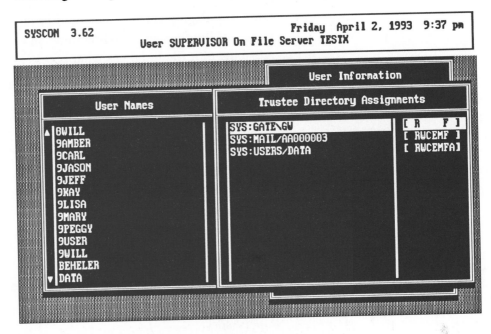

Fig. 11-3. Trustee rights for user DATA.

The rights that can be given are:

1. Read.

   Directory Right: The user can open and read files in the directory. The File Scan right is also needed to view the directory listing for the given directory.

   File Right: The user can see the information in a closed file to use it or to execute it even if the directory does not allow the Read permission.

2. Write.

   Directory Right: The user can change the contents of existing files in the directory.

   File Right: The user can change the contents of the given file even if the directory does not allow the Write permission.

3. Create.

   Directory Right: The user can create files and subdirectories in the directory.

   File Right: The user can salvage a file if it has been deleted.

4. Erase.

   Directory Right: The user can erase files and subdirectories of the directory.

File Right: The user can delete a file even if the directory does not allow the Delete permission.

5. Modify.

Directory Right: The user can modify the Attributes and names of the files and subdirectories in the directory. The Attribute of a file indicates what access anyone has to the file.

File Right: The user can modify the attributes and the name of the file

6. File Scan.

Directory Right: The user can see what files and subdirectories are listed in the directory.

File Right: The user can see the file in the directory listing.

7. Access Control.

Directory Right: The user can grant rights he or she has to the directory to other users.

File Right: The user can grant any right he or she has to the file to other users.

8. Supervisory.

Directory Right: The user has supervisory, and hence, all rights to the directory.

File Right: The user has all rights to the file.

Trustee rights for both directories and files are attached to the user and provide that user with access to certain directories.

Directory Inherited Rights Mask

Normally, if a user has specific trustee rights to a given directory, the user inherits these rights for all subdirectories of the original directory. When a directory is created, it has the same rights as the full set of trustee rights. These directory rights, called the inherited rights mask, are attached to the directory. The inherited rights mask for a directory may be altered using utilities such as Filer to limit any user's inherited rights to that directory, except for the supervisory right. The Supervisor right cannot be eliminated from the Inherited Rights Mask.

Suppose a user is given Read, File scan, Create, and Erase rights to a directory called PROGRAMS. This means that the user will also inherit the same rights for all subdirectories of the directory PROGRAMS unless the inherited rights mask for a subdirectory limits these rights. Suppose that the subdirectory called COBOL under the PROGRAMS directory has the limited inherited rights mask of Read, File Scan, and Modify. This would mean that the user's effective rights for the directory \PROGRAMS\COBOL would be only Read and File Scan because these rights are the only rights the user had to the parent directory (PROGRAMS) that are also present in the inherited rights mask of the subdirectory (PROGRAMS\COBOL).

Note also that when a user is given explicit trustee rights to a directory, these rights override any limitation indicated by the inherited rights mask for the directory. The inherited rights mask has an effect only on those rights which would normally be inherited in a directory.

File Attributes

Information stored on the file server is stored in files. These files can have several different attributes that may further inhibit the user's access or track the use of the file. Attributes limit what a user can do with a file in much the same way that directory rights limit what can be done with the files in a directory. For instance, a file can have a Read Only attribute, which means the user cannot write to it or delete it. The file is said to be "flagged" Read Only. If the user has the Modify File Name/Flags right, he or she can remove the Read Only flag from the file using either the DOS Attrib command or the NetWare Flag command. This allows the supervisor or the user to safeguard certain files against accidental changes or deletions, while still being able to make those changes if necessary. If the user does not have the Modify File Name/Flags right, he or she cannot remove the Read Only attribute. This would give the supervisor the ability to protect individual files in a directory. The file attributes available in NetWare are as follows:

1. Read Only. The file and its file name cannot be changed or deleted.

2. Shareable. The file can be read by several users simultaneously.

3. Hidden. The file name is hidden from directory searches so it is not listed in the DOS DIR command. Unlike the DOS file attribute Hidden, a program file flagged Hidden cannot be executed.

4. System. The file is one of the operating system files. It cannot be deleted or changed by the user.

5. Transactional. This attribute is a safety feature that is usually applied to a database file. NetWare ensures that changes to the file are either completed or not made at all in case of an interruption during the process.

6. Purge. This attribute indicates that the file will be purged from the file system after it has been deleted. It will not be possible to undelete this file later.

7. Archive Needed. Identifies files modified after last backup. It is assigned automatically.

8. Read Audit. The user will be charged for reading this file. This feature is not yet implemented under NetWare.

9. Write Audit. The user will be charged for writing to this file. This feature is not yet implemented under NetWare.

10. Copy Inhibit. The file, which must have an .EXE or .COM extension, can be executed only. The program cannot be copied. This attribute cannot be removed once set.

11. Rename Inhibit. The file cannot be renamed.

12. Delete Inhibit. The file cannot be deleted.

13. Execute Only. The file can only be executed.

Three utility programs can be used to set file attributes, the DOS program ATTRIB.EXE and the NetWare utilities FLAG.EXE and FILER.EXE. Fig. 11-4 shows how the FILER.EXE program displays attribute information for a file. This particular file has only the Read/Only, Shareable, Delete Inhibit, and Rename Inhibit attributes.

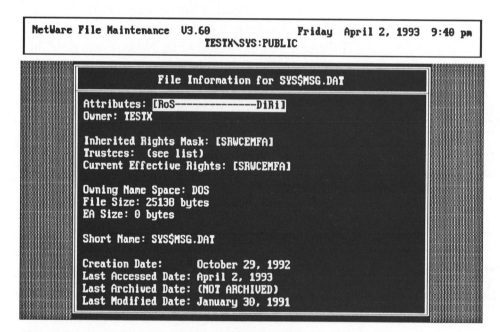

Fig. 11-4. File information about SYS$MSG.DAT.

Organization

Types of Users

When NetWare was installed, it automatically created a user account called SUPERVISOR. The person who assumes the role of supervisor is responsible for the smooth operation of the entire network. It is the supervisor's job to ensure easy and productive access to the network. A user must be given an

322

account with access to the necessary directories and files. Most users will need drive mappings to particular directories. A typist in an office, for example, may need only read access to the directory containing a word processing program and write access to a document directory. A casual user or a user whose uses of the network are not very well defined may also need a menu system and may not be given permission to alter his or her account. A more sophisticated user may want to control as much of his or her account as possible. In addition, this user may want to be able to configure the software he or she is using. A typist probably would not need to be able to change the configuration of the word processing program, but the office manager might.

If it is a large office there may be many people needing the same access rights and menus. One solution is to have all the typists log in under the same user name. An account called TYPIST could be set up which allows several users to be logged in at the same time. This one account could have everything a typist might want, and all the typists would share the same directory space, software, and data. This situation could work well as long as the typists could agree on how their directory space was to be handled. Having everyone login using the same login name can be inconvenient, however. Individual typists may need a more customized environment to work with. Electronic mail and other messages could not be sent to individuals.

Groups

With various users needing different attributes to their accounts, individual accounts would have to be created. But since many users may need the same access rights, it is possible to create groups of users that can be given the same rights. A group could be created called TYPIST rather than an individual account. The group would be given the rights, and then each member of the group TYPIST in the office would be made a user in that group. Each typist in the office could have his or her own login name, login scripts, passwords, and other attributes. Each member of the group TYPIST, for example, may have programs he or she wants in addition to the word processing software provided by the company. If the supervisor sets up the accounts properly, the users could have private areas on the file server to store their programs. Some of the members of the group TYPIST may wish to share some of their private directory space with only certain other individuals, not everyone in the group TYPIST. Users can make these modifications themselves assuming the supervisor has set up their accounts correctly and they know how.

Group Hierarchy

NetWare does not explicitly provide for groups of groups, but the same thing can be accomplished logically. Suppose there were several office managers overseeing the network users. They would need access to everything the members of the group TYPIST have plus additional space for confidential employee information. A group called MANAGER could be created that has only the additional rights needed. A manager would then belong to both groups, MANAGER and TYPIST. A member of the board might need even more information available. That position might need access to pending contracts, for instance. A group called BOARD would give those members access to very critical data only, but since a member of the board might not need to see the work in progress by the members of the group TYPIST, he or she might be a member of the group BOARD and MANAGER and not TYPIST. In this way a hierarchy of users can be established so changes can be made to each group according to the functions they require.

Managers

The supervisor does not have to set up all the user accounts and manage all the groups. NetWare Version 3.11 provides for two additional classifications of managers called Workgroup Managers and User Account Managers. Both the Workgroup Manager and the User Account Manager can give rights to any directory he or she has rights to. The Workgroup Manager can also create new users and give them any subset of the rights the Workgroup Manager has.

For example, if a user, who was designated by the supervisor as a Workgroup Manager, had rights to a directory called ACCOUNTS, he or she could create new users who have access to that directory or a subdirectory of it and assign any access rights the Work Group Manager possesses. For instance, a manager of the directory ACCOUNTS could create a user with rights to only the ACCOUNTS\RECEIVE directory and another user with rights to only the ACCOUNTS\PAYABLE directory.

Data Organization

The way data is organized on the file server hard disk can greatly influence the efficiency of the network. Since the supervisor is responsible for providing the users with a convenient working environment, he or she must arrange the items stored on the server in a way that will make it easy for the user to access them. This implies that it must be easy for the supervisor to assign the proper rights in order to maintain security. The items on the server would need to be arranged by function, as much as possible, with data, application software, operating system software, NetWare public utilities, and NetWare system software in separate areas.

Types of Data

All of the above items may be referred to as data. However, in this context, data is the information created and stored by the user. Application software is the set of programs used to create the data. The operating system consists of DOS and its program utilities such as FORMAT.COM and CHKDSK.COM. NetWare has several public utilities that are intended to be used by any user who knows how, since they cannot harm the accounts of anyone else. Other utilities, software, and data used only by NetWare itself or the supervisor is known as system software.

Suppose a company had the same types of users as above with members of the groups TYPIST, managers, and board members. Since each user has his or her own account, the supervisor might be tempted to arrange the directories something like the way shown in Fig. 11-5.

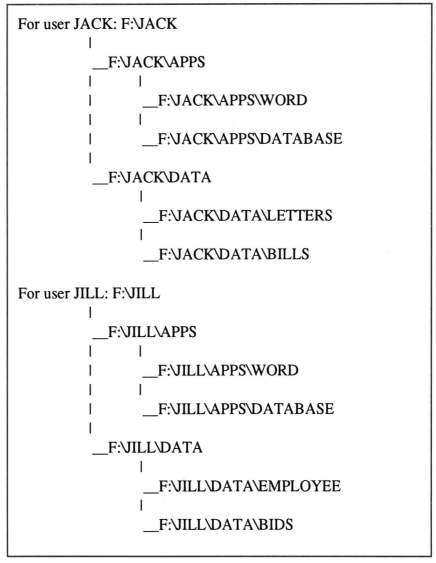

```
For user JACK: F:\JACK
        |
        __F:\JACK\APPS
        |       |
        |       __F:\JACK\APPS\WORD
        |       |
        |       __F:\JACK\APPS\DATABASE
        |
        __F:\JACK\DATA
                |
                __F:\JACK\DATA\LETTERS
                |
                __F:\JACK\DATA\BILLS

For user JILL: F:\JILL
        |
        __F:\JILL\APPS
        |       |
        |       __F:\JILL\APPS\WORD
        |       |
        |       __F:\JILL\APPS\DATABASE
        |
        __F:\JILL\DATA
                |
                __F:\JILL\DATA\EMPLOYEE
                |
                __F:\JILL\DATA\BIDS
```

Fig. 11-5. Directory arrangement.

325

In Fig. 11-5 user JACK is a member of the group TYPIST who needs access to a word processing program and a database program. JACK stores only low security letters and bills in his data directory. JILL on the other hand, is a manager and needs to use the same type of software but must store very sensitive data such as employee evaluations and contract bids. JACK could be made a trustee with full rights in the F:\JACK\DATA directory and only read rights in the F:\JACK\APPS directory. JILL would then need similar rights in the directories under F:\JILL, but she would also need full access to JACK's data directory. Since there are usually more members of the group TYPIST than managers supervising them, JILL would need full rights to all the members of the group TYPIST.

The network supervisor would have to list each of the members of the group TYPIST data directories under JILL's trustee assignments. Also, the software that each of these users needs is being duplicated, wasting space and installation time. A more efficient approach would be to put all the software under one directory and all the data under another.

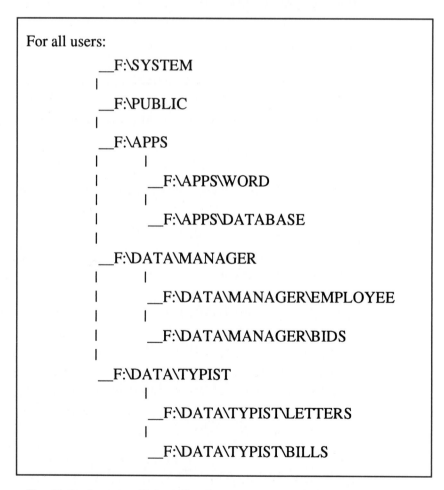

For all users:

```
       __F:\SYSTEM
      |
       __F:\PUBLIC
      |
       __F:\APPS
      |        |
      |         __F:\APPS\WORD
      |        |
      |         __F:\APPS\DATABASE
      |
       __F:\DATA\MANAGER
      |        |
      |         __F:\DATA\MANAGER\EMPLOYEE
      |        |
      |         __F:\DATA\MANAGER\BIDS
      |
       __F:\DATA\TYPIST
               |
                __F:\DATA\TYPIST\LETTERS
               |
                __F:\DATA\TYPIST\BILLS
```

Fig. 11-6. A more efficient directory arrangement.

Fig. 11-6 shows a better directory structure. Under this structure the group called MANAGER would have read and write access to the entire F:\DATA directory and read access to the F:\APPS directory. The group TYPIST would have read and write access to only the F:\DATA\TYPIST directory, and it would also have read access to the F:\APPS directory.

With these groups created, there could be as many members of the group TYPIST and as many managers as necessary. JACK may not have any explicit trustee rights but instead belongs to the group TYPIST. JILL also might have no trustee assignments listed in her account but her membership in the MANAGER group would give her all the rights she needs.

Backing up Data

Often the supervisor must manage all the types of data for the users. Critical data should periodically be stored on a diskette or, more likely, to tape to ensure its safety. Backing up the data, as it is called, serves two main functions. First, it allows the user to retrieve information that may have been changed or deleted in the normal course of operations. Second, it saves information that could be lost if a disaster were to strike the file server. A hardware failure could destroy all the information on the file server. If the data were backed up in a timely manner, it could be restored using the backup diskettes or tapes. Arranging the data so that it can be easily assigned to different users also makes the job of backing up the information easier.

Not only the user's data should be backed up. All types of information should be saved to make the recovery as fast as possible. The time schedule to make these backups will depend on the type of data. Generally, the more often the data changes, the more frequently the backup procedure will need to take place.

In Fig. 11-6, F:\PUBLIC and F:\SYSTEM are directories containing NetWare files. These directories should be backed up at a rate consistent with the changes that are made to the setup of NetWare itself. Such changes would include adding new users and changes to existing user accounts. The files under the F:\APPS will probably not change very often. Also, these programs are probably already stored on the original diskettes as well as on backup diskettes. Unless frequent configuration changes are made to these programs, they will probably be backed up the least often. The files under the F:\DATA directory are the most critical. All the other information could probably be reconstructed if necessary. That might not be the case for important contracts, billing information, or databases that change on an ongoing basis.

Critical data should be backed up frequently and on a rotating schedule. A rotating schedule uses different backup media on different intervals. For instance, a set of tapes could be labeled Monday through Friday. A backup would be made each weekday using the tape labeled for that day. Then, two additional tapes could be used alternately on Saturday. Two or more tapes could be used alternately at the end of each month.

A schedule like this is necessary to be reasonably sure of having a good set of backup tapes at any given moment since the backup hardware and media can also fail, producing unreadable copies. Also, and this is the more frequent problem, a user may ask for a file to be restored that was erased days or weeks ago. With a rotating schedule such as this, the supervisor has a good chance of finding the file the user wanted.

The exact schedule used in a particular installation would of course depend on many factors, including the nature of the business and the amount of data. There may even be data on the server that were placed there for the purpose of being backed up. Many users may wish to copy data from their local hard disk or floppies to the file server for safe keeping. On the server, it becomes the network supervisor's responsibility to back it up. In actual practice there would also be a backup made at regular intervals that would be archived. That is, the tape would not be used to make another backup, but rather it would be placed in long-term storage.

Network Management

Introduction to FCONSOLE

Network control might be considered a fifth level of security. A Novell Network is a very complex system. Almost all of the functions of the system are controlled through the file server. With a program called FCONSOLE, which stands for File Server Console, much of the network activity can be controlled or at least observed. Many of the functions of the FCONSOLE program are available at the file server itself, but in a less attractive format. Also many more functions are available at the file server.

By observing the processes on the server, as well as the activities of the users, a supervisor can sometimes avoid problems or catch them as they start. With FCONSOLE, critical values that may not have been set correctly in installation can be detected. Users can be monitored and disconnected if they cause trouble. Users can also be warned of problems that require their immediate attention.

The SYSCON utility can be used to establish other network control features. User accounts can be set to be restricted to certain workstations or certain times of the day. These restrictions and FCONSOLE's monitoring abilities give the supervisor a great deal of power in determining how, when, and where the network will be used.

FCONSOLE Management Options

Fig. 11-7 shows FCONSOLE's main menu. FCONSOLE is to network management what SYSCON is to network security. The different management options that can be performed with FCONSOLE are explained in the following paragraphs. In NetWare Version 3.11, some of the options available in earlier versions of FCONSOLE are not available. Four of the options (File/Lock Activity, LAN Driver Information, Purge All Salvageable Files, and Statistics) will not work. Equivalent functions are available using V3.11 MONITOR utility, which is run from the server console.

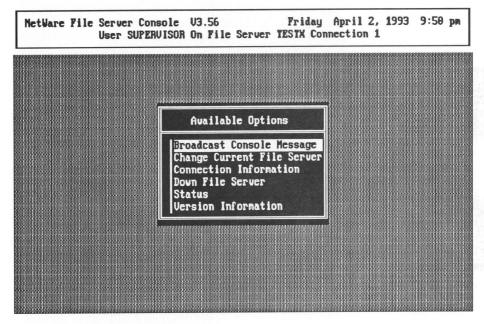

Fig. 11-7. FCONSOLE's main menu.

Broadcast Console Message

The supervisor can send a short message to every workstation attached to the server. The message sent appears on the bottom line of the workstation screen. Any workstation program that may have been running at the time is halted until the user presses the keys CTRL-ENTER. Only very critical messages should be broadcast in this way since it is very interruptive to everyone on the network.

Change Current File Server

The Change Current File Server option displays a list of servers the workstation is attached to as shown in Fig. 11-8. Here the file servers are named IO and TESTX. When a new file server is selected, all the other options pertain to the selected server only.

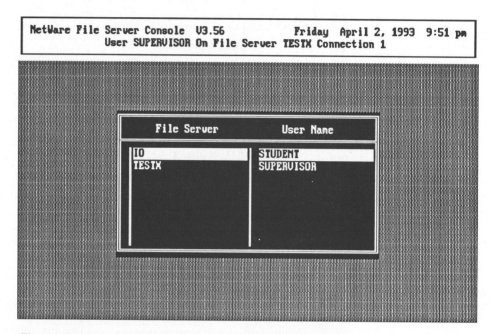

```
NetWare File Server Console  V3.56          Friday  April 2, 1993  9:51 pm
              User SUPERVISOR On File Server TESTX Connection 1
```

```
                    File Server            User Name

                   IO                    STUDENT
                   TESTX                 SUPERVISOR
```

Fig. 11-8. List of servers to which the workstation is attached.

Connection Information

One of FCONSOLE's most important functions is to provide information on the users actually logged in at the moment. When Connection Information is selected a list of users currently logged in appears on the left, as it does in Fig. 11-9. In this case, user SUPERVISOR is the only person logged in. The second column in the Current Connections box shows the connection number. Each station attached to a file server is assigned a connection number. The first workstation to attach is given the value 1, the second 2, and so on. The file server uses these numbers to identify the station. From Fig. 11-9 it can be seen that only the SUPERVISOR's workstation is attached.

The connection number is temporally assigned to a workstation, not a user. Many users may log on and off the same workstation during the day. Assuming the workstation was never disconnected from the file server, all the users would use the same connection number.

When one of the users is selected, the Connection Information menu appears on the right as in Fig. 11-10. These options allow the supervisor to send a message to the user, disconnect the user, or examine various aspects of the user's usage of the file server.

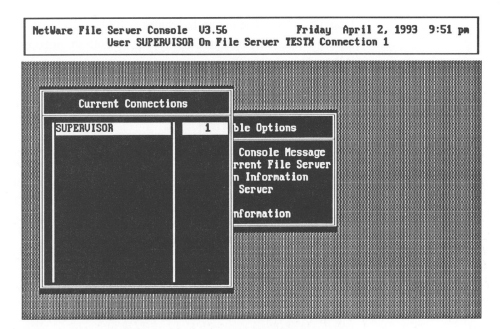

Fig. 11-9. List of current connections to the server.

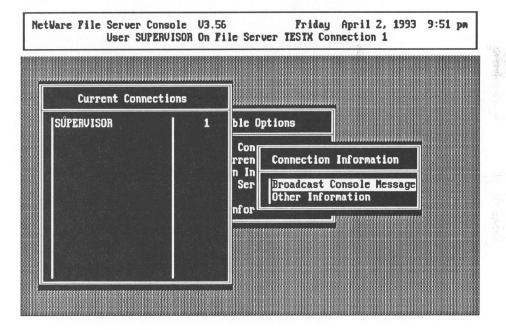

Fig. 11-10. Screen displaying Connection Information.

Down File Server

As noted in Chapter 9, the file server must be properly shut down in order to close any open files. This option shuts down the server after prompting for verification.

Status

The Status option on FCONSOLE's main menu has only four components, as seen in Fig. 11-11: Date, Time, Allow New Users To Login, and Transaction Tracking. These can be changed by highlighting the item and typing in a new value. The date and time will, of course, need occasional adjustment. Allow New Users To Login might be set to No near the end of a day or a few minutes before the server must be brought down for some other reason. Transaction Tracking simply displays the status of this feature.

Version Information

This option displays the exact version the file server is running.

FCONSOLE permits the supervisor to examine some of what the file server is doing at a given moment. In the next section, FCONSOLE and other utilities will be used to demonstrate some of the processes needed to run a secured and well-organized network.

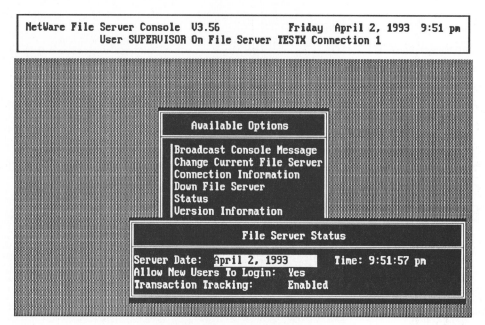

Fig. 11-11. File Server Status Option in FCONSOLE.

Hands-on NetWare

In order to complete the hands-on section of this chapter, the file server and a workstation should be ready to use.

1. The file server must be on.

2. A workstation must be booted and the appropriate network drivers must be loaded.

3. Network Drive F: should be the default drive at the workstation.

4. The user account created in the previous chapter must still be available.

5. In the example below, **<u>TYPE THE NAME OF YOUR AC-COUNT WHERE JSMITH IS USED.</u>** For instance, if the instructions read "Type LOGIN JSMITH", you should type LOGIN followed by the name of the account you created earlier.

Each numbered set of instructions can be completed at different times, as long as they are finished in order. For instance, the exercise on Minimum Password Length must be completed before the exercise on Force Periodic Password Changes.

Levels of Security

As discussed earlier NetWare provides the supervisor with four levels of security. With these four levels, a blanket can be woven around the data providing just the right amount of access for each user. The following instructions will demonstrate the properties of each of the four levels.

Passwords

Passwords are the "first line" of defense against intentional attempts to break network security. Two restrictions that can be placed on the password are Minimum Password Length and Force Periodic Password Changes.

Changing the Password and Minimum Password Length

If a user is allowed to change the password, he or she may be tempted to use very short words to make memorizing it easier. Unfortunately, it also becomes easier to guess. For this reason a minimum length can be set on the password. A program called SETPASS (see Fig. 11-12) is available in the F:\PUBLIC directory that allows the user to quickly change his or her password.

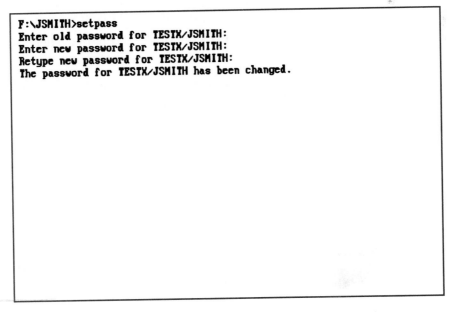

```
F:\JSMITH>setpass
Enter old password for TESTX/JSMITH:
Enter new password for TESTX/JSMITH:
Retype new password for TESTX/JSMITH:
The password for TESTX/JSMITH has been changed.
```

Fig. 11-12. Screen display of output generated by SETPASS.

1. Type **F:** and press the ENTER key

2. Type **LOGIN** and your user name. Then press the ENTER key. The password prompt should appear.

3. Type the original password and press the ENTER key.

4. Type **SETPASS** and press the ENTER key.

5. A prompt should appear asking for your old password. This ensures that no one could change your password while you were momentarily away from your workstation.

6. Type existing password and press the ENTER key. The password will not appear on the screen.

7. Type a new password at least 5 characters in length and press the ENTER key.

8. For verification, type new password again and press the ENTER key.

9. If you are connected to more than one file server, a message asking you if the password should be synchronized on all attached servers should appear. If the account exists on other file servers that are now attached, the SETPASS program can change those passwords as well.

10. Type **LOGOUT** and press the ENTER key to end this session.

Force Periodic Password Changes

Forcing a user to periodically change his or her password is considered an important component of password security. However, changing the password too often makes it difficult to remember. The following steps illustrate the process of setting Force Periodic Password Changes and what happens when the password expires.

1. Type **F:** and press the ENTER key

2. Type **LOGIN** and your user name. Then press the ENTER key. The password prompt should appear.

3. Type your password and press the ENTER key.

4. Type **SYSCON** and press the ENTER key.

5. Use the ARROW KEYS to highlight User Information and press the ENTER key.

6. Type the name of your user account. When your account name is highlighted, press the ENTER key.

7. Press the DOWN ARROW key to highlight Account Restrictions and press the ENTER key.

8. Move the cursor with the ARROW KEYS until the value for Force Periodic Password Changes is highlighted.

9. Press the Y and the ENTER key. The Account Restrictions Dialog Box should appear similar to the one shown in Fig. 11-13. A 40-day interval is the default until the next required change.

10. Highlight the date on the Date Password Expires line using the ARROW KEYS.

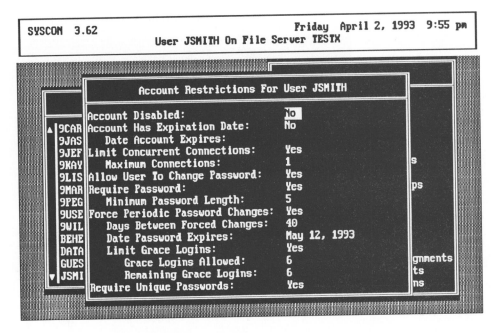

Fig. 11-13. Account Restrictions Dialog.

11. Look at the date shown in the upper right corner of the screen. It should be the current date. Type in the day before the day shown as the current date on your screen. In Fig. 11-14 the current date is April 2, 1993. For the purpose of this exercise, user JSMITH typed in APRIL1, 1993 to indicate that the password has expired.

12. Press the ESC key four times until the EXIT box appears.

13. Press the Y key and then press the ENTER key.

14. Type **LOGOUT** and press the ENTER key. The file server should respond with a message indicating the login time and the logout time.

15. Type **LOGIN** and your user name. Then press the ENTER key. The password prompt should appear.

16. Type your password and press the ENTER key. Since the password expired yesterday, a message will appear asking you if you would like to change it.

17. Press the Y and the ENTER key.

18. Type another new password. The new password will not appear as it is typed. Press the ENTER key.

19. Type the new password and press the ENTER key to verify the change.

20. Type **LOGOUT** and press the ENTER key to end this session.

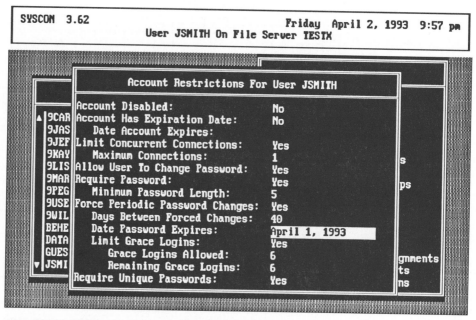

Fig. 11-14. Change Password Expiration Date.

Trustee Rights

The second level of security, trustee rights, requires the most work on the part of the supervisor. SYSCON is used to identify each directory the user or group has trustee rights in. In the following steps you will use your account to give yourself trustee rights in a new directory. This exercise would never be done quite this way in the real world since the supervisor (or a user with supervisor equivalence) does not need to give himself or herself trustee rights. The supervisor would only need to give other users or groups trustee rights.

1. Type **LOGIN** and your user name. Then press the ENTER key. The password prompt should appear.

2. Type your password and press the ENTER key.

3. Type **SYSCON** and press the ENTER key.

4. Use the ARROW KEYS key to highlight User Information and press the ENTER key.

5. Select your user name from the list by typing the name and pressing the ENTER key when it is highlighted.

6. Use the ARROW KEYS to highlight the Trustee Directory Assignments option at the bottom of the User Information menu and press the ENTER key.

7. The Trustee Directory Assignments box should appear, similar to the one in Fig. 11-15. Press the INSERT key.

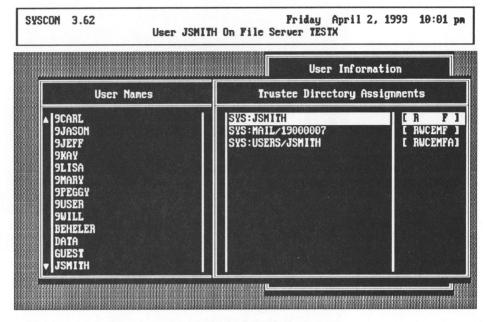

```
┌─────────────────────────────────────────────────────────────────────┐
│ SYSCON   3.62                           Friday  April 2, 1993  10:01 pm│
│                     User JSMITH On File Server TESTX                   │
└─────────────────────────────────────────────────────────────────────┘

                                    ┌──────────────────────────┐
                                    │     User Information      │
          ┌───────────────────┐     ┌───────────────────────────────────┐
          │    User Names     │     │   Trustee Directory Assignments   │
          ├───────────────────┤     ├───────────────────────────────────┤
        ▲ │ 9CARL             │     │ SYS:JSMITH            │  [ R    F ]│
          │ 9JASON            │     │ SYS:MAIL/19000007     │  [ RWCEMF ]│
          │ 9JEFF             │     │ SYS:USERS/JSMITH      │  [ RWCEMFA]│
          │ 9KAY              │     │                       │           │
          │ 9LISA             │     │                       │           │
          │ 9MARY             │     │                       │           │
          │ 9PEGGY            │     │                       │           │
          │ 9USER             │     │                       │           │
          │ 9WILL             │     │                       │           │
          │ BEHELER           │     │                       │           │
          │ DATA              │     │                       │           │
          │ GUEST             │     │                       │           │
        ▼ │ JSMITH            │     │                       │           │
          └───────────────────┘     └───────────────────────────────────┘
```

Fig. 11-15. Trustee Directory Assignments dialog box.

8. A long box labeled Directory In Which Trustee Should Be Added should appear along the top of the screen. The complete directory name can be typed in at this point but SYSCON offers a method for selecting the directory from a list.

9. Press the INSERT key again and the file servers available will be listed.

10. If there is more than one file server listed, use the arrow keys to highlight the one you are using. Fig. 11-16 shows user JSMITH's file server as File Server TESTX at the top of the screen.

11. Press the ENTER key with the proper file server name highlighted.

12. The list of volumes is displayed. Press the ENTER key after highlighting the SYS: volume.

13. The list of directories on the selected volume is displayed. Do not select one of these directories.

14. Press the ESC key. The cursor should return to the long Directory In Which Trustee Should Be Added box.

15. Type the name of your user account and press the ENTER key.

16. Fig. 11-17 shows how SYSCON responds to a new directory. Press the Y and the ENTER key. The new directory is now listed in the Trustee Assignments box with rights Read and File Scan.

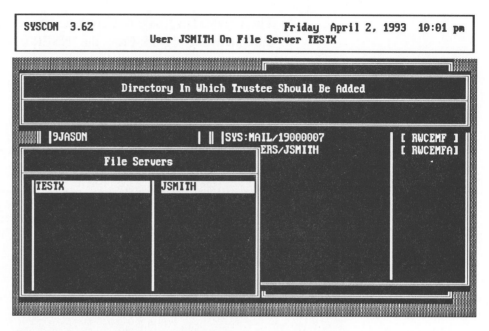

Fig. 11-16. User JSMITH's file server.

17. Highlight the new directory with the ARROW KEYS and press the ENTER key.

18. With the Trustee Rights Granted Box on the left of the screen press the INSERT key.

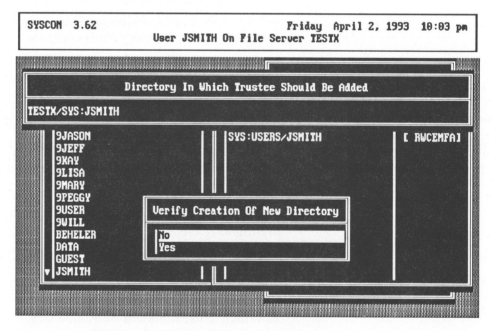

Fig. 11-17. SYSCON's response to a new directory.

19. Press the F5 function key and then the DOWN ARROW key. Continue this until all of the rights listed in the Trustee Rights Not Granted box are marked, except for Supervisory.

20. Press the ENTER key. All of the rights should move to the trustee rights granted box. Press the ESC key again to accept these changes.

21. All of the rights except supervisory should now be listed for the directory with your name as they are for user JSMITH in Fig. 11-18.

22. The user now has complete access to the directory. A directory such as this may be referred to as the user's home directory. It is clearly identified as belonging to this particular user and the user has full rights in it. Press the ESC key four times until the Exit box appears. Then press the Y and the ENTER key.

23. Type **LOGOUT** and press the ENTER key to end this session.

Directory Rights

The supervisor can set each user's access rights to particular values in particular directories. The user automatically has the same rights in any subdirectory. For instance, user JSMITH in the preceding example was given complete rights to the JSMITH directory. If any directories are created below the JSMITH directory, user JSMITH will have complete rights to those as well.

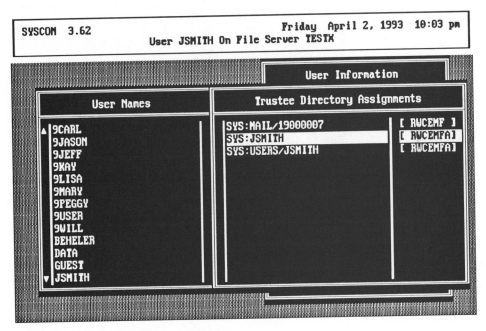

Fig. 11-18. Rights for user JSMITH.

Often, in a large directory structure, one or two directories may need to be restricted so that users have rights to these directories only when they are explicitly given via granting Trustee Directory Rights. Inherited Rights can be restricted by creating an inherited rights mask which restricts all users except those with supervisory authority. The following directions illustrate how the NetWare utility program FILER is used to make the directory rights changes.

1. Type **LOGIN** and your user name. Then press the ENTER key. The password prompt should appear.

2. Type your password and press the ENTER key.

3. Type **CD** and your user name. For user JSMITH the command would be CD\JSMITH. Then press the ENTER key.

4. Type **FILER** and press the ENTER key. Fig. 11-19 shows FILER's main menu.

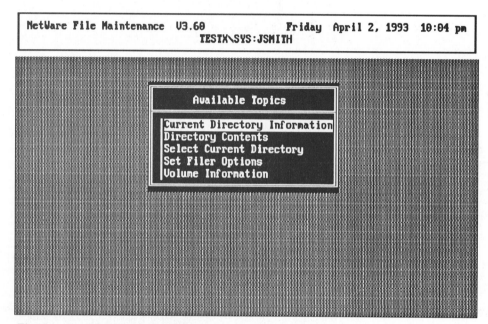

```
NetWare File Maintenance   V3.60              Friday  April 2, 1993  10:04 pm
                            TESTX\SYS:JSMITH

                         ┌─────────────────────────┐
                         │     Available Topics     │
                         ├─────────────────────────┤
                         │Current Directory Information│
                         │Directory Contents         │
                         │Select Current Directory   │
                         │Set Filer Options          │
                         │Volume Information         │
                         └─────────────────────────┘
```

Fig. 11-19. FILER main menu.

5. Press the ENTER key with the Current Directory Information option highlighted. Fig. 11-20 shows the Current Directory Information for the JSMITH directory.

6. Move the highlighted area down to the Inherited Rights Mask field with the ARROW KEYS and press the ENTER key.

7. Highlight Modify Directory/File and press the DELETE key.

8. A box will appear as in Fig. 11-21 asking for confirmation to revoke the right. Press the Y and the ENTER key.

9. Press the ESC key three times until the Exit Filer box appears.

10. Press the Y and ENTER key.

11. Type **LOGOUT** and press the ENTER key to end this session.

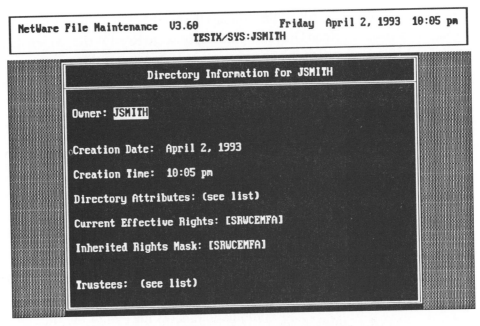

Fig. 11-20. Current directory information for directory SYS:JSMITH.

At this point, any user other than supervisor-equivalent users are not allowed to inherit the Modify Directory/File right unless that right in this directory is listed in their trustee assignments list.

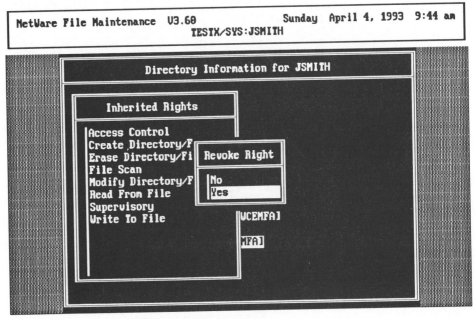

Fig. 11-21. Dialog box to revoke inherited rights.

File Attributes

File attributes could be said to be the last line of defense in security since often they are used to prevent accidental erasure or changes to files. With a file flagged as Read Only, no user, including the supervisor, can change or delete the file. If the user has the Modify File Names/Flags right in the directory, the Read Only attribute can be set to Read Write, which then allows changes. The following short exercise demonstrates this point.

1. Type **LOGIN** and your user name. Then press the ENTER key. The password prompt should appear.

2. Type your password and press the ENTER key.

3. Type **CD** and your user name. For user JSMITH the command would be CD\JSMITH. Then press the ENTER key.

4. Type **COPY CON THIS** and press the ENTER key. This DOS command instructs the computer to copy a file from the console to a file called THIS. In other words the next thing you type will go into the file THIS.

5. Type **THIS IS A TEST** and press the ENTER key.

6. Hold down the CONTROL key and press the Z key. This character combination marks the end of the file.

7. Press the ENTER key. The message 1 File(s) copied should appear.

8. Type **FLAG THIS RO** and press the ENTER key. The utility program FLAG is used solely to change file attributes. The FILER program can also be used to change file attributes. This command tells the FLAG program to set the Read Only flag on the file called THIS.

9. Fig. 11-22 shows the result. Type **DEL THIS** and press the ENTER key to delete the file called THIS. The message Access denied should be displayed. The file was not deleted because of the Read Only attribute assigned to it.

10. Type **LOGOUT** and press the ENTER key to end this session.

Effective Rights

The combination of trustee rights and directory rights is called a user's effective rights. The effective rights are those rights that are granted specifically in the user trustee assignments and/or inherited by a combination of rights inherited from the parent directory which are not limited by the inherited rights mask. To show this, a non-supervisor-equivalent user account is needed. The following steps create such a user.

1. Type **LOGIN** and your user name. Then press the ENTER key. The password prompt should appear.

2. Type your password and press the ENTER key.

3. Type **SYSCON** and press the ENTER key.

4. Press the DOWN ARROW key to highlight the User Information option and press the ENTER key.

```
F:\JSMITH>COPY CON: THIS
THIS IS A TEST
^Z
        1 file(s) copied

F:\JSMITH>FLAG THIS RO
      THIS                    [ Ro - A - - -- - - -- -- -- DI RI ]

F:\JSMITH>
```

Fig. 11-22. Screen displaying rights assigned by the FLAG utility.

5. Press the INSERT key and a box requesting a new user name will appear as it does in Fig. 11-23.

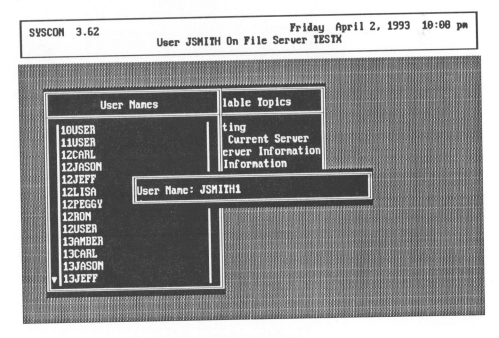

Fig. 11-23. Dialog box to insert a new user name.

6. Type your user name followed by a **1** on the same line. User JSMITH typed JSMITH1 for a new user name. Press the ENTER key after typing the name. Press the ENTER , Y, and ENTER keys again to accept the creation of the Home Directory. Then press the ENTER key again to select the name from the list.

7. Select Account Restrictions from the User Information menu by moving the highlighted bar to that option and pressing the ENTER key.

8. Move the cursor down to the Require Password option with the ARROW KEYS.

9. Press the N key and ENTER key.

10. Press the ESC key to return to the User Information menu.

11. Press the DOWN ARROW key to highlight Login Script and press the ENTER key. A message box will appear as it does in Fig. 11-24.

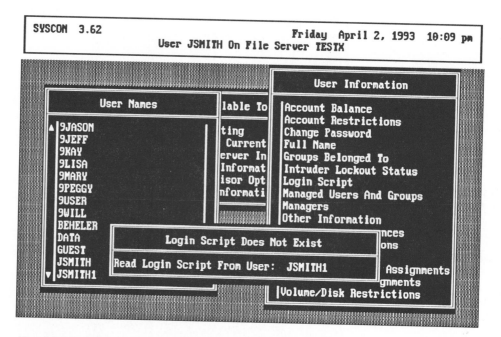

Fig. 11-24. Login script creation.

12. This box allows the supervisor to copy a login script from any other user to the user just created. To copy your login script, simply use the BACKSPACE key to remove the 1 at the end of the name displayed and press the ENTER key.

13. The Login Script editor should now appear. With the cursor in the upper left corner of the box, press the ENTER key once.

14. Move the cursor back up to the top line and type **MAP F:=SYS:**. This line maps the drive letter F to the root directory of the volume SYS.

15. The line MAP S1: = SYS:\PUBLIC should already be there. If not, press ENTER and type it in.

16. The line MAP S2: = SYS:\SYSTEM should already be there. If not, press ENTER and type it in.

17. If the next line is MAP S3:=SYS:\LOGIN change it to read **MAP INS S2: = SYS:\LOGIN** and press ENTER. This command will insert the new mapping for S2: and move the previous mapping for S2: to S3:.

18. Press the ESC key. The Save Changes box should appear.

19. Press the Y and the ENTER key.

20. Next the new user must be given trustee rights. Select Trustee Directory Assignments from the User Information menu by pressing the DOWN ARROW key to highlight the proper line and pressing the ENTER key.

If the directory SYS:USERNAME (where USERNAME is the name of the user you are setting up) is listed in the Trustee Directory Assignments box with rights [RWCEMFA], then skip to step 28.

21. Press the INSERT key.

22. Type **SYS:** followed by your user name. This is the home directory created earlier. For User JSMITH1 you would type SYS:\JSMITH1. Press the ENTER key when the line has been typed in. Press Y and ENTER to verify creation of the new directory.

23. With the new directory in the Trustee Directory Assignments box highlighted, press the ENTER key.

24. With the Trustee Rights Granted Box on the left of the screen, press the INSERT key.

25. Press the F5 key, then the DOWN ARROW key. Continue this until all of the rights listed in the Trustee Rights Not Granted box are marked except for the supervisory right.

26. Press the ENTER key. All of the rights except supervisory should move to the trustee rights granted box.

27. Press the ESC key.

28. Press the INSERT key.

29. Type **SYS:PUBLIC** and press the ENTER key.

30. Press the INSERT key.

31. Type **SYS:SYSTEM** and press the ENTER key.

32. Press the ESC key four times. When the Exit box appears, press Y and press the ENTER key.

33. Create a subdirectory of the JSMITH1 directory called LIMITED.

34. Using FILER, change the inherited rights mask for JSMITH1\LIMITED directory to Read, File Scan, and Supervisory only. (Refer to the steps on page 340 as necessary.)

35. Type **LOGOUT** and press the ENTER key to end this session.

The user JSMITH1 was given all rights except supervisory to the JSMITH1 directory. Normally, he would inherit all these rights in every subdirectory of the JSMITH1 directory. However, the fact that you have created a limited inherited rights mask will alter the effective rights JSMITH1 will have in the directory JSMITH\LIMITED.

The following steps test the effective rights of the new user.

1. Type **LOGIN** followed by your user name and a 1. User JSMITH would type LOGIN JSMITH1. Then press the ENTER key.

2. Type **CD** followed by your user name. User JSMITH1 would type CD \JSMITH1. Then press the ENTER key.

3. Type the command **RIGHTS** followed by the enter key. All rights except supervisory should be displayed because they were explicitly given to the user JSMITH1.

4. Type **CD\JSMITH1\LIMITED** followed by the enter key.

5. Type the command **RIGHTS** followed by the enter key. The effective rights are limited by the inherited rights mask you assigned to this directory.

6. Type **MD \JSMITH1\NEW** followed by the enter key.

7. Type **CD \JSMITH1\NEW** followed by the enter key.

8. Type the command **RIGHTS** followed by the enter key. The effective rights in this subdirectory of JSMITH are the same as the effective rights in JSMITH because a limited inherited rights mask has not been created (see Fig. 11-25).

9. Type **LOGOUT** and press the ENTER key to end this session.

```
F:\JSMITH1\NEW>RIGHTS
TESTX\SYS:JSMITH1\NEW
Your Effective Rights for this directory are [ RWCEMFA]
   * May Read from File.                    (R)
   * May Write to File.                     (W)
     May Create Subdirectories and Files.   (C)
     May Erase Directory.                   (E)
     May Modify Directory.                  (M)
     May Scan for Files.                    (F)
     May Change Access Control.             (A)

 * Has no effect on directory.

     Entries in Directory May Inherit [ RWCEMFA] rights.
```

Fig. 11-25. Display of Effective Rights.

Groups

The new account created in the previous section was not given supervisor equivalence. Therefore, the only rights available were those granted in the Trustee Assignments list. Since it can become tedious to maintain many users' accounts when new directories are added, NetWare provides the ability to assign users to a group, and then simply grant the group trustee rights. The following example illustrates the use of groups when assigning trustee rights.

1. Type **LOGIN** and your user name. Then press the ENTER key. The password prompt should appear. Use the original account, not the username1 account.

2. Type your password and press the ENTER key.

3. Type **SYSCON** and press the ENTER key.

4. Use the DOWN ARROW key to move to the Group Information Option and press the ENTER key.

5. Press the INSERT key and a box asking for a new group name will appear.

6. Type the name of the account you are now using. User names and group names can be the same. Press the ENTER key after typing in the name.

7. With the new group name highlighted, press the ENTER key. The Group Information menu should appear.

8. Use the DOWN ARROW key to highlight Member List and press the ENTER key.

9. Press the INSERT key and a Not Group Members list will appear.

10. Type the name of your user account followed by a 1. In the example the user name is JSMITH1. Press the ENTER key when the name is highlighted.

11. The name should move to the Group Members box as it does in Fig. 11-26. Press the ESC key to return to the Group Information menu.

12. Use the DOWN ARROW key to highlight Trustee Directory Assignments and press the ENTER key. Then press the INSERT key.

13. Type **SYS:** followed by your user name and a **1**. This is the home directory created earlier. User JSMITH1 would type SYS:JSMITH1. Press the ENTER key when the line has been typed.

14. With the new directory in the Trustee Directory Assignments box highlighted, press the ENTER key.

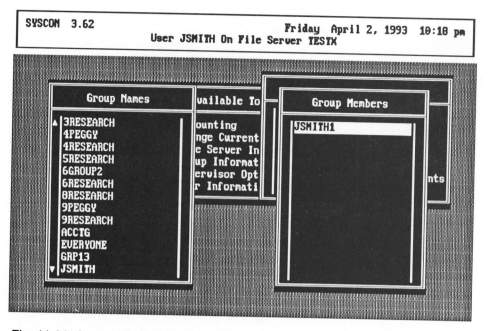

Fig. 11-26. Screen displaying JSMITH1 moved to the Group Members dialog box.

15. With the Trustee Rights Granted box on the left of the screen, press the INSERT key.

16. Press the F5 function key and then the DOWN ARROW key. Continue this until all of the rights listed in the Trustee Rights Not Granted box except supervisory are marked.

17. Press the ENTER key. All of the marked rights should move to the Trustee Rights Granted box. Press the ESC again to accept these changes.

18. Press the ESC key three times to return to SYSCON's main menu called Available Topics.

19. Use the DOWN ARROW key to highlight User Information and press the ENTER key.

20. Type the name of your user account, followed by a **1**. In the example the user name is JSMITH1. Press the ENTER key when the name is highlighted.

21. Use the ARROW KEYS to highlight the Trustee Directory Assignments option and press the ENTER key.

22. Notice one of the directories is a number listed under the MAIL directory. This numbered directory is automatically created for each user and group and contains the login script for the user. The number may contain letters because it is a hexadecimal number. Write down the number for use later in the exercise.

23. Highlight your account's home directory. In the example, user JSMITH1 would highlight SYS:\JSMITH1. Press the DELETE key with the proper directory highlighted.

24. A box asking you if you wish to remove the trustee from the directory will appear as it does in Fig. 11-27. Press the Y key and then press the ENTER key.

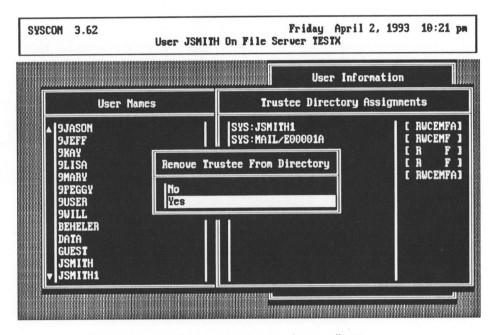

Fig. 11-27. Dialog box used to remove trustee from a directory.

25. Press the ESC key to return to the User Information menu.

26. Use the ARROW keys to highlight Login Script and press the ENTER key.

27. Move the cursor to the end of the last line in the login script and press the ENTER key to create a new line.

28. Type in the new line as it appears in Fig. 11-28, except use the name of the group you created earlier in place of JSMITH. Your group name should also be in quotes.

29. Press the ESC key and then press Y and press the ENTER key to save these changes.

30. Press the ESC key three times until the Exit box appears, then press the Y and the ENTER KEY.

31. Before testing the new login script, it may be of some interest to see where it is located. Type **CD\MAIL** followed by the number you wrote down earlier in this exercise. For user JSMITH1 the command would be CD\MAIL\E00001A. Press the ENTER key at the end of the command.

32. Type **DIR** and press the ENTER key. The login script and a backup of the old login script should appear as files in the directory.

33. Type the command **TYPE LOGIN** and press the ENTER key. This DOS command displays the contents of the file called LOGIN and should appear similar to the one shown in Fig. 11-29.

```
SYSCON  3.62                              Friday  April 2, 1993  10:22 pm
                     User JSMITH On File Server TESTX
```

```
                    Login Script For User JSMITH1

MAP F:=SYS:\
MAP S1:=SYS:\PUBLIC
MAP S2:=SYS:\SYSTEM
MAP INS S2:=SYS:\LOGIN
IF MEMBER OF "JSMITH" THEN WRITE "IN GROUP JSMITH"
```

Fig. 11-28. Login script for user JSMITH1.

```
        3 file(s)        12000 bytes
                       1003520 bytes free

F:\PUBLIC>CD \MAIL\E00001A

F:\MAIL\E00001A>DIR

 Volume in drive F is SYS
 Volume Serial Number is 0B1D-7CD9
 Directory of F:\MAIL\E00001A

LOGIN    OS2        0 04-02-93  10:08p
LOGINBAK           00 04-02-93  10:10p
LOGIN             132 04-02-93  10:22p
        3 file(s)       212 bytes
                     1003520 bytes free

F:\MAIL\E00001A>TYPE LOGIN
MAP F:=SYS:\
MAP S1:=SYS:\PUBLIC
MAP S2:=SYS:\SYSTEM
MAP INS S2:=SYS:\LOGIN
IF MEMBER OF "JSMITH" THEN WRITE "IN GROUP JSMITH"

F:\MAIL\E00001A>
```

Fig. 11-29. Contents of file LOGIN.

34. Type **CD** and press the ENTER key.

35. Type **LOGIN** followed by your account name and a **1**. In the example the command would be LOGIN JSMITH1. Press the ENTER key at the end of the line.

When the new user logs in, the login script will identify the account as a member of the group and print the message:

IN GROUP JSMITH

On your screen JSMITH1 will of course be replaced with the name of your account. JSMITH1 is now a member of the group called JSMITH. It is in the group trustee assignments list where the user is assigned trustee rights to the \JSMITH directory. Many more members could be added to the group without assigning individual trustee rights to that directory.

36. Type **LOGOUT** and press the ENTER key to end this session.

Network Control

The FCONSOLE utility is helpful in observing the functioning of the network as well as establishing control over the use of the network. It provides information on the file server and on the use of the file server. The following instructions illustrate some of the uses of the FCONSOLE utility.

1. Type LOGIN and your user name, then press the ENTER key. The password prompt should appear. Use the original account, not the username1 account.

2. Type your password and press the ENTER key. Then, type CD \PUBLIC and press the ENTER key.

3. Type FCONSOLE and press the ENTER key. The FCONSOLE main menu should appear, similar to the one in Fig. 11-30.

4. Move the highlighted bar down with the ARROW KEYS to highlight the Connection Information option and press the ENTER key.

5. Type the name of your user account. The highlighted bar will move to your name. Press the ENTER key.

6. Highlight the Broadcast Console Message option and press the ENTER key.

7. Type **THIS IS A GREAT DAY** into the broadcast box and press ENTER. Press the CTRL/ENTER keys to return to the Connection Information menu.

8. Use the ARROW keys to highlight the Other Information option and press the ENTER key.

9. The box displayed, similar to the one in Fig. 11-31, shows when and where this user logged in. Write down the number labeled Network Address. Remember to include the ":". The first eight digits of this number indicate the network being used. This is the same network number entered when NetWare was installed. The last twelve digits identify the actual network card in the workstation being used. Ordinarily a supervisor would create a complete map of the network showing the location of every node number.

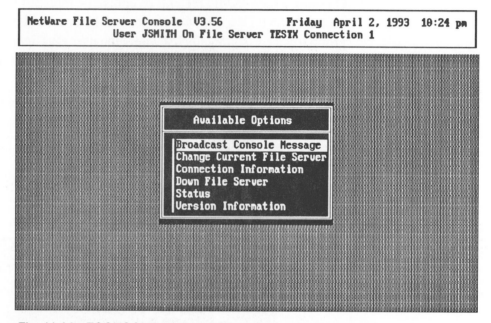

Fig. 11-30. FCONSOLE main menu.

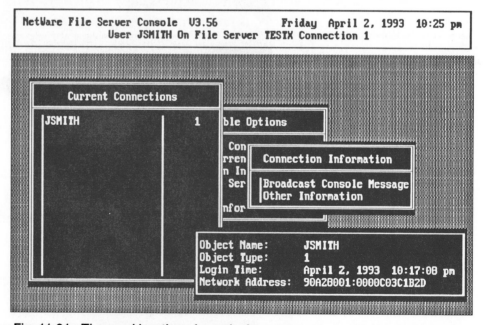

Fig. 11-31. Time and location of user login.

10. Press the ESC key four times, and when the Exit box appears, press Y and press the ENTER key.

11. Type **SYSCON** and press the ENTER key.

12. Use the ARROW keys to highlight User Information and press the ENTER key.

13. Type the name of your account and a **1**. In the example the name is JSMITH1. Press the ENTER key with the correct name highlighted.

14. Use the DOWN ARROW KEY to highlight the Station Restrictions option and press the ENTER key.

15. Press INSERT. A box labeled Network Address will appear as it does in Fig. 11-32. This box allows the supervisor to restrict the user to any workstation on the network indicated by the network number.

16. Type in the first eight digits of the number you wrote down earlier and press the ENTER key.

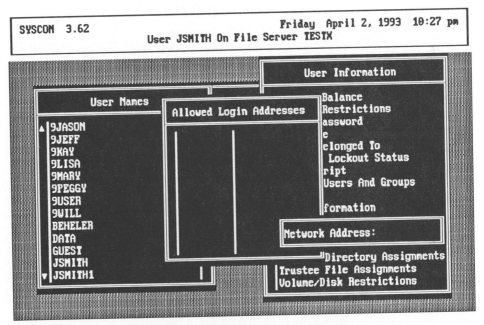

Fig. 11-32. Dialog box used to restrict a user to a specific workstation(s).

17. Type **N** in response to the question regarding allowing the user to log in from any node, and press the ENTER key to indicate that further restrictions apply.

18. A Node Address box will appear below the Network Address box. Type in the last twelve digits of the Network Address you wrote down earlier. Do not include the ":"; it only separates the two components of the number. Press the ENTER key at the end of the number. Notice that Novell is not consistent with what it calls the

Network Address. In FCONSOLE the Network Address was the entire 20-digit number and in SYSCON the Network Address is only the network number portion. Both numbers are represented in hexadecimal format, which is why they contain numbers and letters.

19. The Allowed Login Address box should now show the number you just typed in and no others. Fig. 11-33 shows the only address where user JSMITH1 is allowed to login to be network number 90A28001, node number 0000C03C1B2D.

20. Press the ESC key four times. When the Exit box appears, press Y and press the ENTER key.

21. The Network Address this user is restricted to is the address of the workstation you are now using. Type **LOGOUT** and press the ESC key.

22. Trade workstations with a student next to you or simply move to a vacant workstation. At the new workstation type **LOGIN** followed by your user name and a **1**. User JSMITH would type in LOGIN JSMITH1.

The file server will not allow you to log in with that account at the new workstation because it has a different node number. With this feature, the supervisor can restrict certain user accounts to certain workstations. For maximum security, those workstations could even be diskless.

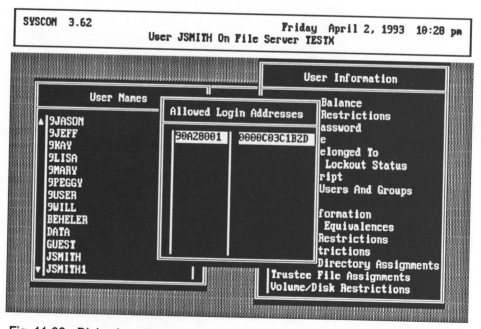

Fig. 11-33. Dialog box displaying the address where user JSMITH1 is allowed.

Summary

Network security is broken down into four levels; passwords, trustee rights, directory rights, and file attributes. The supervisor can put certain restrictions on the password that are intended to force the user to maintain a secure password. The only rights a user has in a given directory are those granted by the supervisor. These rights will be listed in the user's trustee assignments, or the user must belong to a group with the proper rights. The rights granted can be masked by directory rights. The inherited rights for all users except the supervisor are restricted by the inherited rights mask placed on a directory. File attributes are primarily used to prevent accidental damage to files because the attributes apply to the supervisor as well as the other users. With the proper rights in a directory, the file attributes can be changed. The combination of all the rights and restrictions a user has in a given directory is known as the effective rights. Users usually fall into categories that require different rights and restrictions. NetWare provides the ability to put these users into groups that can be given the same rights as the users. The groups can then be structured to allow the supervisor to easily make changes to many user accounts by changing only the group account.

Information on the server must be organized as well. Programs and operating system software should be placed in one region and data created by the users in another. This structure has several advantages. The software and data can be more easily shared. The trustee assignments can be more easily standardized and the supervisor can more easily isolate the data that must be backed up on a regular basis.

Controlling how, when, and where users use the network could be called the fifth level of security. With the FCONSOLE utility the supervisor can observe the files accessed by users and see what workstations they are using. SYSCON can then be used to restrict the user to certain workstations, times, and directories.

Questions

1. Describe the four levels of security.
2. Describe what might be considered a fifth level of security.
3. Can any user change his or her password?
4. What trustee rights are automatically granted to any user?
5. A user has all trustee rights in a directory but still cannot access the files in it. What is preventing him from using the files?

6. A user checks her own Trustee Assignments list and finds that the only directory listed is her MAIL directory, yet she is able to use many different programs on the server. How can this be?

7. Where is a user's login script stored on the server?

8. How can the supervisor identify the workstation a user is logged into?

9. Ordinarily, which should be backed up more often, a database file or the NetWare system files?

Projects

Objective

The following projects provide additional practice in establishing security and trustee rights. Additionally, it provides more hands-on practice with the FCONSOLE utility and login scripts.

Project 1. FCONSOLE and Trustee Rights

1. Use the SYSCON utility to create a new user. Use your initials as the name of the user.

2. Select Trustee Assignments and write down the full MAIL directory path.

3. Give the new user Read and File Scan rights to the SYS:\LOGIN, SYS:\SYSTEM, and SYS:\PUBLIC directories. Do not give the user a login script.

4. Examine the trustee assignments of the account you have been using. Write down the full MAIL directory.

5. Exit the SYSCON utility.

6. Use the DOS COPY command to copy the file called LOGIN from the MAIL directory of the supervisor-equivalent account you have been using to the MAIL directory of the new account.

7. Log in as the new user. Record the results with the Shift Print Screen keys.

8. From another workstation, login under the supervisor-equivalent account.

9. Start the FCONSOLE utility.

10. Use the Connection Information menu to clear the new user account on the other workstation.

11. Use Shift Print Screen keys to record the message that appears at the first workstation.

12. Exit FCONSOLE and start the SYSCON utility.

13. Delete the new user account.

Project 2. Practicing the Login Script Commands

1. Given the following directory structure, write the MAP commands needed to map the drive letters H:, I:, J:, and K: to the numbered directories.

```
F:\___|

|-ACCOUNTS

|   |

|   |-RECEIVE (1)

|   |-PAY (2)

|

|-PERSONEL

|   |

|   |-ARCHIVE

|   |   |

|   |   |-FULLTIME (3)

|   |   |-PARTTIME

|   |

|   |-CURRENT

|       |-FULLTIME

|       |-PARTTIME (4)
```

2. Write the MAP command needed to ensure the correct version of DOS is used with a COMPAQ computer running MS DOS version 3.1. Assume the necessary directories are in place. Also write the MAP command needed to ensure the correct version of DOS is running regardless of the type of computer and version of DOS, assuming the necessary directories are in place.

3. Create a new user. Give the new user a login script that prints "Happy Birthday" on your birthday.

4. Create a directory structure similar to the following:

F:___|

    |-(Your User Name)

      |

      |-SECURE

      | |

       |-DATA

Using the SYSCON utility create a new user with all trustee rights to the directory (Your User Name) except Supervisory and Access Control. Use the Filer utility to make the contents of the SECURE directory inaccessible to the user. Use the Shift Print Screen keys at each step and remove the directories and the user when you are finished.

Workstation Customization

Objectives

After completing this chapter you will

1. Know the command line options available with some versions of IPXODI.COM and NET#.COM.

2. Understand the use of extended and expanded memory by the network driver programs.

3. Understand the use of login script variables to create a search path to DOS directories.

4. Understand the concept of remote reset.

5. Recognize the problems that can occur when using an AUTOEXEC.BAT file during remote reset.

6. Know how to create a boot image file.

7. Know how to use a BOOTCONF.SYS file.

Key Terms

AUTOEXEC.BAT	DOS
DOS Directories	DOSGEN
IPXODI.COM	LSL.COM
MAP	NetBIOS
NET#.COM	Remote Reset
Workstation Shell	

Introduction

In previous chapters, attaching workstations to the network was shown to be simple. Booting the workstation and loading the LSL, NIC driver, IPXODI and NET# programs sufficed to connect the workstation to a file server. This general purpose strategy works well only when the task being done on the network is relatively simple. If the user needs access to DOS programs such as COMMAND.COM, however, the proper DOS version of the program must be stored somewhere on the server and automatically identified by the workstation. Or, the workstation may have extended or expanded memory that could be used to free more conventional memory for application programs. Finally, many workstations could take advantage of a feature known as remote reset. This feature allows workstations to boot from the file server rather than from a diskette in drive A or a hard disk. All these features can be utilized if the workstation is customized, so a few techniques for accomplishing this are well worth learning.

Customizing NetWare

Network Drivers

Access to a Novell network requires four programs to be loaded into memory in the workstation. The programs are LSL.COM, the NIC driver such as PCN2L.COM for IBM PC Baseband Network Interface Cards, IPXODI.COM, and NET#.COM where the # stands for the DOS version used on the workstation. The LSL.COM (Link Support Layer) program allows multiple network protocols to be loaded and have access to the NIC hardware. The NIC driver is designed to operate with only one type of network interface card. Novell ships several standard NIC drivers. Other non-standard drivers are usually shipped with the card. IPXODI.COM provides Novell's IPX protocol. The NET#.COM program is the interface between DOS and the network. It monitors the operations of the user and redirects commands to the network card that involve the network. For this reason the NET#.COM program is generally known as the network redirector, although some literature will call just NET#.COM the shell.

IPXODI.COM

Both IPXODI.COM and NET#.COM have command line parameters that can be used to check or set certain options. The IPXODI.COM file actually contains the IPX protocol, the SPX protocol (used by such NetWare Utilities as RCONSOLE and PSERVER), and the Remote Diagnostics Responder protocol (used for third-party applications that gather diagnostic information). IPX is used for communicating with the workstations, but many applications do not need SPX or the Remote Diagnostics Responder. IP-XODI can be loaded with one or two of these protocols removed. IPXODI.COM's parameters are as follows:

1. Just IPXODI, without any parameter. This command loads IPX, SPX, and the Diagnostic Responder.

2. D. The "D" parameter causes IPXODI to load only IPX and SPX.

3. A. The "A" parameter causes IPXODI to load only IPX.

4. U. The "U" parameter causes IPXODI to unload from memory. Since IPXODI is a TSR (terminate and stay resident program), it is often useful to be able to unload it when it is not in use. Note that it is not automatically unloaded when one Logs out from the network. The other alternative to remove IPXODI from memory is to press CONTROL, ALT, and DELETE to reboot your machine.

5. ?. The "?" parameter causes IPXODI to show what flags are available on the screen.

Note that the IPXODI.COM looks to the SHELL.CFG file for any special information regarding Interrupt setting, I/O setting, and Memory setting for the network interface card. If there is no SHELL.CFG file, then IPXODI uses the default settings for the card, and the card must be physically set up accordingly.

NET#.COM

Since the network redirector or shell must operate in a number of different environments, NET#.COM is actually provided in a number of different forms: NET#.COM, XMSNET#.EXE, and EMSNET#.EXE. The last two of these are used on computers with more than 640K of RAM. XMSNET#.EXE is used on computers with extended memory and EMSNET#.EXE is used on computers with expanded memory. The two types of memory represent two different addressing schemes used to overcome DOS's inherent 640K limit.

The network redirector programs also have command line parameters. NET#.COM, XMSNET#.EXE and EMSNET#.EXE can all use the following parameters.

1. I. The I parameter causes the program to display information about the version of the redirector without loading the program.

2. U. The U parameter unloads the program from memory. This option does not work with some older versions.

3. PS=. In a multi-file-server environment, the network drivers will attach to the first available file server. The PS= parameter is used to indicate a Preferred Server as in PS=SERVER1. This option does not work with some older versions.

Both extended memory and expanded memory require drivers to allow DOS access to these areas. Microsoft's extended memory driver is called HIMEM.SYS and it is included with several software products, including Windows and DOS. The expanded memory driver is very hardware specific and is included only with an expanded memory card. Both drivers are included as statements in the workstation's CONFIG.SYS file. The CONFIG.SYS file is a text file DOS uses for commands that must be executed at the time DOS loads.

The network redirector programs, NET#.COM, XMSNET#.EXE, and EMSNET#.EXE, were included with NetWare for DOS versions 2, 3, and 4, with XMSNET#.EXE and EMSNET#.EXE available for versions 3 and 4 only. NET5.COM is packaged with MS DOS version 5, along with drivers for several other networks. Due to several software bugs, Novell has released NETX.COM, XMSNETX.EXE, and EMSNETX.EXE. These three programs are not DOS version specific. They are available from Novell's Compuserve forum Netwire, or through a Novell authorized dealer.

DOS Directories

In a large network there may be many different types of workstations running many different versions of DOS. The utility programs for each of those DOS versions are sensitive to the version loaded into the computer. Each program, such as FORMAT.COM or CHKDSK.COM, checks which version the computer is running before it executes. For instance, if the FORMAT.COM program from MS DOS 3.1 was started on a computer running PC DOS 3.3 the program would print "Incorrect DOS version." on the screen and then halt.

The result is that if the DOS files for the workstations are to be loaded on the file server, a directory must be created for each of the types of DOS versions that might be used by the workstations. The most critical of the DOS files stored in this way is the DOS command interpreter COMMAND.COM. It is loaded by DOS when the computer is booted and must be frequently reloaded during normal operation. DOS uses the COMSPEC environment variable to record the location of this program. Ordinarily, the COMSPEC variable is set when the computer is booted. If, for instance, the computer was booted from a DOS disk in drive A:, the COMSPEC variable would probably be set to A:\COMMAND.COM. Unfortunately, the DOS disk must often be removed from drive A: to make room for other program or data disks. When DOS needs to reload COMMAND.COM, it will display the message "Insert diskette with COMMAND.COM and strike any key when ready" on the screen and wait for the user to respond.

Network workstations must often be booted from a diskette, so setting the COMSPEC variable to point to a copy of COMMAND.COM on the file server can save a great deal of time for the user. The problem is of course setting it to point to the correct version of COMMAND.COM. NetWare provides facilities for doing just that. The login script variables OS, OS_VERSION, and MACHINE can be used to locate the DOS files at the time the user logs in to the network.

These variables are automatically set when the network drivers are loaded. Once set, they can be used by the login script to MAP network drive letters to appropriate directories. For instance, if an IBM PC running DOS version 3.3 were to login to the network, the OS variable would be set to MSDOS, the OS_VERSION variable would be set to V3.30, and the MACHINE variable would be set to IBM_PC. All the user accounts on the file server could have a line in their login scripts like this:

MAP S1:=SYS:\PUBLIC\%MACHINE\%OS\%OS_VERSION

The search drive, S1, would be mapped to a different directory on the file server for each different value of MACHINE, OS, and OS_VERSION. The supervisor need only ensure that there is a directory containing the correct DOS version for each workstation that logs in. After this line has been executed, the S1 can be used to set the COMSPEC variable.

COMSPEC=S1:COMMAND.COM

In actual practice these two lines would probably be placed in the System Login Script, where they would be executed for every user.

Customizing the Workstation Shell

The network drivers are collectively known as the shell. (Remember, though, that some literature refers to just the NET# module as the shell. Do not let this terminology be confusing. Merely clarify what is meant by the shell in the literature you are reading. This textbook will refer to LSL, the NIC driver, IPXODI, and NET# collectively as the shell.) The shell surrounds the DOS interface to allow commands that should be handled by the network to be rerouted to the network. There are many different ways in which the shell can be customized to work effectively on a given workstation.

The SHELL.CFG File

In addition to running the ODI version of IPX and choosing the correct NET#.COM program, several options can be set using a file called SHELL.CFG. The SHELL.CFG file is a simple text file stored on the workstation computer. Each of the network drivers checks this file for configuration commands. Many of the commands available are quite esoteric and are used primarily to patch compatibility problems with other software running on the workstation. The following is a partial list of SHELL.CFG commands.

1. LONG MACHINE TYPE. Sets the MACHINE login script variable. The default value for this variable is IBM_PC.

2. SHORT MACHINE TYPE. Sets the SMACHINE login script variable. The default value for this variable is IBM. The length cannot exceed four characters. A value of CMPQ, standing for Compaq, will cause the Novell utilities to use a black and white color pallet.

3. LOCAL PRINTERS. Sets the number of printers reserved by the workstation. The most valuable use of this command is to set it to a value of 0 on workstations that do not have any printers. This prevents the computer from locking up when the Print-Screen key is pressed.

4. PREFERRED SERVER. The PREFERRED SERVER command is used to name a specific file server. If the specified file server is not available, the shell will attach to the next available server.

5. SHOW DOTS. An ordinary NetWare directory does not contain the "." and ".." entry as a DOS directory. With the SHOW DOTS command set to ON the "." and ".." entries will be shown. This is especially important when using mouse driven programs that require the user to select ".." to move through the directory structure. Windows 3.11 requires this parameter to be set.

NetBIOS

Novell recognizes the fact that many different networks exist. Among them are networks designed to emulate IBM's original NetBIOS standard. Many network applications were and are written to use the NetBIOS standards for network communications. Novell has provided a program called, not surprisingly, NETBIOS.EXE that emulates the NetBIOS standard. With this program and another called INT2F.EXE installed, application programs can use NetBIOS network function calls or Novell's IPX/SPX network function calls.

Remote Reset

In some environments, strict network security is required. In these situations, diskless workstations can be used to prevent most users from copying data from the server to a diskette on the workstation. The problem, of course, is to boot a computer with no disk drives. The solution is called remote reset, remote boot, or sometimes remote program load. With this feature, a computer can be booted from a file on a network drive rather than from a local disk drive.

Essentially, the workstation is tricked into thinking that the file on the server is a boot disk in drive A. Remote boot is also very helpful for workstations with only floppy disk drives since it eliminates the need for a customized boot diskette to be located near each workstation. Another advantage is that upgrades to a computer's DOS or the network drivers can be made from the network without the need for the supervisor to visit each workstation.

Setting up remote boot involves four steps:

1. The network card must be prepared for remote boot. Only certain network cards can support remote boot. These cards have a ROM (read only memory) chip that requests boot information from the server. Many network cards have sockets for remote boot ROM chips, but the chips are not usually sold with them. Most network cards that are capable of remote boot require a switch to be set on the card or a setup program to be run that sets the card to remote boot mode. It is imperative that the manual for the particular network interface card you are using be consulted to properly set up the card to remote boot.

2. A boot disk must be prepared for the workstation that is to be set for remote boot. DOS, the network drivers, and any other programs that are to be loaded when the computer boots must be copied to the disk. The proper AUTOEXEC.BAT, CONFIG.SYS, and SHELL.CFG files must be prepared and copied to the disk.

3. A program on the file server called DOSGEN must be used to copy all the data on the boot disk to a file on the server called a boot disk image file. The default name for this file is NET$DOS.SYS but it can be changed to something more meaningful such as ROOM1.SYS.

4. If more than one boot image file is needed, another file must be created that indicates which workstations are to use which boot image files. The file, which is named BOOTCONF.SYS, is simply a list of network addresses and the boot image file each needs.

Remote Reset Setup

The Network Card

Preparing the network card for remote boot will be different on each card. Some cards will require only a switch to be set on the card. Many cards have setup programs that are used to set the card to remote boot mode. Other cards will need a remote boot ROM to be inserted in a socket on the card.

The Boot Disk

Some special considerations must be made when preparing a boot disk for remote boot. The problem stems from the unusual behavior of the computer while it is using remote boot.

Without remote boot, the computer will search for a bootable disk. Assuming there is a disk in drive A:, the computer first loads the DOS system files and reads the CONFIG.SYS file for device drivers or other instructions. Next the AUTOEXEC.BAT file is executed. A network boot disk will have an AUTOEXEC.BAT file that loads the appropriate network drivers, LSL.COM, the NIC driver, IPXODI, and NET3.COM, for example. Once these programs are loaded the next line in the AUTOEXEC.BAT file would be executed. Suppose the following lines are in the AUTOEXEC.BAT file.

> LSL
>
> PCN2L (for IBM PC Baseband card)
>
> IPXODI
>
> NET3
>
> LOGIN JSMITH1

Since the computer is booting off the A drive, drive A is the default drive. When the LSL instruction in AUTOEXEC.BAT is executed, the computer will first search only the root directory of drive A to locate and load this program. The same is true for the NIC driver PCN2L, IPXODI, NET3 and LOGIN JSMITH1 instructions. Note that after the NET3 program is loaded, drive letter F: is available to the user. When the LOGIN JSMITH1 instruction is executed, the default drive is still A, even though the workstation has been attached to the server.

The same sequence of events occurs when remote boot is used; however, the computer is "fooled" into reading the boot image file as if it were a disk in drive A. The difference comes after the NET3 program is loaded. As soon as a formal connection is made to the file server, the remote boot process is abandoned and the default drive is left at drive F. Novell considers this a "bug" in the shell software, but new releases of the shell programs have not corrected the problem in all cases.

Even though the remote boot process is essentially over, the AUTOEXEC.BAT file is still executing. Unfortunately DOS has not stored the entire file in memory. Only a byte offset of the next instruction in the batch file is stored. With the remote boot process ended, the AUTOEXEC.BAT file is no longer available since it cannot be read from the boot image file. Additionally, DOS does not recognize that the default drive has been changed. The result is that the computer will attempt to read the next instruction in the AUTOEXEC.BAT from the F:\LOGIN directory.

If there were no more instructions in the file, that is, if NET3 were the last line, the workstation would simply display the F> prompt and be ready for the user to login. Often, however, additional instructions must be executed after the workstation is connected to a file server. In the example above, the command LOGIN JSMITH1 is intended to provide an automatic login at the workstation. To accommodate this one workstation, a copy of the AUTOEXEC.BAT file could be placed in the F:\LOGIN directory. This would not , however, be a satisfactory solution, since every workstation that uses remote boot and needs instructions executed after being connected to the server would encounter the same AUTOEXEC.BAT file.

```
Workstation #1
AUTOEXEC.BAT in boot image file
    LSL
    PCN2L (for IBM PC Baseband Card)
    IPXODI
    NET3
    LOGIN JSMITH1
Workstation #2
AUTOEXEC.BAT in boot image file
    LSL
    PCN2L (for IBM PC Baseband Card)
    IPXODI
    NET3
    LOGIN SUSAN
On file server
F:\LOGIN\AUTOEXEC.BAT
    LSL
    PCN2L
    IPXODI
    NET3
    CAPTURE
```

Fig. 12-1. Different AUTOEXEC.BAT files.

Fig. 12-1 shows three different AUTOEXEC.BAT files. The first two represent files in the boot image prepared for workstations #1 and #2. The third is the file in the F:\LOGIN directory. After the NET3 instruction in each of the workstation files is executed, those workstations are connected to the file server. They will be "fooled" into executing the next line in F:\LOGIN\AUTOEXEC.BAT on the server. The last line in workstation #1's AUTOEXEC.BAT, LOGIN JSMITH1, and the last line in workstation #2's AUTOEXEC.BAT, LOGIN SUSAN would be lost. Each would execute the CAPTURE command in F:\LOGIN\AUTOEXEC.BAT.

There are two solutions to this problem. The first, and most widely used, is to provide a different batch file for each boot disk. The second solution is to ensure that the F:\LOGIN\AUTOEXEC.BAT file will execute different instructions based on information received from the workstation boot image file.

Providing a different batch file for each boot disk is a little more involved than it would first seem. The computer booting up will need to return to the batch file after any programs in it are executed. For instance, if the batch file had a LOGIN statement in it, the computer would need to find the batch file after the LOGIN statement was executed. But the LOGIN script might have changed the current directory. For this reason the batch file being used by the computer during the remote boot process should exist in three places, in the boot disk image file, in the \LOGIN directory, and in the directory that the login script leaves as the default directory when it finishes.

To create the proper boot image file, a complete boot disk should be prepared. DOS, the network shell programs, and an appropriate AUTOEXEC.BAT file should be placed on a disk. To accommodate all of the boot disk image files that might exist on the server, the AUTOEXEC.BAT file is divided into two batch files. AUTOEXEC.BAT simply starts another batch file with a unique name. On the boot disk, the AUTOEXEC.BAT file would have a single line such as JSMITH.BAT. The other file, JSMITH.BAT, would contain all the appropriate instructions for starting the workstation on the network. This file would also be the one that must be duplicated in all three locations mentioned above, the boot disk, the \LOGIN directory, and the default directory left after the login script executes.

The second solution to the problem of multiple boot image files involves the creation of an AUTOEXEC.BAT file on the file server that can accommodate different instructions depending on which boot image file calls it. Creating these batch files requires a better understanding of DOS batch files and the remote boot process.

In Fig. 12-2 all three AUTOEXEC.BAT files have been changed. Three new DOS batch file commands have been used, the SET command, the REM command, and the "%" symbol. The SET command places the text to the right of the "=" in the variable on the left of the "=". This variable is known as an environment variable and is stored in the workstations' memory. The REM command is called a remark and is used simply to put a comment in the file.

It and any text that follows it on the same line are not executed by the computer. The "%" symbol is called a replacement symbol. In a batch file, the environment variable contained inside two "%" symbols is replaced with the contents of the variable. In workstation #1's file, for instance, the last line, %NEXT%, would be replaced with the contents of the variable NEXT, LOGIN JSMITH1.

```
Workstation #1
AUTOEXEC.BAT in boot image file
    SET NEXT=LOGIN JSMITH1
    REM *
    LSL
    PCN2L
    IPXODI
    NET3
    %NEXT%
Workstation #2
AUTOEXEC.BAT in boot image file
    SET NEXT=LOGIN SUSAN
    REM ***
    LSL
    PCN2L
    IPXODI
    NET3
    %NEXT%
On the file server
F:\LOGIN\AUTOEXEC.BAT
    REM ****************
    REM ***
    LSL
    PCN2L
    IPXODI
    NET3
    %NEXT%
```

Fig. 12-2. Updated batch files.

In this case, however, the last line of workstation #1's AUTOEXEC.BAT file will never be executed. But the same replacement will take place when the last line of F:\LOGIN\AUTOEXEC.BAT is executed. The environment variable NEXT will still have the value in it from the first line in workstation #1's AUTOEXEC.BAT.

Followed from the beginning, this is what will happen to workstation #1.

1. When the workstation is turned on or re-booted, the network interface card requests boot information from the server.

2. The file server sends a copy of the boot image file to the workstation. That file is treated as if it were a disk in drive A of the workstation.

3. The workstation loads DOS and begins to execute AUTOEXEC.BAT.

4. The first line, SET NEXT=LOGIN JSMITH1, creates a variable called NEXT and stores the value LOGIN JSMITH1 in it.

5. The second line, REM *, is a remark and is not executed.

6. The third, fourth, fifth, and sixth lines load the network drivers LSL, PCN2L, IPXODI, and NET3.

7. The instant NET3 has loaded successfully, the workstation is attached to the file server and the boot image file is abandoned.

8. The workstation reads its next command from the file server in the file F:\LOGIN\AUTOEXEC.BAT. This is when the REM statements become important. The next command is not necessarily the fifth line in the batch file. It is the command located at the same byte offset as the next command in workstation #1's AUTOEXEC.BAT. There are 44 characters in workstation #1's AUTOEXEC.BAT file up to the end of the sixth line NET3. Adding a carriage return and line feed character to each line brings the total number of bytes to 56 through the end of the sixth line. The REM statements are used to ensure that the seventh line starts at byte offset 57 in each of the three files. The REM statement in the second line of workstation #2's file has two more asterisks in it than the similar line in workstation #1's file because the line SET NEXT=LOGIN SUSAN is two characters less than the line SET NEXT=LOGIN JSMITH1. The first two lines of F:\LOGIN\AUTOEXEC.BAT are there to occupy the space that the first two lines in each of the workstation's files use.

9. Since the byte offsets of the files are aligned properly, the next statement executed by workstation #1 is the fifth line in F:\LOGIN\AUTOEXEC.BAT. The %NEXT% is replaced with the value of the NEXT variable and LOGIN JSMITH1 is executed.

10. The login script for user JSMITH1 takes over and any instructions located there are executed.

The files in this example represent just one way in which environment variables can be used to make individual workstations work differently.

Using DOSGEN

Once created, the information on the boot disk must be converted to a special type of file known as a boot image. The file consists of all the information, including the DOS system files, the network driver programs, and the AUTOEXEC.BAT on the boot disk, converted to a form that the file server can store and send to the workstation when necessary. The NetWare utility program for doing this is called DOSGEN.EXE. The following syntax is used with DOSGEN:

DOSGEN drive [file name]

The drive specified must be a floppy disk drive on the local computer. The file name is optional but must end with a .SYS extension. If no file name is given, DOSGEN will convert the information on the disk to a file called NET$DOS.SYS. The boot disk itself is not changed. NET$DOS.SYS is also the default name that a workstation will use when remote booting. The DOSGEN program is located in the F:\SYSTEM directory on the file server and all boot image files must be stored in the F:\LOGIN directory.

DOSGEN works with any bootable DOS diskette except DOS version 5 and higher. Novell has provided a program called RPLFIX.COM that is used to repair a DOS 5 boot image file already created with DOSGEN. RPLFIX.COM (Remote Program Load Fix) is available on Novell's Compuserve forum Netwire or through a Novell authorized dealer.

BOOTCONF.SYS

Customizing each boot disk means that each workstation will need a separate boot image file. A file called BOOTCONF.SYS is used to store the names of all the boot image files and the network addresses where each will be used. BOOTCONF.SYS must be located in the F:\LOGIN directory and is a simple text file in the form:

0Xnetwork number,node number=boot image file name

A typical line in BOOTCONF.SYS might look something like the following:

0X00D22901,08005A6A34F1=ROOM1.SYS

BOOTCONF.SYS can contain as many lines as needed. When a workstation is using remote boot, BOOTCONF.SYS is searched for a line with that workstation's address. If the address is found, the boot image file specified is used. If the address is not found, the file NET$DOS.SYS is used.

Hands-on NetWare

In order to complete the tutorials in the remaining half of this chapter, the file server and a workstation should be ready to use.

1. The file server must be on.

2. The user account created in the previous chapter must still be available.

3. The network boot disk created earlier must be available.

4. The NetWare WSGEN disk must be available.

5. A complete set of DOS diskettes must be available. DOS version 5 must be used in some sections. The MEM command must be available for these sections.

6. The latest releases of the network shell programs should be obtained. New versions of LSL.COM, your NIC driver, IPXODI.COM, NETX.COM, XMSNETX.EXE, and EMSNETX.EXE are available through Novell's Compuserve forum Netwire or through a Novell authorized reseller.

7. In the examples below TYPE THE NAME OF YOUR ACCOUNT WHERE USER JSMITH IS USED. For instance, if the instructions read "Type LOGIN JSMITH", you should type LOGIN followed by the name of the account you created earlier.

Memory Usage

One of the most important concerns when attaching a DOS computer to any network is the amount of RAM that will be used by the network drivers. In some cases the network drivers use so much memory that application programs cannot run. This of course makes the network worse than useless. The amount of memory used by different networks varies widely from as much as 100K to as little as 10K. Also, the amount of memory used by a single network can vary depending on the options used and the way the drivers are loaded into memory. NetWare is no exception. Many different configurations are possible, and each leaves different amounts of conventional memory free. Conventional memory is all memory up to 640K. All DOS programs must use some of this area during some time in their operation. Other areas of memory, high memory, extended memory, and expanded memory, can only be used in addition to the 640K region, which is what makes it so critical. On a computer with 640K or less of memory, the choices are somewhat limited. The following tutorial demonstrates memory usage in these computers.

Computers with 640K or Less of RAM

In the following tutorial, a workstation with 640K of memory is used. Any workstation with at least 256K could be used. Additional memory will not present a problem.

1. Boot the computer with a DOS diskette by placing the disk in drive A: and pressing the CONTROL, ALT, and DELETE keys simultaneously.

2. Enter the date and time as requested.

3. Type **CHKDSK** and press the ENTER key. The CHKDSK program will show the disk space information and memory usage similar to that in Fig. 12-3. The last two sets of numbers at the bottom show the total amount available to DOS and the amount currently unused. In this case the CHKDSK program shows 575840 bytes of free memory with only DOS loaded.

4. Remove the DOS diskette from drive A and replace it with the network boot disk.

5. Type **LSL** and press the ENTER key.

6. Type the name of your NIC driver. In our example, this was PCN2L for an IBM PC Baseband card, and press the ENTER key.

7. Type **IPXODI** and press the ENTER key.

8. Type **NET#** and press the ENTER key, where the "#" symbol is the DOS version you are currently running. For instance, if you are using DOS 3.1, type NET3. You can type NETX instead of NET# if you have obtained NETX.

9. With the network drivers loaded, return the DOS disk to drive A, type **CHKDSK**, and press the ENTER key. The CHKDSK program should report significantly less memory in the "bytes free" section. The missing memory is being used by the network drivers. Write down the figure shown for "bytes free" for comparison later.

10. Insert the NetWare WSGEN disk. Type **NETBIOS** and press the ENTER key, then type **INT2F** and press the ENTER key. These two programs provide the NetBIOS emulation for application programs that require it.

11. Return the DOS disk to drive A, type **CHKDSK** and press the ENTER key. The "bytes free" figure should be even lower. The memory occupied by these two programs could be significant, and they should not be used unless NetBIOS emulation is required.

The example above represents a worst-case situation in which the drivers must be placed entirely in conventional memory. Many programs not originally intended to operate in a networked environment would not have enough memory to run. A computer with at least 1 megabyte of memory can be configured to preserve much more conventional memory.

```
A:\>CHKDSK

   1457664 bytes total disk space
      7680 bytes in 6 user files
   1449984 bytes available on disk

       512 bytes in each allocation unit
      2847 total allocation units on disk
      2832 available allocation units on disk

    651264 total bytes memory
    575840 bytes free
```

Fig. 12-3. Output produced by the CHKDSK program.

Computers with 1 Megabyte or More of Memory.

DOS programs are typically limited to the 640K conventional memory region, but a number of methods have been created to use more. On a computer with 1 megabyte of memory, some of the 360K (actually 384K) above conventional memory (called high memory) can be used by DOS, if an appropriate extended memory manager program is implemented. Microsoft's HIMEM.SYS device driver is the most readily available of these programs. The following instructions demonstrate how high memory can be used to save conventional memory.

Using HIMEM.SYS and XMSNET#

1. Boot the workstation with the network boot disk by inserting the disk in drive A and simultaneously pressing the CONTROL, ALT, and DELETE keys.

2. Copy the HIMEM.SYS and XMSNET# (use XMSNETX if possible) device drivers to the network boot disk.

3. Ensure that the network boot disk is in drive A.

4. Type the following lines, pressing the ENTER key at the end of each line.

COPY CON CONFIG.SYS

DEVICE=HIMEM.SYS

5. While holding down the CONTROL key, press the Z key, then press the ENTER key.

6. Boot the workstation by simultaneously pressing the CONTROL, ALT, and DELETE keys.

7. Type **LSL** and press the ENTER key.

8. Type the name of your NIC driver and press the ENTER key. Remember, the example is using PCN2L for the IBM PC Baseband card, but you must type the name of the driver for your NIC.

9. Type **IPXODI** and press the ENTER key.

10. Type **XMSNET#** and press the ENTER key where the "#" represents the DOS version number you are using (or use X for the generic version).

11. Replace the network boot disk with a DOS disk containing the CHKDSK program.

12. Type **CHKDSK** and press the ENTER key.

The number of bytes free should be significantly larger in this case than in the previous example with only LSL, the NIC driver, IPXODI, and NET# loaded. The extra space available in conventional memory is made possible by the network shell program XMSNET# loading itself primarily into the high memory region between 640K and 1 megabyte. Write down the figure shown for "bytes free" for comparison later.

DOS Versions 5 and 6

DOS versions 5 and 6 offer other ways to use the high memory area. Most of the DOS code itself, as well as any other memory resident programs such as network drivers can be loaded into the high memory area. The following exercises demonstrate the benefits in conventional memory savings using DOS 5 on a computer with at least 1 megabyte of memory. A bootable DOS 5 disk will be needed.

1. Copy the LSL, the NIC driver, IPXODI.COM, and NET#.COM programs to the bootable DOS 5 disk.

2. Copy the following files from the original DOS 5 disks to the bootable disk: HIMEM.SYS, EMM386.EXE, CHKDSK.EXE, MEM.EXE, and MORE.COM.

3. Ensure that the DOS 5 disk is in drive A and type the following lines, pressing the ENTER key after each line.

COPY CON CONFIG.SYS

DEVICE=HIMEM.SYS

375

DEVICE=EMM386.EXE NOEMS
DOS=HIGH,UMB

4. While holding down the CONTROL key, press the Z key and then the ENTER key.

   The CONFIG.SYS file is being used in this case to load programs that will manage the high memory area and to load DOS into that area. The HIMEM.SYS device driver manages the use of all the memory above 640K. The EMM386.EXE program is being used to allow DOS programs access to the high memory area between 640K and 1 megabyte. The DOS command instructs DOS to load itself into the high memory area and to allow other programs to be loaded there as well.

5. Boot the workstation with the DOS 5 disk by simultaneously pressing the CONTROL, ALT, and DELETE keys.

6. Enter the date and time as requested.

7. Type **LSL** and press the ENTER key.

8. Type the name of your NIC driver and press the ENTER key. Remember, the example is using PCN2L for the IBM PC Baseband card, but you must type the name of the driver for your NIC.

9. Type **LOADHIGH IPXODI** and press the ENTER key. LOADHIGH, which can be abbreviated LH, is a DOS 5 command that attempts to load the program into the high memory area.

10. Type **LOADHIGH NET#** and press the ENTER key.

11. Type **CHKDSK** and press the ENTER key. Compare the "bytes free" figure with the number obtained when using conventional memory only. This amount should be much larger.

12. Type **MEM/C | MORE** and press the ENTER key. The | MORE portion of this command is necessary only because the output from the MEM /C command will be longer than 25 lines displayed on the monitor.

    This command displays memory usage in a more complete form than the CHKDSK command. The first screen shows programs running in conventional memory. MSDOS, HIMEM, EMM386, and COMMAND, LSL, and the NIC driver should be listed there.

13. Strike any key to advance to the next screen of output from the MEM /C command. A list of programs loaded into high memory should appear. SYSTEM, IPXODI, and NET# should be shown in high memory. The MSDOS shown in conventional memory and the SYSTEM shown in high memory are both portions of DOS code.

376

Note that the XMSNET# and the EMSNET# programs are not used in this example because DOS is being used to load the programs in high memory. With this configuration, these programs would not find any memory available for their use.

The previous exercises demonstrate the memory savings using the proper network shell programs, particularly when using DOS 5.

The SHELL.CFG File

When the network shell is loaded, a file called SHELL.CFG is searched for in the current directory. This file contains instructions to the shell programs regarding how they are to be loaded. One of the most important functions of the SHELL.CFG file is to set login script variables to values that reflect the type of computer being used. The variable MACHINE can be used to specify a certain type of computer. This variable can be critical when preparing a login script if the login script needs to set a search drive to a directory containing DOS program files.

In preparation for exercises involving the SHELL.CFG file, directories must be created on the server for each type and version of DOS being used. The following instructions show how this is done. These instructions need to be performed only once on a file server for each DOS version.

1. Boot the workstation with the appropriate network boot disk.

2. Type **LSL** and press the ENTER key.

3. Type the name of the NIC driver (PCN2L in our example) and press the ENTER key.

4. Type **IPXODI** and press the ENTER key.

5. Type the name of the network redirector you will be using and press the ENTER key. NETX will work for all situations but the appropriate NET# program can also be used.

6. Type **F:** and press the ENTER key.

7. Type **LOGIN** followed by the name of the supervisor-equivalent account you created earlier and press the ENTER key.

8. Type **CD\PUBLIC** and press the ENTER key.

9. If your workstation is an IBM computer, type MD IBM_PC and press the ENTER key. If your workstation is an IBM compatible running a machine-specific version of DOS, use the name of the computer shorted to eight characters or less instead of IBM_PC. For instance, if the workstation is a Compaq computer type MD COMPAQ and press the ENTER key.

10. Type **CD** followed by the name of the computer you used in the previous step and press the ENTER key.

11. Type **MD MSDOS** and press the ENTER key. Use MSDOS in the command even if you are using PC DOS.

12. Type **CD MSDOS** and press the ENTER key.

13. Type **MD V** followed by the version number of the DOS you are using and press the ENTER key. For instance if you are using PC DOS version 3.31, type MD V3.31 and press the ENTER key. If you are using MS DOS version 5, type MD V5.00 and press the ENTER key.

14. Type **CD V** followed by the version number you used in the previous command

15. Insert the first DOS disk of the version you are using in drive A:.

16. Type **COPY A:*.* F:** and press the ENTER key.

17. Repeat the previous step for each DOS disk needed for that version of DOS. For instance, PC DOS 3.3 on 3 1/2-inch disks requires two disks to be copied to drive F:.

18. Type **LOGOUT** and press ENTER.

With the appropriate DOS version placed on the file server, the SHELL.CFG file should be created to ensure the correct version is used. Also, additional login script commands should be used to map the DOS directory to a search drive. The following instructions should be used to update the SHELL.CFG file with the appropriate commands:

1. Place the network boot disk in drive A: and set the default drive to A by typing **A:** and pressing ENTER.

2. Type **COPY CON SHELL.CFG** and press the ENTER key.

3. Type **LONG MACHINE TYPE=** followed by the name of the computer used in the creation of the DOS directory and press the ENTER key. For instance, for an IBM PC type LONG MACHINE TYPE=IBM_PC and press the ENTER key.

4. Type **SHOW DOTS ON** and press the ENTER key.

5. Hold down the CONTROL key and press the Z key. Then press the ENTER key.

The SHELL.CFG file should now be on the network boot disk. The next time IPXODI and NETX are loaded, the commands in this file will take effect. In the following steps, SYSCON is used to change the login script to include a map command to COMMAND.COM, the DOS command line interpreter.

1. Boot the workstation with the network boot disk by simultaneously pressing the CONTROL, ALT, and DELETE keys.

2. Enter the date and time as requested.

3. Type **LSL** and press the ENTER key.

4. Type the name of your NIC driver (PCN2L in the example) and press the ENTER key.

5. Type **IPXODI** and press the ENTER key.

6. Type the name of the network redirector you will be using and press the ENTER key. NETX will work for all situations, but the appropriate NET# program can also be used.

7. Type **F:** and press the ENTER key.

8. Type **LOGIN** followed by the name of supervisor-equivalent account you created earlier and press the ENTER key.

9. Type the password used for this account, and press the ENTER key.

10. Type **SYSCON** and press the ENTER key. SYSCON's main menu should appear as shown in Fig. 12-4.

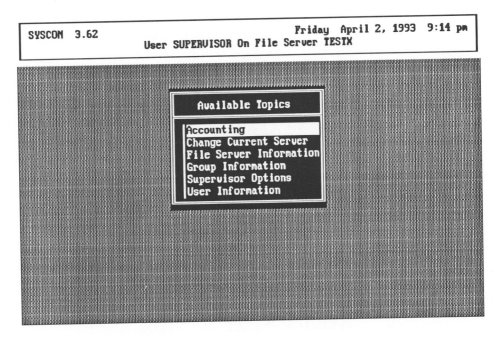

Fig. 12-4. SYSCON's main menu.

11. Move the cursor to the User Information option and press the ENTER key.

12. Type the name of the account you are now using. The cursor should move to highlight the name. Press the ENTER key when the proper name is highlighted.

13. Type **L** to highlight Login Script and press the ENTER key.

14. Within the Login Script editor, move the cursor to the rightmost position in the last line and press the ENTER key.

15. Type the following line exactly as it appears below. Then press the ENTER key.

    MAP S4:=SYS:PUBLIC\%MACHINE\%OS\%OS_VERSION

16. Type the following line exactly as it appears below, then press the ENTER key.

    COMSPEC=S4:COMMAND.COM

17. Press the ESC key.

18. Press the Y key, then press the ENTER key.

19. Press the ESC key three times until the Exit SYSCON menu appears.

20. Press the Y key then press the ENTER key.

21. Type **LOGOUT** and press the ENTER key.

22. Type **LOGIN** followed by the name of your account, and press the ENTER key.

23. Type the password used for this account, and press the ENTER key.

24. The new login script should give you access to the DOS directory appropriate to the version of DOS you are now using. To test the availability of the DOS programs, type **CHKDSK A:** and press the ENTER key. If the drive mapping has been made correctly, the CHKDSK program will report the status of the disk in drive A.

The user now has a search path to the NetWare utility programs as well as DOS programs such as CHKDSK and FORMAT. If appropriate directories are created for all of the DOS versions that might be used on the workstations, the user can login at any workstation and still have a search path to the DOS files needed by that workstation. In other words, the search path to the DOS directory is dependent on the DOS version used at a particular workstation.

Remote Reset

With the remote reset feature, also called remote boot or remote IPL, a workstation can boot from a file on the server rather than from a diskette. This is extraordinarily beneficial in environments where there are many computers without a hard disk to boot from. The supervisor can avoid the tedium of maintaining a boot disk for each workstation which can become lost, damaged, or infected with a computer virus. Remote reset also makes possible a diskless workstation for use in environments where strict data security is required.

Remote reset is only possible when using network interface cards that are specifically designed for it. In addition, most network cards that can employ remote reset require a switch to be physically set on the card. Some network cards require the switch to be set using a program on a setup disk provided with the computer or the card. The following exercises assume the proper hardware settings have been made for remote boot. Remote reset will only work on a computer that has no other physical disk to boot from. Therefore, if the workstation being used to test remote boot has a hard disk, it must be configured as nonbootable.

Installing remote reset will require some cooperation between students using the server. Since there is only one BOOTCONF.SYS file and one AUTOEXEC.BAT file on the server, these files may need to be created only once or updated by an individual for all others. The BOOTCONF.SYS file will contain the network addresses of all the workstations using remote boot. Follow the instructions below to determine the address of the workstation you are currently using.

1. Type **LOGIN** and your user name. Then press the ENTER key. The password prompt should appear.

2. Type the password used for this account and press the ENTER key.

3. Type **FCONSOLE** and press the ENTER key. The FCONSOLE main menu should appear, similar to the one in Fig. 12-5.

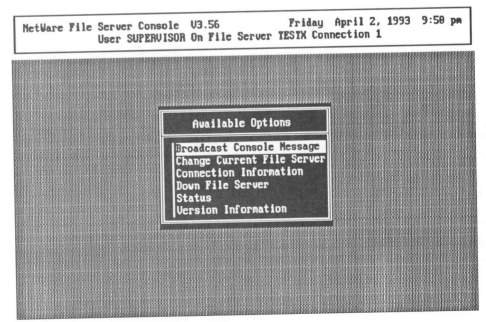

Fig. 12-5. FCONSOLE's main menu.

4. Move the highlighted bar to the Connection Information option and press the ENTER key.

5. Type the name of your user account. The highlighted bar will move to your name. Press the ENTER key.

6. Use the ARROW keys to highlight the Other Information option and press the ENTER key.

7. The box displayed shows when and where this user logged in. Write down the number labeled Network Address. Remember to include the ":". The first eight digits of this number indicate the network being used. This is the same network number entered when NetWare was installed. The last twelve digits identify the actual network card in the workstation being used. Later in this chapter, when this number is used, you must be using the same workstation.

8. Press the ESC key four times until the Exit FCONSOLE menu appears.

9. Press Y, then the ENTER key.

10. Type **LOGOUT** and press the ENTER key to end this session.

For this exercise the last eight digits of the node number will be used as the name for the boot image file. Ordinarily a name would be used that indicates the location or type of computer being used. For instance, the file might be called ROOM222.SYS or COMPAQ#1.SYS. The .SYS extension is required by NetWare. By using a portion of the node number as the name, the chance of accidental duplications of node numbers in the BOOTCONF.SYS file can be greatly reduced.

The next task is to create an appropriate AUTOEXEC.BAT file to be placed on the boot disk. Often a complementary AUTOEXEC.BAT needs to be placed in the F:\LOGIN directory on the file server. The file server AUTOEXEC.BAT must be usable by all the workstations using remote boot. Remember the necessity of a general purpose AUTOEXEC.BAT on the file server is considered to be a bug by Novell and may be fixed in the version of the network shell you are using. To simplify this exercise, a short AUTOEXEC.BAT file will be used that does not have any commands after the network shell is loaded. No file server AUTOEXEC.BAT will then be needed. Follow the steps below to create an AUTOEXEC.BAT file for the boot disk and to create a boot image file on the file server.

1. If necessary, boot the workstation by placing a network boot disk in drive A and pressing the CONTROL, ALT, and DELETE keys simultaneously.

2. Enter the date and time as required.

3. Type the following lines exactly as shown, pressing the ENTER key after each line.

COPY CON AUTOEXEC.BAT

LSL

PCN2L (substitute the name of your NIC driver)

IPXODI

4. Type the name of the network shell program you are using and press the ENTER key. **NETX** will work in all situations.

5. Hold down the CONTROL key and press the Z key. Then press the ENTER key.

6. Type **AUTOEXEC.BAT** and press the ENTER key. This will test the AUTOEXEC.BAT file and load the network driver programs.

7. Type **F:** and press the ENTER key.

8. Type **LOGIN** followed by the name of your account and press the ENTER key.

9. To ensure that you are in the proper directory, type **CD\LOGIN** and press the ENTER key.

10. Verify that the disk in drive A is the network boot disk with the proper network driver programs, the SHELL.CFG file, and the AUTOEXEC.BAT file.

11. Type **DOSGEN A:** followed by the last eight digits of the node number of the workstation you are now using followed by **.SYS**, then press the ENTER key. For example, if the network address written down earlier was 00D22901:08005A5A0123, the command would be DOSGEN A: 5A5A0123.SYS.

An additional step is required for DOS 5 users. A program called RPLFIX.COM must be obtained from Novell's Compuserve forum, Netwire, or from a Novell authorized reseller.

With the RPLFIX program on a disk in drive A:, type A:RPLFIX followed by the name of your boot image file. Then press the ENTER key. For instance, if your boot image file name is 5A5A0123.SYS, the command would be A:RPLFIX 5A5A0123.SYS.

12. A BOOTCONF.SYS file must be created to tell NetWare which boot image file is to be sent to which workstation. This file could be completely entered by an individual using the proper format to indicate the names of the boot image files. A complete BOOTCONF.SYS file might look something like the following.

    0X00D22901,08005A6A3491=5A6A3491.SYS

    0X00D22901,08007A6A44F1=7A6A44F1.SYS

    0X00D22901,08005A6A348B=5A6A348B.SYS

    0X00D22901,08005A6B14FC=5A6B14FC.SYS

    0X00D22901,08005A6A3A11=5A6A3A11.SYS

0X00D22901,08005A6A24F7=5A6A24F7.SYS

0X00D22901,08005B6AF4E1=5B6AF4E1.SYS

0X00D22901,08005A6A34F2=5A6A34F2.SYS

The first two characters of each line, 0X, are required to indicate that the other characters represent a hexadecimal number. The next eight characters are the network number of the network being used. The characters between the "," and the "=" are the individual workstation node numbers and finally, the characters following the "=" are the names of the boot image files.

An alternate method of creating the BOOTCONF.SYS file would be to have each student append the line required for his or her workstation by using a command in the following format.

ECHO 0X00D22901,08005A6A3491=5A6A3491.SYS >> BOOTCONF.SYS

This command must be entered while still logged in under your supervisor-equivalent account and with F:\LOGIN as the current directory. The network address, node address, and boot image file name in the command above would be replaced with the numbers for your workstation.

Testing Remote Reset

With the BOOTCONF.SYS file created, the only step left is to test the remote reset.

1. Type **LOGOUT** and press the ENTER key.

2. Remove any disk that may be in disk drive A.

3. Boot the computer by pressing the CONTROL, ALT, and DELETE keys simultaneously.

4. The workstation should boot as if it were using the boot disk created earlier without prompting for the date and time.

5. To completely test the remote boot feature, type **F:** and press the ENTER key.

6. Type **LOGIN** followed by your account name and press the ENTER key.

7. If the login was successful, type **LOGOUT** and press the ENTER key.

Summary

The workstations on a network may have different types and amounts of memory. To take full advantage of the memory available, these differences must be taken into account when loading the network driver programs. NET# or NETX can be used on any computer, but by using EMSNET# or XMS-NET# the memory available for application programs can be significantly increased. DOS version 5 can also be used to increase available memory by loading the network driver programs into high memory.

Workstations may also use different versions of DOS. Each of the different versions must be loaded onto the file server with appropriate login script commands to make the DOS files available to the user.

Some network cards can take advantage of a NetWare feature called remote reset, which allows the workstation to boot from the file server rather than a floppy or hard disk. In this process, a fully customized boot disk is copied to a file on the server using a program called DOSGEN. If more than one boot image file is needed, a file called BOOTCONF.SYS is used to correlate the workstation with the boot image file.

Questions

1. Can the XMSNETX program be used to conserve memory on a computer with 640K of RAM?

2. Under what situations can the network shell program NETX.COM be used?

3. What are the two ways a particular file server can be specified in a multi-file-server environment?

4. What circumstances would require a user to load the NETBIOS and INT2F programs?

5. Why is it important that the login script variables MACHINE, OS, and OS_VERSION have the proper values for a given workstation?

6. The remote reset process can abandon the AUTOEXEC.BAT file in the boot image file and use another. Where is this other copy of AUTOEXEC.BAT located?

7. What is the name of the program used to create a boot image file?

8. What information does the BOOTCONF.SYS file contain?

Projects

Objective

The following projects provide additional practice creating automated processes in order for users to access the network and to remotely boot a file. They enhance earlier hands-on exercises on these topics.

Project 1. Automating User Logins

1. Create a new user with the SYSCON utility. Use the appropriate login script variables to display the workstation type, operating system, and operating system version each time the user logs in. Do not give the user a password. Use the Shift and Print Screen keys to record the results.

2. Change the login script so that the SET command is executed during the login script. The SET command is an internal DOS command, not a program name. To execute an internal DOS command, use the following syntax:

   COMMAND /C command name

   The COMMAND is the DOS command interpreter COMMAND.COM. The /C tells COMMAND.COM to execute the internal DOS command that follows. Use SHIFT PRINT SCREEN to record the results.

3. Using the DOSGEN program, create a boot image file that logs in the user created above. Use SHIFT PRINT SCREEN to record the results.

Project 2. Creating a Remote Boot File

1. Create a remote boot file for your workstation. Use only one command in the AUTOEXEC.BAT file. That command should be the name of another batch file with a unique name that exists both on the boot disk and in the F:\LOGIN directory.

2. Modify the remote boot file above to login to a user account.

3. Create a login script that assigns the drive letter M: to one of three different subdirectories, MORNING, AFTERNOON, and EVENING, depending on the time of day.

4. Modify the login script of the account used above to start another program such as a word processor or the FILER utility.

Network Printing

Objectives

After completing this chapter you will

1. Understand the concepts of network printing.
2. Know how network printers can be attached to the network.
3. Understand the use of printing structures to direct data and control printers.
4. Know how to install a print server and print queue.
5. Be able to send data to a network printer.

Key Terms

Bridges	Boot Disk
CAPTURE	Print Server
PCONSOLE	PRINTCON
PRINTDEF	Queue
Remote Printing	Server Printing

Introduction

Often an important function of a network is printer sharing. Printing across a network involves loading special software on the workstation that remains resident along with the other network drivers. The software intercepts output that a normal application such as a word processor sends to the workstation's printer port. That data is then sent across the network to a printer attached to another computer. With a network, many users can send output to the same printer. Or, users may wish to select among different types of printers available on the network. NetWare has supported network printing since its earliest versions, but lacked many important features. Several third-party products offered capabilities that made network printing a much more valuable resource. With later versions of NetWare, however, some of these features have been introduced as separate utilities.

Printers can be attached to the network in several ways. They can be connected to the file server, to a NetWare bridge, to a dedicated print server, or to a remote print server. In addition, several third party vendors have produced products that allow even more flexibility in printing. Only the first three methods will be discussed here.

To accommodate the many users and printers that might be on a network, Novell has created a number of structures that are used to control what gets printed and where it gets printed. These structures are print forms, print devices, print queues, and print job configurations.

Printing in a Novell Network

File Server Printing

NetWare networks are very centralized in that almost all activity is handled through the file server. Therefore, the file server is a natural place to begin network printing. In NetWare Version 3.11, printing on printers attached to the file server requires setting up a print server which is loaded via running the PSERVER NLM (NetWare Loadable Module) either as part of the file server's AUTOEXEC.NCF or by loading the NLM manually from the file server's monitor once the file server has booted. The NLM is essentially another program that runs on the server in addition to NetWare.

Print Server Printing

It is often inconvenient for a variety of reasons to use a file server for printing. Perhaps most importantly, the users who may need access to the printer may not be users who should have access to the file server. In other words, it may be dangerous to have the file server where an unskilled individual might try to reboot it in an attempt to restart the printer or run some other software. Physical proximity to the server can also create a noise problem if the network supervisor, the file server, and a loud printer are all located in the same room. Another reason to avoid attaching the printers to the file server is simply that printers usually require a great deal of maintenance while file servers do not. A file server may run for months without being turned off or even touched. Frequent installation and removal of printers or printer ports could disrupt the file server. Additionally, it is often inadvisable to burden an already busy file server with the load of also running as a print server. A dedicated print server can be used to avoid these concerns by placing the printers, paper, cables, and noise in a separate location.

The print server can be any computer on the network with at least 360K of memory and up to five printer ports. The computer runs a program called PSERVER that sends the output to the printers attached to it. Since a print server requires only minimal hardware, it is a good investment to make if there are to be several network printers.

Remote Printing

A print server can direct data to sixteen different printers but those printers do not need to be physically attached to it. In fact, only five printers can be locally attached to the print server. With the proper software loaded on another workstation, the workstation's printer becomes a network printer. Authorized users anywhere on the network can send data to be printed on the workstation's local printer with only a slight slowing of the normal operation of the workstation. The remote printer software is a memory resident program that uses approximately 9K of memory and allows other applications to run. It operates similar to the way the DOS PRINT command works, operating in the background while the workstation's user runs another application in the foreground, such as a word processor. Using remote printing, a printer that is usually accessed by a single workstation can be set up to be accessible by anyone on the network. The greatest disadvantage to this system is its vulnerability. If the user reboots or causes an operating system crash, the remote printing software will no longer be available and will have to be reloaded to continue printing.

Wherever the printer is located, the same tools can be used to access and control it. These tools or printing structures can be used to control all aspects of printing, such as which printer is to be used, what print style is to be used, and who will have access to the printer.

Print Forms

Print forms are the simplest of the printing structures. They represent the type of paper the printer will use. Fig. 13-1 shows a Form Definition dialog box in the Printer Definition utility program PRINTDEF. As seen here, the only important information to the printer is the length and width of the paper. The name of the form might represent much more to the printer operator. For instance, one form might be called CHECK and another BILL. While they may be the same size, they are definitely different.

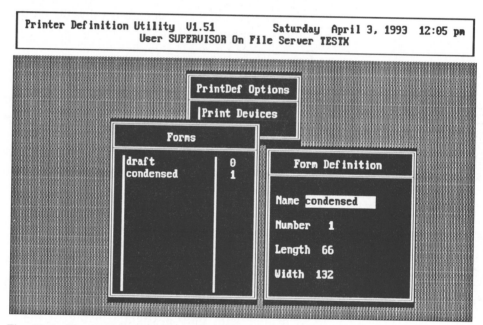

Fig. 13-1. The Form Definition dialog box.

Print Devices

Since each type and brand of printer may have a different set of control codes, NetWare uses the print device structure to define each printer. Fig. 13-2 shows the Print Device Options of the PRINTDEF program. The three options Edit Print Devices, Import Print Device, and Export Print Device refer to the use of printer definition files. When Import Print Device is chosen, the PRINT-DEF program prompts the user for a directory. With the proper directory chosen, the program displays a list of printer definition files. Novell has provided files for most popular printers, and these files are normally stored in the PUBLIC directory. The arrow in the lower left corner of the Available .PDFs box indicates that more files are available than are shown. The files contain the codes that each printer uses for each of its functions. For instance, the CIT120D.PDF file contains the codes a Citizen 120D printer uses for bold, italics, and underline printing. Selecting one of these files causes it to be stored in a separate file, where the information can be used by the other printing structures.

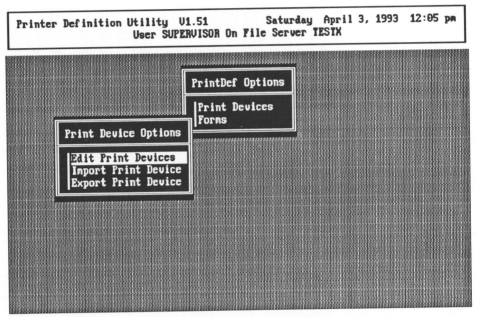

Fig. 13-2. Print Device Options menu.

The print devices can also be edited to provide more functions or to create completely new printer device files. After the Edit Print Devices option is selected, a box containing the Defined Print Devices shows the printers that have already been loaded. Fig. 13-3 shows the Edit Device Options menu that appears when one of the devices is selected. Both of the options listed represent control codes that might be sent to the printer. Device Modes refers to a set of codes that might be sent as a setup before printing, while Device Functions represents the specific codes sent for a single printer command. After selecting Letter Quality, the functions that make up the Letter Quality mode are displayed. In this case it is only one, also called letter quality. Fig. 13-4 shows the control codes for the function letter quality. This box is intended only to display the functions. To edit them, the Edit Print Functions option must be selected from the Edit Device Options menu.

The Printer Definition Utility, PRINTDEF, is used to create and edit print forms and print devices which control the printer. To control how the printers are used, separate utilities are used to create print queues and print job configurations.

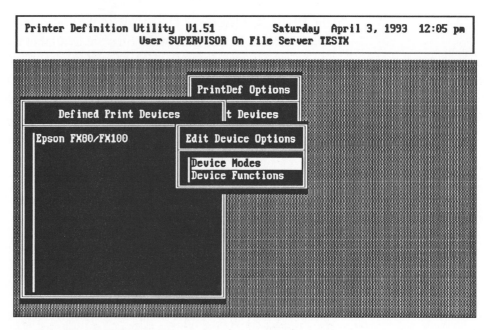

Fig. 13-3. Edit Device Options menu.

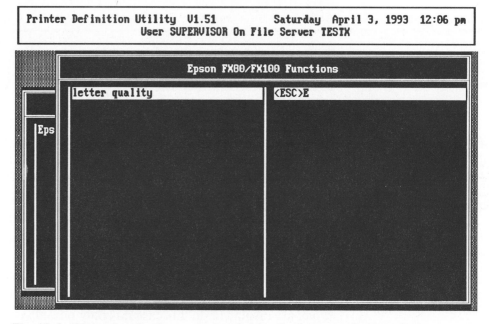

Fig. 13-4. Dialog box for the control codes for the letter quality function.

Print Queues

Obviously, if everyone on the network sent data to a network printer at once, problems would arise. A system had to be created to allow the data from each user to be stored and printed when the printer becomes available. Print queues provide this function and more. The NetWare Print Console utility, PCON-

SOLE, is used to create and maintain print queues and print servers. Fig. 13-5 shows PCONSOLE's main menu. The first option simply allows the user to select another file server. The second option displays a list of existing print queues. When one is selected, the Print Queue Information menu appears. These options control the who, what, where, and when of the queue. The following is a description of each of the selections.

1. Current Print Job Entries. This option displays a list of the print jobs waiting to print from the selected print queue. In this case a print job is data that a user has sent to be printed. A print job is any set of output sent to the printer. This term is easily confused with a print job configuration, which is a certain set of network printing options.

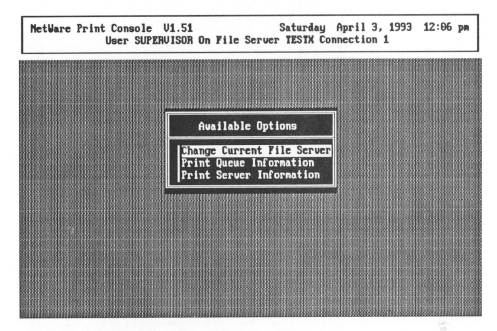

```
NetWare Print Console  V1.51              Saturday  April 3, 1993  12:06 pm
               User SUPERVISOR On File Server TESTX Connection 1
```

```
                          Available Options
                    Change Current File Server
                    Print Queue Information
                    Print Server Information
```

Fig. 13-5. PCONSOLE's main menu.

2. Current Queue Status. Shown in Fig. 13-6, the Current Queue Status box displays how many jobs are waiting to print and how many print servers are attached to the queue. The Operator Flags section allows the operator to turn certain features of the queue on and off. Most importantly, it allows the operator to turn off access to the queue altogether.

3. Currently Attached Servers. It shows the file servers attached to a queue.

4. Print Queue ID. This option displays the eight-digit hexadecimal number that represents the queue on the file server. The number can be used by custom programs to access and control the queue.

393

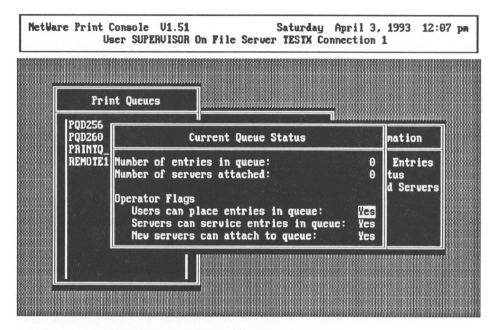

Fig. 13-6. Current Queue Status dialog box.

5. Queue Operators. Each print queue can be controlled by a different set of users. The queue shown in Fig. 13-7 has three operators, MJ, ROOT, and SUPERVISOR. Only these users can make changes to the queue or control jobs in the queue. The word "User" appears next to each name because groups can also be made queue operators.

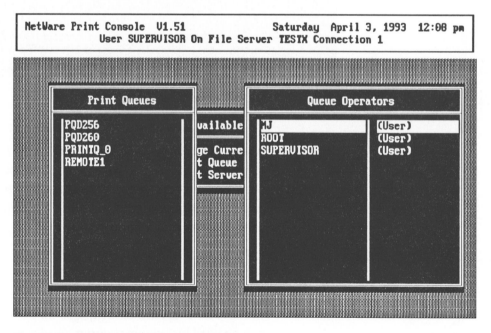

Fig. 13-7. A queue with three operators.

6. Queue Servers. Fig. 13-8 shows the box displayed after selecting Queue Servers. This queue is being serviced by the print server PSERV256. The message "Print Server" appears next to the name because file servers can also service print queues.

7. Queue Users. Each queue can be restricted to certain users or groups of users. This box shows the users and groups who have access to a queue.

The last item on PCONSOLE's main menu is Print Server Information. This item is, of course, quite important in network printing. However, to complete the topic of printing structures, another program, the Configure Print Jobs utility PRINTCON, must be considered.

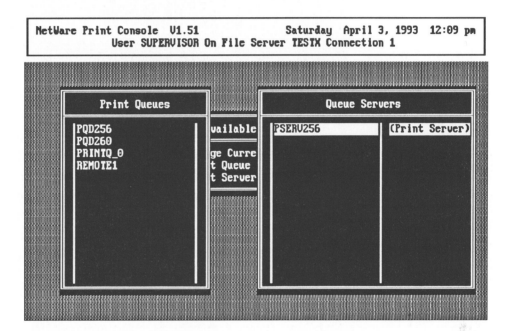

Fig. 13-8. Dialog box displaying a queue and its print server.

Print Job Configurations

PRINTCON allows users to create print job configurations. Notice that this terminology refers to a printing structure, not to individual sets of data that have been sent to the printer. A print job configuration is a set of instructions that are used to create a certain type of output on a certain type of printer. PRINTCON's main menu, shown in Fig. 13-9, has only three selections: Edit Print Job Configurations, Select Default Print Job Configuration, and Copy Print Job Configurations.

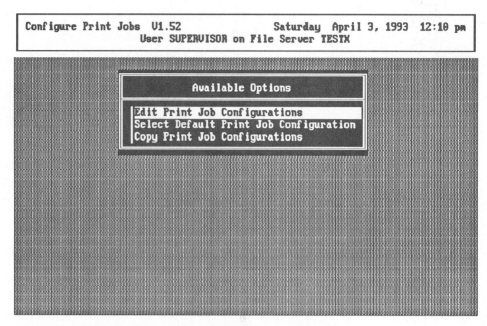

Fig. 13-9. PRINTCON's main menu..

1. Edit Print Job Configurations. When this option is selected, a list of existing print jobs appears. After one has been selected or a new one created, the Edit Print Job Configuration box appears. This is where the power of the print job configuration becomes evident. Every printing option available under NetWare can be set to a specific value or in some cases left to be chosen automatically. For instance, in the left column, the print queue for this job configuration is listed as PQD256 while the print server is left as (Any). This means that the data will be sent to a specific print queue but it may print on any print server serving print queue PQD256.

The options that can be set are as follows:

   a. Number of copies. The user can specify how many times a certain set of data will be printed.

   b. File contents. This option helps NetWare determine how to handle the data.

   c. Tab size. Often in a text document, a tab character is used to represent a certain number of spaces. The number of spaces is then left to the printer to determine. This option tells NetWare to convert those tab characters into the specified number of spaces.

   d. Suppress form feed. Another character often present in text files is the form feed character. It tells the printer to advance to the next page. Since NetWare can handle this function, too many form feeds may be sent to the printer. Suppressing the form feed character allows NetWare to fully control the page advance.

e. Notify when done. When this option is set to "Yes" a message is sent to the user after the data sent has been printed.

f. Local printer. Used with the CAPTURE command to specify which local parallel printer ports the user wishes to redirect to a network printer. Choices are 1, 2, or 3 for LPT1, LPT2, or LPT3.

g. Auto endcap. Output sent to a network printer is stored in the print queue first. The data is not printed until an ENDCAP message is sent. With the Auto endcap feature set to "Yes," output from a certain application is sent to the printer when that application finishes executing. In other words, a word processor such as WordPerfect can send data to the queue, but that data will not be sent to the printer until the user exits WordPerfect. With Auto endcap set to "No," the data would not be printed until the user issues an ENDCAP command.

h. File server. Displays the file server being used.

i. Print queue. Shows which queue the data will be sent to.

j. Print server. Shows which print server the data will be sent to.

k. Device. Shows which device definition will be used, if any. When a device definition is used, it must be one which was set up using the PRINT-DEF command.

l. Mode. Shows which mode the device will be in. The mode is dependent on the device used. The available modes are also set up using the PRINT-DEF command.

m. Form name. Shows which form will be used.

n. Print banner. A banner printed in extra large characters can be printed at the top of the output for identification. Normally when a banner is included, the name of the user and the file name are used in the banner. Here, the name of the user and the file name can be given different values. Print banners waste a sheet of paper for each print job in a small environment. In a large environment, the use of the print banner is highly recommended for separation of print jobs.

o. Enable timeout/timeout count. Used to set the number of seconds to wait after an application has finished sending output to the printer before sending that data on to the print server. If TIMEOUT=0 and AUTO ENDCAP have been selected, printing begins only when the user exits from the application creating the printer output.

2. Select Default Print Job Configuration. PRINTCON's second main menu option allows the user to specify a certain print job configuration to be always used unless another is specified.

3. Copy Print Job Configurations. Print job configurations allow individuals to customize how their output will be printed by the network. Unfortunately, the configuration must be set up for each user and cannot be extended to a group as with most NetWare functions. However, the Copy Print Job Configurations option allows print job configurations to be copied to other users one user at a time.

NetWare offers print forms, print devices, print queues, and print job configurations to allow the process of printing on the network to be completely customized. These features are useless, of course, without printers attached to the network and a means for sending data to them.

Attaching the Printer

The printers can be attached to the network in essentially three different ways: on a print server (which may be the file server or a dedicated workstation), to a NetWork bridge, and on a workstation as a remote printer. By far the most versatile method for attaching printers to the network is to install a print server. The print server is simply a computer running a program called PSERVER.EXE. This program directs the data that has been queued on the file server to the printers that are managed by the print server. The printers may be attached to the print server or they may be attached remotely to workstations. The PCONSOLE program is used again to configure print servers. Fig. 13-10 shows the print servers already available on the file server. Selecting one of them displays the Print Server Information menu, as shown in Fig. 13-11. Each of its options is explained below.

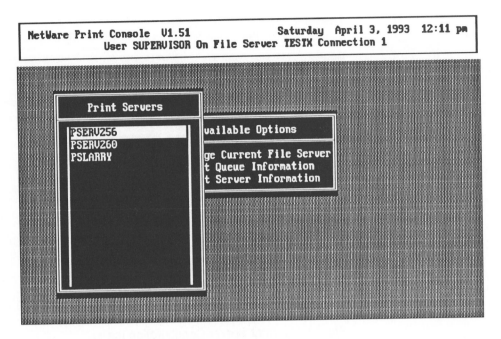

Fig. 13-10. Print servers available to users.

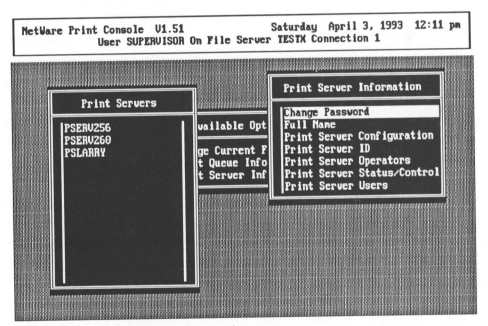

Fig. 13-11. The Print Server Information menu.

1. Change Password. A password can be set on the print server to prevent unauthorized changes.

2. Full Name. The Full Name option can be used to provide a more descriptive name for the print server.

3. Print Server Configuration. This option displays another menu as shown in Fig. 13-12. Its four options are as follows:

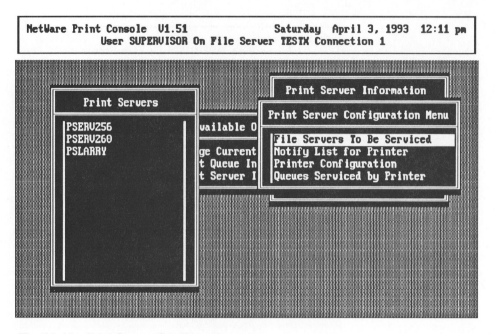

Fig. 13-12. Print Server Configuration menu.

a. File Servers to Be Serviced. Displays the file servers this print server will accept print jobs from. The current file server does not need to be listed.

b. Notify List for Printer. Printers require frequent maintenance. A print server can detect when a printer goes off-line and notify a user. The Notify List for Printer option is used to set which users will be notified about problems with each printer.

c. Printer Configuration. When selected, this option displays a list of the sixteen printers that can be managed by a single print server. By selecting any of these, a Printer Configuration box appears. These options tell the print server how the printer is physically attached to either the print server or to a remote workstation.

d. Queues Serviced by Printer. When this option is selected, a list of defined printers appears. Selecting a printer shows which print queues send data to that printer and allows the user to add a print queue to a given printer by pressing the INS key and then selecting the queue to be attached.

4. Print Server ID. This option simply displays the NetWare Object Identification number.

5. Print Server Operators. This option displays a list of users or groups authorized to change the status of the print server selected. Users can be added to or deleted from this option.

6. Print Server Status/Control. Displays status and allows some control over the print server.

7. Print Server Users. Displays a list of users and groups allowed to send data to the selected print server. Users can be added to or deleted from this option.

The PRINTDEF, PCONSOLE, and PRINTCON utilities are used to manipulate how data is to be sent to the available network printers. Sending the data to be printed can be accomplished in four ways: using the PCONSOLE utility, using a command line utility called NPRINT, using a command line utility called CAPTURE, or by using an application program designed to use network printers.

Printing with PCONSOLE

The PCONSOLE program provides much of the control needed for network printing, including manipulating the jobs waiting to be printed. With it, print jobs can be added to or deleted directly from the print queue. Selecting Current Print Job Entries in the Print Queue Information menu of PCONSOLE displays the print jobs printing or waiting to be printed. Pressing the INSERT key allows the user to select a file to be printed. This method of sending data to be printed assumes that a file has been created that contains any special characters that may be needed for underlining, boldface fonts, or other special effects. Such a file is known as a print file. Many application programs allow their output to be sent to a print file.

Printing with NPRINT

The NPRINT utility also requires a print file to already exist. A command of NPRINT THISFILE would send the file called THISFILE to the default print queue. The NPRINT program has several command line options that allow the print forms, print queues, and print job configurations to be specified.

Printing with CAPTURE

Almost any application can be used with network printers using the CAPTURE program. It is a memory resident program that intercepts data that the workstation sends to its printer ports, and redirects that data to a print queue. The CAPTURE program can be used in three different ways: in conjunction with the ENDCAP program, with the AUTO ENDCAP feature, or with the TIMEOUT feature.

The ENDCAP program is used to turn off redirection of the printer data. It essentially unloads the CAPTURE program from memory and places the data in the print queue. Notice that the data is only stored, not put in the queue, until the ENDCAP program is run. This way a user may send data to the network printer in many separate pieces. When the ENDCAP command is given, all the data is placed in the queue.

With the AUTO ENDCAP feature of the CAPTURE program enabled, the printer output data is sent on to the print queue when the application which created the print job terminates. For instance, if a user wants to send data to a network printer using a word processor, he or she would first run the CAPTURE program, then start the word processing program. Any printing that is done from the word processing program is stored until the user exits the word processing program. It is only then that the data is placed in the print queue.

Using the TIMEOUT feature allows the user's data to be sent to the print queue while the user is still in the application program. A timeout period is given in seconds and tells the CAPTURE program when to send the data that it has captured on to the print queue. The CAPTURE program waits the time specified after the last output has been captured before placing the data in the print queue.

Suppose a spreadsheet program is being used with the TIMEOUT feature set to 15 seconds. When the user requests a chart to be printed, the output is stored, and a timer starts counting after the last byte is captured. If the user prints another chart less than 15 seconds later, the data will continue to be stored. The data will be sent to the print queue only when a time longer than 15 seconds passes between print requests.

Making the timeout period too short may break up data that should be printed together. For instance, it may take longer than 15 seconds for the second chart in a single report to be calculated. Someone else's data could be placed in the queue between the first and second charts.

Making the period too long may cause data that the user intended to be printed separately to be printed together instead. If the user wanted the charts to be printed separately, he or she would have to watch the clock until the 15 seconds had passed before printing the second chart. This is not usually a problem since most applications would advance to the next page before printing the second time. A period longer than a few seconds may also be a source of frustration for the user. Even when only one person is sending data to be printed, he or she must wait for the data to be captured, wait the timeout period, then wait for the print server to start processing the data in the queue. These delays can add up to a long enough time that the user may wonder if there is a problem with the printer.

The last and easiest way to send data to a network printer is to use an application program that is designed to send its output to a print queue on a NetWare network.

Hands-on NetWare

In order to complete the following exercises, the file server and at least two workstations should be ready to use.

1. The file server should be on.
2. The boot disk created earlier should be available.
3. The accounts created earlier should be available.

Preparing the Boot Disk

A new line must be added to the SHELL.CFG file on the boot disk in order for the print server to operate properly. The print server software will not be loaded for several steps to come, but the change will not affect normal operation of the workstation. The following instructions prepare the network boot disk for use by a print server.

1. Boot the workstation with the appropriate network boot disk by placing the disk in drive A and simultaneously pressing the CTRL/ALT/DEL keys.
2. Enter the date and time if prompted.
3. Ensure that the network boot disk is in drive A and that it is not write protected.
4. Type ECHO SPX=60 >> A:SHELL.CFG and press the ENTER key.

The >> symbol in the command appends SPX=60 to the end of the existing SHELL.CFG file.

Configuring the Print Server and Print Queue

The long list of steps below create a new print server and a new print queue. These operations can be carried out at any workstation which is logged into the network.

1. Boot the workstation with the appropriate network boot disk by placing the disk in drive A and simultaneously pressing the CTRL/ALT/DEL keys. Enter the date and time if prompted.
2. The network driver programs should have been loaded by the AUTOEXEC.BAT file on the diskette. If they were not, type LSL and press the ENTER key. Then type the name of your network card driver and press ENTER. Next type **IPXODI** and press

ENTER. Then type **NETX** and press the ENTER key. NETX can be replaced with the appropriate network shell program for your memory configuration and DOS version.

3. Type **F:** and press the ENTER key.

4. Type **LOGIN** followed by your supervisor-equivalent login name and press the ENTER key.

5. Type the password for this account, and press the ENTER key.

6. Type **CD\PUBLIC** and press the ENTER key

7. Type **PCONSOLE** and press the ENTER key.

8. Select Print Server Information by using the cursor keys to highlight that option and pressing the ENTER key.

9. Press the INSERT key. A box requesting a new print server name should appear, as shown in Fig. 13-13. Here the print server name LASER has been added.

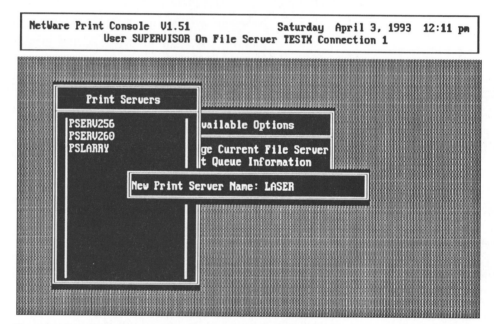

Fig. 13-13. Dialog box to request a new print server.

10. Type **PS** followed by your login name. For instance, if your login name is JSMITH, type PSJSMITH and press the ENTER key. The PS is simply used to indicate Print Server; it is not a required prefix.

11. With the new name highlighted, press the ENTER key.

12. Select Print Server Configuration in the Print Server Information box by using the cursor keys to highlight that option and pressing the ENTER key.

13. Select Printer Configuration in the Print Server Configuration menu by highlighting that option with the cursor keys and pressing the ENTER key. Your screen should appear similar to Fig. 13-14.

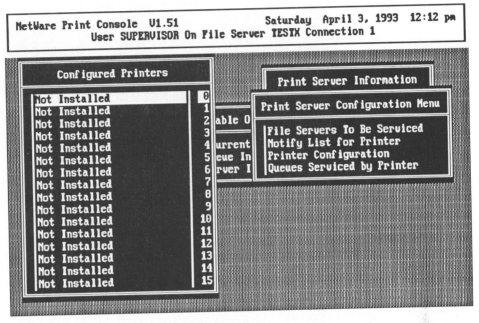

Fig. 13-14. Printer Configuration option.

14. With the first Not Installed message highlighted, press the ENTER key.

15. Move the cursor to the field labeled Name: and type **PRINTER 0** and press the ENTER key. Press the ENTER key again on the Defined elsewhere option.

16. A list of possible printer ports should be displayed as they are in Fig. 13-15. Use the cursor keys to highlight the printer port your printer is attached to. The first one on the list, Parallel, LPT1, is the most common. This means that the printer is attached to the LPT1 port on the workstation to be used as a print server.

17. With the correct printer port highlighted, press the ENTER key.

18. If the printer port you selected was Serial, additional options will have to be set. Only if you have selected a Serial port, use the cursor keys to move to the fields labeled Baud rate:, Data bits:, Stop bits:, Parity:, and Use X-On/X-Off: and place the correct values in each.

19. Press the ESC key to leave the Printer 0 configuration menu.

20. Press the Y and ENTER keys to save the changes.

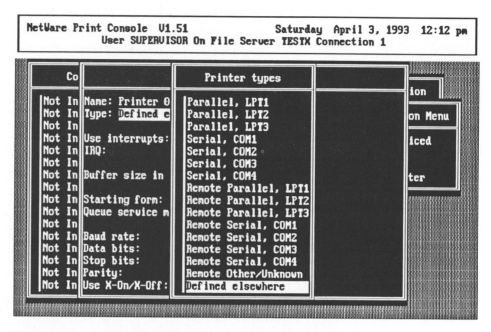

Fig. 13-15. List of printer ports.

21. Press the ESC key twice to return to the Print Server Information box.

22. Use the cursor keys to highlight Print Server Operators and press the ENTER key.

23. Press the INSERT key.

24. Type the name of your user account. The highlighted bar should move to your name. Highlight the correct account name with (User) displayed in the right column and press the ENTER key.

25. Press the ESC key to return to the Print Server Information box.

26. Highlight Print Server Users and press the ENTER key.

27. Verify that the group EVERYONE has been made a user of this print server and press the ESC key.

28. Press the ESC key twice to return to PCONSOLE's main menu.

When creating a new print server and print queue combination, something of a chicken and egg problem arises. You cannot finish configuring the print server without the print queue, and you cannot finish configuring the print queue without the print server. The reason for this complexity is that one queue can send data to several print servers and one print server can receive data from several queues. The following instructions create a new print queue and assign it to the new print server.

29. Highlight the Print Queue Information Option and press the ENTER key.

30. Press the INSERT key.

31. Type **Q**, followed by your account name, and press the ENTER key. For instance, if your account name is JSMITH, type QJSMITH and press the ENTER key. The "Q" is simply used to indicate a queue. It is not a required prefix.

32. With the new print queue name highlighted, press the ENTER key. The Print Queue Information box should appear as shown in Fig. 13-16.

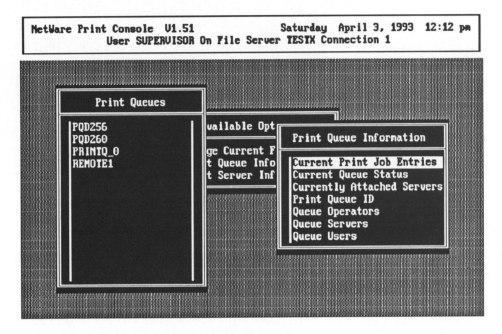

Fig. 13-16. The Print Queue Information menu.

33. Highlight Queue Servers and press the ENTER key.

34. Press the INSERT key to view the list of available servers, as shown in Fig. 13-17.

35. Type the name of your print server and press the ENTER key. Your print server's name is PS, followed by your account name.

36. Press the ESC key.

37. Highlight Queue Operators and press the ENTER key.

38. Press the INSERT key.

39. Type the name of your user account. The highlighted bar should move to your name, but it will stop when it reaches the group of the same name. Highlight the correct account name with (User) displayed in the right column and press the ENTER key.

40. Press the ESC key to return to the Print Queue Information box.

41. Highlight Print Queue Users and press the ENTER key.

42. Verify that the group EVERYONE has been made a user of this print queue and press the ESC key.

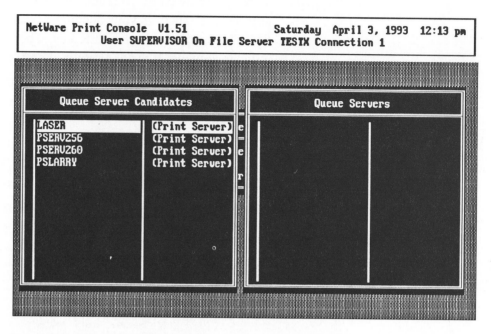

```
NetWare Print Console  V1.51              Saturday  April 3, 1993  12:13 pm
                    User SUPERVISOR On File Server TESTX Connection 1
```

Queue Server Candidates | Queue Servers

```
LASER       (Print Server)
PSERV256    (Print Server)
PSERV260    (Print Server)
PSLARRY     (Print Server)
```

Fig. 13-17. List of available servers.

43. Press the ESC key twice to return to PCONSOLE's main menu.

44. Highlight Print Server Information again and press the ENTER key.

45. Type the name of your print server and press the ENTER key. Your print server's name is PS, followed by your account name.

46. In the Print Server Information box, move the cursor down to the Print Server Configuration option and press the ENTER key.

47. In the Print Server Configuration menu, move the cursor down to the Queues Serviced by Printer option and press the ENTER key.

48. Press the ENTER key with the printer you defined earlier highlighted.

49. Press the INSERT key to view the list of available queues.

50. Type the name of your print queue and press the ENTER key. Its name is Q followed by the name of your account.

51. Since several queues can be assigned to a single server, a priority number can be given to each queue. This feature permits a special queue to be created for "rush" print jobs. Press the ENTER key to accept the priority shown.

52. Press the ESC key six times until the Exit PCONSOLE prompt appears.

53. Press the Y and ENTER keys. The print server is now ready for operation.

54. Type **LOGOUT** and press the ENTER key to end this session.

Running PSERVER

With the Print Server software loaded onto the file server hard disk and configured using the PCONSOLE program, the print server can be started by running the PSERVER program on any workstation. The following operations start the print server.

1. Boot the workstation to be used as a print server with the appropriate network boot disk (with SPX=60 in the SHELL.CFG file) by placing the disk in drive A and simultaneously pressing the CTRL/ALT/DEL keys. Enter the date and time if prompted.

2. The network driver programs should have been loaded by the AUTOEXEC.BAT file on the diskette. If they were not, type LSL and press the ENTER key. Then type the name of your network card driver and press ENTER. Next type **IPXODI** and press ENTER. Then type **NETX** and press the ENTER key. NETX can be replaced with the appropriate network shell program for your memory configuration and DOS version.

3. Type **F:** and press the ENTER key.

4. Type **LOGIN** followed by the name of your non-supervisor-equivalent account and press the ENTER key. This account name was created using your first initial, last name, and a 1. For instance, if your supervisor-equivalent account was called JSMITH, the non-supervisor account was called JSMITH1.

5. Type the password for this account and press the ENTER key.

6. Type **CD\PUBLIC** and press the ENTER key.

7. Type **PSERVER** followed by the name of your print server and press the ENTER key. Your print server's name is PS followed by your account name. PSERVER's screen should appear.

8. The status of the printer is displayed in the upper left corner of the screen. Press any key to display the status of the eight other possible printers. Press any key again to return to the first eight printers.

9. The boot disk may be removed from disk drive A.

Sending Output to the Print Server

The Print Server is up and running. All that remains is to test it. Leave the print server software running and move to another workstation. Follow the directions below to send data to the print server.

1. Boot the workstation with the appropriate network boot disk by placing the disk in drive A and simultaneously pressing the CRTL/ALT/DEL keys.

The network driver programs should have been loaded by the AUTOEXEC.BAT file on the diskette. If they were not, type LSL and press the ENTER key. Then type the name of your network card driver and press ENTER. Next type IPXODI and press ENTER. Then NETX and press the ENTER key. NETX can be replaced with the appropriate network shell program for your memory configuration and DOS version.

2. Type **F:** and press the ENTER key.

3. Type **LOGIN** followed by your supervisor-equivalent login name and press the ENTER key.

4. Type the password for this account, and press the ENTER key.

5. Type **NPRINT A:SHELL.CFG /Q=** followed by the print queue created earlier. Then press the ENTER key. For example, if your supervisor-equivalent account is JSMITH, the command would be NPRINT A:SHELL.CFG /Q=QJSMITH.

6. In a few moments the contents of the SHELL.CFG file should print on the printer attached to the print server. Note that this method of network printing does not interfere with the use of the printer on the workstation.

7. Type **CAPTURE /Q=** followed by the print queue name and /**NA**. Then press the ENTER key. For instance, the command might look like CAPTURE /Q=QJSMITH /NA. The CAPTURE program loads into memory and remains resident. The /NA option indicates that the auto endcap feature is disabled.

8. Type **COPY A:SHELL.CFG LPT1:** and press the ENTER key. Ordinarily, this DOS command would send the contents of the SHELL.CFG file to the local printer. With the CAPTURE program loaded, the output is stored until the ENDCAP command is issued.

9. Type **ENDCAP** and press the ENTER key. The contents of the SHELL.CFG file will print at the print server in a few moments.

10. To end this session, type **LOGOUT** and press the ENTER key. The print server can be turned off or re-booted.

Configuring the Print Server for Remote Printing

Additional printers can be connected to the print server, even printers that are not physically attached to it. With a program called RPRINTER running on a workstation, the workstation's local printer becomes a network printer. Use the directions below to configure the print server for a remote printer, restart the print server, and start the RPRINTER program on a workstation.

1. Boot the workstation with the appropriate network boot disk by placing the disk in drive A and simultaneously pressing the CTRL/ALT/DEL keys.

The network driver programs should have been loaded by the AUTOEXEC.BAT file on the diskette. If they were not, type LSL and press the ENTER key. Then type the name of your network card driver and press ENTER. Next type IPXODI and press ENTER. Then NETX and press the ENTER key. NETX can be replaced with the appropriate network shell program for your memory configuration and DOS version.

2. Type **F:** and press the ENTER key.

3. Type **LOGIN** followed by your supervisor-equivalent login name and press the ENTER key.

4. Type the password for this account, and press the ENTER key.

5. Type **PCONSOLE** and press the ENTER key.

6. Move the cursor to Print Server Information and press the ENTER key.

7. Type the name of your print server. Press the ENTER key when the proper name is highlighted.

8. Move the cursor to the Print Server Configuration option and press the ENTER key.

9. Move the cursor to the Printer Configuration option of the Print Server Configuration Menu and press the ENTER key. A list of printers attached to this print server should appear as it does in Fig. 13-18.

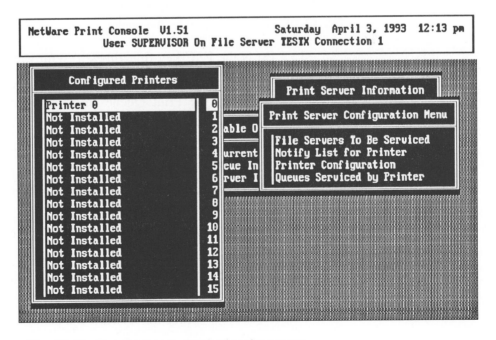

Fig. 13-18. List of printers attached to the server.

10. Move the cursor to the first available Not Installed message and press the ENTER key.

11. Move the cursor to the Name: and type **Remote printer** and press the ENTER key. Press the ENTER key again to select the Defined elsewere option.

12. Move the cursor to the Remote Parallel, LPT1 option in the Printer types box, as shown in Fig. 13-19. Then press the ENTER key.

13. Press the ESC key until the Save Changes menu appears.

14. Press the Y and ENTER keys.

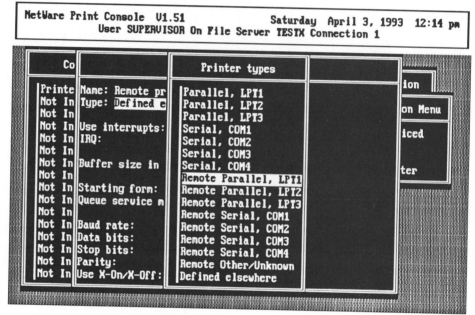

Fig. 13-19. Selecting a port for the printer.

15. Press the ESC key four times to return to PCONSOLE's main menu of available topics.

16. Highlight the Print Queue Information option and press the ENTER key.

17. Press the INSERT key to enter a new print queue name.

18. Type **R** followed by your account name and press the ENTER key. For instance, user JSMITH would type RJSMITH and press the ENTER key.

19. With the new print queue name highlighted, press the ENTER key.

20. Move the cursor to highlight Queue Servers and press the ENTER key.

21. Press the INSERT key to view the list of available servers.

22. Type the name of your print server and press the ENTER key. Your print server's name is PS, followed by your account name.

23. Press the ESC key.

24. Move the cursor up to highlight Queue Operators and press the ENTER key.

25. Press the INSERT key.

26. Type the name of your user account. The highlighted bar should move to your name. Highlight the correct account name with (User) displayed in the right column and press the ENTER key.

27. Press the ESC key to return to the Print Queue Information box.

28. Highlight Queue Users and press the ENTER key.

29. Verify that the group EVERYONE has been made a user of this print queue and press the ESC key.

30. Press the ESC key twice to return to PCONSOLE's main menu.

31. Highlight Print Server Information again and press the ENTER key.

32. Type the name of your print server and press the ENTER key. Your print server's name is PS, followed by your account name.

33. In the Print Server Information box, move the cursor to the Print Server Configuration option and press the ENTER key.

34. In the Print Server Configuration menu, move the cursor down to the Queues Serviced by Printer option and press the ENTER key.

35. Move the cursor down to the remote printer defined as Printer 1 earlier and press the ENTER key.

36. Press the INSERT key to view the list of available queues.

37. Type the name of your remote printer queue and press the ENTER key. The remote printer queue name is R followed by your account name.

38. Press the ENTER key to verify the Priority.

39. Press the ESC key six times until the "Exit PCONSOLE" menu appears.

40. Press the Y and ENTER keys.

Running PSERVER with a Remote Printer

The print server now has the capability of supporting a remote printer anywhere on the network. Any workstation that loads the RPRINTER program and selects the proper print server and printer will operate as the remote print server. The following steps restart the print server, which will control the remote printer.

1. Boot the print server workstation with the appropriate network boot disk by placing the disk in drive A and simultaneously pressing the CRTL/ALT/DEL keys. Enter the date and time if prompted.

2. The network driver programs should have been loaded by the AUTOEXEC.BAT file on the diskette. If they were not, type LSL and press the ENTER key. Then type the name of your network card driver and press ENTER. Next type **IPXODI** and press ENTER. Then type **NETX** and press the ENTER key. NETX can be replaced with the appropriate network shell program for your memory configuration and DOS version.

3. Type **F:** and press the ENTER key.

4. Type **LOGIN** followed by the name of your non-supervisor-equivalent account and press the ENTER key. This account name was created using your first initial, last name, and a 1. For instance, if your supervisor-equivalent account was called JSMITH, the non-supervisor account was called JSMITH1.

5. Type **CD\PUBLIC** and press the ENTER key.

6. Type **PSERVER** followed by the name of your print server and press the ENTER key. Your print server's name is PS, followed by your account name.

7. Remove the boot disk from drive A.

Running RPRINTER

With the new improved version of the Print Server program running, move to a new workstation that has a local printer. Follow the instruction below to install the RPRINTER program.

1. Boot the workstation attached to the printer that you are going to use with the appropriate network boot disk by placing the disk in drive A and simultaneously pressing the CTRL, ALT, and DEL keys.

2. Type **F:** and press the ENTER key.

3. Type **LOGIN** followed by your supervisor-equivalent login name and press the ENTER key.

4. Type the password for this account, and press the ENTER key.

5. Type **RPRINTER** and press the ENTER key. The remote printer program should display a list of print servers.

6. Type the name of your print server and press the ENTER key. The remote printers available for that print server should be displayed.

7. Select the name of your remote printer by pressing the ENTER key. The message "*** Remote Printer "Printer 1" (printer 1) installed **" indicates that the RPRINTER program has been successfully installed.

Sending Output to the Remote Printer

The printer attached to the workstation can still be used by the workstation, but data being sent to the workstation by the print server will also be printed. Two methods can be used to test this situation. One is to have another student at another workstation send data to the remote printer. The other method is to use a network printing utility to send data to the same workstation as a remote printer. The following steps will work equally well at another workstation or at the same workstation. These instructions assume the workstation is still logged in.

1. Type **NPRINT A:SHELL.CFG /Q=** followed by the remote print queue created earlier, then press the ENTER key. For example, if your supervisor equivalent account is JSMITH, the command would be

   NPRINT A:SHELL.CFG /Q=RJSMITH.

2. In a few moments the contents of the SHELL.CFG file should print on the printer attached to the remote print server. Note that this method of network printing does not interfere with the use of the printer on the workstation.

3. Type **CAPTURE /Q=** followed by the remote print queue name and /NA, and then press the ENTER key. For instance, the command might look like

   CAPTURE /Q=RJSMITH /NA.

   The CAPTURE program loads into memory and remains resident. The "/NA" stands for No Autoendcap.

4. Type **COPY A:SHELL.CFG LPT1:** and press the ENTER key. Ordinarily, this DOS command would send the contents of the SHELL.CFG file to the local printer. With the CAPTURE program loaded, the output is stored until the ENDCAP command is issued.

5. Type **ENDCAP** and press the ENTER key. The contents of the SHELL.CFG file will print at the remote print server in a few moments.

6. To end this session, type **LOGOUT** and press the ENTER key. The print server can be turned off or rebooted.

Summary

One of the most often used features of a network is sharing printers. A Novell network allows printers located on the file server, on a dedicated print server, or on a remote print server to be accessed by any user or group with authorization. Print forms, print devices, print queues, and print job configurations are all tools that can be used to control how and where data is to be printed. Data can be sent to a network printer in four ways: with the PCONSOLE utility, with the NPRINT command, with the CAPTURE command, or with an application program designed to send data to a network printer.

Questions

1. What is considered to be the most versatile way to attach a printer to the network?
2. Can a print form be used to specify which printer will be used?
3. Can a print device be used to define a special font such as bold?
4. Can a print job configuration be used by a group?
5. How many printers can be attached to a print server?
6. If a print server has only one printer port, but two printers attached, where is the second printer?
7. Can a single print queue feed data to more than one printer?
8. In what ways is a remote printer vulnerable?

Projects

Objective

The following projects provide additional practice with the basic networking printing facilities of NetWare. Additionally, the second project provides more hands-on training in creating print queues and sending print jobs across the network.

Project 1. Basic Network Printing

1. Use the PRINTDEF utility to ensure that the driver for the printer attached to the print server created earlier is available on the system. The driver will need to be imported only once for the file server being used.

2. Use the PRINTDEF utility to create a print form called 132_COL that uses a form width of 132 columns. The form will need to be created only once for the file server being used.

3. Use the PRINTCON utility to create a print job configuration called CONDENSED that specifies the print device, the print mode, and the print form. Use the print device name of the printer attached to your print server, the condensed mode of that printer, and the 132-column form.

4. Use the NPRINT utility to print the AUTOEXEC.BAT file on your boot disk with the print job CONDENSED. The syntax of the NPRINT command is

   NPRINT filename /J=print_job_name

Project 2. Advanced Network Printing

1. Create a print queue with a unique name on an existing print server. Be sure to include your user name as a print queue operator.

2. Set the printer to OFF LINE. Send a file to the print queue. Then use the PCONSOLE utility to remove the file from the queue. Put the printer back on line.

3. Try the same operation as above, but send your data to a class-mates' print queue. You should not be able to remove the print job.

Project 3. Setting up a Print Server with One Locally Attached Printer and Two Remote Printers

1. Following instructions given in the Hands-On section of this chapter, modify your print server to have one more remote printer.

2. Assign a new queue to this printer and test its operation.

Customizing NetWare

Objectives

After completing this chapter you will

1. Understand the benefits of using menus.

2. Know several techniques to create menus.

3. Know different techniques to make LANs more accessible to users.

Key Terms

Application Software

Menu

Server

Variables

Batch File

Network Software

Submenu

Introduction

Assuming Novell NetWare has been installed correctly, that appropriate users and login scripts have been created, and all network printing functions needed have been installed, there is only one item missing — application software. The primary purpose of the network is to deliver the software that users need to their workstations. All of the other setup involved means nothing to the users if they cannot easily access the word processors, databases, spreadsheets, and other programs they need to do their jobs. Novell supplies a program with NetWare called MENU.EXE that can produce attractive, easy to use menus that blend smoothly with the other Novell utilities. Unfortunately, it does not work in all situations. In some cases, it is necessary to use DOS batch files to serve as menus. It is also possible to purchase programs designed specifically to operate as NetWare menus.

The software that is to be accessed by these menus falls into three categories: network incompatible, network compatible, and network aware. Network incompatible software is software that cannot be run from the file server. It might, however, still need to be called from the workstation's local hard disk in a menu system. Network compatible programs have no difficulty running on the file server, but they do not take advantage of the network for services such as network printing or mail. Programs that do take advantage of these services are known as network aware.

Customizing NetWare

All programs in a NetWare file server should be made easy to access by all users. The process followed in accessing network-based software consists of the following steps.

1. The user workstation must attach to the file server that contains the shared programs.

2. A drive letter must be mapped to the directory where the required program resides.

3. The mapped drive should be made the default drive.

4. The command required to start a program must be given.

5. After the program is exited, the drive letter mapped in step 2 needs to be deleted.

6. The user logs out of the file server that contains the shared software.

These steps are difficult to perform by most users, in addition to being cumbersome to use on a continuous basis. The solution is to create a batch file and place it in the SYS:PUBLIC where all users can have access to it.

An example of a typical batch file to start a copy of Lotus 123 from a server named SERVER2 may consist of the following lines.

```
ATTACH SERVER2/GUEST
MAP H:=SERVER2/SYS:SHARESOF\LOTUS123
H:
LOTUS
MAP DEL H:
LOGOUT SERVER2
```

In this example, the first line attaches a user who has the login name GUEST to the server whose network name is SERVER2. A drive H is mapped to the directory that stores Lotus 123, and the program is executed with the command LOTUS, and when the user exits the program, the drive mapping is deleted, and the user is logged out of the server SERVER2.

Batch files are used when shared programs are stored on special servers to which the user must attach in order to run the programs. Although network managers create much more complicated batch files, the above example illustrates the use of such a file to access programs stored in a network file server.

Although batch files protect the user from needing to know the intricacies of NetWare commands to attach to file servers and map directories, the use of menus further enhances the usability of the network. Using menus provides easy access to shared software for new or inexperienced users.

Novell has a menu-building system that can be used for most situations and needs. Many commercially available programs can also be used for this purpose. With menus, users can start batch files by selecting a letter or a number from a list of choices. The menu then transfers execution to the batch file. When the batch file terminates executing, control is returned to the menu and it is automatically displayed back on the screen. Creating menus requires extra effort from the network administrator, but in the long run menus tend to increase network usage by making users feel comfortable with the hardware.

The Novell Menu System

Novell provides a program with NetWare called MENU.EXE that can be used to create custom menus. MENU.EXE is placed in the \PUBLIC directory. The program uses ASCII script files to display colorful menus similar to those used in the NetWare utilities. The script files can be written with any ASCII text editor. Once written, the MENU program is used to interpret them. For example, suppose an ASCII text file called START.MNU contains the following:

%Available Options

1. Syscon

　　SYSCON

2. Fconsole

　　FCONSOLE

The command MENU START would load and execute the MENU program. The MENU program would load and interpret the instructions in the START.MNU file.

1. MENU.EXE assumes the file name listed on the command line has a .MNU extension.

2. The "%" on the first line indicates the title of the menu.

3. Text that begins in the first column without a "%" indicates a menu selection.

4. Any other text that does not start in the first column is considered the instructions that are to be executed for the preceding menu selection.

   The instructions can be any legal DOS command or program name with three exceptions. First the LOGOUT command must be preceded by a "!" to operate properly. Second, DOS batch files should not be called by the menu. Third, memory resident programs should not be loaded from the menu. The file shown above results in the menu shown in Fig. 14-1.

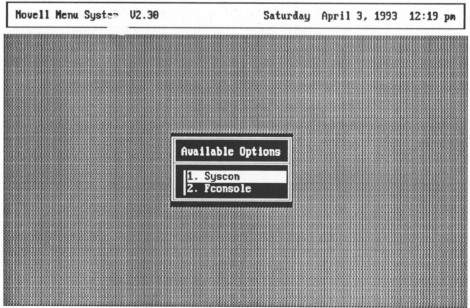

Fig. 14-1. Menu created by batch file.

The menu thus created follows many of the same rules as other Novell menus. For instance, the "2." on the line with the Fconsole menu option does not have any special meaning to the MENU.EXE program but by typing a "2" in the menu, the Fconsole line is highlighted. This is because, as in any Novell menu, typing the menu selection highlights the option. The arrow keys can also be used to move the highlighted area to the desired option. In either case, ENTER is pressed to select the option highlighted. Even the F1 key operates the same as in other Novell menus. Fig. 14-2 shows the first panel of the help screen shown when F1 is pressed in the START.MNU menu. Pressing F1 again displays the second help panel as in Fig. 14-3. Unfortunately not all of the keys listed work when using custom menus. To exit a custom menu such as START.MNU, the ESCAPE key is pressed. A familiar "Exit" menu will be displayed as it is in Fig. 14-4.

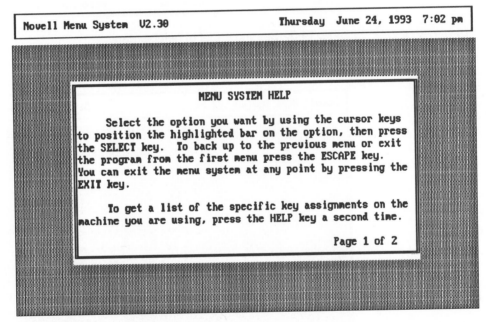

Fig. 14-2. First panel of help screen.

The menus created with MENU.EXE can be customized further by using parameters on the menu title line. Three parameters can be used to indicate the vertical placement of the menu, the horizontal placement, and the color palette used. For instance, if the first line in START.MNU were changed to "%Available Options,10,60,5", the center of the menu would be placed 10 lines from the top of the screen and 60 columns from the left edge of the screen. The "5" on the end of the line indicates that color palette 5 is to be used. Palette 5 denotes black and white text only. Note that the vertical and horizontal distances are measured from the center of the menu. The result is shown in Fig. 14-5. Additional color palettes can be created using the NetWare COLORPAL program.

```
Novell Menu System  V2.30                      Thursday  June 24, 1993  7:02 pm
```

```
The function key assignments on your machine are:

ESCAPE          Esc              Back up to the previous level.
EXIT            Alt F10          Exit the program.
CANCEL          F7               Cancel markings or edit changes.
BACKSPACE       Backspace        Delete the character to the left of
                                 the cursor.
INSERT          Ins              Insert a new item.
DELETE          Del              Delete an item.
MODIFY          F3               Rename/modify/edit the item.
SELECT          Enter            Accept information entered or select
                                 the item.
HELP            F1               Provide on-line help.
MARK            F5               Toggle marking for current item.
CYCLE           Tab              Cycle through menus or screens.
MODE            F9               Change Modes.
UP              Up arrow         Move up one line.
DOWN            Down arrow       Move down one line.
LEFT            Left arrow       Move left one position.
RIGHT           Right arrow      Move right one position
```

Fig. 14-3. Second panel of help screen.

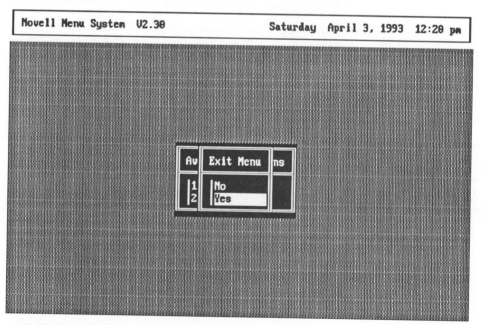

Fig. 14-4. Exit menu created by the batch file.

424

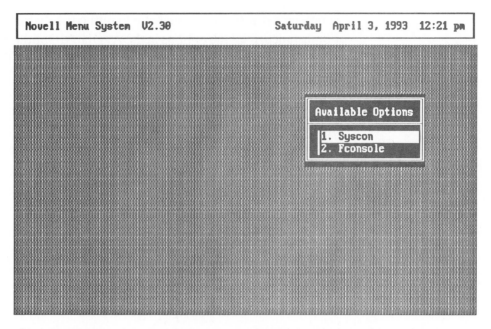

```
Novell Menu System  V2.30        Saturday  April 3, 1993  12:21 pm



                                  ┌─────────────────────┐
                                  │  Available Options  │
                                  ├─────────────────────┤
                                  │ 1. Syscon           │
                                  │ 2. Fconsole         │
                                  └─────────────────────┘
```

Fig. 14-5. Screen generated by the command %Available Options,10,60,5.

Submenus

The START.MNU example above is, of course, a very simple menu. The MENU.EXE program is capable of producing much more complex menus through the use of submenus. Suppose the file START.MNU is expanded to indicate the submenu "Other Options," as shown below.

```
%Available Options,10,60,5

1. Syscon

  SYSCON

2. Fconsole

  FCONSOLE

3. Other Options

   %Other Options

%Other Options

1. Filer

  FILER

2. Session

  SESSION
```

The third option in the Available Options menu executes something called "%Other Options." The definition for the menu "Other Options" immediately follows. A line starting with a % in the first column defines a menu. A line that starts with a % but does not begin in column one calls the submenu. The submenu definition does not have to immediately follow the line that calls it. For instance, if all the options in the Available Options menu were submenus, all three definitions would be listed at the bottom of the file.

Menu Variables

The Novell menu system also allows the user to enter text that the menu can then take some action on. Variables can be used to force the menu to stop and require input from the user. The menu file below uses variables to perform DOS functions.

%DOS functions

1. Directory

   DIR   @1"Directory of"

   pause

2. Check Disk

   CHKDSK   @1"Check Disk"

   pause

In the line that reads DIR   @1"Directory of", the @1 is recognized by the MENU.EXE program as a variable. Rather than attempting to execute the line exactly as it is, the program stops and asks the user to input a value. The "Directory of" in quotes is used as a prompt for the user. When selected, the user is prompted as shown in Fig. 14-6.

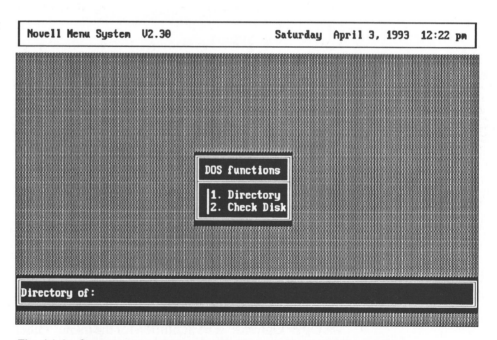

Fig. 14-6. Screen generated by batch file in menu variables section.

Only after the user has entered a value does the MENU.EXE program execute the command. For instance, if the user enters *.EXE, the command would be executed as DIR *.EXE. The user prompt is not used in the command. In the second option, Check Disk, the @1 variable is used again but the MENU.EXE program will prompt the user again so its value will not be retained from the first option. Both options in this menu have a pause statement to halt execution, so the result of the command can be read from the screen before the menu screen returns.

Problems with MENU.EXE

As impressive as MENU.EXE is at creating menus, it has two significant flaws. First, memory resident applications cannot be loaded from it. Attempting to load a resident program can cause the computer to "crash." Second, it does not operate well with DOS batch files. If a batch file calls MENU.EXE, the first menu option selected causes control to be returned to the batch file. When the batch file finishes, control goes back to MENU.EXE, and the menu screen reappears. Also, if a menu file calls a batch file, only the batch file will be executed in that menu option. Commands that appear after the batch file name in a certain menu option will not be executed. Other commercial programs are available for creating menus on a Novell network.

Batch File Menus

Novell's menu system is colorful and allows the supervisor to create menus that match the NetWare Utilities, but its inability to load memory resident programs makes it impossible to use in many situations. In a diverse environment where there may be dozens of programs available on the file server, loading and unloading memory resident programs become quite important. The NetWare CAPTURE program is a good example. In a truly friendly environment, the user would need the option of redirecting the printer output to a network printer or a local printer. This is accomplished by either loading the CAPTURE program or unloading it with the ENDCAP program. Such memory resident programs also use memory that then cannot be used by the primary application.

General purpose resident programs such as Sidekick can consume a large amount of memory, too much for some other programs to run in what is left. In addition, memory resident programs often collide with each other or with the primary application, causing a system crash. For example, many programs require a mouse and a memory resident mouse driver program, but others such as Microsoft Windows are capable of running without a memory resident mouse driver program and will crash if one is present. If the user is not permitted to install memory resident programs as they are needed and remove them when possible, he or she will be forced to logout and re-boot the workstation frequently, causing frustration and delays.

Fortunately, complex menus can be created using only DOS batch commands. Consider the batch file, MYMENU.BAT below.

```
@ECHO OFF
IF "%1" == "" GOTO SCREEN
IF "%1" == "a" GOTO A
IF "%1" == "A" GOTO A
IF "%1" == "b" GOTO B
IF "%1" == "B" GOTO B
IF "%1" == "c" GOTO C
IF "%1" == "C" GOTO C
ECHO %1 is not a valid menu option.
goto screen
:A
CAPTURE
CD Z:\SHARESOF\WORDSTAR
WORDSTAR %2
CD\
ENDCAP
GOTO SCREEN
:B
CD Z:\SHARESOF\LOTUS
 LOTUS %2
GOTO SCREEN
:C
CD Z:\SHARESOF\WP
WP %2
GOTO SCREEN
:SCREEN
CLS
ECHO Type MENU followed by:
ECHO _____
ECHO   A     for WordStar
ECHO   B     for Lotus
ECHO   C     for WordPerfect
ECHO _____
```

This batch file starts three different programs when the user types MYMENU A, MYMENU B, or MYMENU C. The menu screen itself is displayed when the user types MENU. Any DOS commands can be used to start the program or prepare for it. For example, the WORDSTAR option includes the CAPTURE and ENDCAP commands. The %1 in the first few lines of the batch file represents the item typed immediately after the word MENU. The %2 in the lines that call the application programs represents the second item typed after the word MYMENU. For instance, if the user types MYMENU A LETTER.DOC, the WORDSTAR program would execute with the word LETTER.DOC as its parameter. Notice that no PATH statement is used and no MAP statement is used. Instead, the drive letter Z, which is assumed to have been created earlier, is moved to point to the appropriate directory. When a search drive is created, it starts at the end of the alphabet to choose an available drive letter, in this case drive letter Z. By simply changing the directory that drive letter Z points to, the search path is changed as well.

Hands-on Creating Menus

The Novell Menu System

The following instructions offer practice in using the Novell menu program.

1. Boot the workstation, if not already on, with the appropriate network boot disk by placing the disk in drive A and simultaneously pressing the CONTROL, ALT, and DELETE enter keys. Enter the date and time if prompted.

2. The network driver programs should have been loaded by the AUTOEXEC.BAT file on the diskette. If they were not, type LSL and press the ENTER key. Then the name of your network card driver and the ENTER key. Next type **IPXODI**, press the ENTER key. Then type **NETX** and press the ENTER key. NETX can be replaced with the appropriate network shell program for your memory configuration and DOS version.

3. Type **F:** and press the ENTER key.

4. Type **LOGIN** followed by your supervisor-equivalent login name and press the ENTER key.

5. Type the password for this account, and press the ENTER key.

6. Type **CD** followed by your account name and press the ENTER key. For instance if the account name is JSMITH, the command would be CD\JSMITH followed by the ENTER key.

7. A menu file can be created with any ASCII text editor or by using the DOS COPY CON command. If you do not have an appropriate text editor, type COPY CON MYMENU.MNU and press the ENTER key.

8. Type the following lines, either immediately following the COPY CON MYMENU.MNU command or in your text editor. Type each line exactly as it appears, pressing the ENTER key at the end of each line.

   %Available Options,10,20

   1. Syscon

     SYSCON

   2. Fconsole

     FCONSOLE

   3. Other Options

     %Other Options

   4. Filer

     FILER

   %Other Options,17,60

   1. Directory

     DIR @1"Directory of"

     PAUSE

   2. Check Disk

     CHKDSK @1"Chkdsk"

     PAUSE

9. If you are using the COPY CON MYMENU.MNU command, hold down the CONTROL key and press the Z key and then press the ENTER key. If you are using a text editor, save the file under the name MYMENU.MNU.

10. Type **MENU MYMENU** and press the ENTER key. The Available Options menu should appear as it does in Fig. 14-7.

11. With the Syscon option highlighted, press the ENTER key. Syscon's main menu should appear.

12. Press the ESC key, then the Y and ENTER keys. You should return to your menu.

13. Press the DOWN ARROW key two times and then the ENTER key. The Other Options menu should appear in the lower right of the screen as it does in Fig. 14-8.

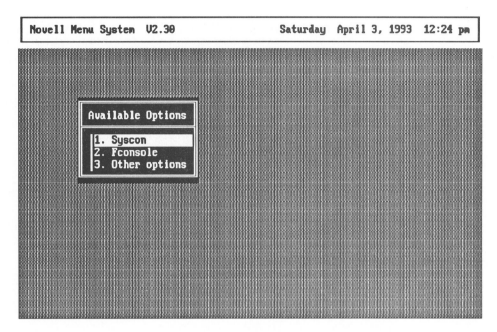

Fig. 14-7. Available options menu created by the MYMENU.MNU.

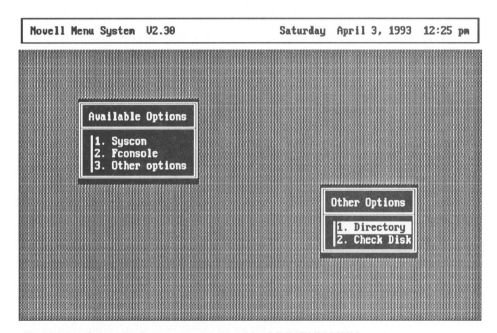

Fig. 14-8. Other Options menu created by MYMENU.MNU.

14. Highlight the Check Disk option and press the ENTER key. The Chkdsk : prompt should appear at the bottom of the screen as in Fig. 14-9.

15. Ensure that a diskette is in drive A and type **A:**, and press the ENTER key. The CHKDSK program should run and display data about your diskette.

16. Press any key to return to the Other Options menu.

431

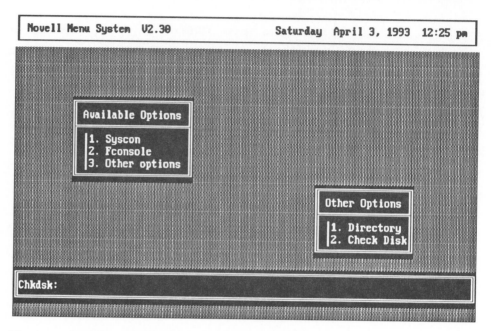

Fig. 14-9. Screen displaying the Chkdsk: prompt.

17. Press the ESC key to return to the Available Options menu.

18. Press the ESC key.

19. Press the Y key, then the ENTER key to exit your menu.

20. To end this session, type **LOGOUT** and press the ENTER key.

Batch Files

The following steps demonstrate how some of the same features can be built into a batch file rather than the Novell menu program. It is often necessary to use batch files, even if they are not as attractive as the menus created with MENU.EXE.

1. Boot the workstation, if not already on, with the appropriate network boot disk, by placing the disk in drive A and simultaneously pressing the CONTROL, ALT, and DELETE keys. Enter the date and time if prompted.

2. The network driver programs should have been loaded by the AUTOEXEC.BAT file on the diskette. If they were not, type LSL and press the ENTER key. Then the name of your network card driver and the ENTER key. Next type **IPXODI** and press the ENTER key. Then type **NETX** and press the ENTER key. NETX can be replaced with the appropriate network shell program for your memory configuration and DOS version.

3. Type **F:** and press the ENTER key.

4. Type **LOGIN** followed by your supervisor-equivalent login name and press the ENTER key.

5. Type the password for this account, and press the ENTER key.

6. Type **CD** followed by your account name and press the ENTER key. For instance if the account name is JSMITH, the command would be CD\JSMITH followed by the ENTER key.

7. The batch file can be created with any ASCII text editor or by using the DOS COPY CON command. If you do not have an appropriate text editor, type COPY CON M.BAT and press the ENTER key.

8. Type the following lines, either immediately following the COPY CON M.BAT command or in your text editor. Type each line exactly as it appears, pressing the ENTER key at the end of each line.

@ECHO OFF

IF "%1" == "" GOTO SCREEN

IF "%1" == "a" GOTO A

IF "%1" == "A" GOTO A

IF "%1" == "b" GOTO B

IF "%1" == "B" GOTO B

IF "%1" == "c" GOTO C

IF "%1" == "C" GOTO C

ECHO %1 is not a valid menu option.

PAUSE

GOTO SCREEN

:A

SYSCON

GOTO SCREEN

:B

FCONSOLE

GOTO SCREEN

:C

CHKDSK %2 %3

PAUSE

GOTO SCREEN

:SCREEN

CLS

ECHO Type M followed by:

ECHO _____

ECHO	**A**	**Syscon**
ECHO	**B**	**Fconsole**
ECHO	**C:**	**Chkdsk**
ECHO	_____	

9. If you are using the COPY CON M.BAT command, hold down the CONTROL key and press the Z key. Then, press the ENTER key. If you are using a text editor, save the file under the name M.BAT.

10. Press M and press the ENTER key. A menu should appear at the top of the screen.

11. Type **M A** and press the ENTER key. Syscon's main menu should appear.

12. Press the ESC key and then press the ENTER key. The batch file menu should be displayed.

13. To end this session, type **LOGOUT** and press the ENTER key.

Summary

The efficiently installed network is useless without easy access to the application programs it is intended to deliver. Often this implies that a menu system is needed to allow users to select the programs they need. Novell supplies a program that can be used to create such menus, but it does not work in all situations. Often, batch files must be used instead.

Most programs can be put into one of three categories: network incompatible, network compatible, and network aware. The network incompatible software might be installed on the workstation's local hard disk where it could be included in the menu system. Network compatible programs are often the easiest to install but are the most dangerous from a legal perspective, because a copy of the software must be purchased for each user accessing the program on the server. Network aware software often eliminates the legal issue by using the network to restrict the number of users accessing it. Network aware programs can also offer features such as electronic mail and can provide easier network printing.

Questions

1. Can a menu created with MENU.EXE have submenus?
2. Can a menu created with MENU.EXE call a batch file?

3. What is the most common problem that makes a program incapable of running on the file server?

4. What can be done to force a program that looks for its files on drive C, to operate on the file server?

5. What type of software cannot be used with MENU.EXE?

6. If the Novell menu system cannot be used, what are two other ways menus might be created?

Projects

Objective

The following projects provide additional practice in creating menus using Novell's NetWare menu facility.

Project. Creating Directories and Menus

1. A company has three divisions, Sales, Manufacturing, and Business Services. The Sales division has two departments, Accounting and Transportation. The Manufacturing division has three departments, Accounting, Transportation, and Quality Control. The Business Services division has three departments, Accounting, Personnel, and Secretarial. Each division stores its own data but they share all the software possible. Draw a directory structure that might be suitable for this company's file server.

2. In this company, the Business Services division collects all the data it needs from the other divisions directly from their directories. The other divisions, however, should not be able to read each other's data or modify Business Services' data. Write the trustee rights that should be given to a typical user from each of the divisions.

3. Use the MENU program to create a menu that provides access to at least three other programs.

4. Create a menu that prompts the user for a single local drive to be mapped to a network directory. The options should be as follows:

      a. Map drive A: to the LOGIN directory.

      b. Map drive B: to the LOGIN directory.

      c. Map drive C: to the LOGIN directory.

      d. Delete local drive mapping.

Use the @1 construction or the IF - GOTO menu construct for this menu.

Microsoft Windows 3.1 and Networking

Objectives

After completing this chapter you will

1. Be familiar with the process of installing software in a network.
2. Understand the different modes that applications may have when working in a network.
3. Be familiar with the installation process of Windows 3.1.
4. Understand the different options in installing Windows 3.1.
5. Be familiar with some of the problems associated with running Windows 3.1 and Novell NetWare.

Key Terms

Application Software
MS-DOS
Network Security
Trustee Rights

File Attributes
Network Applications
Server
Windows

Introduction

Personal computers derive their usefulness from the software that they are capable of running. This software includes word processors, spreadsheets, databases, graphics, and others. Local area networks enhance the usefulness of the personal computer. Therefore, it is important to understand the capability of the personal computer in running applications in a local area network environment.

One type of software system that many network users are using is Microsoft Windows. Microsoft Windows is a graphical environment for IBM personal computers and compatibles running under the MS-DOS operating system. Windows creates a new working environment on top of MS-DOS, thus shielding the user from having to memorize operating system commands.

It is important to understand that Windows is not a replacement for MS-DOS. It is just a graphical shell that becomes the interface between the computer and the user. Additionally, individuals who plan to use Microsoft Windows should have some knowledge of the basic input/output operations performed by the computer.

Microsoft Windows 3.1 contains many features that can be used to navigate through a network environment and to perform many functions that used to be done from the DOS command prompt. When a network and Windows are properly installed, Windows will automatically make a network connection and related menu items appear on the Windows menu. These menus can then be used to assist network administrators with network management and related activities such as printing.

Using Application Software in a Network

Benefits

There are many reasons for using network versions of software on a local area network. Some of the most compelling are

1. Sharing of software.
2. Sharing of data.
3. Sharing system resources.
4. Security and backups.
5. Easier maintenance and upgrades.

Sharing Software

Imagine an office that has 20 employees, all using personal computers with word processing, spreadsheet, and database software. If each user is to have individual copies of software, there must a legally purchased copy of each package for each user.

Another solution is to purchase network versions of all software products and install a single copy of each on a local area network connecting all users. Purchasing a network version of a software product is, in many situations, less expensive than buying individual copies for each user.

Additionally, there isn't the need to keep track of 20 copies of the same software product. Only one copy needs to be administered, maintained, and updated.

Sharing Data

With Network copies of software programs, the data generated by one user can be used by other users in a "transparent" mode. That is, all users can work with the same data file as if it were their own. With individual copies of software, data generated on one workstation must be physically moved from one machine to another. In the case of sales, inventory departments, and others, this type of data transfer creates problems with outdated versions of files and with duplication of efforts and data.

Sharing System Resources

Network versions of software also save on hard disk space. Instead of using space on multiple users' hard disks, the software can be placed on the network server's hard disk. This allows the software and data to be shared by everyone in a local area network.

Security and Backups

Individual copies of software on multiple workstations are difficult to safeguard from unauthorized individuals. It is relatively easy to go to a person's desk and damage or change data files.

Using the security resources of a network, software can be safeguarded by installing passwords, trustee rights, and file attributes. This enhances the safety of data files and programs in a manner that is almost impossible with individual software.

With multiple users working with stand-alone programs, backing up software becomes a difficult task. Users are not always prompt when it comes to backing up important software and data. Using the network resources, software and data can be backed up from a single location with a minimal amount of effort. This also enhances security since the latest copy of a file is assured when using the latter method.

Easy Maintenance and Upgrades

In many situations users of a particular package do not have the latest updates or modifications. Sometimes this is due to a lack of time to install software upgrades, and other times there is a lack of funding to purchase the latest release of a product.

If network software is used, only one upgrade copy of the software needs to be installed and/or modified to get the latest features. Also, in large corporations with many users, the cost of upgrading a network version of a software product can be substantially less than purchasing individual copies of the same program.

Choosing Servers

If the network consists of only one server, then the choice of where to install shared software is easy. However, if multiple servers are available, a decision must be made as to which server will hold the shared software.

There are several possibilities for multiple server networks. Assume that a network consists of two servers. One possibility is to purchase two copies of the software and install one on each server. Another possibility is to purchase a third server and place all shared software on it. Or all shared software can be installed in one of the servers and let users of the other server attach themselves to the one that has the software (see Fig. 15.1).

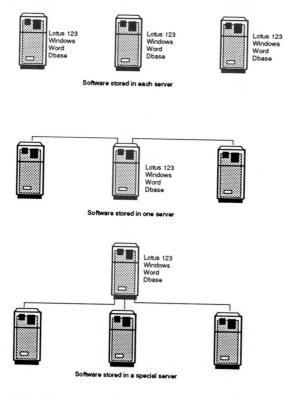

Fig. 15-1. Possible combinations of shared servers.

Each of these approaches has its pros and cons. If a copy is purchased for each server, then the expense of the extra copy may be higher than having a network version of the software and a license for all possible users. Additionally, there is the need to keep security and maintenance of the same software product on multiple servers.

Placing all shared software on a single server may prove to be too much for a computer acting as the server. Too many users can slow the response time of the server to unacceptable levels.

Acquiring an individual server on which to place all shared software is the most elegant solution. However, in many situations this is not economically feasible.

A final possibility is to spread all shared software among the available servers. This allows the purchase of a single network version of a software product along with a license for the number of users involved. This method also allows the load created by the shared software to be spread evenly among all available servers (see Fig. 15.2).

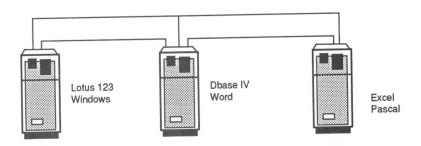

Fig. 15-2. Dividing software evenly among three servers.

Choosing a Directory for Shared Software

In addition to choosing the server where the shared software is to reside, the directory structure of this server must be determined. There are several possibilities. One is to place all shared programs under the main or root directory. The other possible solution is to create a directory under the root directory and name this subdirectory SHARESOF, PROGRAMS, or something that indicates its purpose (see Fig. 15.3 for two such subdirectories).

The first solution is usually not the best approach. One problem is that the root directory may become cluttered as new programs are added to the server. This makes the task of maintenance and backup more difficult since each shared program name must be identified during backups using some backup schemes.

The second method is the better one. During backup procedures the entire shared software subdirectory can be backed up with a single command. Additionally, establishing security rights over one subdirectory is easier than over multiple subdirectories.

A more complex task is when some software is supposed to be "public domain" and other software is to be secured. The words "public domain" mean that all programs or data in the subdirectory are available to all users for use at their workstation, and there are no restrictions imposed on how they use it. Even though such software is shared, it should not share a parent directory with programs and data that require large measures of security.

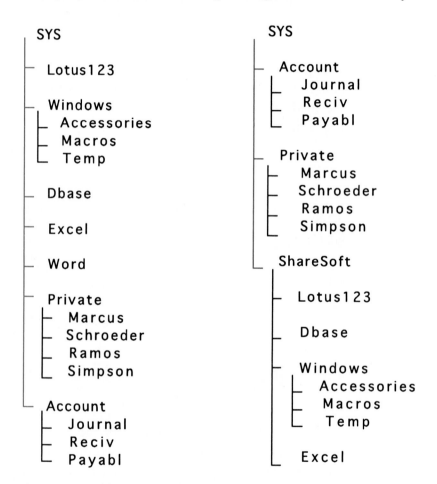

Fig. 15-3. Directory structure for shared programs.

Accessing Shared Programs

Several NetWare tools allow a system manager to determine the access rights and privileges of the network users. As a rule, users should be able to work with networked software as if it were an individual program on their workstation. They should be able to change certain software parameters, such as type of printer, in the same manner as if they had a personal copy of the program. Also, users should be able to create data files and store them without the need to learn complex network commands. All of this should take place with the shared programs safeguarded from accidental deletions or deliberate alterations by users without the proper authorization.

A list of all users must be made, specifying their software needs, hard disk space, requirements, and rights. Also, for each data file and software program, attributes such as Shareable or Read Only need to be identified. This also must be performed for all subdirectories and the programs stored inside of them. When a program is Shareable, its parent directory should also be Shareable. The parent directory attributes typically determine what can be done with the programs and files stored inside of it.

Granting NetWare Rights

Most shared network software comes with documentation that indicates in detail the types of rights to provide to program users. If a list is not available, the network administrator must decide what rights to provide.

The goal is to provide users access to the program without allowing them to change or delete the files that make up the program. If the software package to be installed provides no documentation, then a possible model is to place the software in the SYS:PUBLIC directory. This directory contains program files that all users must be able to run but not change.

All users on a NetWare system have, by default, Read, and File Scan rights to the SYS:PUBLIC directory. If the shared software to be installed provides little or no information as to the rights to provide to programs and files, the rights of Read, and File Scan can be provided as a first try. The programs should then be tested to make sure that they perform correctly. If errors are encountered, a trial and error procedure of assigning rights may have to be undertaken until the proper rights are provided.

Group Rights

If a large number of users have the same rights, such as a class in a college, a group can be created instead of creating individual users. Then group rights can be provided that affect all the users that belong to the group. For example, if an accounting class needs access to an accounting package, and no one else needs to use the programs, a group ACCOUNTING can be created. When a user who is a member of the ACCOUNTING group logs in, he or she will be granted all rights for the group and access to the programs accordingly. This eliminates the need to grant rights to several dozen accounts, thus reducing the overhead of the network and making maintenance less difficult for network administrators.

Many network administrators create a group for each program that requires some type of access control. Each group is then given rights to its respective program. Finally, users are placed in the appropriate groups.

Program File Attributes

Files in a NetWare-based network can be given any of the file attributes outlined in earlier chapters. Generally, most files are made Shareable and Read Only. Files that are shareable are available to multiple users at the same time. If a file is not Shareable and a user is accessing the file, other users must wait for the first user to complete using the file before they can gain access to it. In other words, it can be used by only one user at a time.

Making a program Read Only protects it from accidental deletion and modification, even by users who have delete privileges, such as the supervisor.

Another type of file attribute is Execute Only. This attribute can be given to executable files in order to prevent them from being copied. While this attribute is on, users can execute the program but cannot copy it to their own disks or subdirectories.

Using Application Programs in a Network Environment

Most software written for IBM compatibles can be divided into three categories: network incompatible, network compatible, and network aware.

Network incompatible software cannot be used at all while it is stored on a file server. Usually the problem involves the program's use of low-level operations to control the disk drive or access its own files. These low-level operations access the hardware of the computer directly, rather than using the DOS function calls that NetWare has redirected to the file server. Other problems can arise when the program is simply incompatible with the resident network driver programs, although this situation is rare. In that case the program cannot be run on a computer that is attached to the network. When the software can be run with the network drivers loaded, but not on the network, it is necessary to install it on the workstation's hard disk. A complete menu system would also offer selections to the user to run this software, as well as network software.

Network compatible software includes all programs that can be run on the network, even though they might not be network specific versions. Many programs have no install options that indicate what drive letter the program is running on. These programs can simply be copied to a network directory. Others, such as older versions of WordStar, can be installed on any drive letter A - Z using the appropriate install procedures. This is often the easiest type of program for the network supervisor to install. Still others may be programmed to always look on a certain disk drive for their files, for instance on drive C. In this case, the NetWare MAP command can be used to map drive letter C to the appropriate network directory. The programs in this category must be handled very carefully in regard to federal copyright laws. Under almost all license agreements accompanying the software, one copy of the software must be owned for each user accessing the program.

Network aware programs have been written to detect and sometimes take advantage of a network. Many programs released in the last few years are designed specifically to detect that they are running on a network and to allow only one user to access them. This prevents users from illegally using more copies of the software than they own. Usually, special multiuser versions of such programs are available that allow five, ten or some other number of users to access the software simultaneously. The multiuser versions are always more expensive than single-user versions, of course. But they are less expensive than an equal number of single-user copies. Other programs are written to take advantage of the network environment. These programs offer electronic mail, quick messages, easy use of network printers, or network use of a common database.

Installing Microsoft Windows

To install Windows on a Novell network, a shared copy of the program can be placed in the network. Then copies of some Windows files need to be placed on user disks. This is done by using the command SETUP /X where X is one of three switches that the installer will have to choose from. These switches are as follows:

1. /a. This is the Windows Administrative Setup. When this option is used, Windows files are copied to a network server so users can run the Setup program from the network.

2. /n. This is the Windows Network Setup. When this option is used, the setup system sets up a workstation to run a shared copy of Windows. In this case only a few of the Windows system files are copied to the workstation's hard disk. The rest of the files reside in the server's hard disk. The files copied to the user's workstation allow the user to customize the Windows environment.

3. /h. This is the Windows Automated Setup. This option allows the automated or easy installation of Windows by invoking an automated Setup routine.

Before installing Windows on a network, make sure that any network messaging services and TSRs used for sending messages are turned off. This type of application can cause the Setup program to fail during installation.

Using the Setup /a Option

By using the Setup /a (Windows Administrative Setup) option, the system administrator can place Windows files on a network server. However, this option doesn't create a usable copy of Windows. This option only transfers files from the Windows disks to the server's hard disk. All the files copied are expanded, renamed, and placed on the server's disk as read-only files. This is done so they can be accessed by more than one user or application at a time.

To use this option:

1. From the user's workstation, connect to the network where the copy of Windows is going to be installed. Make sure that you have the rights to perform this operation.

2. Insert Windows 3.1 disk #1 into drive A and set the drive pointer to this drive.

3. Type Setup /a and press the ENTER key.

4. Follow the instructions on the screen.

5. After the installation is complete, mark all Windows files as shareable.

To copy Windows to another network drive that is part of the same network as the one where Windows was just installed, you can run the setup procedure using the /a option from the shared directory that was previously created.

After all Windows files are placed on a network server, users can connect to that server and install Windows in their workstations by running Setup /n from their workstations. However, at this point the network administrator must decide whether to allow users to share Windows from the network server, or copy all Windows files to their workstation using the Automated Setup option.

Using the Setup /n Option

Users can set up their workstations so they have access to a shared copy of Windows by running Setup /n. By using this option, some of the Windows files are copied to the user's hard disk. The directory where some of the Windows files are placed is a personal directory for the user that must be present in order to run Windows.

By maintaining their own copies of these files, users can customize the Windows environment without affecting the shared files located in the network and used by all individuals working with Windows.

To set up a shared copy of Windows on a workstation:

1. From the user's workstation, connect to the network where the copy of Windows is going to be installed. Make sure that you have the rights to perform this operation.

2. Change to the network directory where Windows is located.

3. Type Setup /n and press the ENTER key.

4. Follow the instructions on the screen.

This option copies only the files that pertain to the user's system, such as the group (GRP) and initialization (INI) files.

Using the Setup /h Option

This option uses the information stored in a system settings file to install Windows without much user intervention. The installation is performed quickly and easily. This option is usually preferred if there are many workstations to set up or if users will be performing their own installations.

To use the Automated Setup option:

1. Create a system settings file for each workstation configuration and place the files in a directory where users have access to it and can open, read, and copy the file to the workstation.

2. From the workstation, the users can set up Windows by typing Setup /h and pressing the ENTER key.

If a shared copy of Windows is to be installed using this option, then

3. Type Setup /h:[drive:\path]\filename /n, where filename is the name of the system configuration settings file that contains the details required by the installation program.

Windows comes with a system setting file called SETUP.SHH that can be found in disk #1 of the Windows system disks. The sections in this file are

1. [sysinfo]. This determines if a System Configuration screen will appear during Setup.

2. [configuration]. Determines the various devices on the user's system.

3. [windir]. Determines where to put the Windows files.

4. [userinfo]. Determines the user and company name.

5. [doninstall]. Determines which Windows components shouldn't be installed.

6. [options]. Determines various options such as setting up existing applications, starting the Windows tutorial, and loading the RE-ADME files.

7. [printers]. Determines the printer to be used by Windows.

8. [endinstall]. Determines if Setup will modify the CONFIG.SYS and AUTOEXEC.BAT files and if the system is to be rebooted after the installation of Windows.

The basic SETUP.SHH file is displayed below. These settings can be customized to the environment where it will be used.

```
[sysinfo]
;
; Use this section to specify whether you want Setup to  display the
; System Configuration screen. Specify "yes" to display the screen and "no"
; if you don't want the screen displayed. (The default value is "no".)
;
; You may want to display and review the System Configuration screen so
; that you can confirm the configuration settings before continuing with
; Setup.
showsysinfo=yes
[configuration]
;
; Use this section to specify the various devices on your system. You can
; find the values for each variable in the SETUP.INF file. If you omit an
; entry, Windows uses the detected or default device.
;
; If you are updating Windows, some of these entries will be ignored and
; Windows will use the devices that are already installed. If you want to
; force the update and override the installed device, precede the value
; with an exclamation point (!), for example, display = !vga. Only the
; Machine, Display, Mouse, and Network devices require an exclamation point
; for overriding the installed device during an upgrade.
; Machine profile string from [machine] section of SETUP.INF
machine = ibm_compatible
; Display profile string from [display] section of SETUP.INF
display = vga
; Mouse profile string from [pointing.device] section of SETUP.INF
mouse = ps2mouse
; Network profile string from [network] section of SETUP.INF
; followed by version profile string from the appropriate
; [xxxxxxx.versions] section which identifies the network  version.
; The following example will setup Windows using
; "Microsoft LAN Manager version 2.0 Enhanced".
network = lanman/01020000
; Keyboard profile string from [keyboard.types] section of SETUP.INF
keyboard = t4s0enha
; Language profile string from [language] section of SETUP.INF
language = enu
;  Keyboard Layout profile  string  from  [keyboard.tables]  section  of
SETUP.INF
kblayout = nodll
[windir]
;
; Use this section to specify where to put Windows files. If a previous
; version of Windows is already set up in the specified directory, Setup
; will update it. If you do not specify a directory, or if the specified
; directory is not valid, Setup displays a dialog box asking you to specify
; the directory in which you want to set up Windows.
c:\windows
[userinfo]
;
; Use this section to specify the user and company name. The first line
; specifies the user's name. This line is required. The second specifies
; the company name, and is optional. Both names can be up to 30 characters
; long and must be enclosed in double quotation marks (" ") if they include
; blank spaces.
```

```
;
; If you do not specify a user name, a dialog box appears during Setup asking
; for the user's name.
;
; If you are setting up Windows across a network, the [userinfo] section
; will be ignored.
;
"John Q. Public"              ; User Name    (30 chars MAX) (required)
"Microsoft Corporation"      ; Company Name (30 chars MAX) (optional)
[dontinstall]
;
; Use this section to specify components that you do not want to set up
; on your system. By default, all components will be installed. If you do
; not want to set up a particular component, include it in this section.
accessories                  ; Do NOT install accessories
readmes                      ; Do NOT install readme files
games                        ; Do NOT install games
screensavers                 ; Do NOT install screen savers
bitmaps                      ; Do NOT install bitmaps
[options]
;
; Use this section to specify whether you want to set up applications
; during Setup, and/or start the Windows Tutorial at the end of Setup.
; If you don't want any of these options, you can omit this section.
;
; If you choose to set up applications, you can either set them up
; interactively during Setup (you choose which applications you want to
; set up,) or you can specify that you want Setup to automatically set up
;all applications found on your hard disk.
;
; If you specify both "setupapps" and "autosetupapps", all applications
; on your hard disk will be set up.
;
setupapps                    ; Setup applications already on hard disk
autosetupapps                ; Set up all applications on hard disk
tutorial                     ; Start Windows Tutorial at the end of Setup
[printers]
;
; Use this section to specify any printers you want to set up. You specify
; a printer description and a port. Values for the printer description
; variable are listed in the [io.device] section of the CONTROL.INF file.
; Values for the port variable are listed in the [ports] section of the
; WIN.INI file.
;
; The printer description must be enclosed in double quotation marks ("
; ")
; if it contains blank spaces. The port value must appear exactly as it
;does in the WIN.INI file. If you do not want to set up a printer, omit
;this section.
;
"HP LaserJet III",LPT1:
[endinstall]
;
; Use this section to specify whether you want Setup to make modifications
; to the CONFIG.SYS and AUTOEXEC.BAT files and whether you want Setup to
; exit to DOS, restart Windows, or restart your system when it has finished
; installing Windows.
;
; The "configfiles" entry specifies whether Setup should modify the
; CONFIG.SYS and AUTOEXEC.BAT with the necessary changes, or whether Setup
```

```
; should save the proposed changes in separate files called CONFIG.WIN and
; AUTOEXEC.WIN in your WINDOWS directory. If you choose the latter, you
;must make the changes yourself.
;
; You can specify one of the following entries.
;
; configfiles = modify              ;writes modifications back to source.
; configfiles = save                ;saves changes to alternate (*.win)
;files.
;
; If  you do not specify a "configfiles" entry, the CONFIG.SYS and
; AUTOEXEC.BAT files will be modified by Setup.
;
; The "endopt" entry specifies what happens at the end of  Setup. You can
; specify one of the following entries.
;
;     endopt = exit       ; Setup exits to DOS
;     endopt = restart    ; Setup restarts Windows
;     endopt = reboot     ; Setup reboots your computer
;
; If you do not specify an "endopt" entry, a dialog box appears at the end
; of Setup asking the user to choose from the three options.
;
; If you are using the network option for setting up Windows (Setup /n),
;the reboot option is not valid. Setup will exit to DOS instead of rebooting
; your system.
;
configfiles = save
endopt        = restart
```

Accessing Windows

Users can access Windows applications easier by placing entries in the SETUP.INF file that indicate the application and the access mechanism for a specific program. The SETUP.INF file is included with Windows and becomes a permanent file in the shared Windows directory.

By placing entries in the SETUP.INF file, applications can be added to the Program Manager's groups and their settings can also be modified or customized. In this manner, if an application needs to be added to the user's Program Manager window, a title and the path for the application must be placed in the SETUP.INF file.

In addition to the title and path, an icon file name or icon number may also be included in the SETUP.INF file entry for a program application. If an icon is not specified, the displayed icon will be one from the application file.

The SETUP.INF file also has a network section that can be identified by looking for the keyword [network] within the file. This section contains information for specific versions of network drivers and specific network sections that describe SYSTEM.INI entries and other information for specific networks such as Novell NetWare.

Guidelines for Using Windows on a Novell Network

Using Windows on a Novell network is simplified by following these steps:

1. Start the network first; then start Windows. That is, make sure that the workstation is attached to the network server, and that the user is logged in.

2. Personal files should not be kept in a shared file directory.

3. Always use the same network drive letter used when Windows was installed. If Windows was installed in drive H, use drive H when trying to access Windows.

4. When attaching to a printer, always use the same port for that specific printer.

By following these guidelines, using Windows in a Novell network becomes a much simpler task.

When running Novell NetWare, Windows Setup copies the following files to the Windows directory:

1. NETX.COM

2. IPXODI.COM

3. TBMI2.COM

4. IPX.OBJ

5. LSL.COM.

If Windows is running from a shared copy on the network, these five files are located in the shared network directory. Before running Windows, the following steps should be taken.

1. Replace the NetWare shell with the NETX.COM provided.

2. IPXODI.COM and LSL.COM should be upgraded to the version provided.

3. If Windows is to run in standard mode, then TBMI2 should be loaded. It is recommended that a batch file be created to load this utility. The batch file could look like this one:

tbmi2

win

tbmi2 /u

The last line unloads TBIM2 from memory when Windows exits.

4. A new version of IPX.COM needs to be built using the IPX.OBJ provided (or use the IPXODI version discussed earlier).

5. Increase the number of file handles to at least 60 in the SHELL.CFG file or the NET.CFG file.

6. Increase the number of files in the CONFIG.SYS to 60.

7. Turn SHOW DOTS to ON in SHELL.CFG or NET.CFG.

8. When mapping a connection in File Manager use the MAP ROOT function. This simulates the MS-DOS subst command which sets the root of a given drive to a directory designated by the user instead of setting it to the true root of the volume. For example, instead of the usual command in the AUTOEXEC.BAT file of

   map f:=io\sys:home\acc

   you should provide the mapping as

   map root f:=io\sys:home\acc

9. Make sure that the entry

   load=nwpopup.exe

   is added to the [Windows] section of the user's WIN.INI file. This entry automatically starts the NetWare popup utility.

10. Care should be taken when running Printer Assistant with Windows 3.1 and Novell NetWare. Some Windows applications print garbage mixed with correct output when this TSR is in use.

If the system administrator needs to have a greater depth of knowledge about Windows 3.1 and the different options that can be set in it, an inexpensive product from Microsoft called the Microsoft Windows Resource Kit should be obtained. This is an in-depth coverage of Windows installation and operating procedures for stand-alone and network implementations. At a price under $20 it is one resource that a system administrator working with Windows shouldn't be without.

Hands-on Installing Microsoft Windows

Installing Microsoft Windows 3.1

To install shared software on a Novell network, you should login as the supervisor.

1. Type **LOGIN SUPERVISOR** and press the ENTER key.

2. Type the password required to login as the supervisor.

We are going to install Windows as a shared program to be used by all network users. Therefore, a good place to put the Windows files is a subdirectory that branches off from the main directory or one that branches off from the public directory. For this exercise you will take the latter approach.

We may decide later to install additional shared software; therefore, we will create a subdirectory called SHARESOF. The subdirectory SHARESOF will contain subdirectories for each shared application that may need to be installed.

3. Type **CD\PUBLIC** and press the ENTER key.

4. Type **MD SHARESOF** and press the ENTER key.

This creates the shared directory where all the applications subdirectories will reside.

5. Type **CD SHARESOF** and press the ENTER key.

6. Type **MD WINDOWS** and press the ENTER key.

This creates the Windows subdirectory.

7. Type **CD WINDOWS** and press the ENTER key.

8. Insert the Microsoft Windows 3.1 Disk 1 in disk drive A:

9. Type **A:SETUP /A** and press the ENTER key.

10. Windows will ask for a directory in which to install. Type **F:\PUBLIC\SHARESOF\WINDOWS** for the directory name.

Installing Windows on Users' Disks

Microsoft Windows is now installed in the file server under the subdirectory Windows. The actual path to the Windows files is

F:\PUBLIC\SHARESOF\WINDOWS

Users will need only a few of the files residing in the above directory in order to use the application. These files will reside in the user's directory or on the hard disk. To prepare Windows in a user directory or hard disk follow these steps:

1. Login to the network with the user name and password.

2. Type **CD\PUBLIC\SHARESOF\WINDOWS** and press the ENTER key.

3. Type **SETUP /N** and press the ENTER key.

4. Press the ENTER key.

The computer will respond with a default path and directory suggesting where files should reside.

5. Type the path and name of the directory where Windows will be installed. In this example we assume that the user has a hard disk on his or her workstation. Therefore, type **C:\WINDOWS** and press the ENTER key.

6. Continue to follow the installation instructions displayed on the screen by the setup program. You will need to verify the equipment that the setup program thinks you have and plan to use with

453

Windows. If there are no hardware problems, Windows will install some required files on the user's disk and the installation will stop normally.

To facilitate using the Windows program, an entry should be made in the login script for this user. This entry will map a search drive to the Windows subdirectory. This helps in accessing the shared files required to run the application.

7. Logout of the user account and login as a supervisor.

8. Type **SYSCON** and press the ENTER key.

9. Highlight User Information from the SYSCON menu and press the ENTER key.

10. Highlight the name of the user to receive the changes in the login script and press the ENTER key.

11. Highlight Login Script and press the ENTER key.

12. Type

    MAP S4:=SYS:\PUBLIC\SHARESOF\WINDOWS

    and highlight Yes when asked if you want to save the changes.

13. Press the ESC key three times.

14. Highlight Yes when asked if you want to exit SYSCON.

Windows is now installed. To access it, type C: and press the ENTER key. Then type CD\WINDOWS and press the ENTER key. Finally, type WIN and press the ENTER key.

To make it a little easier, a batch file as the one below can be placed in the PUBLIC directory and be given the attributes Shareable and Read Only. The batch file is

```
C:
CD\WINDOWS
WIN
F:
```

Summary

Microsoft Windows is a graphical environment for IBM personal computers and compatibles running under the MS-DOS operating system. Windows creates a new working environment on top of MS-DOS, thus shielding the user from having to memorize operating system commands.

Microsoft Windows 3.1 contains many features that can be used to navigate through a network environment and to perform many functions that used to be done from the DOS command prompt. When a network and Windows are properly installed, Windows will automatically make a network connection and related menu items appear automatically on the Windows menu. These menus can then be used to assist network administritators with network management and related activities such as printing.

To install Windows on a Novell network, a shared copy of the program can be placed in the network. Then copies of some Windows files need to be placed on user disks. This is done by using the command SETUP /X during the installation process. In this case the /X option refers to one of three switches that the installer will have to choose from. These switches are as follows:

1.   /a. Windows Administrative Setup.
2. /n. Windows Network Setup.
3. /h. Windows Automated Setup.

Questions

1. Why use Windows 3.1 in a Novell network?
2. What are the options when installing Windows on a network?
3. What are the network drivers provided with Windows?
4. What is the purpose of the SYSTEM.INF file?
5. Which of the installation options is best for the normal user?

Projects

Objectives

These projects are designed to provide the student with hands-on practice on installing software application using Novell NetWare.

Project 1. Installing Microsoft Excel on the File Server

Excel is a spreadsheet developed by Microsoft Corporation to run under the Microsoft Windows environment. Before Excel can be installed, a shared version of Windows needs to be present in a network file server. Excel can be installed in a directory in the file server. Then it can be executed on any computer that has access to this file directory.

To install Excel on a Novell network server, the Microsoft Excel Setup program needs to be executed. When the Setup program asks for the name of a directory where Excel is to be installed, the name of a previously created and shareable directory has to be provided to the program.

All files in the above directory can have the attributes of Shareable, Execute, and Read Only. This will allow multiple network users to access the program simultaneously.

In addition to using Novell's network security mechanisms to protect Excel generated documents, users can provide additional safeguards using one or more of the following methods:

1. Allow only authorized users to open a document. This is done by saving the document with a password using the Save As command. Only people who are given the password can access the document.

2. Prevent unauthorized editing of a document. Using the Format Cell Protection command, cells can be locked. Then using the Options Protect Document command, the document should be given a password for further security.

3. Hide cells by setting the column width or row height to zero for the columns containing the cells to be protected.

Project 2. Installing Microsoft Word for Windows on the File Server

Microsoft Word for Windows is a word processor that runs under the Microsoft Windows environment. The Word program files can be stored in a shareable directory in the file server. Any workstation that has access to the directory can run the Word program.

For Word to work properly, an entry needs to be made in the file WIN.INI that indicates the Word options. Word also has its own version of WIN.INI. It is called WINWORD.INI. This file contains the settings for some Word menus and utilities.

Microsoft Word for Windows looks for WINWORD.INI in the directory specified in WIN.INI, the Word directory, or the directory from which Word was executed. If it doesn't find one, it will create it. Finally, the entry "NOVELLNET=YES" needs to be added to the Word for Windows section of the WIN.INI file.

Appendix

Vendors of Gateways and Related Products

Access Server
Novell Inc. Comm. Products
890 Ross Dr.
Sunnyvale, CA 94089
800-453-1267

C-Slave/286 and XBUS4/AT
Alloy Computer Products Inc.
165 Forest St.
Marlboro, MA 01752
508-481-8500

Chatterbox4000
J&L Information Systems Inc.
9238 Deering Ave.
Chatsworth, CA 91311
818-709-1778

ComBridge
Cubix Corp.
2800 Lockheed Way
Carson City, NV 89706
800-829-0550

FlexCom
Evergreen Systems Inc.,
120 Landing Ct.
Suite A
Novato, CA 94945
415-897-8888

MultiComAsyncGateway
Multi-Tech Systems Inc.
2205 Woodale Dr.
Mounds View, MN 55112
800-328-9717

Telebits ACS
Telebit Corp
115 Chesapeake Terr.
Sunnyvale, CA 94089
800-835-3248

386/Multiware
Alloy Computer Products Inc.
165 Forest St.
Marlboro, MA 01752
508-481-8500

Vendors of EBBS and Related Products

Accunet
The Major BBS
Galacticom Inc.
4101 SW 47th Ave., #101
Fort Lauderdale, FL 33314
305-583-5990

Oracomm-Plus
Surf Computer Services, Inc.
71-540 Gardess Rd.
Rancho Mirage, CA 92270
619-346-1608

PCBoard
Clark Development Co.
3950 S. 700 East, #303
Murray, UT 84107
800-356-1686

RemoteAccess
Continental Software
195 Adelaide Terr.
Perth, Australia, 6000
USA contact 918-254-6618

Searchlight
Searchlight Software
Box 640
Stony Brook, NY 11790
516-751-2966

TBBS
eSoft Inc.
15200 E. Girard Ave., #2550
Aurora, CA 80014
303-699-6565

Vendors of Routers, Bridges, and Related Products

Eicon Router for NetWare
Eicon Technology Corp.
2196 32nd Ave.
Montreal, Quebec H8T 3H7 Canada
514-631-2592

G/X25 Gateway & Bridge 64
Gateway Communicatons Inc.
2941 Alton Ave.
Irvine, CA 92714
800-367-6555

LAN2LAN/Mega Router
Newport Systems Solutions Inc.
4019 Westerley Pl, #103
Newport Beach, CA 92660
800-368-6533

Microcom LAN Bridge 6000
Microcom Systems Inc.
500 River Ridge Dr.
Norwood, MA 02062
800-822-8224

NetWare Link/X.25
Novell Inc.
122 East 1700 South
Provo, UT 84606
800-638-9273

NetWare Link/T1
Novell Inc.
122 East 1700 South
Provo, UT 84606
800-638-9273

POWERbridge
Performace Technology
7800 IH 10, W. 800
Lincoln Center
San Antonio, TX 78230
800-825-5267

Vendors of E-Mail Products

Beyond Mail
Beyond Inc.
38 Sidney St.
Cambridge, MA 02139
617-621-0095

cc:Mail Gateway
Lotus Development Corp.
2141 Landings Dr.
Mountain View, CA 94043
800-448-2500

@Mail
Beyond Inc.
38 Sidney St.
Cambridge, MA 02139
617-621-0095

MailMAN
Reach Soft. Corp.
330 Portrero Ave.
Sunnyvale, CA 94086
408-733-8685

Microsoft Mail for PC Networks
Microsoft Corp.
1 Microsoft Way
Redmont, WA 98052
206-882-8080

Microsoft Mail
Microsoft Corp.
1 Microsoft Way
Redmont, WA 98052
206-882-8080

Office Works Comm. Option
Data Access Corp.
14000 SW 119 Ave.
Miami, FL 33186
800-451-3539

WordPerfect Office
WordPerfect Corp.
1555 N. Technology Way
Orem, UT 84057
800-451-5151

3+Open Mail
3Com Corp.
3165 Kifer Rd.
Santa Clara, CA 95052
800-638-3266

Vendors of Fax Gateways and Related Products

FaxPress 2000
Castelle
3255-3 Scott Blvd.
Santa Clara, CA 95051
800-359-7654

GammaFax CPD
GammaLink
133 Caspian Court
Sunnyvale, CA 94089
408-744-1430

Facsimile Server
Interpreter, Inc.
11455 West 48th Ave.
Wheat Ridge, CO 80033
800-232-4687

NetFax Board
All the Fax, Inc.
917 Northern Blvd.
Great Neck, NY 11021
800-289-3329

Vendors of Network Management Products

PreCursor
The Alridge Co.
2500 City West Blvd., Suite 575
Houston, TX 77042
800-548-5019

StopCopy Plus
BBI Computer Systems
14105 Heritage Lane
Silver Spring, MD 20906
301-871-1094

Stop View
BBI Computer Systems
14105 Heritage Lane
Silver Spring, MD 20906
301-871-1094

SiteLock
Brightwork Development, Inc.
766 Shrewsbury Ave.
Jerral Center West
Trenton Falls, NJ
800-552-9876

Certus LAN
Certus International
13110 Shaker Sq.
Cleveland, OH 44120
800-722-8737

Saber Meter
Saber Software Corp.
Box 9088
Dallas, TX 75209
800-338-8754

EtherPeek
AG Group
2540 Camino Diablo
Walnut Creek, CA 94596
415-937-2479

LocalPeek
AG Group
2540 Camino Diablo
Walnut Creek, CA 94596
415-937-2479

NetPatrol Pack
AG Group
2540 Camino Diablo
Walnut Creek, CA 94596
415-937-2479

Net Watchman
AG Group
2540 Camino Diablo
Walnut Creek, CA 94596
415-937-2479

ARCserve for NetWare 286
Cheyenne Software, Inc.
55 Bryant Ave.
Roslyn, NY 11576
800-243-9462

ARCserve for NetWare 386
Cheyenne Software, Inc.
55 Bryant Ave.
Roslyn, NY 11576
800-243-9462

Network Supervisor
CSG Technologies, Inc.
530 William Penn Place
Suite 329
Pittsburgh, PA 15219
800-366-4622

Retrospect Remote
Dantz Development Corp.
1400 Shattuck Ave., Suite 1
Berkeley, CA 94709
415-849-0293

LANVista 100
Digilog, Inc.
1370 Welsh Rd.
Montgomeryville, PA 18936
800-344-4564

PhoneNET Manager's Pack
Farallon Computing, Inc.
2000 Powell St.
Emeryville, CA 94608
415-596-9000

NetWare Early Warning System
Frye Computer Systems, Inc.
19 Temple Place, 4th Floor
Boston, MA 02111
800-234-3793

NetWare Management
Frye Computer Systems, Inc.
19 Temple Place, 4th. Floor
Boston, MA 02111
800-234-3793

LANWatch
FTP Software, Inc.
26 Princess St.
Wakefield, MA 01880
617-246-0900

LANprobe
Hewlett-Packard Co.
5070 Centennial Blvd.
Colorado Springs, CO 80919
719-531-4000

Network Advisor
Hewlett-Packard Co.
5070 Centennial Blvd.
Colorado Springs, CO 80919
719-531-4000

OpenView
Hewlett-Packard Co.
5070 Centennial Blvd.
Colorado Springs, CO 80919
719-531-4000

ProbeView
Hewlett-Packard Co.
5070 Centennial Blvd.
Colorado Springs, CO 80919
719-531-4000

LANanlyzer
Novell, Inc.
122 East 1700 South
Provo, UT 84606
800-453-1267

Lantern
Novell, Inc.
122 East 1700 South
Provo, UT 84606
800-453-1267

Lantern Service Monitor
Novell, Inc.
122 East 1700 South
Provo, UT 84606
800-453-1267

Access/One
Ungermann-Bass, Inc.
3900 Freedom Cir.
Santa Clara, CA 95052
800-873-6381

NetDirector
Ungermann-Bass, Inc.
3900 Freedom Cir.
Santa Clara, CA 95052
800-873-6381

LattisNet Advanced Network Management
Synoptics Communication, Inc.
Box 58185
Santa Clara, CA 95052
408-988-2400

LattisNet Basic Network Management
Synoptics Communication, Inc.
Box 58185
Santa Clara, CA 95052
408-988-2400

LattisNet System 3000
Synoptics Communication, Inc.
Box 58185
Santa Clara, CA 95052
408-988-2400

Network Control Engine
Synoptics Communication, Inc.
Box 58185
Santa Clara, CA 95052
408-988-2400

Vendors of Network Operating Systems and Related Products

LANtastic
Artisoft, Inc.
575 E. River Rd., Artisoft Plaza
Tucson, AZ 85704
602-293-6363

LANsoft
ACCTON Technology Corp.
46750 Fremont Blvd., Suite 104
Fremont, CA 94538
415-226-9800

VINES
Banyan Systems, Inc.
120 Flanders Rd.
Westboro, MA 01581
508-898-1000

PC/NOS
Corvus Systems, Inc.
160 Great Oaks Blvd.
San Jose, CA 95119
800-426-7887

LANsmart
D-Link Systems, Inc.
5 Musick
Irvine, CA 92718
714-455-1688

OS/2 Ext. Ed.
IBM Corp.
Old Orchard Rd.
Armonk, NY 10504
800-426-2468

EasyNet NOS/2 Plus
LanMark Corp.
Box 246, Postal Station A
Mississauga, ON
CD L5A 3G8
416-848-6865

LAN Manager
Microsoft Corp.
One Microsoft Way
Redmont, WA 98052
800-426-9400

NetWare
Novell, Inc.
122 East 1700 South
Provo, UT 84606
800-453-1267

Commercial Information Services

BIX
One Phoenix Mill Lane
Peterborough, NH 03458
800-227-2983

Compuserve
Box 20212
Columbus, OH 43220
800-848-8199

Dialog Information Service, Inc.
3460 Hillview Ave.
Palo Alto, CA 94304
800-334-2564

General Videotext Corp.
Three Blackstone St.
Cambridge, MA 02139
800-544-4005

GEnie
401 N. Washington St.
Rockville, MD 20850
800-638-9636

NewsNet
945 Haverford Rd.
Bryn Mawr, PA 19010
800-345-1301

Prodigy Services Co.
445 Hamilton Ave.
White Plains, NY 10601
800-776-3449

Quantum Computer Services
8619 Westwood Center Dr., Suite 200
Vienna, VA 22182
800-227-6364

SprintMail
12490 Sunrise Valley Dr.
Reston, VA 22096
800-736-1130

SprintNet Data Network
US Sprint
12490 Sunrise Valley Dr.
Reston, VA 22096
800-736-1130

Public Communication Networks
Accunet
AT&T Computer Systems
295 N. Maple Ave.
Basking Ridge, NJ 07920
800-222-0400

Tymnet Global Network
BT North America Inc.
2560 N. 1st St., Box 49019
San Jose, CA 94161
800-872-7654

CompuServe Network Services
CompuServe Inc.
5000 Arlington Centre Blvd.
Columbus, OH 43220
800-848-8199

Vendors of Data Switches, PBXs, and Related Products

AISwitch Series XXX
Applied Innovation, Inc.
651-C Lakeview Plaza Blvd.
Columbus, OH 43085
800-247-9482

IBM Information Network
IBM Corp
3405 W. Dr. Martin Luther King, Jr.
Blvd.
Tampa, FL 33607
800-727-2222

MDX
Equinox Systems, Inc.
14260 Southwest 119th Ave.
Miami, FL 33186
800-328-2729

Infonet
Infonet Services Corp.
2100 East Grand Ave.
El Segundo, CA 90245
800-342-5272

Instanet6000
MICOM Communications Corp.
Box 8100
4100 Los Angeles Ave.
Simi Valley, CA 93062-8100
800-642-6687

Mark*Net
GE Corp.
Information Services Div.
401 N. Washington St.
Rockville, MD 20850
800-433-3683

Data PBX Series
Rose Electronics
Box 742571
Houston, TX 77274
800-333-9343

Gateway Data Switch
SKP Electronics
1232-E S. Village Way
Santa Ana, CA 92705
714-972-1727

INCS-64
Western Telematic, Inc.
5 Sterling
Irvine, CA 92178
800-854-7226

Slimline Data Switches
Belkin Components
14550 S. Main St.
Gardena, CA 90248
800-223-5546

MetroLAN
Datacom Technologies, Inc.
11001 31st Place, West
Everett, WA 98204
800-468-5557

Intelligent Printer Buffer
Primax Electronics Inc.
2531 West 237th St., Suite 102
Torrance, CA 90505
213-326-8018

Data Switches
Rose Electronics
Box 742571
Houston, TX 77274
800-333-9343

ShareNet 5110
McComb Research
Box 3984
Minneapolis, MN 55405
612-527-8082

Aura 1000
Intran Systems, Inc.
7493 N. Oracle Rd., Suite 207
Tucson, AZ 85704
602-797-2797

Logical Connection
Fifth Generation Systems, Inc.
10049 N. Reiger Rd.
Baton Rouge, LA 70809
800-873-4384

Vendors of Network Remote Access Software and Related Products

Distribute Console Access Facility
IBM Corp.
(Contact IBM sales rep.)
800-426-2468

PolyMod2
Memsoft Corp.
1 Park Pl.
621 NW 53rd St., #240
Boca Raton, FL 33487
407-997-6655

Remote-OS
The Software Lifeline Inc.
Fountain Square, 2600 Military Trail, #290
Boca Raton, FL 33531
407-994-4466

Vendors of TCP/IP Hardware and Related Products

Isolink PC/TCP
BICC Data Networks
1800 W. Park Dr., Suite 150
Westborough, MA 01581
800-447-6526

PC/TCP Plus
FTP Software, Inc.
26 Princess St.
Wakefield, MA 01880
617-246-0900

TCP/IP for OS/2 EE
IBM
Old Orchard Rd.
Armonk, NY 10504
800-426-2468
10Net TCP

Digital Comm. Assoc.
10NET Comm. Div.
7887 Washington Village Dr.
Dayton, OH 45459
800-358-1010

WIN/TCP for DOS
Wollongong Group, Inc.
Box 51860
1129 San Antonio Rd.
Palo Alto, CA 94303
800-872-8649

PC/TCP Thernet Comm.
UniPress Software, Inc.
2025 Lincoln Hwy.
Edison, NJ 08817
800-222-0550

Vendors of Zero Slot LANs, Media Transfer Hardware and Software, and Related Products

LANtastic Z
Artisoft, Inc.
575 E. River Rd.
Artisoft Plaza
Tucson, AZ 85704
602-293-6363

PC-Hookup
Brown Bag Software
2155 S. Bascom, Suite 114
Campbell, CA 95008
800-523-0764

Brooklyn Bridge
Fifth Generation Systems
10049 N. Reiger Rd.
Baton Rouge, LA 70809

LapLink
Traveling Software, Inc.
18702 N. Creek Pkwy.
Bothell, WA 98011
800-662-2652

FastLynx
Rupp Corp.
7285 Franklin Ave.
Los Angeles, CA 90046
800-852-7877

MasterLink
U.S. Marketing, Inc.
1402 South St.
Nashville, TN 37212
615-242-8800

Glossary

Account Boot Disk. A disk used to load DOS into the computer when it is turned on.

ASCII. The acronym for American Standard Code for Information Interchange. This is a standard code for the transmission of data within the US. It is composed of 128 characters in a 7-bit format.

Asynchronous. A communication that places data in discrete blocks that are surrounded by framing bits. These bits show the beginning and ending of a block of data.

Bandwidth. This is the capacity of a cable to carry data on different channels or frequencies.

Baseband. A network cable that has only one channel for carrying data signals.

Baud. The rate of data transmission.

Bit. An abbreviation for binary digit. A bit is the smallest unit of data.

BOOTCONF.SYS. A file on the file server used to indicate which boot image file each workstation will use.

Bridge. A device that connects different LANs so a node on one LAN can communicate with a node on another LAN.

Broadband. A network cable with several channels of communication.

Bus Topology. A physical layout of a LAN where all nodes are connected to a single cable.

Byte. Normally a combination of 8 bits.

CAPTURE. A NetWare utility program used to redirect output from a printer port on the workstation to a network printer.

Coaxial Cable. A cable consisting of a single metal wire surrounded by insulation, which is itself surrounded by a braided or foil outer conductor.

Computer. An electronic system that can store and process information under program control.

CONSOLE. The file server.

Control Code. Special nonprinting codes that cause electronic equipment to perform specific actions.

CPU. Central processing unit. The "brains" of the computer; that section where the logic and control functions are performed.

Device Driver. A software program that enables a network operating system and the DOS operating system to work with NICs, disk controllers, and other hardware.

Directory Rights. Access attached to directories on a NetWare file server.

Driver. A memory resident program usually used to control a hardware device.

FCONSOLE. A NetWare utility program used to monitor file server and workstation activity.

Fiber-Optic Cable. A data transmitting cable that consists of plastic or glass fibers.

File Attributes. Access rights attached to each file.

File Server. A computer running a network operating system that enables other computers to access its files.

Full Duplex. In full duplex communication, the terminal transmits and receives data simultaneously.

Gateway. A device that acts as a translator between networks that use different protocols.

Group. A collection of users.

Group Rights. Rights given to a collection of users.

Half Duplex. In half duplex communication, the terminal transmits and receives data in separate, consecutive operations.

Handshaking. A set of commands recognized by the sending and receiving stations that control the flow of data transmission.

Interface. A communication channel that is used to connect a computer to an external device.

Internetwork Packet Exchange (IPX). One of the data transmission protocols used by NetWare.

LAN. Local area network. A network that encompasses a small geographical area.

LOGIN. A NetWare utility program that allows users to identify themselves to the network.

Login Script. A series of statements executed each time a user logs into a NetWare network.

MAP. Association of a logical NetWare drive letter with a directory.

Modem. An electronic device that converts digital data (modulates) from a computer into analog signals that the phone equipment can understand. Additionally, the modem converts analog (demodulates) data into digital data.

NetBIOS. A network communication protocol that NetWare can emulate.

NETGEN. A NetWare utility program used to configure and load NetWare onto a file server.

NetWare. A network operating system produced by Novell Incorporated.

Network Address. A hexadecimal number used to identify a network cabling system.

NIC. The network interface card is a circuit board that is installed in the file server and workstations that make up the network. It allows the hardware in the network to send and receive data.

Node. A workstation, file server, bridge, or other device that has an address on a network.

Novell. A company based in Provo, Utah, that produces the NetWare network operating system.

NPRINT. A NetWare utility program used to send a file directly to a network printer. Its name stands for Network PRINT.

Packet. A discrete unit of data bits transmitted over a network.

Password. A secret word used to identify a user.

PCONSOLE. A NetWare utility program used to configure and operate print servers. Its name stands for Print server CONSOLE

PRINTCON. A NetWare utility program used to create print job configurations.

PRINTDEF. A NetWare utility program used to create and edit print device files.

Print Devices. Definition files for different type of printers to be used on a print server.

Print Forms. Definitions of different types of paper size to be used on a print server.

Print Job Configurations. Complete descriptions of how a file is to be printed on the network.

Print Queues. Definitions of the order and location in which a file is to be printed on the network.

Print Server. A computer running the PSERVER program that allows it to accept files to be printed from other workstations.

Protocol. The conventions that must be observed in order for two electronic devices to communicate with each other.

PSERVER. The NetWare Print SERVER program.

RAM. Random access memory.

Remote Print Server. A computer running the RPRINTER program, enabling it to print output from other network workstations and operate as a normal workstation.

Remote Reset. The process of loading DOS and the network drivers from the file server.

Ring Topology. A network configuration that connects all nodes in a logical ring-like structure.

ROM. Read only memory

RPRINTER. The program that allows other workstations to print to a workstation's printer.

Shell. Under NetWare, the network drivers.

SHELL.CFG. A file used on a workstation to configure the network drivers as they are loaded into memory.

Star Topology. A network configuration where each node is connected by a single cable link to a central location, called the hub.

Synchronous. A method of communication using a time interval to distinguish between transmitted blocks of data.

SYSCON. A NetWare utility program used to establish users and their rights on the file server. Its name stands for SYStem CONfiguration.

Token. The data packet used to carry information on LANs using the ring topology.

Topology. The manner in which nodes are connected on a LAN.

Trustee Rights. Rights given to users to access directories on the file server.

Uninterruptible Power Supply. A device that keeps computers running after a power failure, providing power from batteries for a short period of time.

User. Under NetWare, the definition of a set of access rights for an individual.

VAP. A value-added process to the NetWare operating system provided by a third party vendor.

Wide Area Network. A network that encompasses a large geographical area.

Workstation. A computer attached to the network.

X.25. A communication protocol used on public data networks.

Index